OXFORD READINGS IN SOCIO-LEGAL STUDIES

A Reader on Punishment

OXFORD READINGS IN SOCIO-LEGAL STUDIES

Forthcoming titles in this series

Criminal Justice
Edited by Nicola Lacey

Family Law
Edited by John Eekelar and Mavis Maclean

The Law of the Business Enterprise
Edited by Sally Wheeler

A Reader on
Punishment

EDITED BY

R. A. Duff and David Garland

OXFORD UNIVERSITY PRESS

Oxford University Press, Walton Street, Oxford OX2 6DP

Oxford New York
Athens Auckland Bangkok Bombay
Calcutta Cape Town Dar es Salaam Delhi
Florence Hong Kong Istanbul Karachi
Kuala Lumpur Madras Madrid Melbourne
Mexico City Nairobi Paris Singapore
Taipei Tokyo Toronto

and associated companies in
Berlin Ibadan

Oxford is a trade mark of Oxford University Press

Published in the United States
by Oxford University Press Inc., New York

British Library Cataloguing in Publication Data
Data available

Library of Congress Cataloging in Publication Data
Data available
ISBN 0–19–876352–2
ISBN 0–19–876353–0 (pbk.)

Printed in Great Britain
on acid-free paper by
Bookcraft Ltd.
Midsomer Norton, Bath

Contents

Introduction: Thinking about Punishment

R. A. DUFF and D. GARLAND

1. Philosophical and Sociological Perspectives on Punishment

This volume brings together writings on the philosophy of punishment, penology, and the sociology of punishment. All too often these different ways of writing about punishment are treated as if they are separate disciplines which can proceed independently of one another. The result is that philosophical discussions are often far removed from the realities of penal practice, while penology and the sociology of punishment are frequently crude or evasive in their handling of complex normative issues.

Our collection aims to show the value of establishing a dialogue between these closely related endeavours. We have made no attempt to survey the whole range of penal topics. Instead, we have focused on some central themes in penal jurisprudence—concerning the proper aims and justification of the practice of state punishment—and tried to show that these issues can be adequately considered only when normative and empirical issues are combined. Serious thought about punishment must focus on 'working social categories' (HIRST: 267)[1] and institutional practices, rather than on merely abstract ideas or disembodied theories: but that focus must be informed by an adequate understanding of normative theories.

Philosophies of punishment must therefore be assessed not merely as they appear on the page, but as they are (or could practicably be) realized in specific practices. Pragmatic penology must be subjected to close moral and political scrutiny as well as to rigorous empirical testing. And sociologists of punishment must remember that what they are trying to describe, analyse, and explain is itself a normative practice which must be understood accordingly. State punishment is a practice that claims to be structured by certain definite aims and values. Its officials justify the institution, and their activities within it, by reference to those legitimating aims and values, and often draw on normative philosophical theories of punishment to do so. Philosophy thus enters directly into this practical context, though rarely in a very coherent or elaborated way, and any sociology which disregards this normative dimension, or treats it as mere rhetoric, is liable to misunderstand the nature of the institution. No doubt there is usually some discrepancy between the declared aims of a practice and its actual operations; no doubt there are often latent objectives which officials are reluctant to articulate. But any adequate analysis of penal practice will still need to understand the normative rationales which structure official conduct; and any serious critique will have to articulate and defend normative arguments of its own.

The division of academic labour might try to set them apart, but philosophers and sociologists need each other if they are to make sense of the world. And anyone with a practical interest in penal matters— whether as policy-maker or as practitioner; as someone subject to penal measures, or as a member of the public in whose name state punishments are imposed—will need to draw upon a whole range of relevant materials, rather than on just one particular specialism. In this Introduction, and in the brief remarks which precede each of the collected essays, we offer a philosophical and sociological framework which should enable readers to relate the essays to each other, and to the intellectual and practical contexts from which they emerge.

2. Philosophical Issues

Punishment requires justification because it is morally problematic. It is morally problematic because it involves doing things to people that (when not described as 'punishment') seem morally wrong. It is usually wrong to lock people up, to take their money without return, or put them to death. But the state imprisons and fines offenders, and some states still execute them. How can such coercive and violent practices be justified?

Different kinds of moral theory generate different accounts of just why punishment is morally problematic, and thus of the kind of justification it requires. To classical utilitarians, for whom happiness (pleasure) is the only intrinsic good, and unhappiness (pain) the only intrinsic evil, punishment is morally problematic because it involves the infliction of pain or suffering. For such thinkers, a system of punishment can be justified only by showing that it produces sufficient pleasures, or prevents sufficient pains, to outweigh this evil (see Bentham 1789: ch. 13.2; on punishment as 'pain-delivery' see Christie 1981). By contrast, moralists who follow Kant in taking the values of autonomy and freedom to be central will see punishment as problematic because it is coercive, being inflicted on offenders against their manifest will. On this view, a system of punishment can be justified only by showing such coercion to be consistent with a proper respect for the offender as a rational and autonomous agent (see MURPHY).

Since state punishment is an exercise of state power, theories of punishment generally entail or rely upon some broader political theory of the state. Once again, different political theories will generate different justifications of punishment, since they involve different accounts of the legitimate role and scope of the state, and prescribe different relationships between the state authorities and individual citizens (see Philips 1986; Lacey 1988; but contrast Davis 1989). Liberal theories are concerned above all with individual rights and freedoms, and see the state's purpose as being to provide individuals with a secure framework within which they can pursue their own lives and their own choices of the good. From this perspective, punishment can be justified in so far as it protects the freedom of individual citizens to go about their lives safe from the threat of crime. But the state's power must also be strictly limited to ensure that it enhances rather than improperly constrains individual freedom. The liberal principles which permit the state to punish thus also set definite constraints on its power. It must punish no more than is necessary to secure the proper aims of punishment, and its penal institutions must not intrude too far on individual privacy and freedom (see Murphy 1985). By contrast, communitarian theories of the state are less inclined to view individuals in isolation from one another, or to distinguish so sharply the interests of individual citizens from those of the state. They place more emphasis on collective goods, and give the state a larger and more positive role in nurturing communal welfare and securing social values. Penal theories drawing on this tradition of political thought may thus support a more interventionist and welfarist form of penal system, and uphold a set of communitarian values and objectives (such as the rehabilitation and reintegration of offenders) which will seem quite inappropriate to strict liberals (see Lacey 1988: chs. 7–8; Norris 1991: ch. 5).

It follows that a justification of state punishment must show not merely that punishment achieves some good, but that it is a proper task of the state to pursue that good by these means. Much debate in recent years has questioned the right of the state to pursue penal aims—such as moral censure or education, or individual reform and rehabilitation—

which might otherwise seem desirable (see Murphy 1985; Shafer-Landau 1991; von Hirsch 1993: ch. 8; Rothman 1978).

A justification of punishment also presupposes some conception of crime. Punishment is inflicted on alleged offenders, for their alleged crimes; so we must ask what it is about crime that makes punishment an appropriate response to it. Consequentialists who take the prevention of crime to be the main aim of punishment may say that what matters is that crime is (actually or potentially) harmful: we may therefore cause harm (by punishment) in order to prevent the greater harms that would otherwise be caused by crime. Non-consequentialists who insist that punishment must be justified as an intrinsically appropriate response to crime (see below, s. 3) must offer an account of crime which shows how and why it requires a punitive response. They may argue, for instance, that crime involves taking an unfair advantage over the law-abiding—an advantage that punishment removes (see MURPHY); or that crimes are wrongdoings which deserve censure—a censure that punishment administers (see VON HIRSCH); or that crime separates the offender from the good and from the community—a separation which punishment can repair (see H. MORRIS). Such accounts of the character of crime are often implicit rather than clearly elaborated, but they require critical scrutiny if they are to form the basis for an account of the punitive response. Criminologists warn us that 'crime' is a misleading general term covering a wide range of very different kinds of conduct (see Walker 1987), so we should be careful of unexplicated assumptions about what crime is. Moreover, our common patterns of thought lead us to link 'crime' with 'punishment' in an apparently obvious and natural way; but as we will argue later, there is reason to doubt that the two concepts need always be combined in this manner (see BIANCHI; Hulsman 1986; de Haan 1990: chs. 1–2, 8).

To talk of 'the justification' of punishment might suggest that we need a unitary theory—one that founds the practice of punishment on some single value or on a set of non-conflicting values. For much of its history the philosophy of punishment was indeed presented as an opposition between 'consequentialists' and 'retributivists', each providing coherent but radically incompatible normative foundations for the institution. But is it plausible to suppose that any unitary justification can be provided? Should we not rather accept Hart's argument that 'any morally tolerable account' of punishment 'must exhibit it as a compromise between distinct and partly conflicting principles' (Hart 1968: 1; and see TONRY)? On Hart's own 'mixed' theory, the 'general justifying aim' of a system of punishment should be understood in consequentialist terms of crime reduction, but our pursuit of that aim should be subject to 'side-constraints' of justice, which forbid the punishment of the innocent or the disproportionately severe punishment of the guilty. These retributivist constraints should govern decisions in the individual case, even if they tend to obstruct the system's ability to pursue its general consequential aims. (On Hart see Ten 1987: 81–5; Morison 1988; Lacey 1988: 46–56; Primoratz 1989: 137–43. For other species of mixed account, see VON HIRSCH, TONRY.)

One question about any mixed theory is whether the 'mixture' is a stable one that can be consistently applied, rather than a shifting patchwork of compromises and arbitrary decisions. Can we so rank the different values that one will always take priority—by insisting, for instance, that the demands of justice always override those of crime prevention? Or must we recognize that in a complex institution of this kind decision-makers will always face normative conflicts which cannot be generally resolved or settled in advance (see Goldman 1979; Robinson 1987; von Hirsch 1993: ch. 6)?

Finally, we should note that philosophical accounts of punishment are ideal theories, which tell us what aims and values a system of punishment must embody if it is to be unqualifiedly justified. No actual system will fully match that ideal; all will be to a greater or lesser degree defective. Indeed, a crucial function of normative theories of punishment is to provide a critical standard against which actual practices can be measured—and found wanting. But what if theorists who recognize that existing practices fall well short of the appropriate normative standards also believe that there is no immediate prospect of reforming them so that they can be justified? Must they then hold that punishment as now practised is unjustified? And if it is, should we simply abandon the practice of punishment? Or perhaps seek to undermine its claims to legitimacy and the popular and political support on which it depends? And if one pursues this radical aim, what is to be done about law-breaking in the meantime, and about all the harms that flow from unchecked criminal conduct?

Or alternatively, should such theorists compromise, and accept that punishment is a practical necessity which, though unjust, must be accepted for fear of the consequences of abandoning it? But if so, where and how can we draw the line between an institution which we declare unjust and one which is altogether intolerable (see MURPHY; Lacey 1988: 195–8; Duff 1991; Tunick 1992)?

Some thinkers do of course argue that punishment *should* be abolished (see the abolitionist perspective discussed in s. 8 below). But it is a fair criticism of too many philosophers that they do not think radically enough about the institution of punishment. They implicitly assume that there *must* be some adequate justification for state punishment, if only one can find it, rather than asking seriously whether such an institution can be justified at all. The most important task for philosophy in this context is perhaps not to 'justify' the penal system, but to ensure that the massive power of the penal state is subjected to constant normative scrutiny and criticism, by articulating the values against which it must be judged, and by questioning the assumptions on which it rests (for a critical overview of recent work in the philosophy of punishment, see Duff 1995).

3. Consequentialism and Non-Consequentialism

Normative theories of punishment are typically classified as either 'consequentialist' or 'non-consequentialist', or as a mixture of the two. Non-consequentialist theories are often called 'retributivist', although this label has been applied to such different theories that its utility might now be doubted (see Cottingham 1979).

A consequentialist holds that the rightness or wrongness of any action or practice depends solely on its overall consequences. It is right if its consequences are good (at least as good as those of any available alternative), and wrong if its consequences are bad (worse than those of some available alternative). So to justify a system of punishment we must show not only that it does some good, or prevents some evil, but also that no available alternative practice would achieve as much or more good at lower cost. Consequentialists differ in their accounts of what makes consequences good or bad. Classical utilitarians see practices as right or wrong in so far as they promote or destroy 'the greatest happiness of the greatest number'. Recent consequentialists have offered different criteria. Thus Braithwaite and Pettit (1990: ch. 5) posit 'dominion' (the assured liberty of citizens living under the rule of law) as the good to be maximized; whilst Lacey (1988: chs. 5, 8) identifies 'autonomy' and 'welfare' as the two central goods within a communitarian view of the state.

The common feature of all consequentialist accounts is that they justify punishment by its contingent, instrumental, contribution to some independently identifiable good. That is to say, the good that punishment is to promote—whether this is happiness, dominion, autonomy, welfare, or crime prevention—can be identified without reference to punishment itself. It is then a contingent question whether punishment is a necessary or efficient means of achieving such goods. Empirical information about the effects of punishment, and about possible alternatives, is crucial to any justification of the institution (see, for instance, WILSON and MATHIESEN on the efficacy of punishment as a deterrent). The contingency of the link between punishment and its consequentialist aims gives rise to the most familiar objection to purely consequentialist accounts of punishment: that they would justify manifestly unjust punishments (scapegoating the innocent, or 'making an example' of the guilty, for instance) if such measures would efficiently serve the system's consequentialist aims. Consequentialists have responded, however, by arguing that a proper view of the full range of ends that penal systems must serve (which includes maintaining public confidence in the law) and of the ways in which such ends can practicably be served, will generate a purely consequentialist justification for a strict prohibition on punishing the innocent. (See Rawls 1955; Hare 1981: chs. 3, 9.7; Braithwaite and Pettit 1990: 72–6. On Rawls, see Duff 1986: 162–4. On Hare, see Primoratz 1989: 129–37.)

A non-consequentialist, on the other hand, insists that actions may be right or wrong in virtue of their intrinsic character, independently of their consequences. This approach is expressed most prominently in the retributivist claim that the guilty, and only the guilty, deserve to be punished, and that punishment is justified if, or only if, it inflicts on the guilty the suffering they deserve. We should distinguish here between negative retributivism, which holds that *only* the guilty may be punished, and then *only* to the extent of their desert—which does not imply that such punishments *must* be imposed—and positive retributivism, which holds that the guilty must always be punished, to the full extent of their desert (see Mackie 1982; Dolinko 1991: 539–43). Positive retributivism offers a complete justification of punishment: negative retributivism cannot offer this, but may figure as a side-constraint on consequentialist accounts of the positive aims of punishment (see for instance Hart 1968; Walker 1991: ch. 11; neither Hart nor Walker, however, found their negative principles on the notion of 'desert').

The central problem for any retributivist, whether negative or positive, is to explain the idea of desert. Punishment is supposed to be justified as an intrinsically appropriate response to crime; the notion of 'desert' is supposed to indicate that justificatory link between past crime and present punishment. But just what is that link? What is 'desert', which supposedly makes punishment the appropriate response to crime (see Honderich 1984: 26–33; Ardal 1984)? Some writers appeal to the supposedly shared intuition that the guilty 'deserve to suffer' (see Moore

1987). But that intuition, however widely shared, requires explanation and justification. A common criticism of retributivist theories is that they fail to provide any clear account of this central concept, or any genuinely non-consequentialist account of the justificatory relationship between crime and punishment (see Honderich 1984: ch. 2). Different versions of retributivism try to meet this criticism, by explaining why the guilty deserve to suffer punishment (see for instance MURPHY; VON HIRSCH; Duff 1986; Hampton 1992a, 1992b).

Consequentialist theories of punishment are instrumentalist and forward-looking: they justify punishment as a contingently efficient technique for achieving certain beneficial effects. Retributivist theories are intrinsicalist and backward-looking: they justify punishment in terms of its relation to a past offence. But there is a third kind of theory which differs from both these approaches, and is not merely a mixture of the two. Theories of this third kind—which are variously referred to as educative or communicative—give punishment a forward-looking purpose, linking it to a goal (such as moral reform or education) which it might or might not achieve. They thus differ from purely retributivist theories, which hold that the purpose of punishment is fulfilled by the fact of punishment itself. However, they also differ from consequentialist theories in that the link between punishment and its purpose is not purely contingent. Punishment, on such accounts, is an intrinsically appropriate (not merely a contingently efficacious) means of pursuing that goal (see below, 14–16; H. MORRIS; Duff 1986).

4. The Decline of Consequentialism

In the 1950s and 1960s, penal discourse was predominantly, although never exclusively, consequentialist. In the course of the twentieth century, the rise of new professional groups, such as social workers, psychologists and criminologists, gradually transformed the character of criminal justice and the ideologies of punishment held by its practitioners. They became less reliant on traditional legalistic and moralistic absolutes, and more committed to the idea of basing penal practice upon scientific research into the causes of crime and the crime-preventive impact of particular penal measures. The same programmes and attitudes which fostered 'the Welfare State' sought to make the penal system an instrument of social engineering through which crime could be prevented. Punishment could prevent crime by deterring potential offenders or by incapacitating actual offenders: but it could achieve even greater goods, it was hoped, by reforming and rehabilitating offenders. Retributivist ideas still influenced sentencing decisions, and the negative retributivist principle that only the guilty should be punished was still implicitly accepted. But positive retributivism was typically dismissed as outmoded and reactionary: the reigning consensus was that penal policy should be oriented towards the treatment and training of offenders, and the main debate was about which techniques would best promote these reformative ambitions. Some theorists indeed argued that punishment was not an effective technique for promoting such ends: instead of punishing criminals, we should 'treat' them in whatever way would be humanely effective (see Wootton 1963; Menninger 1968).

One of the most striking changes of the last twenty years has been the extent to which consequentialist ideas have been abandoned, and retributivist ideas revived (see Tonry and Morris 1978; Bottoms and Preston 1980: chs. 1–3; Radzinowicz and Hood 1981; Galligan 1981; von Hirsch 1985; ch. 1; Hudson 1987). 'Just deserts' has again become a respectable and prominent rationale for punishment (and indeed for the administration of prison and probation regimes), and the most innovative philosophical work has tended to focus on the reworking of retributivist and other non-consequentialist theories.

This change is a philosophical corollary of institutional and ideological changes which have affected the penal system since the late 1960s. The perceived failure of many rehabilitative programmes, widespread concern that such programmes were open to administrative abuse, and the politically damaging fact that crime rates rose dramatically in many jurisdictions just at the time when a more reformative penal system was emerging, combined to undermine the optimistic ideal of a reformative penality (see Allen 1981; Bottoms 1980). This process of disillusionment was to a degree inevitable. For one thing, reformers' claims about the efficacy of the treatment approach were overblown and unrealistic. The penal system deals with only a small proportion of the total population of offenders, and generally does so only for short and intermittent periods. It was always unlikely that such measures could have a major impact on the crime rates, or even upon individual offenders after their release. For another, contemporary penal systems have developed careful methods of monitoring their own practices, so that any failures cannot be ignored for long. The same scientific methods and criminological knowledge which were intended to make the penal system a system of correction and rehabilitation would subsequently show how rarely those goals were actually achieved. By the mid-1970s, the rehabilitative ideal had thus come under serious attack, as had penal consequentialism more generally. The pessimistic belief that 'nothing works' became almost as widespread as penological optimism had been in the previous decades (see Martinson 1974; Brody 1976; Wilson 1975).

This sea-change was part of a larger reaction against the consequentialist mentality and the kind of scientistic social engineering which often accompanied it. It was a critical reaction to the by-now established institutions of the welfare state which, during the 1970s, began to be viewed by some not as necessary responses to grave social problems, but as interfering bureaucracies which were themselves a source of problems and oppressions. This reaction focused not only on the perceived failure of consequentialist strategies to achieve their declared goals, but also on the perceived moral costs of such strategies. Liberal theorists especially began to reassert the importance of justice over utility, and of individual rights against the claims of the state (Rawls 1972 and Dworkin 1978 are two seminal works in this movement). Thus after a brief period when the optimism of the New Deal and the Beveridge Report made it possible to think of the state as a benevolent, competent authority promoting social welfare, by the 1970s this view gave way to a neo-liberalism that saw big government as a threat to individual freedom and moral agency.

One manifestation of this moral shift was that theorists began to focus on the rights of the guilty as well as those of the innocent. This new focus was reinforced by the rise of a prisoners' rights movement, in the USA and elsewhere, which was critical of the treatment approach, particularly of indeterminate sentencing and of the apparently arbitrary discretion involved in executive decisions concerning release on parole (see Fitzgerald 1977; Jacobs 1983b). Where once the offender was regarded by progressives as a misfit in need of reform, there now arose a new conception which thought in terms of the offender's civil rights and of the need to protect prisoners and others from an over-intrusive state and from the discretionary powers of treatment professionals. These objections applied most immediately to 'rehabilitative' practices which, at their worst, were capable of rank injustices and inhumanity under the guise of individualized treatment and, even at their best, were liable to treat the offender as an object to be manipulated rather than as a responsible moral agent (see Morris 1968; American Friends Service Committee 1971; Fogel 1975; Jackson 1971; Allen 1981. For defences of 'rehabilitation' against these criticisms see CARLEN; ROTMAN; Cullen and Gilbert 1982; Palmer 1992).

The objection that a consequentialist approach fails to respect the offender's moral status was also brought against policies which emerged

in the 1970s and 1980s—for instance, against strategies of 'selective incapacitation' which aim to incarcerate 'high rate' or 'dangerous' offenders
for extended periods, whilst permitting much more lenient sentences for
occasional or 'non-dangerous' offenders, even though the offence committed had been the same (see Greenwood and Abrahamse 1982; also
N. MORRIS). The most immediate problem for such policies is that given
the inaccuracy of our predictive techniques as applied to individual cases,
too many 'false positives'—i.e. individuals mistakenly identified as 'career
criminals' or 'dangerous offenders'—are liable to be detained. But the
deeper objection is that such preventive detention, even if based on accurate predictions, denies the moral status (the moral rights) of those
detained. They are imprisoned not for what they have done, but because
of what they might subsequently do if not detained. But giving individuals their due as responsible moral agents requires that we leave them free
to choose for themselves whether to obey the law, and subject them to
the coercive attentions of the state only if and when they choose to
disobey. (For the arguments on either side of this debate, see Floud and
Young 1981; Bottoms and Brownsword 1982; Lacey 1983; Honderich
1982; von Hirsch 1985; Duff 1986: 170–8; von Hirsch and Ashworth 1992:
ch. 3. N. MORRIS offers a highly qualified defence of selective incapacitation.)

As for deterrent policies, these seem to treat offenders and potential
offenders as rational and responsible agents in so far as a deterrent strategy assumes that individuals are capable of acting prudently—of seeing
the threat of punishment as a reason not to break the law and of acting
accordingly. And if we could be reasonably sure that punishment is effective as a deterrent (on this see WILSON, MATHIESEN), there would be consequentialist arguments justifying its use as a proper means of reducing
crime (see WALKER). But it might be objected that in using an offender's
punishment as a means to deter others we are improperly treating the
offender 'merely as a means' to that end, so violating the Kantian moral
imperative that individuals should be treated as 'ends' and never 'merely
as means'. (See Kant 1785: 90–3; Kant 1797: 99–100; MURPHY: 48. For discussions of this notoriously obscure slogan see Murphy 1979; Honderich
1984: 60–1; WALKER; Walker 1991: ch. 6.) Furthermore, in trying to dis-
suade the citizen from breaking the law by threats of suffering (rather
than by urging the moral reasons which support the claim that the law
ought to be obeyed), we face the charge that we are treating him or her
'like a dog instead of with the freedom and respect due' to a human being
(Hegel 1821: 246; see Duff 1986: 178–86; see also MATHIESEN).

Some consequentialist theorists have responded to such criticisms by arguing that a properly structured consequentialist penal system can avoid improperly violating individual rights (see for instance WALKER; Walker 1991; Braithwaite and Pettit 1990). Others argue that the state has the right to threaten punishment as a means of social defence, and that this is compatible with respect for individual rights so long as potential offenders are given fair warning of penalties, and are punished only if they voluntarily break the law (see Nino 1983; Quinn 1985; Farrell 1985). But to many critics of consequentialism the problem of reconciling punishment with a proper respect for the rights and integrity of the person punished is central to penal philosophy, and is one which no purely or primarily consequentialist theory can resolve. Some of the most interesting and innovative work of the past twenty-five years has been directed to dealing with this problem, and it has done so by drawing upon the resources of the retributivist tradition (for a critical survey of some of the early contributions to this 'new retributivism', see Honderich 1984: Postscript).

5. The Retributivist Revival

A common theme amongst the new retributivists is that the primary aim of the penal system should be to ensure that offenders receive their 'just deserts': that they should suffer fair and determinate punishments proportionate to the seriousness of their crimes. This 'just deserts' principle, which was current in the eighteenth century, gained new popularity in reaction to the perceived unfairness of the treatment-oriented system that had gradually developed during the first half of the twentieth century—in particular, the indeterminate sentence (which left the prisoner's date of release in the hands of the parole board), and the practice of individualized sentencing (which purportedly sentenced according to the treatment needs of the offender rather than the seriousness of the offence). During the 1970s and 1980s 'just deserts' became a key slogan in the movement for determinate sentencing in the USA—a movement that led many states, and the federal sentencing authorities, to repeal their indeterminate sentencing laws in favour of new codes which aimed to reduce judicial discretion and to promote greater consistency and certainty in sentencing (see von Hirsch 1976; Tonry and Morris 1978; Radzinowicz and Hood 1981; Tonry 1988; von Hirsch and Ashworth 1992: ch. 5).

These new sentencing codes have been the subject of much debate and criticism in recent years—particularly from judges who claim that their ability to deliver just sentences in individual cases has been undermined by statutory guide-lines. Even their proponents admit that the political and administrative processes that shaped the new systems have sometimes undermined the reformers' intentions (see Greenberg and Humphries 1980). As ZIMRING points out, the task of structuring and regulating punishment is a highly complex one, which must engage *de facto* sentencers such as prosecutors and parole boards as well as trial judges, and which runs up against problems such as the open-ended character of legal categories, and the conflicting motivations that influence different decision-makers in the criminal justice process. Despite these difficulties, many commentators still see sentencing guide-lines and fixed tariffs as being preferable to the system of largely uncontrolled discretion which still operates in the UK and elsewhere. Indeed, the Criminal Justice Act 1991 (for England and Wales) took a small step towards such an approach (see Wasik and Taylor 1991; Ashworth 1992). As the White Paper preceding the Act stated, 'The aim of the Government's proposals is better justice through a more consistent approach to sentencing, so that convicted criminals get their "just desserts" [*sic*]. The severity of the sentence of the court should be directly related to the seriousness of the offence' (Home Office 1990: para. 1.6). As we noted above, a central question for retributivists concerns the meaning and foundations of this slogan. Why do offenders deserve to be punished? How are their 'just deserts' to be calculated, and translated into specific sentences?

One answer is that the offender takes an unfair advantage over the law-abiding in breaking the law, and that this unfair advantage can be annulled by a proportionate punishment (see MURPHY, and the Editors' Preface to his essay). This is a non-consequentialist account: the annulment of the offender's unfair advantage or benefit is not a contingent consequence of the punishment, but is achieved by the very fact of punishment. It is, moreover, a positive retributivism: punishment is not merely permissible, but is required by justice, since law-abiding citizens suffer injustice if offenders are allowed to get away with their unfair advantage. For some time, this account was widely seen as the most plausible version of retributivism, but it has more recently been subjected to stringent criticism (see the Editors' Preface to MURPHY).

Another kind of answer to this question begins by emphasizing the expressive character of punishment. Punishment consists not merely in hard treatment or deprivation, but involves an essential element of condemnation: this is what distinguishes a fine from a tax, for instance, or penal imprisonment from other kinds of detention such as psychiatric detention or quarantine (see FEINBERG, and the Editors' Preface to his essay). We can understand how crime, if it involves genuine wrongdoing, deserves to be condemned or censured. Moreover, censure or condemnation is backward-looking, focusing on the wrongdoing that has already occurred. The expressive character of punishment might thus provide the basis for a more plausible version of retributivism which explains the justifying relation between crime and punishment in terms of the relation between wrongdoing and the condemnation it deserves.

But any such account faces two problems. First, even if a crime deserves censure, why should it be the state's job to administer that censure? Why not leave that task to the victim, or to other individual citizens? Second, why should that censure be expressed by means of penal sanctions which inflict hard treatment and suffering on the offender? Could it not be conveyed merely by a conviction, or by some other purely symbolic means, such as a badge which offenders might be ordered to wear? To justify state punishment in its present forms, we would need to show not only that the condemnation of crime is an appropriate task for the state, but that that condemnation is properly expressed by means of such hard treatments as imprisonment, fines, or even death (see Christie 1977, 1981; he argues for the necessity of blame, but against 'pain-delivering' punishment).

One could offer purely consequentialist reasons both for formally censuring criminal conduct, and for doing so through punishments which involve hard treatment. Censure can be an effective way of changing someone's future conduct (see Brandt 1961), and hard treatment can make the censure more effective as a deterrent (see Walker 1991: 21–33, 78–82; for a sophisticated consequentialist account of punishment as 'stigmatizing' see Braithwaite and Pettit 1990; Braithwaite 1989). Others argue, however, that censure should be understood (and must be understood, if it is to respect the offender as a responsible agent) as an intrinsically appropriate response to wrongdoing, and that punishment as censure must be justified in non-consequentialist terms (see VON HIRSCH; Duff 1986: chs. 2, 9). As for hard treatment, some retributivists argue that it is necessary if the particular kind of censure which the offender deserves is to be appropriately communicated (for a sophisticated argument of this sort see Hampton 1992a, 1992b; for criticism see Dolinko 1991; Marshall 1992). Others instead offer a mixed theory: punishment is justified primarily in retributivist terms, as appropriate censure, but hard treatment is used to convey that censure for consequentialist reasons—to add a deterrent force to what would otherwise be merely a moral appeal, and thus to increase the crime-preventive efficacy of the law (see VON HIRSCH for a sophisticated version of this argument).

Other communicative theories of punishment (as we can term them) portray punishment as an educative or reformative process that aims, through the hard treatment which it involves, to induce the offender to repent, to reform, and so to become reconciled with the community. (See H. MORRIS, and the Preface to his essay. See also Hampton 1984; Falls 1987; Duff 1986; for criticisms see Bickenbach 1988; Ten 1990; Shafer-Landau 1991; Baker 1992; von Hirsch 1993: ch. 8; Narayan 1993.) Such accounts differ from those which portray punishment as a matter of imposing 'just deserts'. They ascribe a further aim to punishment—an aim which is not achieved by the very fact of punishment, but depends on how the punishment is received, since the possibility of moral repentance and reform depends on how the offender understands and responds to the punishment. They thus seek not merely to impose just deserts, or to express censure: they aim to enter into a moral dialogue, a communicative enterprise, with the offender.

Nor, however, are such communicative theories straightforwardly consequentialist. For one thing, some such theorists hold that we should make the communicative effort which punishment involves even if we are certain that it will fail: even if we are sure that the offender will remain unmoved and unreformed, we owe it both to the victim who has been wronged, and to the offender as a moral agent and fellow citizen, to make that effort (see Duff 1986: 264–6). For another thing, the process must address offenders as rational moral agents, and appeal to their moral understanding: the aim should not be merely to 're-form' offenders by whatever effective means we can find (as on a purely consequentialist approach), but to persuade offenders to reform themselves (see H. MORRIS; Duff 1986: 261–2).

As Morris makes clear in his essay, such an approach involves a species of paternalism, albeit one that seeks to nurture the moral autonomy of the individual. Some liberals will find it objectionable to allow the state thus to 'impinge on the inner citadels of [the offender's] soul' (Lucas 1968: 221; and see Murphy 1985), and here the disagreement is essentially a political one. For behind many of the new theories which stress moral communication or education lies a more communitarian conception of society, which sees individuals' well-being as crucially dependent on their place within a community and their attachment to its shared values, and which would allow the state an active role in integrating individuals (and reintegrating offenders) into the moral community. One key question here concerns the feasibility, as well as the desirability, of such a political conception in today's heterogenous, pluralistic, and 'multi-cultural' societies.

6. The Philosophy of Punishment and Penal Theory

As Nigel Walker points out (1969: 1), there is a difference between the philosophy of punishment, which is what we have been discussing so far, and the more practically-oriented discourse of penal theory. The latter is more directly concerned with the practical ends of penal action than with the attempt to articulate a general normative theory of punishment—particularly with the aims of sentencing, but also with the aims of prison or probation administration. When penologists and penal practitioners engage in explicitly normative discourse (which they perhaps do too rarely), it is this latter genre that tends to be employed (see Walker 1980; Ashworth 1992; von Hirsch and Ashworth 1992; Morris 1974).

There are, of course, close links between these two kinds of discourse. The aims which penal theory has traditionally held out as proper objectives to be pursued in sentencing include retribution, deterrence, reform, denunciation or condemnation, and incapacitation or 'social defence'—aims which are articulated and debated in the philosophy of punishment. And just as retributivist philosophers of punishment find its justification in its backward-looking focus on the past crime, so the pursuit of retribution or denunciation in sentencing prompts an 'offence-centred' approach which attends only to the nature and seriousness of the offence for which the offender is being sentenced. (One recurrent issue in this context concerns the relevance of the offender's prior record: see von Hirsch 1981, and TONRY's discussion of the Minnesota sentencing guide-lines; also the provisions of s. 29 of the Criminal Justice Act 1991, which were much criticized and soon abandoned; see Criminal Justice Act 1993, s. 66(6).) Similarly, just as consequentialist theories of punishment look forward to its effects, so the pursuit of such aims as individual deterrence, reform, and incapacitation prompts a more 'offender-centred' mode of reasoning in sentencing, which requires more information about the offender, and about the likely effects on him or her of different possible sentences.

We noted above that the recent history of the philosophy of punishment has seen a shift from consequentialist towards retributivist theories of punishment. A parallel trend can be observed in the recent history of penal policy, which has seen a shift of official and academic emphasis away from the 'reductionist' concerns of deterrence, reform, and social defence toward the more retributivist concerns of just deserts or denunciation. However, the connections between the philosophy of punishment, penal policy, and actual penal practice are neither straightforward nor particularly close, for a variety of reasons.

First, penal decision-makers (both legislators and sentencers) tend to draw eclectically upon the broad normative arguments which the philosophy of punishment provides, employing different kinds of reasoning for what they see as different kinds of case. Thus, at the level of official policy, the renewed emphasis on just deserts in the UK is accompanied by an incapacitative approach for violent or high-rate offenders, and a residual treatment framework for certain groups such as sex offenders and drug addicts: but little attempt is made to reconcile these apparently contradictory retributivist and consequentialist modes of reasoning, beyond the blank assertion that sentencing can serve both kinds of aim (see for instance Home Office 1988: para. 1.5). Similarly, though judicial discretion in sentencing has been increasingly constrained (more so in the USA than in the UK), sentencers still typically retain a discretion which allows them to choose between various possible goals, or to construct for themselves homespun compromises between different goals which would not stand up to close philosophical scrutiny (see Hogarth 1974).

Second, the choices which sentencers have to make are not, in any immediate sense, choices about the general purposes of punishment. They must decide which of a restricted range of possible sanctions (imprisonment, a fine, a community service order, probation . . .) is the appropriate kind of penalty for the case at hand, and what level of the chosen sanction should be imposed. Sometimes this choice will involve a choice between different penal aims or purposes, as when retribution might require a custodial sentence but a probation order would be more likely to reform the offender and reduce future crime (see TONRY: 155–8). But it is by no means clear that such specific sentencing choices can or should be guided directly by a particular philosophical theory of punishment (see Morris and Tonry 1990: 90–2 on the distinction between 'purposes at sentencing' and 'the general . . . purposes of sentencing (or punishment)'. For a criticism of Morris and Tonry's distinction, see von Hirsch 1993: 64–8).

Third, the standard kinds of sanction can usually be portrayed as serving any one, or several, of those general aims which figure in the philosophy of punishment. This makes it possible for sentencers to believe that the particular sentence they pass will inflict just deserts, denounce, deter, reform, and incapacitate all at the same time. It allows policy-makers to relate particular sanctions to a whole series of claimed 'purposes', or rationalizations, some of which are bogus, and others of which depend heavily upon the character of the local regime. It is a characteristic of penal rhetoric that favoured kinds of sanction are portrayed as achieving currently fashionable ends—ends which in practice tend to be somewhat elusive. Even the apparently most readily attainable goals, such as the infliction of retributive suffering or the incapacitation of the offender, may not always be realized (see HIRST; Brody and Tarling 1980); and it is notoriously difficult to implement deterrent or rehabilitative regimes that will 'work' for the majority of those sentenced to them (see below, 24–5).

Fourth, the actual effects of developments in the philosophy of punishment, or in penal theory, on the practices of penal decision-makers and functionaries are complex and unpredictable. Sentencers are not automatically responsive to shifts in philosophical fashion or to changes of official government policy; and when penal regimes are affected by the prevailing philosophy, the consequent changes are not always intended or foreseen. For example, many commentators have noted that during the post-war era in which a consequentialist, treatment philosophy held sway, prison reformers and administrators tended to use rehabilitative arguments to justify the liberalization and humanization of prison life, rather than apply penal treatment in its strictest sense (see Cressey 1983; Cullen and Gilbert 1982). Indeed, it is a fair criticism of the critics of rehabilitation that they tended to examine the *logic* of the rehabilitative approach, and some extreme examples of its application, rather than the way it was routinely put into practice. Similarly, while the early advocates of 'just deserts' were typically liberal reformers who hoped to reduce the general severity of punishment, and especially of imprisonment (see for instance von Hirsch 1976), the rhetoric of 'just deserts' can also be used to rationalize increased levels of punishment by 'law and order' politicians (see Hudson 1987). It is as yet unclear whether the current emphasis on 'just deserts' by the UK government will lead to prison and probation regimes in which offenders' rights are better respected and justice is given greater priority, or will become a licence for a more harshly punitive style of dealing with offenders (see Woolf and Tumim 1991, and Coyle 1991, on justice in prisons; Rees and Hall Williams 1989, and Bottoms and McWilliams 1979, on similar debates about the future of probation).

One general point which these considerations highlight is that there is a large gap between the general normative theorizing about punishment in which philosophers typically engage, and the kinds of decision which penal policy-makers and practitioners have to make. No general theory of punishment can apply itself, and philosophers who wish to influence penal policy would do well to think through their normative principles to show how they could be embodied in specific practices, rather than assuming that thinking about implementation can simply be left to others (but see von Hirsch 1993 for a sustained attempt to bring general theory to bear on practical policy; and Braithwaite and Pettit 1990). Government policy-makers are learning this lesson, and now draw up action plans and detailed implementation strategies to ensure that legislative intentions are carried through into the daily routines of practitioners. Whilst philosophers may lack the skills and knowledge required for detailed policy-making, they must recognize that effective philosophy, like effective government, requires a combination of broad vision with close attention to practical detail.

But how far should we even hope, or aim, for a penal system which is structured by just one coherent normative theory of punishment? Should we not rather recognize that punishment is inevitably a locus both of conflicting principles, and of conflicts between principles and more pragmatic considerations? Von Hirsch argues, for instance, that the principle of proportionality should be the primary guide to sentencing: legislators, policy-makers, and sentencers should strive to ensure that each offender receives a sentence whose severity is proportionate to the seriousness of the crime, in order that the punishment can express the appropriate degree of censure (von Hirsch 1993). Critics have objected, first, that we cannot in practice hope to achieve a proper proportionality between crime and punishment; second, that there are other principles such as that of parsimony in punishment which may conflict with the demands of proportionality; and third that an undue emphasis on strict proportionality stands in the way of making effective use of the wide range of 'intermediate sanctions' which are finding favour amongst penal policy-makers (see TONRY).

The role of 'intermediate sanctions' (sanctions such as intensive probation or supervision, substantial fines, and community service, which fall between imprisonment and traditional probation) is one of the main focuses of current debate in penal policy. Interest in such sanctions, both in the UK and in the USA, was sparked partly by the spiralling costs of an ever-increasing prison population (see Mathiesen 1990; Zimring and Hawkins 1990), and partly by the growing recognition that prison is a counter-productive measure which tends to reinforce rather than to weaken criminal tendencies. On both sides of the Atlantic governments have sought to persuade sentencers to reduce their use of imprisonment as a sanction. In the USA, this has been done by the use of statutory sentencing guide-lines (see von Hirsch and Ashworth 1992: ch. 5); while in the UK governments have sought to influence sentencers by the provision of a wider range of 'alternatives to imprisonment' such as community service, house arrest, curfews, and intensive probation, as well as by specifying certain conditions which must be satisfied before a prison sentence is imposed (see Criminal Justice Act 1991; Home Office 1990). These reductionist efforts are frequently undercut by the law and order rhetoric which ministers deploy in public: but they also pose new kinds of problem for penal philosophy. What role should such sanctions play (and correlatively, what role should imprisonment play) in the penal armoury? What goals or principles should guide their use? In what kinds of case should they be used? Can we, or should we, try to apply them in accordance with the principle of proportionality—which would require us to rank these very different kinds of sanction on a single scale of severity, in order to ensure that the severity of the punishment is proportionate to the seriousness of the crime? This also raises the issue of how 'severity' is to be measured. Tonry notes the different impacts which the 'same' sentence can have (TONRY 150; see Morris and Tonry 1990: 82–97); and the controversy aroused in the UK by the introduction of 'unit fines' shows how different understandings of the notion of 'severity' can be (the unit fine provisions of s. 18 of the Criminal Justice Act 1991 were rapidly abolished by s. 65 of the Criminal Justice Act 1993; on unit fines generally, see Gibson 1990; Greene 1988).

What is needed is a principled discussion not only of the role of intermediate sanctions, but more generally of the appropriate modes of punishment. What kinds of punishment should be at the disposal of the courts? This is an issue too rarely tackled in the philosophy of punishment (though see Morris and Tonry 1990; von Hirsch 1993; Adler 1992: Part II; Duff 1992), but we do need to ask whether we can find any principled foundations either for the provision of a particular range of penalties, or for decisions about what kinds of penalty are appropriate for what kinds of offence. However, once we begin to ask such questions, we must also attend more carefully to the ways in which the uses of particular kinds of penalty are related to complex webs of social, political, and economic factors; we must, that is, attend to the social determinants of penal practice.

7. An Empirical Grounding for the Philosophy of Punishment

We have so far been concerned with current debates in the philosophy of punishment, and with the relationship between these philosophical debates and the actual practices of penal institutions and policy-makers. We have suggested that effective thinking about punishment requires a closer relationship between high-level normative theory and ground-level practical decision-making. We now turn to some of the ways in which the philosophy of punishment should interact with penology and the sociology of punishment.

Penology is a practically-oriented form of social science which emerged in the early nineteenth century, developing alongside the prison and the other emergent institutions of modern criminal justice. Its primary concern has always been to monitor the practices of penal institutions, tracing and evaluating their effects, and suggesting ways in which institutional objectives might be more efficiently achieved. This was at first an in-house activity, undertaken by officials who developed 'penitentiary science' as a tool with which to rationalize and legitimate their activities (see, for instance, Ruggles-Brise 1924; Wines 1895). Later, during the twentieth century, it broadened its scope beyond the prison (studying the administration of probation, fines, the prosecution, and the court process, etc.) and began to establish a base in universities as well as in government institutions, becoming an important element in the new discipline of criminology (see Garland 1994). Today, penological research covers the entire range of penal practice and administration, down to the most minute details, providing policy-makers with a form of self-consciousness or reflexivity which feeds into the policy-making process— although research findings are of course rarely the sole basis of policy-making (on the reflexivity of modern institutions, see Giddens 1990; on the role of penological research in policy formation see Hood 1974; Bottomley 1989). Like all knowledges tied to specific institutions, penology has a critical dimension, in so far as it identifies problems and suggests improvements which would enhance the system's effectiveness and thus help to rationalize it. But most penology takes the existing institutions for granted, and situates itself within them, so that more radical questions about alternative ways of responding to crime or administering punishment tend not to be part of its research agenda (see Garland 1990: ch. 1; Garland and Young 1983: ch. 1).

The sociology of punishment, in contrast, is less closely tied to the existing institutions and more willing to raise basic questions about the ways in which society organizes and deploys its power to punish. Its main concern is not to promote the efficient functioning of penal institutions, but instead to explore the relations between punishment and society, to understand how punishment functions as a social institution, and to trace its broader role in social life (see Garland 1990). Sociologists ask why particular societies adopt particular modes of punishment, and investigate the conditions which make certain styles of sanctioning both possible and desirable in particular social situations (see HIRST). Much of that research is historical: it investigates, for instance, the genealogy of the modern prison (see Durkheim 1902; Foucault 1977; Ignatieff 1978; Spierenburg 1984); the growth of the generalized use of fines (see Rusche and Kirchheimer 1968; Young forthcoming); and the development of the modern 'penal-welfare' system which combines punishment with more positive forms of social regulation (see Garland 1985; Rothman 1980). Comparative analysis is also used to explore why particular jurisdictions differ in their use of penal measures, for instance their rates of imprisonment (see Rutherford 1984; Zimring and Hawkins 1990; and especially Downes 1988), or their reliance upon fines (see Young forthcoming), or their continued use of capital punishment (see Zimring and Hawkins 1986: 3–25). A sophisticated combination of comparative and historical methods is used to study correlations between penal phenomena (e.g. rates of imprisonment) and other social indices such as unemployment rates, demographic variables, crime rates, and shifts in political and public opinion (see Zimring and Hawkins 1990: ch. 5; Box 1987; Melossi 1989). There is also a strong tradition of sociological investigation of the inner life of the prison and other 'total institutions', tracing the characteristic dynamics and relationships of the world that inmates and captors construct for themselves while inside (see Goffman 1968; Sykes 1958; Cressey 1961; Clemmer 1958; Jacobs 1977, 1983a; Carlen 1983; Mathiesen 1965). At a more general level, sociologists also examine the relations between normative theories of punishment and the social, political, and economic contexts in which they emerge (see for instance Garland 1985, 1990; Norrie 1991).

Such studies frequently have a critical bite which derives not so much from explicit moral argument as from the unsettling character of the facts that they reveal. Practices which we take for granted may be shown to be quite recent inventions, or to be limited to particular kinds of society; and any assumption that punishment is justly distributed may be disturbed by evidence that its use is correlated not with criminal guilt, but with economic status or membership of a particular social class (Foucault 1977; Platt and Takagi 1980; Box 1987; Jacobs 1983*b*).

Not all of these inquiries are relevant to the philosophy of punishment. But some of them are, and normative philosophy must take account of penological and sociological studies if it is to ground its arguments successfully and apply them to the actual world. In part, this is a matter of maintaining a sharper awareness of the historical contingency both of penal practices and of normative penal theories. It involves recognizing that 'punishment' is not an abstract ahistorical structure, but a social institution which takes different forms in different social contexts. It also involves an awareness that the normative theories which philosophers articulate—and which they may purport to found on entirely abstract or a priori principles—grow out of particular traditions of political, social, and moral thought which themselves depend upon particular social, political, and economic contexts (see MacIntyre 1985). We need at least to ask what kinds of political and social structure, and what conceptions of the state and the citizen, are presupposed by any normative theory; and to ask too how far any such theory can claim to be doing more than reflect the political structures of the particular society in which it emerges.

But even once we accept some normative theory of punishment, we need to attend to sociological studies if we are to apply it to the actual world. This is true even of non-consequentialist theories which do not found the justification of punishment on its beneficial effects. If punishment is, for instance, to deprive offenders of the unfair advantage they gain in breaking the law, we must ask whether criminals in our societies can plausibly be said to gain any such unfair advantage (see MURPHY). If it is to communicate the censure which offenders deserve for their wrongdoing, we must ask whether in our societies offenders do generally deserve such censure, whether it is actually and justly administered to those who deserve it, and whether our existing penal institutions are effective vehicles for such communication (see CARLEN; MATHIESEN).

It is obvious too that consequentialist approaches to punishment must be informed by adequate sociological knowledge. In insisting that penal measures should be used to achieve positive benefits such as deterrence, reformation, or incapacitation, they presuppose that specific practices exist, or could be created, by which such benefits could be achieved. But despite the common assumption, by theorists, politicians, and the public, that such goals *are* attainable through our present penal institutions, the findings of empirical research suggest a rather more complex picture.

To begin with, empirical inquiry has shown how crucial it is to provide a clear definition of the end being sought, and the indices by which its achievement can be measured. Generations of research on the 'rehabilitative' effects of penal measures, or the deterrent impacts of specific policies or penalties, have not produced clear conclusions about what 'works' and what does not—largely because so many factors and variations are involved in the processes whereby different offenders choose to desist from criminal conduct (see Martinson 1974; Lipton *et al.* 1975; Brody 1976; Wilson 1983: ch. 9; Palmer 1992). The initial response to these findings, when the first surveys of research began to appear in the 1970s, was the cry that 'Nothing Works!', and the argument that ambitious reformative approaches should be abandoned in favour of the more straightforward strategies of punishment and incapacitation (see e.g. Cohen 1985: 30–5). Subsequently, however, researchers have come to realize that the phenomena in question, the rehabilitative or deterrent effects of punishment, had been unrealistically conceptualized and measured, and that much more refined conceptions would be necessary in order to trace the operations of what are actually very subtle social processes (see Pawson and Tilley, forthcoming).

Thus, if 'rehabilitation' is taken to be a kind of transformation of character in which offenders are turned into law-abiding citizens by the application of some generalizable penal technique, then the reconviction rates alone indicate that rehabilitation remains an impossible goal. But if one works instead with a yardstick which measures rehabilitative effects in more partial, qualitative ways—such as a slowing down in subsequent rates of offending, or a decrease in the seriousness of subsequent crimes, or even collateral improvements in aspects of the offender's conduct and life-style—it becomes clear that in certain circumstances, with certain kinds of offender, these more modest goals can sometimes be achieved (see Maguire and Priestley 1985; Palmer 1992)—though much seems to depend on the quality of interpersonal relationships, which are difficult to replicate for the purposes of comparative research. The issues here are normative as well as empirical. We need to ask not just 'what works' to bring about for instance a reduction in the frequency of future offending, but also what we should count as 'working'. Should the penal system be concerned only with reducing future offending, or also with other kinds of improvement in offenders' conduct and circumstances? Should attention focus on individual offenders, and the attempt to change their behaviour; or should more attention be paid to the social and economic circumstances which encourage crime, and upon which remedial efforts are too rarely focused (see CARLEN; ROTMAN)?

Similarly, research on deterrence has shown that this apparently simple concept is actually rather complex and difficult to define, and that deterrent effects are notoriously difficult to establish, since they involve counterfactuals—'would these individuals have acted differently had the threat of criminal penalties been other than it was?' (see Beyleveld 1979; 1980; Zimring and Hawkins 1973; Blumstein *et al.* 1978).

Even the standard examples of outbreaks of mass criminality during police strikes, or power failures, or the collapse of ruling powers, are not fully convincing as evidence that deterrence normally works, since so many other variables are at work in these highly unusual situations (see Mathiesen 1990). It is worth noting too that most penological research on deterrence tries to measure the marginal deterrent effect of increasing the likelihood that offenders will be apprehended, or will receive severer sentences, thus comparing one penal regime with another, rather than comparing penal deterrents with non-penal methods of restraining conduct such as positive socialization. The latter kind of comparison tends to interest the system's critics more than its administrators (see Marshall 1985; Abel 1991). However, as with rehabilitation, what reliable evidence we have suggests that deterrence is not an all or nothing matter. It is rather a variable which operates to some extent, in some situations, with respect to certain kinds of individual. It is an instrument whose efficacy is context-specific, depending for its success upon a set of background conditions and local circumstances (the extent of public awareness and information, the degree of calculation and rationality exercised by potential offenders, the probabilities of apprehension, the operations of other restraints on criminal conduct), and therefore not easily generalizable from one situation to others (see WILSON).

Doubts abut the efficacy or costs of strategies of deterrence or rehabilitation led some to advocate a policy of incapacitation as a response to serious crime (see Greenwood and Abrahamse 1982; Moore *et al.* 1984; Wilson 1983: ch. 8). One attraction of this approach is that it seems to guarantee straightforward and unconditional efficacy. Offenders who are locked up are thus kept off the streets and out of trouble, and such positive benefits in crime reduction and public protection offer a justification for the suffering and costs involved in large-scale, long-term imprisonment. But research on incapacitation suggests that even this apparently straightforward goal is not always readily attainable in practice. Incapacitation only 'works' as a crime control strategy if the offenders whom we lock up are indeed repeaters who would commit further offences if left free (see Monahan 1981 on the problem of 'false positives'); if they are not immediately replaced on the streets by new recruits; and if their post-release criminal activity is not so high as to off-set the crimes which their incapacitation prevented. Indeed, it only works in the more limited sense of physically restraining 'dangerous' individuals if we can ensure that they do not commit offences against other inmates or staff whilst in prison (see Wilson 1983: ch. 8; and N. MORRIS's highly qualified defence of a very limited strategy of incapacitation). Several recent studies have suggested that the effectiveness of incapacitation poli-cies in reducing crime rates is likely to be much less than was estimated by early proponents, and have emphasized the high financial costs of using long-term custodial sentences as a means of controlling crime (see Brody and Tarling 1980; Blumstein *et al.* 1986; and von Hirsch and Ashworth 1992: ch. 3).

Similarly, those who insist that punishment should be, above all, a matter of 'just deserts', of distributing proportionate penalties in a consis-tent and non-discriminatory way, should be aware of the many sources of inequality in sentencing and of the ways in which justice can be under-mined by the penal process. 'Sentencing' is merely part of an extended process which begins when the police or prosecution authorities decide how to process suspects, and which extends beyond the formal stage of sentencing at the trial to such matters as the allocation of prisoners to different kinds of prison, and decisions on early release. Many key deci-sions in this process are much less visible than the trial judge's formal sentence: but if 'just deserts' are to be secured, we need ways of ensuring that such decisions are made in a spirit of justice—that they are not discriminatory, nor based simply on administrative convenience (see ZIMRING; Feeley 1979; Skolnick 1975; Blumberg 1967; Moody and Tombs 1982; McConville *et al.* 1991; Adler and Longhurst forthcoming; Jacobs 1982). There is, for instance, a massive research literature which traces the operation of bias, of discrimination of grounds of race, gender, or social class, in the official treatment of suspects and offenders from disad-vantaged or less powerful sections of the community (see CARLEN; Reiner 1992; Hood 1992; Carlen 1988; Allen 1987; Cook 1989; Cashmore and McLaughlin 1991). Normative theories which advocate justice and equal respect for persons cannot afford to neglect the patterns of discrimination which routinely detract from these ideals.

Furthermore, retributivists who insist on the importance of respecting 'moral autonomy' should recognize that the day-to-day reality of life under our existing penal institutions (in prison, or under intensive proba-tion, for instance) can easily make a mockery of this ideal (see Cohen and

Taylor 1972; Bottoms and McWilliams 1979). It makes little sense to insist on a framework of sentencing which treats offenders as moral agents, responsible for their actions, but then to subject them to infantilizing, disciplinary regimes in which all opportunities for responsible conduct and moral choice are removed (see Carlen 1983; Scottish Prison Service 1990; Morgan 1994).

Finally, even the simple retributivist aim of inflicting hard treatment on the guilty depends for its realization upon certain empirical conditions: particularly upon the relationship between penal regime and the offender's normal standard of living. As HIRST points out, some offenders may not experience the suffering which their punishments are supposed to inflict, because their normal conditions of life are hardly better than those of the prison, or because they are so wealthy that any fine imposed has little impact on them. Rusche and Kirchheimer pointed out long ago (1968; see Garland 1985) that penal regimes must be made 'less eligible' than the lives of the poorest free citizens if their punitive effect is to be sustained: if punishments are to be experienced as punitive even by the worst off in the society then the standard of living in penal institutions must be markedly lower than that in normal society. (This principle of 'less eligibility' has made its mark not only on our penal institutions, but in the field of social security, motivating a concern to make the status of social security claimant an unattractive one (see Dean and Taylor-Goodby 1992).) However, in societies where large groups of people are markedly poorer than the average working-class household, and where the conditions of life of some (such as addicts, vagrants, the homeless) are below that required for minimal health, punitive 'less eligibility' will be difficult or impossible to achieve without grotesque inhumanity. The existence of what one might call punitive social conditions can thus undermine the punitiveness of formal punishments. So too, the fact that many offenders are social security claimants whose benefits are set at a low, 'less eligible' level makes it impractical to impose the fines which might otherwise be seen as the appropriate, just punishment. And if such fines are imposed, many offenders will—despite instalment options and means inquiries—be imprisoned for failing to pay them, thus receiving punishments which the original court did not think were deserved (see CARLEN on the importance of feasibility; Moxon 1983 on fine default, unemployment, and imprisonment; and Carlen and Cook 1989).

Under the influence of 'just deserts' thinking, penologists and practitioners have now begun to consider these kinds of issue, creating a type of middle-range theorizing which asks what 'just deserts' means in practice for specific institutions (see Bottoms and McWilliams 1979; Hudson 1987; Cavadino and Dignan 1992; de Haan 1990). This kind of work, combining the normative with the practical in a principled way, should play a much more central role in our thinking about punishment.

8. Sociology and the Critique of Philosophy's Foundations

There is another respect in which philosophical thinking about punishment would benefit from a more direct engagement with penological and sociological evidence, and this concerns the empirical validity of the premises and presuppositions entailed in normative theory. There are a number of important 'givens' in the philosophy of punishment—premises which are present but unstated, assumptions which are simply taken for granted—which need to be deconstructed and subjected to scrutiny. Some of these 'givens' are of a quite fundamental kind, so that if we do bring them into question, this can prompt a radical critique of our ways of dealing with crime and criminals.

For instance, normative theories of punishment often presuppose that 'crime' must be punished: the important issue is then to work out an adequate justificatory theory of punishment (since it is now assumed that there must be such a justification), and to establish which forms of punishment are appropriate. But, as abolitionist writers point out, there are prior questions to be asked both about the concept of 'crime', and about whether we should respond to social harms and disputes by invoking the criminal law and its penal armoury (see BIANCHI, and the Preface to his essay). Societies vary considerably in their reliance on penal controls (see Roberts 1979; Schwartz and Miller 1964), and there is no reason to suppose that our existing balance between formal and informal controls, or between criminal and civil law responses, is the most appropriate one. Even if we do not, or cannot, travel the radical abolitionist's road towards the 'abolition' of punishment as such, we need to look critically at the distinction between 'crimes' and 'civil wrongs'; at the prospects for limiting the scope of the criminal law (see Mathiesen 1974; Cohen 1985); at the possibility of diverting certain kinds of offender, especially children, out of the criminal justice system into less stigmatizing and punitive alternatives (see Rutherford and McDermott 1976; Morris 1978); and at the possibility of expanding various modes of 'informal justice' and of mediation (see Abel 1982; Matthews 1988; Marshall and Merry 1990; Dignan 1994). Such alternative strategies inevitably have drawbacks and problems (see Lemert 1981; Cohen 1985; Abel 1982). But our point is that punishment is only one of a range of possible strategies, involving one of a range of possible conceptualizations of the 'problem' of crime: such a strategy, and such a conceptualization, must be argued for rather than simply assumed.

Nor, of course, should we simply assume that the state is the natural and proper penal authority, to be entrusted with the task of regulating conduct and punishing deviance (see Garland and Young 1983: Introduction; Carlen 1983; de Haan 1990; BIANCHI). One problem here concerns the very authority of the criminal law. It presents itself as the legitimate embodiment of the community's fundamental values, as if these values are shared by the whole community (as if there is indeed a genuine community united in allegiance to such values): but that claim to normative authority is questionable in societies which exhibit no such consensus on fundamental values, or in which large sectors of the population are so marginalized from the mainstream of social life that they cannot be expected to recognize the law as 'theirs' (see BIANCHI; Bauman 1992; Smart 1993; MacIntyre 1985). Another point is that, historically, the state has only recently come to claim a monopoly in the regulation of crime or deviance. Until the nineteenth century, many of the kinds of conduct which are now dealt with by the criminal justice system were dealt with by private or non-state authorities such as churches, guilds, landlords, families, and employers (see Spierenburg 1984: ch. 1; Gatrell *et al.* 1980); 'criminal' conduct is still often dealt with outside the formal legal system (see Macaulay 1963; Henry 1983); and the recent re-emergence of mediation, restitution, and compensation schemes at the fringes of the penal system reminds us that the criminal justice system is only one amongst many possible strategies for dealing with 'crime'. Before we try to determine the proper ends of punishment, we need to ask more fundamental questions about the nature and structure of society; about what kinds of social order should be maintained; about how we should conceptualize 'deviance' (see Christie 1977 on 'conflicts'; Hulsman 1986 on 'troubles'); and about whether and when the social response to deviant conduct should be formal and punitive rather than informal and/or non-punitive (see Garland 1990: ch. 12).

We should also examine the conceptions of the individual offender which underpin much normative theorizing.[2] The criminal law tends to assume that individuals can be regarded as 'free' and 'responsible' unless extreme mental disorder or some other excusing condition renders them unfree. It thus sets up a rather strict dichotomy, with little room for variation between the two poles of freedom and determinism.

Individuals who do not fall into the narrow excusing categories are treated as equally free and responsible agents who can choose whether to obey the law or not; and are judged and convicted without detailed regard to their particular social circumstances (see Norrie 1991). But we need to attend to the sociological argument that 'freedom', of the kind which properly bears on the individual's criminal liability, is a contingent social good rather than an essential property of all sane individuals. Like most social goods freedom is unequally distributed in our societies, with those at the upper end of the social hierarchy having more options and opportunities, and thus more freedom and more room for genuine choice, than those lower down (see MURPHY; Bauman 1992: 219; Bauman 1988). Crime is typically the outcome not of the wholly unconstrained choices of free individuals, but of the socially constrained choices of socially situated individuals (see Matza 1964); and obeying the law (or even recognizing that it properly claims one's obedience) may be considerably harder for those who are hard-pressed by poverty and other social disadvantages.

We need then to ask what difference this should make to our penal practices. Should social disadvantage serve as an excuse, or as a mitigating factor at the sentencing stage (see Hudson 1987: ch. 4; contrast von Hirsch 1993: 106–8)? One danger here is that social disadvantage might also be seen as increasing the offender's 'dangerousness', and thus lead to a harsher incapacitative penalty (see N. MORRIS; Box 1987). Should we go further than this, and argue that rather than punishing the individuals whose crimes reflect (at least in part) their restricted freedom and limited life-chances, we should seek instead to ameliorate their social conditions, increase their opportunities, and reduce social and economic inequalities (see MURPHY; CARLEN)? This was indeed the aim of much of the rehabilitative penology of the mid-twentieth century (see above, pp. 8–9). What its critics portrayed as an attempt to manipulate offenders into conformity, in ways which failed to respect them as moral agents, was often in fact an attempt to provide the disadvantaged with the education and social resources that would allow them the freedom which the better-off take for granted (see ROTMAN; CARLEN; Rotman 1990; Taylor 1981: ch. 2). What is at stake here is not just the question of what kinds of technique or strategy will be most effective in preventing crime. It is rather a question of what the state owes to its citizens, and of the extent to which responses to crime should assume (as our penal system assumes) that crimes can properly be attributed simply to individual agents who can then be held responsible, and punished, for them. It is also a question of how far the criminal justice system should treat those who come into its hands as responsible individuals, abstracted from their social circumstances, and how far it should attend to their concrete social situation in determining culpability and sentence (see TONRY). While some would argue that conviction and punishment must, if they are to be just, be founded on as complete an understanding as possible of the individual offender, their particular crime, and the social circumstances of that crime, liberals might argue that we should not allow the state such an extensive power to inquire into every aspect of the offender's life.

Work in the sociology and history of punishment, though it is not often directly focused on such normative issues as these, can raise questions about the legitimacy of our current institutions and the rationality of current practices. David Downes's (1988) comparison of the post-war penal policies of the Netherlands with those of England and Wales is a good example. He asks why the prison population in the Netherlands was greatly reduced during this period, while that in England and Wales increased greatly, although both jurisdictions experienced a sharp increase in the crime rate; and he shows clearly the extent to which penal policy is determined not by the demands of the 'crime problem', but by other social and political factors. In particular, he shows how the attitudes of political and judicial élites, formed by education and historical experience, have a marked impact on penal policy, producing average levels of punishment in one jurisdiction which are markedly lower than those in the other. Work of this kind reminds us that levels of punishment can vary substantially, and are often the product of political habits or forces which have little directly to do with the necessities of punishment. (The radical shift in government rhetoric and policy in England between 1988 and 1993 is another illustration of this point). This then renders problematic the ambition of fixing levels of punishment which will impose 'just deserts' on offenders. If the 'just' or 'proportionate' sentence for a particular offence is seen in one jurisdiction as being five years' imprisonment, while in a neighbouring jurisdiction it is seen as one year in prison, how can we hope to develop a rational system of just penalties, one that does not simply reflect the contingencies of our particular system? (See Rutherford 1984; see also von Hirsch 1993: ch. 5, for an attempt to provide rational grounds for determining appropriate levels of punishment.)

More generally, Downes's work shows how heavily the development of penal policy is influenced by political and cultural circumstances, and by the institutional frameworks in which penal decisions are made. In seeking to relate normative theory to actual practice, we must attend to the ways in which penal policy is determined by political forces and the struggle of contending interests, rather than by normative argument or relevant empirical evidence (see Hood 1974; Scheingold 1991; Hall *et al.* 1978; Ryan 1983; Windlesham 1993; for an historical perspective see Garland 1985).

The bearing of external forces and interests on penal practice is in fact the stock-in-trade of much sociology of punishment. There is, for example, an interesting literature on the 'latent functions' of punishment, identifying the ways in which penal practice may come to serve ends other than those that are officially declared as its objectives. The most familiar example of this kind of account is Durkheim's argument that the rituals of punishment serve to reaffirm the core beliefs of the society and reinforce feelings of solidarity amongst the law-abiding (see Durkheim 1984; also Mead 1918; Erikson 1966; Garfinkel 1956; for a critical discussion see Garland 1990: ch. 3). This kind of account can be seen as the sociological counterpart of the 'expressive' or 'communicative' theories of punishment which we discussed earlier (see above, pp. 13–16). But there are other kinds of 'latent function' analysis which are less familiar—and less easily absorbed into current normative thinking.

For instance, Rusche and Kirchheimer (1968) maintain that the penal practice of a society is functionally adapted to the needs of the labour market: changing forms and uses of punishment can, they argue, be explained by reference to the changing character of the economy and to oscillations in the labour market (see also Box 1987; Melossi and Pavarini 1981; Melossi 1989). This kind of theory is probably too general and too economistic to provide any complete explanation of historical developments in penal practice and policy (see Garland 1990: ch. 4): but it rightly draws attention to the influence which economic factors have on penal institutions and practices.

Another 'latent function' which some have ascribed to punishment is that of 'managing the rabble' (Irwin 1990: 2). According to John Irwin, the modern American jail should be understood not by reference to its supposed penological goals, but instead as a device for controlling the 'underclass' of the poor, unemployed and potentially disorderly (see also Simon 1993 on the functions of parole supervision in the USA). Mathiesen (1974, 1990) offers a similarly critical analysis of European uses of imprisonment. The official rationales for prison as a punishment (deterrence, reform, incapacitation, retribution) cannot, he argues, explain our heavy reliance on imprisonment as a sanction. We must rather look to the hidden social functions of the prison: to its 'expurgatory' function (removing the unproductive or disruptive from circulation); its 'power-draining' function (disempowering inmates, and thus reducing any threat they may pose to the social order); its 'symbolic' function (epitomizing the stigma of criminality, and thus enabling those outside to distance themselves from those inside); its 'diverting' function (focusing our anxieties on 'crime' and the individual street criminal, thus diverting our attention from the illegal or socially harmful conduct of the powerful); and finally its 'action' function (reassuring us that 'something is being done' about crime, even when those who seek thus to reassure us are aware of the very limited penological efficacy of imprisonment). Mathiesen suggests that we might explain the persistence of high rates of imprisonment, amidst extensive criticism of the institution, by seeing that prison may have a political effectiveness which compensates for its penological failure.

The most sophisticated and influential social analysis of modern penality was developed by Michel Foucault (1977, 1980, 1989). He argued that the emergence of imprisonment as the characteristic penal sanction in modern society can be explained by reference to the prison's role in a wider network of disciplinary institutions and practices designed to govern individuals for a variety of purposes. Foucault's meticulous examination of the power relations involved in the practice of imprisonment— as well as his account of how scientific knowledge about the individual offender is used to extend the hold of power upon the inmate—provide us with a way of thinking about the prison (and about penal control) as a particular manifestation of a distinctively modern style of constructing and regulating the individual as a self-controlled subject. We should thus view the prison alongside the school, the hospital, the asylum, the factory, and the barracks as an institution in which bodies and spaces are carefully articulated in ways which permit the exercise of constant surveillance, and the application of disciplinary technologies designed to create docile, disciplined, productive individuals (for discussions of Foucault see Ignatieff 1983; Minson 1985; Garland 1990: chs. 6–7). Like Mathiesen, Foucault suggests that the prison fails to achieve its specifically penological objectives, there being little evidence that the discipline and orderliness even of a well-run penitentiary will continue to influence convicts after their release. But even a penologically ineffective prison has some uses, he argues (such as the maintenance of a clear-cut division between the respectable and the disreputable poor, and the concentration of criminality in a closely monitored 'criminal class' composed largely of ex-convicts); and the disciplinary principles on which the prison is based are now so engrained in our institutions and culture that it is very hard to imagine a serious alternative (see BIANCHI for an abolitionist attempt to imagine an alternative—which none the less still relies on the use of detention).

Sociological analyses of this kind must, of course, face various critical questions. We must ask how far the 'latent functions' they identify can plausibly be seen as the real determinants of penal practice. How far do such analyses undercut normative theorizing about the proper aims of punishment, by showing such theorizing to be, in the actual world, impotent or practically irrelevant? What role there is for effective rational discussion of penal policy? They might also be accused of concluding too readily that the prison is a penological failure, by starting with unrealistic conceptions of what would count as 'success' for an institution which is usually dealing with offenders who already have a long criminal record. It should be no surprise that the prison fails to reform the majority of inmates or to deter them from future crimes; and we should not ignore the extent to which prison 'succeeds' in its function of delivering pain (see Christie 1981) and imposing suffering on offenders. This might suggest that it does operate effectively to serve the ends of a crude retributivism—by inflicting suffering in ways which are sufficiently painful to satisfy the popular and political desires for vengeance which survive in even the most 'civilized' penal systems (see Elias 1938, 1939; Durkheim 1984; Ranulf 1964). Moreover, and unlike capital or corporal punishment, the behind-the-scenes character of imprisonment ensures that its infliction of pain is sufficiently sanitized and invisible to be tolerated by a society which pretends to disavow violence (see Garland 1990: ch. 10).

Sociological analyses such as these present a serious challenge to normative penal theorizing. They remind us that punishment is a social institution which can be understood only within the social context which gives it its practical meaning and determines its social effects. And while they make it plain that normative theory is not the only determinant of our institutions of punishment, they nevertheless demonstrate that our discourses and conceptions do make a difference at the level of practice. Their lesson is not that normative theorizing and argument are futile, but rather that we need to address our arguments and our principles about penal justice to the broader set of social institutions and relations which ultimately affect the ways that we punish.

Notes

1. Capitalized references are to items in this volume.
2. Not to mention the assumption that offenders are typically individual human beings, which raises problems for the punishment of corporate criminals; see Schwendinger and Schwendinger 1975; Wells 1993.

References

ABEL, R. (1982), *The Politics of Informal Justice* (New York).

——— (1991), 'The Failure of Punishment as Social Control', *Israel Law Review*, 25/3, 4: 740–52.

ADLER, J. (1992), *The Urgings of Conscience* (Philadelphia).

ADLER, M., and LONGHURST, B. (forthcoming), *Power, Discourse and Justice: Towards a New Sociology of Imprisonment* (London).

ALLEN, F. A. (1981), *The Decline of the Rehabilitative Ideal* (New Haven, Conn.).

ALLEN, H. (1987), *Justice Unbalanced: Gender, Psychiatry and Judicial Decisions* (Milton Keynes).

American Friends Service Committee (1971), *Struggle for Justice* (New York).

ARDAL, P. (1984), 'Does Anyone ever Deserve to Suffer?', *Queen's Quarterly*, 91–2: 241–57.

ASHWORTH, A. J. (1992), *Sentencing and Criminal Justice* (London).

BAKER, B. M. (1992), 'Consequentialism, Punishment, and Autonomy', in Cragg 1992: 149–61.

BAUMAN, Z. (1988), *Freedom* (Milton Keynes).

——— (1992), *Intimations of Postmodernity* (London).

BENTHAM, J. (1789), *An Introduction to the Principles of Morals and Legislation*, ed. J. H. Burns and H. L. A. Hart (London, 1970).

BEYLEVELD, D. (1979), 'Identifying, Explaining and Predicting Deterrence', *British Journal of Criminology*, 19: 205–24.

——— (1980), *A Bibliography on General Deterrence* (Farnborough, Hants).

BICKENBACH, J. (1988), 'Critical Notice of R. A. Duff, Trials and Punishments', *Canadian Journal of Philosophy*, 18: 765–86.

BLUMBERG, A. (1967), *Criminal Justice* (Chicago).

BLUMSTEIN, A., COHEN, J., and NAGIN, D. (1978) (eds.), *Deterrence and Incapacitation: Estimating the Effects of Criminal Sanctions on Crime Rates* (Washington, DC).

BLUMSTEIN, A., COHEN, J., ROTH, J. and VISHER, C. (1986) (eds.), *Criminal Careers and 'Career Criminals'*, i (Washington, DC).

BOTTOMLEY, A. K. (1989), *Crime and Penal Politics: The Criminologist's Dilemma* (Hull).

BOTTOMS, A. E. (1980), 'An Introduction to "The Coming Crisis" ', in Bottoms and Preston (1980), 1–24.

Bottoms, A. E. and Brownsword, R. (1982), 'The Dangerousness Debate after the Floud Report', *British Journal of Criminology*, 22: 229–54.

—— and McWilliams, W. (1979), 'A Non-Treatment Paradigm for Probation Practice', *British Journal of Social Work*, 9: 159–202.

—— and Preston, R. H. (1980) (eds.), *The Coming Penal Crisis: A Criminological and Theological Exploration* (Edinburgh).

Box, S. (1987), *Recession, Crime and Punishment* (Basingstoke).

Braithwaite, J. (1989), *Crime, Shame and Reintegration* (Cambridge).

—— and Pettit, P. (1990), *Not Just Deserts* (Oxford).

Brandt, R. B. (1961), 'Determinism and the Justifiability of Moral Blame', in S. Hook (ed.), *Determinism and Freedom in the Age of Modern Science* (New York), 149–54.

Brody, S. R. (1976), *The Effectiveness of Sentencing: A Review of the Literature* (London).

—— and Tarling, R. (1980), *Taking Offenders out of Circulation* (London).

Carlen, P. (1983), *Women's Imprisonment: A Study in Social Control* (London).

—— (1988), *Women, Crime and Poverty* (Milton Keynes).

—— and Cook, D. (1989) (eds.), *Paying for Crime* (Milton Keynes).

Cashmore, E., and McLaughlin, E. (1991) (eds.), *Out of Order? Policing Black People* (London).

Cavadino, M., and Dignan, J. (1992), *The Penal System: An Introduction* (London).

Christie, N. (1977), 'Conflicts as Property', *British Journal of Criminology*, 17: 1–15.

—— (1981), *Limits to Pain* (London).

Clemmer, D. (1958), *The Prison Community* (New York).

Cohen, S. (1985), *Visions of Social Control* (Cambridge).

—— and Taylor, L. (1972), *Psychological Survival: The Experience of Long Term Imprisonment* (Harmondsworth).

Cook, D. (1989), *Rich Law, Poor Law* (Milton Keynes).

Cottingham, J. (1979), 'Varieties of Retribution', *Philosophical Quarterly*, 29: 238–46.

Coyle, A. (1991), *Inside: Rethinking Scotland's Prisons* (Edinburgh).

Cragg, W. (1992) (ed.), *Retributivism and its Critics* (Stuttgart).

Cressey, D. (1961) (ed.), *The Prison: Studies in Institutional Organisation and Change* (New York).

—— (1983), 'Interview' in J. Laub, *Criminology in the Making* (Boston, Mass.), 131–65.

Cullen, F. T., and Gilbert, K. E. (1982), *Reaffirming Rehabilitation* (Cincinnati).

Davis, M. (1989), 'The Relative Independence of Punishment Theory', *Law and Philosophy*, 7: 321–50.

Dean, H., and Taylor-Gooby, P. (1992), *Dependency Culture: The Explosion of a Myth* (London).

de Haan, W. (1990), *The Politics of Redress: Crime, Punishment and Penal Abolition* (London).

DIGNAN, J. (1994), 'Reintegration through Reparation: A Way Forward for Restorative Justice?' in Duff *et al.* 1994: 231–44.

DOLINKO, D. (1991), 'Some Thoughts about Retributivism', *Ethics*, 101: 537–59.

DOWNES, D. (1988), *Contrasts in Tolerance* (Oxford).

DUFF, R. A. (1986), *Trials and Punishments* (Cambridge).

—— (1991), 'Retributive Punishment: Ideals and Actualities', *Israel Law Review*, 25: 422–51.

—— (1992), 'Alternatives to Punishment or Alternative Punishments?', in Cragg 1992: 43–68.

—— (1995), 'Penal Communications: Recent Work in the Philosophy of Punishment', *Crime and Justice: An Annual Review of Research*, 20.

—— , MARSHALL, S. E., DOBASH, R. E., and DOBASH, R. P. (1994) (eds.), *Penal Theory and Practice* (Manchester).

DURKHEIM, E. (1902), 'Two Laws of Penal Evolution', *Année Sociologique*, 4: 65–95. Repr. as 'The Evolution of Punishment', in S. Lukes and A. Scull (eds.) *Durkheim and the Law* (Oxford, 1983), 102–32.

—— (1984), *The Division of Labour* (1893), trans. W. D. Halls (London).

DWORKIN, R. (1978), *Taking Rights Seriously* (London).

ELIAS, N. (1938), *The Civilizing Process*, i: *The History of Manners* (Oxford).

—— (1939), *The Civilizing Process*, ii: *State Formation and Civilization* (Oxford).

ERIKSON, K. (1966), *Wayward Puritans: A Study in the Sociology of Deviance* (New York).

FALLS, M. M. (1987), 'Retribution, Reciprocity, and Respect for Persons', *Law and Philosophy*, 6: 25–51.

FARRELL, D. M. (1985), 'The Justification of General Deterrence', *Philosophical Review*, 94: 367–94.

FEELEY, M. (1979), *The Process is the Punishment* (New York).

FITZGERALD, M. (1977), *Prisoners in Revolt* (Harmondsworth).

FLOUD, J., and YOUNG, W. (1981), *Dangerousness and Criminal Justice* (London).

FOGEL, D. (1975), *We Are the Living Proof: The Justice Model for Corrections* (Cincinnati).

FOUCAULT, M. (1977), *Discipline and Punish: The Birth of the Prison* (London).

—— (1980), 'Prison Talk' in M. Foucault, *Power/Knowledge: Selected Interviews*, ed. by C. Gordon (New York), 37–54.

—— (1989), 'What Calls for Punishment?', in *Foucault Live (Interviews 1966–84)* (New York), 275–92.

GALLIGAN, D. J. (1981), 'The Return to Retribution in Penal Theory', in Tapper 1981: 144–71.

GARFINKEL, H. (1956), 'Conditions of Successful Degradation Ceremonies', *American Journal of Sociology*, 61: 420–24.

GARLAND, D. (1985), *Punishment and Welfare* (Aldershot).

—— (1990), *Punishment and Modern Society: A Study in Social Theory* (Oxford).

—— (1994), 'Of Crimes and Criminals: The Development of Criminology in

Britain', in M. Maguire, R. Morgan, and R. Reiner (eds.), *The Oxford Handbook of Criminology* (Oxford), 17–68.

GARLAND, D. and YOUNG, P. (1983) (ed.), *The Power to Punish* (London).

GATRELL, V. A. C., LENMAN, B., and PARKER, G. (1980), *Crime and the Law: The Social History of Crime in Western Europe since 1500* (London).

GIBSON, B. (1990), *Unit Fines* (Winchester).

GIDDENS, A. (1990), *The Consequences of Modernity* (Cambridge).

GOFFMAN, E. (1968), *Asylums* (Harmondsworth).

GOLDMAN, A. H. (1979), 'The Paradox of Punishment', *Philosophy and Public Affairs*, 9: 42–58.

GREENBERG, D., and HUMPHRIES, D. (1980), 'The Co-optation of Fixed Sentencing Reform', in *Crime and Delinquency*, 26: 206–25.

GREENE, J. (1988), 'Structuring Criminal Fines: Making an "Intermediate" Penalty More Useful and Equitable', *Justice System Journal*, 13: 37–48; excerpted in von Hirsch and Ashworth 1992: 344–54.

GREENWOOD, P., and ABRAHAMSE, A. (1982), *Selective Incapacitation* (Santa Monica, Calif.).

HALL, S., CRITCHER, C., JEFFERSON, T., CLARKE, J., and ROBERTS, B. (1978), *Policing the Crisis: Mugging, the State, and Law and Order* (London).

HAMPTON, J. (1984), 'The Moral Education Theory of Punishment', *Philosophy and Public Affairs*, 13: 208–38.

—— (1992a), 'An Expressive Theory of Retribution', in Cragg 1992: 1–25.

—— (1992b), 'Correcting Harms versus Righting Wrongs: The Goal of Retribution', *UCLA Law Review*, 39: 201–44.

HARE, R. M. (1981), *Moral Thinking: Its Levels, Methods and Point* (Oxford).

HART, H. L. A. (1968), 'Prolegomenon to the Principles of Punishment', in H. L. A. Hart, *Punishment and Responsibility* (Oxford), 1–27.

HEGEL, G. W. F. (1821), *The Philosophy of Right*, trans. T. Knox (Oxford, 1942).

HENRY, S. (1983), *Private Justice* (London).

HOGARTH, J. (1974), *Sentencing as a Human Process* (Toronto).

Home Office (1988), *Punishment, Custody and the Community* (London).

—— (1990), *Crime, Justice and Protecting the Public* (London).

HONDERICH, T. (1982), 'On Justifying Protective Punishment', *British Journal of Criminology*, 22: 268–78.

—— (1984), *Punishment: The Supposed Justifications* (rev. ed., Harmondsworth).

HOOD, R. (1974), 'Criminology and Penal Change', in R. Hood (ed.), *Crime, Criminology, and Public Policy* (London), 375–417.

—— (1992), *Race and Sentencing: A Study in the Crown Court* (Oxford).

HUDSON, B. (1987), *Justice through Punishment: A Critique of the 'Justice' Model of Corrections* (London).

HULSMAN, L. (1986), 'Critical Criminology and the Concept of Crime', *Contemporary Crises*, 10: 63–80.

IGNATIEFF, M. (1978), *A Just Measure of Pain* (New York, 1989).

—— (1983), 'State, Civil Society and Total Institutions: A Critique of Recent Histories of Punishment', in S. Cohen and A. Scull (eds.), *Social Control and the State* (Oxford), 75–105.

IRWIN, J. (1990), *The Jail: Managing the Underclass in American Society* (Berkeley, Calif.).

JACKSON, G. (1971), *Soledad Brother: The Prison Letters of George Jackson* (Harmondsworth).

JACOBS, J. B. (1977), *Stateville: The Penitentiary in Mass Society* (Chicago).

—— (1982), 'Sentencing by Prison Personnel: Good Time', *UCLA Law Review*, 30/2: 217–70.

—— (1983a), *New Perspectives on Prisons and Imprisonment* (Ithaca, NY).

—— (1983b), 'The Prisoners' Rights Movement and its Impacts', in Jacobs (1983a), 33–60.

—— (1983c), 'Macrosociology and Imprisonment', in Jacobs (1983a), 17–32.

KANT, I. (1785), *Groundwork of the Metaphysic of Morals*, trans. H. Paton as *The Moral Law* (London, 1948).

—— (1797), *The Metaphyical Elements of Justice*; Part I of *The Metaphysic of Morals*, trans. J. Ladd (Indianapolis, 1965).

LACEY, N. (1983), 'Dangerousness and Criminal Justice: The Justification of Preventive Detention', *Current Legal Problems*, 36: 31–49.

—— (1988), *State Punishment* (London).

LEMERT, E. (1981), 'Diversion in Juvenile Justice: What Hath Been Wrought?', *Journal of Research on Crime and Delinquency*, 18: 34–45.

LIPTON, D., MARTINSON, R., and WILKS, J. (1975), *The Effectiveness of Correctional Treatment* (New York).

LUCAS, J. R. (1968), 'Or Else', *Proceedings of the Aristotelian Society*, 69: 207–22.

MACAULAY, S. (1963), 'Non-contractual Relations in Business: A Preliminary Study' *American Sociological Review*, 28: 55–67.

MCCONVILLE, M., and BALDWIN, J. (1981), *Courts, Prosecution and Conviction* (Oxford).

—— SANDERS, A., and LENG, R. (1991), *The Case for the Prosecution* (London).

MACINTYRE, A. (1985), *After Virtue: A Study of Moral Theory* (2nd edn. London).

MACKIE, J. L. (1982), 'Morality and the Retributive Emotions', *Criminal Justice Ethics*, 1: 3–10.

MAGUIRE, J., and PRIESTLEY, P. (1985), *Offending Behaviour: Skills and Strategems for Going Straight* (London).

MARSHALL, S. E. (1992), 'Harm and Punishment in the Community', in Cragg 1992: 75–82.

MARSHALL, T. F. (1985), *Alternatives to Criminal Courts: The Potential for Non-Judicial Settlement* (Aldershot).

—— and MERRY, S. (1990), *Crime and Accountability* (London).

MARTINSON, R. (1974), 'What Works? Questions and Answers about Prison Reform', *Public Interest*, 35: 22–54.

MATHIESEN, T. (1965), *The Defences of the Weak: A Sociological Study of a Norwegian Correctional Institution* (London).

—— (1974), *The Politics of Abolition* (London).

—— (1990), *Prison on Trial: A Critical Assessment* (London).

MATTHEWS, R. (1988) (ed.), *Informal Justice* (London).

MATZA, D. (1964), *Delinquency and Drift* (New York).

MEAD, G. H. (1918), 'The Psychology of Punitive Justice', *American Journal of Sociology*, 23: 577–602.

MELOSSI, D. (1989) (ed.), Special Issue of *Contemporary Crises* on 'Punishment and Social Structure'.

—— and PAVARINI, M. (1981), *The Prison and the Factory* (London).

MENNINGER, K. (1968), *The Crime of Punishment* (New York).

MINSON, J. (1985), *The Genealogy of Morals: Nietzsche, Foucault and Donzelot and the Eccentricity of Ethics* (London).

MONAHAN, J. (1981), *Predicting Violent Behavior: An Assessment of Clinical Techniques* (New York).

MOODY, S., and TOMBS, J. (1982), *Prosecution in the Public Interest* (Edinburgh).

MOORE, M. H., ESTRICH, S., McGILLIS, D., and SPELMAN, W. (1984), *Dangerous Offenders: The Elusive Target of Justice* (Cambridge, Mass.).

MOORE, M. S. (1987), 'The Moral Worth of Retribution', in F. Schoeman (ed.), *Responsibility, Character and the Emotions* (Cambridge), 179–219.

MORGAN, R. (1994), 'Just Prisons and Responsible Prisoners' in Duff *et al.* (1994: 127–45).

MORISON, J. (1988), 'Hart's Excuses: Problems with a Compromise Theory of Punishment', in P. Leith and P. Ingram (eds.), *The Jurisprudence of Orthodoxy* (London), 117–46.

MORRIS, A. (1978), 'Diversion of Juvenile Offenders from the Criminal Justice System' in N. Tutt (ed.), *Alternative Strategies for Coping with Crime* (Oxford), 45–63.

MORRIS, H. (1968), 'Persons and Punishment', *Monist*, 52: 475–501.

MORRIS, N. (1974), *The Future of Imprisonment* (Chicago).

—— and TONRY, M. (1990), *Between Prison and Probation: Intermediate Punishments in a Rational Sentencing System* (New York).

MOXON, D. (1983), 'Fine Default, Unemployment and the Use of Imprisonment', *Home Office Research Bulletin*, 16: 38–44.

MURPHY, J. G. (1979), 'Kant's Theory of Criminal Punishment', in J. G. Murphy, *Retribution, Justice, and Therapy* (Dordrecht), 82–92.

—— (1985), 'Retributivism, Moral Education and the Liberal State', *Criminal Justice Ethics*, 4: 3–11.

NARAYAN, U. (1993), 'Appropriate Responses and Preventive Benefits: Justifying

Censure and Hard Treatment in Legal Punishment', *Oxford Journal of Legal Studies*, 13: 166–82.

NINO, C. S. (1983), 'A Consensual Theory of Punishment', *Philosophy and Public Affairs*, 12: 289–306.

NORRIE, A. W. (1991), *Law, Ideology and Punishment* (Dordrecht).

PALMER, T. (1992), *The Effectiveness of Correctional Intervention* (London).

PAWSON, R., and TILLEY, N. (forthcoming), 'What Works in Evaluation Research?', *British Journal of Criminology*.

PHILIPS, M. (1986), 'The Justification of Punishment and the Justification of Political Authority', *Law and Philosophy*, 5: 393–416.

PLATT, T., and TAKAGI, P. (1980) (eds.), *Punishment and Penal Discipline* (Berkeley, Calif.).

PRIMORATZ, I. (1989), *Justifying Legal Punishment* (Atlantic Highlands, NJ).

QUINN, W. (1985), 'The Right to Threaten and the Right to Punish', *Philosophy and Public Affairs*, 14: 327–73.

RADZINOWICZ, L., and HOOD, R. (1981), 'The American Volte-Face in Sentencing Thought and Practice', in Tapper (1981), 127–43.

RANULF, S. (1964), *Moral Indignation and Middle Class Psychology* (New York).

RAWLS, J. (1955), 'Two Concepts of Rules', *The Philosophical Review*, 64: 3–32.

—— (1972), *A Theory of Justice* (Oxford).

REES, H., and HALL WILLIAMS, E. (1989), *Punishment, Custody and the Community: Comments and Reflections on the Green Paper* (London).

REINER, R. (1992), *The Politics of the Police* (Hemel Hempstead).

ROBERTS, S. (1979), *Order and Dispute: An Introduction to Legal Anthropology* (Harmondsworth).

ROBINSON, P. H. (1987), 'Hybrid Principles for the Distribution of Criminal Sanctions', *Northwestern University Law Review*, 82: 19–42.

ROTHMAN, D. (1978), 'Introduction' to W. Gaylin, I. Glasser, S. Marcus, and D. Rothman, *Doing Good: The Limits of Benevolence* (New York), pp. ix–xv.

—— (1980), *Conscience and Convenience: The Asylum and its Alternatives in Progressive America* (Boston).

ROTMAN, E. (1990), *Beyond Punishment: A New View of the Rehabilitation of Offenders* (Westport, Conn.).

RUGGLES-BRISE, E. (1924), *Prison Reform at Home and Abroad* (London).

RUSCHE, G., and KIRCHHEIMER, O. (1968), *Punishment and Social Structure* (New York; 1st edn. 1939).

RUTHERFORD, A. (1984), *Prisons and the Process of Justice: The Reductionist Challenge* (London).

—— and MCDERMOTT, R. (1976), *Juvenile Diversion* (Washington, DC).

RYAN, M. (1983), *The Politics of Penal Reform* (London).

SCHEINGOLD, S. (1991), *The Politics of Street Crime: Criminal Process and Cultural Obsession* (Philadelphia).

SCHWARTZ, R. D., and MILLER, J. C. (1964), 'Legal Evolution and Societal Complexity', *American Journal of Sociology*, 70: 159–69.

SCHWENDINGER, H., and SCHWENDINGER, J. (1975), 'Defenders of Order or Guardians of Human Rights?', in I. Taylor, P. Walton, and J. Young (eds.), *Critical Criminology* (London), 113–46.

Scottish Prison Service (1990), *Opportunity and Responsibility: Developing New Approaches to the Management of the Long Term Prison System in Scotland* (Edinburgh).

SHAFER-LANDAU, R. (1991), 'Can Punishment Morally Educate?', *Law and Philosophy*, 10: 189–219.

SIMON, J. (1993), *Poor Discipline: Parole and the Social Control of the Underclass, 1890–1990* (Chicago).

SKOLNICK, J. (1975), *Justice Without Trial* (2nd edn., New York).

SMART, B. (1993), *Postmodernity* (London).

SPIERENBURG, P. (1984), *The Spectacle of Suffering: Executions and the Evolution of Repression* (Cambridge).

SYKES, G. M. (1958), *The Society of Captives* (Princeton, NJ).

TAPPER, C. F. H. (1981) (ed.), *Crime, Proof and Punishment* (London).

TAYLOR, T. (1981), *Law and Order: Arguments for Socialism* (London).

TEN, C. L. (1987), *Crime, Guilt and Punishment* (Oxford).

—— (1990), 'Positive Retributivism', *Social Philosophy and Policy*, 7: 194–208.

TONRY, M. (1988), 'Structuring Sentencing', *Crime and Justice*, 12: 267–337.

—— and MORRIS, N. (1978), 'Sentencing Reform in America', in P. R. Glazebrook (ed.), *Reshaping the Criminal Law* (London), 434–48.

TUNICK, M. (1992), *Punishment: Theory and Practice* (Berkeley, Calif.).

VON HIRSCH, A. (1976), *Doing Justice: The Choice of Punishments* (New York).

—— (1981), 'Desert and Previous Convictions in Sentencing', *Minnesota Law Review*, 65: 591–634.

—— (1985), *Past or Future Crimes* (Manchester).

—— (1993), *Censure and Sanctions* (Oxford).

—— and ASHWORTH, A. J. (1992) (eds.), *Principled Sentencing* (Boston, Edinburgh).

WALKER, N. (1969), *Sentencing in a Rational Society* (Harmondsworth).

—— (1980), *Punishment, Danger and Stigma* (Oxford).

—— (1987), *Crime and Criminology: An Introduction* (Oxford).

—— (1991), *Why Punish?* (Oxford).

WASIK, M., and TAYLOR, R. D. (1991), *Blackstone's Guide to the Criminal Justice Act of 1991* (London).

WELLS, C. (1993), *Corporations and Criminal Responsibility* (Oxford).

WILSON, J. Q. (1975), *Thinking about Crime* (New York).

—— (1983), *Thinking about Crime* (rev. edn., New York).

WINDLESHAM, LORD (1993), *Responses to Crime, ii: Penal Policy in the Making* (Oxford).

WINES, F. H. (1895), *Punishment and Reformation: An Historical Sketch of the Rise of the Penitentiary* (New York).

WOOLF, H., and TUMIM, S. (1991), *Prison Disturbances April 1990* (London).

WOOTTON, B. (1963), *Crime and the Criminal Law* (London).

YOUNG, P. (forthcoming), *Punishment, Money and Legal Order* (Edinburgh).

ZIMRING, F., and HAWKINS, G. (1973), *Deterrence: The Legal Threat in Crime Control* (Chicago).

—— —— (1986), *Capital Punishment and the American Agenda* (Cambridge).

—— —— (1990), *The Scale of Imprisonment* (Chicago).

Preface: J. G. Murphy, 'Marxism and Retribution'

Murphy offers a retributivist, rights-based objection to utilitarian theories of punishment. He argues that utilitarian punishment fails to respect the rights of those who are punished, treating them as 'mere means' to some social good, rather than as 'ends in themselves' (see WALKER for a response to this criticism). Only a retributivist theory, Murphy argues, takes rights sufficiently seriously. But how does it do so?

A central task for retributivism is to explain why crime deserves or requires punishment. Murphy provides one influential answer to this question. A system of law brings the benefits of protected freedom to each of its citizens, by imposing on them all the burden of self-restraint which obedience to law involves. Offenders accept the benefits which flow from the law-abiding self-restraint of others, but refuse to accept the burden of obeying the law themselves. They take an unfair advantage for themselves, over all who obey the law: an advantage consisting not in any material profit their crimes may bring, but in their very avoidance of the burden of self-restraint. Punishment deprives them of that unfair advantage, by imposing an extra burden on them. It restores that fair balance of benefits and burdens which crime disturbs (see also Morris 1968; von Hirsch 1976; Sadurski 1989; Dagger 1993). And punishments of this kind, Murphy argues, respect the offender's rights and autonomy, since the offender has, as a rational agent, willed such a system of punishment—a system which ensures that no one profits from their own wrongdoing.

This account has been subjected to fierce criticism, even by some of its early adherents, including Murphy himself (Murphy 1985; von Hirsch 1990: 264–9; VON HIRSCH: 116–18; Burgh 1982; Duff 1986: ch. 8; Falls 1987; Hudson 1987; Dolinko 1991). Critics argue that the theory distorts the essential character of crime (the wrongfulness of rape, for instance, does not consist in taking an 'unfair advantage' over those who obey the law); and the liberal social contract theory to which Murphy appeals cannot show that offenders have in any real sense 'willed' their own punishment. A further crucial question concerns the applicability of the theory to 'the actual social world in which we live'. It is one thing to offer an ideal theory of how punishment could be justified in a just society of free, autonomous agents: but can such a theory justify punishment in our own actual societies? Do those who break our laws culpably take an unfair advantage for themselves? Can a retributivist system of punishment 'do justice' in a society which is itself unjust (see CARLEN: 316–18)? Unlike many philosophers, Murphy takes such questions seriously. He concludes that punishment in our contemporary societies lacks moral legitimacy, because the empirical preconditions necessary for penal justice are lacking.

Murphy draws on the work of the Dutch criminologist Willem Bonger, who argued that most criminality has its roots in relative deprivation and in the aggressive values of a competitive society. This reliance upon Bonger may seem strange, since criminological theory has come a long way since the publication of Bonger's book in 1916 (see Taylor *et al.* 1973 for a sympathetic modern discussion of Bonger's thesis). The links between deprivation and crime in competitive societies are far more complex, and less direct, than Bonger suggested; nor is crime predominantly committed by the socially deprived, although they tend to bear the brunt of criminalization and punishment (see Currie 1986 and Reiman 1979 on the links between crime, punishment, and social disadvantage; see Braithwaite 1979 and Pearce 1976 on crimes of the powerful). But Bonger's work none the less presents a challenge that Murphy thinks confronts any ideal theory of just punishment. For if crime represents not the free choices of errant individuals, but the structurally shaped outcomes of an unjust social system; and if, as Bonger claims, injustice and crime are essential rather than contingent aspects of a capitalist society, in which the idea of universal autonomy is an ideological fiction (since freedom and autonomy are socially distributed goods, more readily available to those at the top than to those at the bottom); then in such a society punishment cannot be justified as a system which inflicts 'just deserts' on individuals who have freely broken just laws which are binding on them as rational agents.

Such an outright denial that punishment can be justified in contemporary capitalist societies might seem too sweeping. Social science suggests that the empirical data are varied and complex, but the philosophical conclusion which Murphy draws is stark and simple. And unless we are willing to hold that punishment must simply be abandoned until it can satisfy the demands of an ideal theory, we must ask whether punishment cannot be to some degree justified even in an admittedly unjust society (see Duff 1986: ch. 10.3; TONRY; von Hirsch 1976: ch. 17, 1993: epilogue). Murphy does, however, sharply remind us of the importance of bringing empirical actuality to bear on ideal normative theories; of asking whether any ideal theory can justify punishment in 'the actual world in which we live'.

References

BRAITHWAITE, J. (1979), *Inequality, Crime and Public Policy* (London).

BURGH, R. W. (1982), 'Do the Guilty Deserve Punishment?', *Journal of Philosophy*, 79: 193–210.

CURRIE, E (1986), *Confronting Crime* (New York).

DAGGER, R. (1993), 'Playing Fair with Punishment', *Ethics*, 103: 73–88.

DOLINKO, D. (1991), 'Some Thoughts about Retributivism', *Ethics*, 101: 537–59.

DUFF, R. A. (1986), *Trials and Punishments* (Cambridge).

FALLS, M. M. (1987), 'Retribution, Reciprocity, and Respect for Persons', *Law and Philosophy*, 6: 25–51.

HUDSON, B. (1987), *Justice through Punishment* (London).

MORRIS, H. (1968), 'Persons and Punishment', *Monist*, 52: 475–501.

MURPHY, J. G. (1985), 'Retributivism, Moral Education and the Liberal State', *Criminal Justice Ethics*, 4: 3–11.

PEARCE, F. (1976), *Crimes of the Powerful* (London).

REIMAN, J. H. (1979), *The Rich Get Richer and the Poor Get Prison: Ideology, Class and Criminal Justice* (New York).

SADURSKI, W. (1989), 'Theory of Punishment, Social Justice, and Liberal Neutrality', *Law and Philosophy*, 7: 351–73.

TAYLOR, I., WALTON, P., and YOUNG, J. (1973), *The New Criminology* (London).

VON HIRSCH, A. (1976), *Doing Justice: The Choice of Punishments* (New York).

—— (1990), 'Proportionality in the Philosophy of Punishment: From "Why Punish?" to "How Much?" ', *Criminal Law Forum*, 1: 259–90.

—— (1993), *Censure and Sanctions* (Oxford).

Marxism and Retribution

J. G. MURPHY

Punishment in general has been defended as a means either of ameliorating or of intimidating. Now what right have you to punish me for the amelioration or intimidation of others? And besides there is history—there is such a thing as statistics—which prove with the most complete evidence that since Cain the world has been neither intimidated nor ameliorated by punishment. Quite the contrary. From the point of view of abstract right, there is only one theory of punishment which recognizes human dignity in the abstract, and that is the theory of Kant, especially in the more rigid formula given to it by Hegel. Hegel says: 'Punishment is the *right* of the criminal. It is an act of his own will. The violation of right has been proclaimed by the criminal as his own right. His crime is the negation of right. Punishment is the negation of this negation, and, consequently an affirmation of right, solicited and forced upon the criminal by himself.'

There is no doubt something specious in this formula, inasmuch as Hegel, instead of looking upon the criminal as the mere object, the slave of justice, elevates him to the position of a free and self-determined being. Looking, however, more closely into the matter, we discover that German idealism here, as in most other instances, has but given a transcendental sanction to the rules of existing society. Is it not a delusion to substitute for the individual with his real motives, with multifarious social circumstances pressing upon him, the abstraction of 'free will'—one among the many qualities of man for man himself? . . . Is there not a necessity for deeply reflecting upon an alteration of the system that breeds these crimes, instead of glorifying the hangman who executes a lot of criminals to make room only for the supply of new ones?

Karl Marx, 'Capital Punishment'
New York Daily Tribune (18 February 1853)[1]

Philosophers have written at great length about the moral problems involved in punishing the innocent—particularly as these problems raise

An earlier version of this essay was delivered to the Third Annual Colloquium in Philosophy ('The Philosophy of Punishment') at the University of Dayton in October 1972. I am grateful to the Department of Philosophy at the University of Dayton for inviting me to participate and to a number of persons at the Colloquium for the useful discussion on my paper at the time. I am also grateful to Anthony D. Woozley of the University of Virginia and to two of my colleagues, Robert M. Harnish and Francis V. Raab, for helping me to clarify the expression of my views.

obstacles to an acceptance of the moral theory of utilitarianism. Punishment of an innocent man in order to bring about good social consequences is, at the very least, not always clearly wrong on utilitarian principles. This being so, utilitarian principles are then to be condemned by any morality that may be called Kantian in character. For punishing an innocent man, in Kantian language, involves using that man as a mere means or instrument to some social good and is thus not to treat him as an end in himself, in accord with his dignity or worth as a person.

The Kantian position on the issue of punishing the innocent, and the many ways in which the utilitarian might try to accommodate that position, constitute extremely well-worn ground in contemporary moral and legal philosophy.[2] I do not propose to wear the ground further by adding additional comments on the issue here. What I do want to point out, however, is something which seems to me quite obvious but which philosophical commentators on punishment have almost universally failed to see—namely, that problems of the very same kind and seriousness arise for the utilitarian theory with respect to the punishment of the *guilty*. For a utilitarian theory of punishment (Bentham's is a paradigm) must involve justifying punishment in terms of its social results—e.g. deterrence, incapacitation, and rehabilitation. And thus even a guilty man is, on this theory, being punished because of the instrumental value the action of punishment will have in the future. He is being used as a means to some future good—e.g., the deterrence of others. Thus those of a Kantian persuasion, who see the importance of worrying about the treatment of persons as mere means, must, it would seem, object just as strenuously to the punishment of the guilty on utilitarian grounds as to the punishment of the innocent. Indeed the former worry, in some respects, seems more serious. For a utilitarian can perhaps refine his theory in such a way that it does not commit him to the punishment of the innocent. However, if he is to approve of punishment at all, he must approve of punishing the guilty in at least some cases. This makes the worry about punishing the guilty formidable indeed, and it is odd that this has gone generally unnoticed.[3] It has generally been assumed that if the utilitarian theory can just avoid entailing the permissibility of punishing the innocent, then all objections of a Kantian character to the theory will have been met. This seems to me simply not to be the case.

What the utilitarian theory really cannot capture, I would suggest, is the notion of persons having rights. And it is just this notion that is central to any Kantian outlook on morality. Any Kantian can certainly agree that punishing persons (guilty or innocent) may have either good or bad or indifferent consequences and that in so far as the consequences (whether in a particular case or for an institution) are good, this is something in favour of punishment. But the Kantian will maintain that this consequential outlook, important as it may be, leaves out of consideration entirely that which is most morally crucial—namely, the question of rights. Even if punishment of a person would have good consequences, what gives us (i.e. society) the moral right to inflict it? If we have such a right, what is its origin or derivation? What social circumstances must be present for it to be applicable? What does this right to punish tell us about the status of the person to be punished—e.g., how are we to analyse his rights, the sense in which he must deserve to be punished, his obligations in the matter? It is this family of questions which any Kantian must regard as morally central and which the utilitarian cannot easily accommodate into his theory. And it is surely this aspect of Kant's and Hegel's retributivism, this seeing of rights as basic, which appeals to Marx in the quoted passage. As Marx himself puts it: 'What right have you to punish me for the amelioration or intimidation of others?' And he further praises Hegel for seeing that punishment, if justified, must involve respecting the rights of the person to be punished.[4] Thus Marx, like Kant, seems prepared to draw the important distinction between (a) what it would be good to do on grounds of utility and (b) what we have a right to do. Since we do not always have the right to do what it would be good to do, this distinction is of the greatest moral importance; and missing the distinction is the Achilles heel of all forms of Utilitarianism. For consider the following example: A Jehovah's Witness needs a blood transfusion in order to live; but, because of his (we can agree absurd) religious belief that such transfusions are against God's commands, he instructs his doctor not to give him one. Here is a case where it would seem to be good or for the best to give the transfusion and yet, at the very least, it is highly doubtful that the doctor has a right to give it. This kind of distinction is elementary, and any theory which misses it is morally degenerate.[5]

To move specifically to the topic of punishment: how exactly does retributivism (of a Kantian or Hegelian variety) respect the rights of persons? Is Marx really correct on this? I believe that he is. I believe that retributivism can be formulated in such a way that it is the only morally defensible theory of punishment. I also believe that arguments, which may be regarded as Marxist at least in spirit, can be formulated which show that social conditions as they obtain in most societies make this form of retributivism largely inapplicable within those societies. As Marx says, in those societies retributivism functions merely to provide a 'transcendental sanction' for the status quo. If this is so, then the only morally defensible theory of punishment is largely inapplicable in modern societies. The consequence: modern societies largely lack the moral right to punish.[6] The upshot is that a Kantian moral theory (which in general seems to me correct) and a Marxist analysis of crime (which if properly qualified, also seems to me correct) produces a radical and not merely reformist attack not merely on the scope and manner of punishment in our society but on the institution of punishment itself. Institutions of punishment constitute what Bernard Harrison has called structural injustices[7] and are, in the absence of a major social change, to be resisted by all who take human rights to be morally serious—i.e. regard them as genuine action guides and not merely as rhetorical devices which allow people to morally sanctify institutions which in fact can only be defended on grounds of social expediency.

Stating all of this is one thing and proving it, of course, is another. Whether I can ever do this is doubtful. That I cannot do it in one brief article is certain. I cannot, for example, here defend in detail my belief that a generally Kantian outlook on moral matters is correct.[8] Thus I shall content myself for the present with attempting to render at least plausible two major claims involved in the view that I have outlined thus far: (1) that a retributive theory, in spite of the bad press that it has received, is a morally credible theory of punishment—that it can be, H. L. A. Hart to the contrary,[9] a reasonable general justifying aim of punishment; and (2) that a Marxist analysis of crime can undercut the practical applicability of that theory.

The Right of the State to Punish

It is strong evidence of the influence of a utilitarian outlook in moral and legal matters that discussions of punishment no longer involve a consideration of the right of anyone to inflict it. Yet in the eighteenth and nineteenth centuries, this tended to be regarded as the central aspect of the problem meriting philosophical consideration. Kant, Hegel, Bosanquet, Green—all tended to entitle their chapters on punishment along the lines explicitly used by Green: 'The Right of the State to Punish'.[10] This is not just a matter of terminology but reflects, I think, something of deeper philosophical substance. These theories, unlike the utilitarian, did not view man as primarily a maximizer of personal satisfactions—a maximizer of individual utilities. They were inclined, in various ways, to adopt a different model of man—man as a free or spontaneous creator, man as autonomous. (Marx, it may be noted, is much more in line with this tradition than with the utilitarian outlook.[11]) This being so, these theorists were inclined to view punishment (a certain kind of coercion by the state) as not merely a causal contributor to pain and suffering, but rather as presenting at least a prima facie challenge to the values of autonomy and personal dignity and self-realization—the very values which, in their view, the state existed to nurture. The problem as they saw it, therefore, was that of reconciling punishment as state coercion with the value of individual autonomy. (This is an instance of the more general problem which Robert Paul Wolff has called the central problem of political philosophy—namely, how is individual moral autonomy to be reconciled with legitimate political authority?[12]) This kind of problem, which I am inclined to agree is quite basic, cannot even be formulated intelligibly from a utilitarian perspective. Thus the utilitarian cannot even see the relevance of Marx's charge: even if punishment has wonderful social consequences, what gives anyone the right to inflict it on me?

Now one fairly typical way in which others acquire rights over us is by our own consent. If a neighbour locks up my liquor cabinet to protect me against my tendencies to drink too heavily, I might well regard this as a presumptuous interference with my own freedom, no matter how good the result intended or accomplished. He had no right to do it and indeed violated my rights in doing it. If, on the other hand, I had asked him to do this or had given my free consent to his suggestion that he do it, the same sort of objection on my part would be quite out of order. I had given him the right to do it, and he had the right to do it. In doing it, he violated no rights of mine—even if, at the time of his doing it, I did not desire or want the action to be performed. Here then we seem to have a case where my autonomy may be regarded as intact even though a desire of mine is thwarted. For there is a sense in which the thwarting of the desire can be imputed to me (my choice or decision) and not to the arbitrary intervention of another.

How does this apply to our problem? The answer, I think, is obvious. What is needed, in order to reconcile my undesired suffering of punishment at the hands of the state with my autonomy (and thus with the state's right to punish me), is a political theory which makes the state's decision to punish me in some sense my own decision. If I have willed my own punishment (consented to it, agreed to it) then—even if at the time I happen not to desire it—it can be said that my autonomy and dignity remain intact. Theories of the General Will and Social Contract theories are two such theories which attempt this reconciliation of autonomy with legitimate state authority (including the right or authority of the state to punish). Since Kant's theory happens to incorporate elements of both, it will be useful to take it for our sample.

Moral Rights and the Retributive Theory of Punishment

To justify government or the state is necessarily to justify at least some coercion.[13] This poses a problem for someone, like Kant, who maintains that human freedom is the ultimate or most sacred moral value. Kant's own attempt to justify the state, expressed in his doctrine of the *moral title* (*Befugnis*),[14] involves an argument that coercion is justified only in so far as it is used to prevent invasions against freedom. Freedom itself is the only value which can be used to limit freedom, for the appeal to any other value (e.g. utility) would undermine the ultimate status of the value of freedom. Thus Kant attempts to establish the claim that some forms of coercion (as opposed to violence) are morally permissible because, contrary to appearance, they are really consistent with rational freedom. The argument, in broad outline, goes in the following way. Coercion may keep people from doing what they desire or want to do on a particular occasion and is thus prima facie wrong. However, such coercion can be shown to be morally justified (and thus not absolutely wrong) if it can be established that the coercion is such that it could have been rationally willed even by the person whose desire is interfered with:

Accordingly, when it is said that a creditor has a right to demand from his debtor the payment of a debt, this does not mean that he can *persuade* the debtor that his own reason itself obligates him to this performance; on the contrary, to say that he has such a right means only that the use of coercion to make anyone do this is entirely compatible with everyone's freedom, *including the freedom of the debtor*, in accordance with universal laws.[15]

Like Rousseau, Kant thinks that it is only in a context governed by social practice (particularly civil government and its Rule of Law) that this can make sense. Laws may require of a person some action that he does not desire to perform. This is not a violent invasion of his freedom, however, if it can be shown that in some antecedent position of choice (what John Rawls calls 'the original position'),[16] he would have been rational to adopt a Rule of Law (and thus run the risk of having some of his desires thwarted) rather than some other alternative arrangement such as the classical State of Nature. This is, indeed, the only sense that Kant is able to make of classical Social Contract theories. Such theories are to be viewed, not as historical fantasies, but as ideal models of rational decision. For what these theories actually claim is that the only coercive institutions that are morally justified are those which a group of rational beings could agree to adopt in a position of having to pick social institutions to govern their relations:

The contract, which is called *contractus originarius*, or *pactum sociale* . . . need not be assumed to be a fact, indeed it is not [even possible as such. To suppose that would be like insisting] that before anyone would be bound to respect such a civic constitution, it be proved first of all from history that a people, whose rights and obligations we have entered into as their descendants, had *once upon a time* executed such an act and had left a reliable document or instrument, either orally or in writing, concerning this contract. Instead, this contract is a *mere idea* of reason which has undoubted practical reality; namely, to oblige every legislator to give us laws in such a manner that the laws *could* have originated from the united will of the entire people and to regard every subject in so far as he is a citizen as though he had consented to such [an expression of the general] will. This is the testing stone of the rightness of every publicly-known law, for if a law were such that it was impossible for an entire people to give consent to it (as for example a law that a certain class of subjects, by inheritance, should have the privilege of the *status of lords*), then such a law is unjust. On the other hand, if there is a mere *possibility* that a people might consent to a (certain) law, then it is a duty to consider that the law is just even though at the moment the people might be in such a position or have a point of view that would result in their refusing to give their consent to it if asked.[17]

The problem of organizing a state, however hard it may seem, can be solved even for a race of devils, if only they are intelligent. The problem is: 'Given a multiple of rational beings requiring universal laws for their preservation, but each of whom is secretly inclined to exempt himself from them, to establish a constitution in such a way that, although their private intentions conflict, they check each other, with the result that their public conduct is the same as if they had no such intentions.'[18]

Though Kant's doctrine is superficially similar to Mill's later self-protection principle, the substance is really quite different. For though Kant in some general sense argues that coercion is justified only to prevent harm to others, he understands by 'harm' only certain invasions of freedom and not simply disutility. Also, his defence of the principle is not grounded, as is Mill's, on its utility. Rather it is to be regarded as a principle of justice, by which Kant means a principle that rational beings could adopt in a situation of mutual choice:

The concept [of justice] applies only to the relationship of a will to another person's will, not to his wishes or desires (or even just his needs) which are the concern of acts of benevolence and charity . . . In applying the concept of justice we take into consideration only the form of the relationship between the wills insofar as they are regarded as free, and whether the action of one of them can be conjoined with the freedom of the other in accordance with universal law. Justice is therefore the aggregate of those conditions under which the will of one person can be conjoined with the will of another in accordance with a universal law of freedom.[19]

How does this bear specifically on punishment? Kant, as everyone knows, defends a strong form of a retributive theory of punishment. He holds that guilt merits, and is a sufficient condition for, the infliction of punishment. And this claim has been universally condemned—particularly by utilitarians—as primitive, unenlightened, and barbaric.

But why is it so condemned? Typically, the charge is that infliction of punishment on such grounds is nothing but pointless vengeance. But what is meant by the claim that the infliction is 'pointless'? If 'pointless' is tacitly being analysed as 'disutilitarian', then the whole question is simply being begged. You cannot refute a retributive theory merely by noting that it is a retributive theory and not a utilitarian theory. This is to confuse redescription with refutation and involves an argument whose circularity is not even complicated enough to be interesting.

Why, then, might someone claim that guilt merits punishment? Such a claim might be made for either of two very different reasons. (1) Someone (e.g. a Moral Sense theorist) might maintain that the claim is a primitive and unanalysable proposition that is morally ultimate—that we can just intuit the 'fittingness' of guilt and punishment. (2) It might be maintained that the retributivist claim is demanded by a general theory of political obligation which is more plausible than any alternative theory. Such a theory will typically provide a technical analysis of such concepts as crime and punishment and will thus not regard the retributivist claim as an indisputable primitive. It will be argued for as a kind of theorem within the system.

Kant's theory is of the second sort. He does not opt for retributivism as a bit of intuitive moral knowledge. Rather he offers a theory of punishment that is based on his general view that political obligation is to be analysed, quasi-contractually, in terms of reciprocity. If the law is to remain just, it is important to guarantee that those who disobey it will not gain an unfair advantage over those who do obey voluntarily. It is important that no man profit from his own criminal wrongdoing, and a certain kind of 'profit' (i.e., not bearing the burden of self-restraint) is intrinsic to criminal wrongdoing. Criminal punishment, then, has as its object the restoration of a proper balance between benefit and obedience. The criminal himself has no complaint, because he has rationally consented to or willed his own punishment. That is, those very rules which he has broken work, when they are obeyed by others, to his own advantage as a citizen. He would have chosen such rules for himself and others in the original position of choice. And, since he derives and voluntarily accepts benefits from their operation, he owes his own obedience as a debt to his fellow-citizens for their sacrifices in maintaining them. If he chooses not to sacrifice by exercising self-restraint and obedience, this is tantamount to his choosing to sacrifice in another way—namely, by paying the prescribed penalty:

A transgression of the public law that makes him who commits it unfit to be a citizen is called . . . a crime . . .

What kind and what degree of punishment does public legal justice adopt as its principle and standard? None other than the principle of equality (illustrated by the pointer of the scales of justice), that is, the principle of not treating one side more favorably than the other. Accordingly, any undeserved evil that you inflict on someone else among the people is one you do to yourself. If you vilify him, you vilify yourself; if you steal from him, you steal from yourself; if you kill him, you kill yourself . . .

To say, 'I will to be punished if I murder someone' can mean nothing more than, 'I submit myself along with everyone else to those laws which, if there are any criminals among the people, will naturally include penal laws.'[20]

This analysis of punishment regards it as a debt owed to the law-abiding members of one's community; and, once paid, it allows re-entry into the community of good citizens on equal status.

Now some of the foregoing no doubt sounds implausible or even obscurantist. Since criminals typically desire not to be punished, what can it really mean to say that they have, as rational men, really willed their own punishment? Or that, as Hegel says, they have a right to it? Perhaps a comparison of the traditional retributivist views with those of a contemporary Kantian—John Rawls—will help to make the points clearer.[21] Rawls (like Kant) does not regard the idea of the social contract as a historical fact. It is rather a model of rational decision. Respecting a man's autonomy, at least on one view, is not respecting what he now happens, however uncritically, to desire; rather it is to respect what he desires (or would desire) as a rational man. (On Rawls's view, for example, rational men are said to be unmoved by feelings of envy; and thus it is not regarded as unjust to a person or a violation of his rights, if he is placed in a situation where he will envy another's advantage or position. A rational man would object, and thus would never consent to, a practice where another might derive a benefit from a position at his expense. He would not, however, envy the position *simpliciter*, would not regard the position as itself a benefit.) Now on Kant's (and also, I think, on Rawls's) view, a man is genuinely free or autonomous only in so far as he is rational. Thus it is man's rational will that is to be respected.

Now this idea of treating people, not as they in fact say that they want to be treated, but rather in terms of how you think they would, if rational, will to be treated, has obviously dangerous (indeed Fascistic) implications. Surely we want to avoid cramming indignities down the throats of people with the offhand observation that, no matter how much they scream, they are really rationally willing every bit of it. It would be particularly ironic for such arbitrary repression to come under the mask of respecting autonomy. And yet, most of us would agree, the general principle (though subject to abuse) also has important applications—for example, preventing the suicide of a person who, in a state of psychotic depression, wants to kill himself. What we need, then, to make the general view work, is a check on its arbitrary application; and a start toward providing such a check would be in the formulation of a public, objective theory of rationality and rational willing. It is just this, according to both Kant and Rawls, which the social contract theory can provide. On this theory, a man may be said to rationally will X if, and only if, X is called for by a rule that the man would necessarily have adopted in the original position of choice—i.e., in a position of coming together with others to pick rules for the regulation of their mutual affairs. This avoids arbitrariness because, according to Kant and Rawls at any rate, the question of whether such a rule would be picked in such a position is objectively determinable given certain (in their view) non-controversial assumptions about human nature and rational calculation. Thus I can be said to will my own punishment if, in an antecedent position of choice, I and my fellows would have chosen institutions of punishment as the most rational means of dealing with those who might break the other generally beneficial social rules that had been adopted.

Let us take an analogous example: I may not, in our actual society, desire to treat a certain person fairly—e.g., I may not desire to honour a contract I have made with him because so doing would adversely affect my own self-interest. However, if I am forced to honour the contract by the state, I cannot charge (1) that the state has no right to do this, or (2) that my rights or dignity are being violated by my being coerced into doing it. Indeed, it can be said that I rationally will it since, in the original position, I would have chosen rules of justice (rather than rules of utility) and the principle, 'contracts are to be honoured,' follows from the rules of justice.

Coercion and autonomy are thus reconciled, at least apparently. To use Marx's language, we may say (as Marx did in the quoted passage) that one virtue of the retributive theory, at least as expounded by Kant and Hegel on lines of the General Will and Social Contract theory, is that it manifests at least a formal or abstract respect for rights, dignity, and autonomy. For it at least recognizes the importance of attempting to construe state coercion in such a way that it is a product of each man's rational will. Utilitarian deterrence theory does not even satisfy this formal demand.

The question of primary interest to Marx, of course, is whether this formal respect also involves a material respect; i.e., does the theory have application in concrete fact in the actual social world in which we live? Marx is confident that it does not, and it is to this sort of consideration that I shall now pass.

Alienation and Punishment

What can the philosopher learn from Marx? This question is a part of a more general question: what can philosophy learn from social science? Philosophers, it may be thought, are concerned to offer a priori theories, theories about how certain concepts are to be analysed and their application justified. And what can the mundane facts that are the object of behavioural science have to do with exalted theories of this sort?

The answer, I think, is that philosophical theories, though not themselves empirical, often have such a character that their intelligibility depends upon certain empirical presuppositions. For example, our moral language presupposes, as Hart has argued,[22] that we are vulnerable creatures—creatures who can harm and be harmed by each other. Also, as I have argued elsewhere,[23] our moral language presupposes that we all share certain psychological characteristics—e.g., sympathy, a sense of justice, and the capacity to feel guilt, shame, regret, and remorse. If these facts were radically different (if, as Hart imagines for example, we all developed crustaceanlike exoskeletons and thus could not harm each other), the old moral language, and the moral theories which employ it, would lack application to the world in which we live. To use a crude example, moral prohibitions against killing presuppose that it is in fact possible for us to kill each other.

Now one of Marx's most important contributions to social philosophy, in my judgment, is simply his insight that philosophical theories are in peril if they are constructed in disregard of the nature of the empirical world to which they are supposed to apply.[24] A theory may be formally correct (i.e., coherent, or true for some possible world) but materially incorrect (i.e., inapplicable to the actual world in which we live). This insight, then, establishes the relevance of empirical research to philosophical theory and is a part, I think, of what Marx meant by 'the union of theory and practice'. Specifically relevant to the argument I want to develop are the following two related points:

(1) The theories of moral, social, political, and legal philosophy presuppose certain empirical propositions about man and society. If these propositions are false, then the theory (even if coherent or formally correct) is materially defective and practically inapplicable. (For example, if persons tempted to engage in criminal conduct do not in fact tend to calculate carefully the consequences of their actions, this renders much of deterrence theory suspect.)

(2) Philosophical theories may put forth as a necessary truth that which is in fact merely a historically conditioned contingency. (For example, Hobbes argued that all men are necessarily selfish and competitive. It is possible, as many Marxists have argued, that Hobbes was really doing nothing more than elevating to the status of a necessary truth the contingent fact that the people around him in the capitalistic society in which he lived were in fact selfish and competitive.[25])

In outline, then, I want to argue the following: that when Marx challenges the material adequacy of the retributive theory of punishment, he is suggesting (*a*) that it presupposes a certain view of man and society that is false and (*b*) that key concepts involved in the support of the theory (e.g., the concept of 'rationality' in Social Contract theory) are given analyses which, though they purport to be necessary truths, are in fact mere reflections of certain historical circumstances.

In trying to develop this case, I shall draw primarily upon Willem Bonger's *Criminality and Economic Conditions* (1916), one of the few sustained Marxist analyses of crime and punishment.[26] Though I shall not have time here to qualify my support of Bonger in certain necessary ways, let me make clear that I am perfectly aware that his analysis is not the whole story. (No monolithic theory of anything so diverse as criminal behaviour could be the whole story.) However, I am convinced that he has discovered part of the story. And my point is simply that, in so far as

Bonger's Marxist analysis is correct, then to that same degree is the retributive theory of punishment inapplicable in modern societies. (Let me emphasize again exactly how this objection to retributivism differs from those traditionally offered. Traditionally, retributivism has been rejected because it conflicts with the moral theory of its opponent, usually a utilitarian. This is not the kind of objection I want to develop. Indeed, with Marx, I have argued that the retributive theory of punishment grows out of the moral theory—Kantianism—which seems to me generally correct. The objection I want to pursue concerns the empirical falsity of the factual presuppositions of the theory. If the empirical presuppositions of the theory are false, this does indeed render its application immoral. But the immorality consists, not in a conflict with some other moral theory, but immorality in terms of a moral theory that is at least close in spirit to the very moral theory which generates retributivism itself—i.e., a theory of justice.[27])

To return to Bonger. Put bluntly, his theory is as follows. Criminality has two primary sources: (1) need and deprivation on the part of disadvantaged members of society, and (2) motives of greed and selfishness that are generated and reinforced in competitive capitalistic societies. Thus criminality is economically based—either directly in the case of crimes from need, or indirectly in the case of crimes growing out of motives or psychological states that are encouraged and developed in capitalistic society. In Marx's own language, such an economic system alienates men from themselves and from each other. It alienates men from themselves by creating motives and needs that are not 'truly human'. It alienates men from their fellows by encouraging a kind of competitiveness that forms an obstacle to the development of genuine communities to replace mere social aggregates.[28] And in Bonger's thought, the concept of community is central. He argues that moral relations and moral restraint are possible only in genuine communities characterized by bonds of sympathetic identification and mutual aid resting upon a perception of common humanity. All this he includes under the general rubric of reciprocity.[29] In the absence of reciprocity in this rich sense, moral relations among men will break down and criminality will increase.[30] Within bourgeois society, then, crimes are to be regarded as normal, and not psychopathological, acts. That is, they grow out of need, greed, indifference to others, and sometimes even a sense of indignation—all, alas, perfectly typical human motives.

To appreciate the force of Bonger's analysis, it is necessary to read his books and grasp the richness and detail of the evidence he provides for his claims. Here I can but quote a few passages at random to give the reader a tantalizing sample in the hope that he will be encouraged to read further into Bonger's own text:

The abnormal element in crime is a social, not a biological, element. With the exception of a few special cases, crime lies within the boundaries of normal psychology and physiology . . .

We clearly see that [the egoistic tendencies of the present economic system and of its consequences] are very strong. Because of these tendencies the social instinct of man is not greatly developed; they have weakened the moral force in man which combats the inclination towards egoistic acts, and hence toward the crimes which are one form of these acts—Compassion for the misfortunes of others inevitably becomes blunted, and a great part of morality consequently disappears . . .

As a consequence of the present environment, man has become very egoistic and hence more *capable of crime*, than if the environment had developed the germs of altruism . . .

There can be no doubt that one of the factors of criminality among the bourgeoisie is bad [moral] education . . . The children—speaking of course in a general way—are brought up with the idea that they must succeed, no matter how; the aim of life is presented to them as getting money and shining in the world . . .

Poverty (taken in the sense of absolute want) kills the social sentiments in man, destroys in fact all relations between men. He who is abandoned by all can no longer have any feelings for those who have left him to his fate . . .

[Upon perception that the system tends to legalize the egoistic actions of the bourgeoisie and to penalize those of the proletariat], the oppressed resort to means which they would otherwise scorn. As we have seen above, the basis of the social feeling is reciprocity. As soon as this is trodden under foot by the ruling class the social sentiments of the oppressed become weak towards them . . .[31]

The essence of this theory has been summed up by Austin J. Turk. 'Criminal behavior', he says, 'is almost entirely attributable to the combination of egoism and an environment in which opportunities are not equitably distributed.'[32]

No doubt this claim will strike many as extreme and intemperate—a sample of old-fashioned Marxist rhetoric that sophisticated intellectuals have outgrown. Those who are inclined to react in this way might consider just one sobering fact: of the 1.3 million criminal offenders handled each day by some agency of the United States correctional system, the vast majority (80 per cent on some estimates) are members of the lowest 15 per cent income level—that per cent which is below the 'poverty level' as defined by the Social Security Administration.[33] Unless one wants to embrace the belief that all these people are poor because they are bad, it might be well to reconsider Bonger's suggestion that many of them are 'bad' because they are poor.³⁴ At any rate, let us suppose for purposes of discussion that Bonger's picture of the relation between crime and economic conditions is generally accurate. At what points will this challenge the credentials of the contractarian retributive theory as outlined above? I should like to organize my answer to this question around three basic topics:

(1) *Rational Choice*. The model of rational choice found in Social Contract theory is egoistic—rational institutions are those that would be agreed to by calculating egoists ('devils' in Kant's more colourful terminology). The obvious question that would be raised by any Marxist is: why give egoism this special status such that it is built, a priori, into the analysis of the concept of rationality? Is this not simply to regard as necessary that which may be only contingently found in the society around us? Starting from such an analysis, a certain result is inevitable—namely, a transcendental sanction for the status quo. Start with a bourgeois model of rationality and you will, of course, wind up defending a bourgeois theory of consent, a bourgeois theory of justice, and a bourgeois theory of punishment.

Though I cannot explore the point in detail here, it seems to me that this Marxist claim may cause some serious problems for Rawls's well-known theory of justice, a theory which I have already used to unpack some of the evaluative support for the retributive theory of punishment. One cannot help suspecting that there is a certain sterility in Rawls's entire project of providing a rational proof for the preferability of a certain conception of justice over all possible alternative evaluative principles, for the description which he gives of the rational contractors in the original position is such as to guarantee that they will come up with his two principles. This would be acceptable if the analysis of rationality presupposed were intuitively obvious or argued for on independent grounds. But it is not. Why, to take just one example, is a desire for wealth a rational trait whereas envy is not? One cannot help feeling that the desired result dictates the premisses.³⁵

(2) *Justice, Benefits, and Community*. The retributive theory claims to be grounded on justice; but is it just to punish people who act out of those very motives that society encourages and reinforces? If Bonger is correct, much criminality is motivated by greed, selfishness, and indifference to one's fellows; but does not the whole society encourage motives of greed and selfishness ('making it', 'getting ahead'), and does not the

competitive nature of the society alienate men from each other and thereby encourage indifference—even, perhaps, what psychiatrists call psychopathy? The moral problem here is similar to one that arises with respect to some war crimes. When you have trained a man to believe that the enemy is not a genuine human person (but only a gook, or a chink), it does not seem quite fair to punish the man if, in a war situation, he kills indiscriminately. For the psychological trait you have conditioned him to have, like greed, is not one that invites fine moral and legal distinctions. There is something perverse in applying principles that presuppose a sense of community in a society which is structured to destroy genuine community.[36]

Related to this is the whole allocation of benefits in contemporary society. The retributive theory really presupposes what might be called a 'gentlemen's club' picture of the relation between man and society—i.e., men are viewed as being part of a community of shared values and rules. The rules benefit all concerned and, as a kind of debt for the benefits derived, each man owes obedience to the rules. In the absence of such obedience, he deserves punishment in the sense that he owes payment for the benefits. For, as a rational man, he can see that the rules benefit everyone (himself included) and that he would have selected them in the original position of choice.

Now this may not be too far off for certain kinds of criminals—e.g., business executives guilty of tax fraud. (Though even here we might regard their motives of greed to be a function of societal reinforcement.) But to think that it applies to the typical criminal, from the poorer classes, is to live in a world of social and political fantasy. Criminals typically are not members of a shared community of values with their gaolers; they suffer from what Marx calls alienation. And they certainly would be hard pressed to name the benefits for which they are supposed to owe obedience. If justice, as both Kant and Rawls suggest, is based on reciprocity, it is hard to see what these persons are supposed to reciprocate for. Bonger addresses this point in a passage quoted earlier: 'The oppressed resort to means which they would otherwise scorn . . . The basis of social feelings is reciprocity. As soon as this is trodden under foot by the ruling class, the social sentiments of the oppressed become weak towards them.'

(3) *Voluntary Acceptance.* Central to the Social Contract idea is the claim that we owe allegiance to the law because the benefits we have derived have been voluntarily accepted. This is one place where our autonomy is supposed to come in. That is, having benefited from the Rule of Law when it was possible to leave, I have in a sense consented to it and to its

consequences—even my own punishment if I violate the rules. To see how silly the factual presuppositions of this account are, we can do no better than quote a famous passage from David Hume's essay 'Of the Original Contract':

Can we seriously say that a poor peasant or artisan has a free choice to leave his country—when he knows no foreign language or manners, and lives from day to day by the small wages which he acquires? We may as well assert that a man, by remaining in a vessel, freely consents to the dominion of the master, though he was carried on board while asleep, and must leap into the ocean and perish the moment he leaves her.

A banal empirical observation, one may say. But it is through ignoring such banalities that philosophers generate theories which allow them to spread iniquity in the ignorant belief that they are spreading righteousness.

It does, then, seem as if there may be some truth in Marx's claim that the retributive theory, though formally correct, is materially inadequate. At root, the retributive theory fails to acknowledge that criminality is, to a large extent, a phenomenon of economic class. To acknowledge this is to challenge the empirical presupposition of the retributive theory—the presupposition that all men, including criminals, are voluntary participants in a reciprocal system of benefits and that the justice of this arrangement can be derived from some eternal and ahistorical concept of rationality.

The upshot of all this seems rather upsetting, as indeed it is. How can it be the case that everything we are ordinarily inclined to say about punishment (in terms of utility and retribution) can be quite beside the point? To anyone with ordinary language sympathies (one who is inclined to maintain that what is correct to say is a function of what we do say), this will seem madness. Marx will agree that there is madness, all right, but in his view the madness will lie in what we do say—what we say only because of our massive (and often self-deceiving and self-serving) factual ignorance or indifference to the circumstances of the social world in which we live. Just as our whole way of talking about mental phenomena hardened before we knew any neurophysiology—and this leads us astray, so Marx would argue that our whole way of talking about moral and political phenomena hardened before we knew any of the relevant empirical facts about man and society—and this, too, leads us astray. We all suffer from what might be called the *embourgeoisement* of language, and thus part of any revolution will be a linguistic or conceptual revolution. We have grown accustomed to modifying our language or conceptual structures under the impact of empirical discoveries in physics. There is no reason why discoveries in sociology, economics, or psychology could not and should not have the same effect on entrenched patterns of thought and speech. It is important to remember, as Russell remarked, that our language sometimes enshrines the metaphysics of the Stone Age.

Consider one example: a man has been convicted of armed robbery. On investigation, we learn that he is an impoverished black whose whole life has been one of frustrating alienation from the prevailing socio-economic structure—no job, no transportation if he could get a job, substandard education for his children, terrible housing and inadequate health care for his whole family, condescending-tardy-inadequate welfare payments, harassment by the police but no real protection by them against the dangers in his community, and near total exclusion from the political process. Learning all this, would we still want to talk—as many do—of his suffering punishment under the rubric of 'paying a debt to society'? Surely not. Debt for what? I do not, of course, pretend that all criminals can be so described. But I do think that this is a closer picture of the typical criminal than the picture that is presupposed in the retributive theory—i.e., the picture of an evil person who, of his own free will, intentionally acts against those just rules of society which he knows, as a rational man, benefit everyone including himself.

But what practical help does all this offer, one may ask. How should we design our punitive practices in the society in which we now live? This is the question we want to ask, and it does not seem to help simply to say that our society is built on deception and inequity. How can Marx help us with our real practical problem? The answer, I think, is that he cannot and obviously does not desire to do so. For Marx would say that we have not focused (as all piecemeal reform fails to focus) on what is truly the real problem. And this is changing the basic social relations. Marx is the last person from whom we can expect advice on how to make our intellectual and moral peace with bourgeois society. And this is surely his attraction and his value.

What does Bonger offer? He suggests, near the end of his book, that in a properly designed society all criminality would be a problem 'for the physician rather than the judge'. But this surely will not do. The therapeutic state, where prisons are called hospitals and gaolers are called psychiatrists, simply raises again all the old problems about the justification of coercion and its reconciliation with autonomy that we faced in worrying about punishment. The only difference is that our coercive practices are now surrounded with a benevolent rhetoric which makes it even harder to raise the important issues. Thus the move to therapy, in my judgment, is only an illusory solution—alienation remains and the problem of reconciling coercion with autonomy remains unsolved. Indeed, if the alternative is having our personalities involuntarily restructured by some state psychiatrist, we might well want to claim the 'right to be punished' that Hegel spoke of.[37]

Perhaps, then, we may really be forced seriously to consider a radical proposal. If we think that institutions of punishment are necessary and desirable, and if we are morally sensitive enough to want to be sure that we have the moral right to punish before we inflict it, then we had better first make sure that we have restructured society in such a way that criminals genuinely do correspond to the only model that will render punishment permissible—i.e., make sure that they are autonomous and that they do benefit in the requisite sense. Of course, if we did this then—if Marx and Bonger are right—crime itself and the need to punish would radically decrease if not disappear entirely.

Notes

1. In a sense, my paper may be viewed as an elaborate commentary on this one passage, excerpted from a discussion generally concerned with the efficacy of capital punishment in eliminating crime. For in this passage, Marx (to the surprise of many I should think) expresses a certain admiration for the classical retributive theory of punishment. Also (again surprisingly) he expresses this admiration in a kind of language he normally avoids—i.e., the moral language of rights and justice. He then, of course, goes on to reject the applicability of that theory. But the question that initially perplexed me is the following: what is the explanation of Marx's ambivalence concerning the retributive theory; why is he both attracted and repelled by it? (This ambivalence is not shared, for example, by utilitarians—who feel nothing but repulsion when the retributive theory is mentioned.) Now except for some very brief passages in *The Holy Family*, Marx himself has nothing more to say on the topic of punishment beyond what is contained in this brief *Daily Tribune* article. Thus my essay is in no sense an exercise in textual scholarship (there are not enough texts) but is rather an attempt to construct an assessment of punishment, Marxist at least in spirit, that might account for the ambivalence found in the quoted passage. My main outside help comes, not from Marx himself, but from the writings of the Marxist criminologist Willem Bonger.

2. Many of the leading articles on this topic have been reprinted in H. B. Acton (ed.), *The Philosophy of Punishment* (New York: St Martin's Press, 1969). Those papers not included are cited in Acton's excellent bibliography.

3. One writer who has noticed this is Richard Wasserstrom. See his 'Why Punish the Guilty?', *Princeton University Magazine*, 20 (1964), 14–19.

4. Marx normally avoids the language of rights and justice because he regards such language to be corrupted by bourgeois ideology. However, if we think very broadly of what an appeal to rights involves—namely, a protest against unjustified coercion—there is no reason why Marx may not legitimately avail himself on occasion of this way of speaking. For there is surely at least some moral overlap between Marx's protests against exploitation and the evils of a division of labour, for example, and the claims that people have a right not to be used solely for the benefit of others and a right to self-determination.

5. I do not mean to suggest that under no conceivable circumstances would the doctor be justified in giving the transfusion even though, in one clear sense, he had no right to do it. If, for example, the Jehovah's Witness was a key man whose survival was necessary to prevent the outbreak of a destructive war, we might well regard the transfusion as on the whole justified. However, even in such a case, a morally sensitive man would have to regretfully realize that he was sacrificing an important principle. Such a realization would be impossible (because inconsistent) for a utilitarian, for his theory admits only one principle—namely, do that which on the whole maximizes utility. An occupational disease of utilitarians is a blindness to the possibility of genuine moral dilemmas—i.e., a blindness to the possibility that important moral principles can conflict in ways that are not obviously resolvable by a rational decision procedure.

6. I qualify my thesis by the word 'largely' to show at this point my realization, explored in more detail later, that no single theory can account for all criminal behaviour.

7. Bernard Harrison, 'Violence and the Rule of Law', in Jerome A. Shaffer (ed.), *Violence* (New York: McKay, 1971), 139–76.

8. I have made a start toward such a defence in my 'The Killing of the Innocent', *The Monist*, 57/4 (Oct. 1973).

9. H. L. A. Hart, 'Prolegomenon to the Principles of Punishment', from *Punishment and Responsibility* (Oxford: Oxford University Press, 1968), 1–27.

10. Thomas Hill Green, *Lectures on the Principles of Political Obligation* (1885) (Ann Arbor, Mich.: University of Michigan Press, 1967), 180–205.

11. For an elaboration of this point, see Steven Lukes, 'Alienation and Anomie', in Peter Laslett and W. G. Runciman (eds.), *Philosophy, Politics and Society* (3rd series) (Oxford: B. H. Blackwell, 1967), 134–56.

12. Robert Paul Wolff, *In Defense of Anarchism* (New York: Harper, 1970).

13. In this section, I have adapted some of my previously published material: *Kant: The Philosophy of Right* (London: Macmillan, 1970), 109–12 and 140–4; 'Three Mistakes about Retributivism', *Analysis*, 31 (Apr. 1971), 166–9; and 'Kant's Theory of Criminal Punishment', in *Proceedings of the Third International Kant Congress*, ed. Lewis White Beck (Dordrecht: D. Reidel,

1972), 434–41. I am perfectly aware that Kant's views on the issues to be considered here are often obscure and inconsistent—e.g. the analysis of 'willing one's own punishment' which I shall later quote from Kant occurs in a passage the primary purpose of which is to argue that the idea of 'willing one's own punishment' makes no sense! My present objective, however, is not to attempt accurate Kant scholarship. My goal is rather to build upon some remarks of Kant's which I find philosophically suggestive.

14. Immanuel Kant, *The Metaphysical Elements of Justice* (1797), trans. John Ladd (Indianapolis: Bobbs-Merrill, 1965), 35 ff.

15. Ibid. 37.

16. John Rawls, 'Justice as Fairness', *Philosophical Review*, 67 (1958), 164–97; and *A Theory of Justice* (Cambridge, Mass.: Harvard University Press, 1971), esp. 17–22.

17. Immanuel Kant, 'Concerning the Common Saying: This May be True in Theory but Does not Apply in Practice' (1793), in *The Philosophy of Kant*, ed. and trans. Carl J. Friedrich (New York: Random House, 1949), 421–2.

18. Immanuel Kant, *Perpetual Peace* (1795), trans. Lewis White Beck in the Kant anthology *On History* (Indianapolis: Bobbs-Merrill, 1963), 112.

19. Kant, *The Metaphysical Elements of Justice*, 34.

20. Ibid. 99, 101, and 105, in the order quoted.

21. In addition to the works on justice by Rawls previously cited, the reader should consult the following for Rawls's application of his general theory to the problem of political obligation: John Rawls, 'Legal Obligation and the Duty of Fair Play', in Sidney Hook (ed.), *Law and Philosophy* (New York: New York University Press, 1964), 3–18. This has been reprinted in my anthology *Civil Disobedience and Violence* (Belmont, Calif.: Wadsworth Publishing Company, 1971), 39–52. For a direct application of a similar theory to the problem of punishment, see Herbert Morris, 'Persons and Punishment', *The Monist*, 52/4 (Oct. 1968), 475–501.

22. H. L. A. Hart, *The Concept of Law* (Oxford: Oxford University Press, 1961), 189–95.

23. Jeffrie G. Murphy, 'Moral Death: A Kantian Essay on Psychopathy', *Ethics*, 82/4 (July 1972), 284–98.

24. Banal as this point may seem, it could be persuasively argued that all Enlightenment political theory (e.g., that of Hobbes, Locke, and Kant) is built upon ignoring it. For example, once we have substantial empirical evidence concerning how democracies really work in fact, how sympathetic can we really be to classical theories for the justification of democracy? For more on this, see C. B. Macpherson, 'The Maximization of Democracy', in Laslett and Runciman (eds.), *Philosophy, Politics and Society* 83–103. This article is also relevant to the point raised in n. 11 above.

25. This point is well developed in C. B. Macpherson, *The Political Theory of Possessive Individualism* (Oxford: Oxford University Press, 1962). In a sense,

this point affects even the formal correctness of a theory. For it demonstrates an empirical source of corruption in the analyses of the very concepts in the theory.

26. The writings of Willem Adriaan Bonger (1876–1940), a Dutch criminologist, have fallen into totally unjustified neglect in recent years. Anticipating contemporary sociological theories of crime, he was insisting that criminal behaviour is in the province of normal psychology (though abnormal society) at a time when most other writers were viewing criminality as a symptom of psychopathology. His major works are: *Criminality and Economic Conditions* (Boston: Little, Brown, 1916); *An Introduction to Criminology* (London: Methuen, 1936); and *Race and Crime* (New York: Columbia University Press, 1943).

27. I say 'at least in spirit' to avoid begging the controversial question of whether Marx can be said to embrace a theory of justice. Though (as I suggested in n. 4) much of Marx's own evaluative rhetoric seems to overlap more traditional appeals to rights and justice (and a total lack of sympathy with anything like Utilitarianism), it must be admitted that he also frequently ridicules at least the terms 'rights' and 'justice' because of their apparent entrenchment in bourgeois ethics. For an interesting discussion of this issue, see Allen W. Wood, 'The Marxian Critique of Justice', *Philosophy and Public Affairs*, 1/3 (Spring 1972), 244–82.

28. The importance of community is also, I think, recognized in Gabriel de Tarde's notion of 'social similarity' as a condition of criminal responsibility. See his *Penal Philosophy* (Boston: Little Brown, 1912). I have drawn on de Tarde's general account in my 'Moral Death: A Kantian Essay on Psychopathy'.

29. By 'reciprocity' Bonger intends something which includes, but is much richer than, a notion of 'fair trading or bargaining' that might initially be read into the term. He also has in mind such things as sympathetic identification with others and tendencies to provide mutual aid. Thus, for Bonger, reciprocity and egoism have a strong tendency to conflict. I mention this lest Bonger's notion of reciprocity be too quickly identified with the more restricted notion found in, for example, Kant and Rawls.

30. It is interesting how greatly Bonger's analysis differs from classical deterrence theory—e.g., that of Bentham. Bentham, who views men as machines driven by desires to attain pleasure and avoid pain, tends to regard terror as the primary restraint against crime. Bonger believes that, at least in a healthy society, moral motives would function as a major restraint against crime. When an environment that destroys moral motivation is created, even terror (as statistics tend to confirm) will not eradicate crime.

31. *Introduction to Criminology*, 75–6, and *Criminality and Economic Conditions*, 532, 402, 483–4, 436, and 407, in the order quoted. Bonger explicitly attacks Hobbes: 'The adherents of [Hobbes's theory] have studied principally men

who live under capitalism, or under civilization; their correct conclusion has been that egoism is the predominant characteristic of these men, and they have adopted the simplest explanation of the phenomenon and say that this trait is inborn.' If Hobbists can cite Freud for modern support, Bonger can cite Darwin. For, as Darwin had argued in the *Descent of Man*, men would not have survived as a species if they had not initially had considerably greater social sentiments than Hobbes allows them.

32. Austin J. Turk, in the Introduction to his abridged edition of Bonger's *Criminality and Economic Conditions* (Bloomington, Ind.: Indiana University Press, 1969), 14.

33. Statistical data on characteristics of offenders in America are drawn primarily from surveys by the Bureau of Census and the National Council on Crime and Delinquency. While there is of course wide disagreement on how such data are to be interpreted, there is no serious disagreement concerning at least the general accuracy of statistics such as the one I have cited. Even government publications openly acknowledge a high correlation between crime and socio-economic disadvantages. 'From arrest records, probation reports, and prison statistics a "portrait" of the offender emerges that progressively highlights the disadvantaged character of his life. The offender at the end of the road in prison is likely to be a member of the lowest social and economic groups in the country, poorly educated and perhaps unemployed . . . Material failure, then, in a culture firmly oriented toward material success, is the most common denominator of offenders' (*The Challenge of Crime in a Free Society: A Report by the President's Commission on Law Enforcement and Administration of Justice* (US Government Printing Office, Washington, DC, 1967), 44 and 160). The Marxist implications of this admission have not gone unnoticed by prisoners. See Samuel Jorden, 'Prison Reform: In Whose Interest?' *Criminal Law Bulletin*, 7/9 (Nov. 1971), 779–87.

34. There are, of course, other factors which enter into an explanation of this statistic. One of them is the fact that economically disadvantaged guilty persons are more likely to wind up arrested or in prison (and thus be reflected in this statistic) than are economically advantaged guilty persons. Thus economic conditions enter into the explanation, not just of criminal behaviour, but of society's response to criminal behaviour. For a general discussion on the many ways in which crime and poverty are related, see Patricia M. Wald, 'Poverty and Criminal Justice', *Task Force Report: The Courts* (US Government Printing Office, Washington, DC, 1967), 139–51.

35. The idea that the principles of justice could be proved as a kind of theorem (Rawls's claim in 'Justice as Fairness') seems to be absent, if I understand the work correctly, in Rawls's recent *A Theory of Justice*. In this book, Rawls seems to be content with something less than a decision procedure. He is no longer trying to pull his theory of justice up by its own bootstraps, but now seems concerned simply to *exhibit* a certain elaborate conception of justice in the

belief that it will do a good job of systematizing and ordering most of our considered and reflective intuitions about moral matters. To this, of course, the Marxist will want to say something like the following: 'The considered and reflective intuitions current in our society are a product of bourgeois culture, and thus any theory based upon them begs the question against us and in favour of the status quo.' I am not sure that this charge cannot be answered, but I am sure that it deserves an answer. Someday Rawls may be remembered, to paraphrase Georg Lukacs's description of Thomas Mann, as the last and greatest philosopher of bourgeois liberalism. The virtue of this description is that it perceives the limitations of his outlook in a way consistent with acknowledging his indisputable genius. (None of my remarks here, I should point out, are to be interpreted as denying that our civilization derived major moral benefits from the tradition of bourgeois liberalism. Just because the freedoms and procedures we associate with bourgeois liberalism—speech, press, assembly, due process of law, etc.—are not the only important freedoms and procedures, we are not to conclude with some witless radicals that these freedoms are not terribly important and that the victories of bourgeois revolutions are not worth preserving. My point is much more modest and non-controversial—namely, that even bourgeois liberalism requires a critique. It is not self-justifying and, in certain very important respects, is not justified at all.)

36. Kant has some doubts about punishing bastard infanticide and duelling on similar grounds. Given the stigma that Kant's society attached to illegitimacy and the halo that the same society placed around military honour, it did not seem totally fair to punish those whose criminality in part grew out of such approved motives. See *Metaphysical Elements of Justice*, 106–7.

37. This point is pursued in Herbert Morris, 'Persons and Punishment'. Bonger did not appreciate that 'mental illness', like criminality, may also be a phenomenon of social class. On this, see August B. Hollingshead and Frederick C. Redlich, *Social Class and Mental Illness* (New York: Wiley, 1958). On the general issue of punishment versus therapy, see my *Punishment and Rehabilitation* (Belmont, Calif.: Wadsworth Publishing Company, 1973).

Preface: J. Feinberg, 'The Expressive Function of Punishment'

Murphy's version of retributivism portrayed punishment as a burden imposed on the offender; and many theories of punishment portray it simply as something done to, or inflicted on, offenders. A rather different strand of penal thought, however, portrays punishment as an essentially *expressive* or *communicative* enterprise: as an activity whose meaning is as important as its effects. Feinberg's paper played a central role in bringing the idea of punishment as expression back into the centre of normative theorizing about punishment (see H. MORRIS; VON HIRSCH; Primoratz 1989; Duff 1995; for critical discussion see MATHIESEN; Hart 1963: 60–9; Walker 1978; Skillen 1980). The expressive or communicative dimension of punishment has also been a central theme in sociological work on punishment: from the classic works of Durkheim, Mead, and Garfinkel, to the contemporary analyses of Foucault and Garland (Foucault 1977; Garland 1990). These writings have emphasized the symbolic, communicative aspects of penal ceremonies, and the social and psychological effects which they entail.

If we suggest that punishment is essentially expressive, the obvious questions are: what is being expressed, to whom, and why? The obvious answer to the 'what' question is that punishment expresses the community's condemnation of the crime being punished. This then raises the question of whether and how far the law can claim to embody the shared values of the society. That condemnation can be expressed to the criminal, to the victim, and to the community at large; but we have to ask whether, and under what conditions, this communicative process can be effective—how far is the right message communicated to the right people (see MATHIESEN)? Feinberg suggests various goals which such expression can serve, and various reasons why the state ought to engage in such formal condemnations of crime (see also VON HIRSCH: 119–21). One central question here is whether we should understand the rationale for expressive punishments in *consequentialist* terms (the state should impose expressive punishments because they will or might bring about certain beneficial consequences), or in *intrinsicalist* terms (it is intrinsically right that criminals should suffer such condemnation; see Primoratz 1989 on 'extrinsic' and 'intrinsic' expressionism).

But, as Feinberg argues, an account of the expressive function of punishment, of the benefits which are gained or the values which are respected by the formal condemnation of criminals, is not yet a justification of punishment as we know it. For a condemnation of the criminal's crime could be expressed by a formal declaration at the end of the criminal trial, or by a purely symbolic punishment which is painful solely in virtue of its symbolic meaning. But the kinds of punishment which our penal systems impose are not merely formal or symbolic: they inflict 'hard treatment'—they impose burdens (the loss of liberty, money, time, or even life) which are onerous or painful quite independently of their symbolic meaning. We must ask what justifies the state in choosing these methods of expression. Why should condemnation be expressed through hard treatment?

Feinberg himself rejects traditional retributivist accounts of why offenders should suffer hard treatment. But some retributivists argue that punishment should take the form of hard treatment because only then will it effectively communicate to offenders the condemnation which they deserve (the problem with purely symbolic measures being that offenders may not take them seriously) (see Lucas 1980: 132–6; Falls 1987; Primoratz 1989; Kleinig 1991: for criticism see VON HIRSCH: 121–2; Duff 1986: 240–5). Other theorists argue that hard treatment must be justified in consequentialist terms. Most obviously, it can serve to deter, by the fear of hard treatment, those who would not be dissuaded from crime merely by a symbolic condemnation (see VON HIRSCH for a sophisticated version of this kind of argument). Others suggest that hard treatment punishments can serve as modes of moral reform of education (see H. MORRIS; Hampton 1984), or as penances by which the criminal may be brought to repentance (see Duff 1986). The point which must be emphasized, however, is that hard treatment does need justification: even if offenders should be formally condemned, and even if that condemnation can be expressed by penal hard treatment, we must still ask why it should be expressed in that way.

References

DUFF, R. A. (1986), *Trials and Punishments* (Cambridge).
—— (1995), 'Penal Communications: Recent Work in the Philosophy of Punishment', in *Crime and Justice: An Annual Review of Research*, 20.
FALLS, M. M. (1987), 'Retribution, Reciprocity, and Respect for Persons', *Law and Philosophy*, 6: 25–51.
FOUCAULT, M. (1977), *Discipline and Punish: The Birth of the Prison* (London).
GARLAND, D. (1990), *Punishment and Modern Society: A Study in Social Theory* (Oxford).
HAMPTON, J. (1984), 'The Moral Education Theory of Punishment', *Philosophy and Public Affairs*, 13: 208–38.
HART, H. L. A. (1963), *Law, Liberty and Morality* (Oxford).
KLEINIG, J. (1991), 'Punishment and Moral Seriousness', *Israel Law Review*, 25: 401–21.
LUCAS, J. R. (1980), *On Justice* (Oxford).
PRIMORATZ, I. (1989), 'Punishment as Language', *Philosophy*, 64: 187–205.
SKILLEN, A. J. (1980), 'How to Say Things with Walls', *Philosophy*, 55: 509–23.
WALKER, N. (1978), 'Punishing, Denouncing or Reducing Crime', in P. R. Glazebrook (ed.), *Reshaping the Criminal Law* (London), 391–403.

The Expressive Function of Punishment

JOEL FEINBERG

It might well appear to a moral philosopher absorbed in the classical literature of his discipline, or to a moralist sensitive to injustice and suffering, that recent philosophical discussions of the problem of punishment have somehow missed the point of his interest. Recent influential articles[1] have quite sensibly distinguished between questions of definition and justification, between justifying general rules and particular decisions, between moral and legal guilt. So much is all to the good. When these articles go on to *define* 'punishment', however, it seems to many that they leave out of their ken altogether the very element that makes punishment theoretically puzzling and morally disquieting. Punishment is defined in effect as the infliction of hard treatment by an authority on a person for his prior failing in some respect (usually an infraction of a rule or command).[2] There may be a very general sense of the word 'punishment' which is well expressed by this definition; but even if that is so, we can distinguish a narrower, more emphatic sense that slips through its meshes. Imprisonment at hard labour for committing a felony is a clear case of punishment in the emphatic sense. But I think we would be less willing to apply that term to parking tickets, offside penalties, sackings, flunkings, and disqualifications. Examples of the latter sort I propose to call *penalties* (merely), so that I may inquire further what distinguishes punishment, in the strict and narrow sense that interests the moralist, from other kinds of penalties.[3]

One method of answering this question is to focus one's attention on the class of non-punitive penalties in an effort to discover some clearly identifiable characteristic common to them all, and absent from all punishments, on which the distinction between the two might be grounded. The hypotheses yielded by this approach, however, are not likely to survive close scrutiny. One might conclude, for example, that mere penalties are less severe than punishments, but although this is generally true, it is not necessarily and universally so. Again, we might be tempted to interpret penalties as mere 'pricetags' attached to certain types of behaviour that are generally undesirable, so that only those with especially strong motivation will be willing to pay the price.[4] In this way deliberate efforts on the part of some Western states to keep roads from urban centres to wilderness areas few in number and poor in quality would be viewed as essentially no different from various parking fines and football penalties. In each case a certain kind of conduct is discouraged without being absolutely prohibited: anyone who desires strongly enough to get to the wilderness (or park overtime, or interfere with a pass) may do so provided he is willing to pay the penalty (price). On this view, penalties are in effect licensing fees, different from other purchased permits in that the price is often paid afterward rather than in advance. Since a similar interpretation of punishments seems implausible, it might be alleged that this is the basis of the distinction between penalties and punishments. However, even though a great number of penalties can no doubt plausibly be treated as retroactive licensing fees, it is hardly possible to view all of them as such. It is certainly not true, for example, of most demotions, firings, and flunkings that they are 'prices' paid for some already consumed benefit; and even parking fines are sanctions for rules 'meant to be taken seriously as ... standard[s] of behaviour'[5] and thus are more than mere public parking fees.

Rather than look for a characteristic common and peculiar to the penalties on which to ground the distinction between penalties and punishments, we would be better advised, I think, to turn our attention to the examples of punishments. Both penalties and punishments are authoritative deprivations for failures; but, apart from these common features, penalties have a miscellaneous character, whereas punishments have an important additional characteristic in common. That characteristic, or specific difference, I shall argue, is a certain expressive function: punishment is a conventional device for the expression of attitudes of resentment and indignation, and of judgments of disapproval and reprobation, on the part either of the punishing authority himself or of those 'in whose name' the punishment is inflicted. Punishment, in short, has a *symbolic significance* largely missing from other kinds of penalties.

The reprobative symbolism of punishment and its character as 'hard treatment', though never separate in reality, must be carefully distinguished for purposes of analysis. Reprobation is itself painful, whether or not it is accompanied by further 'hard treatment', and hard treatment, such as fine or imprisonment, because of its conventional symbolism, can itself be reprobatory. Still, we can conceive of ritualistic condemnation unaccompanied by any *further* hard treatment, and of inflictions and deprivations which, because of different symbolic conventions, have no reprobative force. It will be my thesis in this essay that (1) both the 'hard treatment' aspect of punishment and its reprobative function must be part of the *definition* of legal punishment, and that (2) each of these aspects raises its own kind of question about the *justification* of legal punishment as a general practice. I shall argue that some of the jobs punishment does, and some of the conceptual problems it raises, cannot be intelligibly described unless (1) is true, and that the incoherence of a familiar form of the retributive theory results from failure to appreciate the force of (2).

I

That the expression of the community's condemnation is an essential ingredient in legal punishment is widely acknowledged by legal writers. Henry M. Hart, for example, gives eloquent emphasis to the point:

> What distinguishes a criminal from a civil sanction and all that distinguishes it, it is ventured, is the judgment of community condemnation which accompanies ... its imposition. As Professor Gardner wrote not long ago, in a distinct but cognate connection:
>
> 'The essence of punishment for moral delinquency lies in the criminal conviction itself. One may lose more money on the stock market than in a court-room; a prisoner of war camp may well provide a harsher environment than a state prison; death on the field of battle has the same physical characteristics as death by sentence of law. It is the expression of the community's hatred, fear, or contempt for the convict which alone characterizes physical hardship as punishment.'
>
> If this is what a 'criminal' penalty is, then we can say readily enough what a 'crime' is. ... It is conduct which, if duly shown to have taken place, will incur a formal and solemn pronouncement of the moral condemnation of the community. ... Indeed the condemnation plus the added [unpleasant physical] consequences may well be considered, compendiously, as constituting the punishment.[6]

Professor Hart's compendious definition needs qualification in one respect. The moral condemnation and the 'unpleasant consequences' that he rightly identifies as essential elements of punishment are not as distinct and separate as he suggests. It does not always happen that the convicted prisoner is first solemnly condemned and then subjected to unpleasant physical treatment. It would be more accurate in many cases to say that the unpleasant treatment itself expresses the condemnation, and that this expressive aspect of his incarceration is precisely the element by reason of which it is properly characterized as punishment and not mere penalty. The administrator who regretfully suspends the license of a conscientious but accident-prone driver can inflict a deprivation without any scolding, express or implied; but the reckless motorist who is sent to prison for six months is thereby inevitably subject to shame and ignominy—the very walls of his cell condemn him, and his record becomes a stigma.

To say that the very physical treatment itself expresses condemnation is to say simply that certain forms of hard treatment have become the conventional symbols of public reprobation. This is neither more nor less paradoxical than to say that certain words have become conventional vehicles in our language for the expression of certain attitudes, or that champagne is the alcoholic beverage traditionally used in celebration of great events, or that black is the colour of mourning. Moreover, particular kinds of punishment are often used to express quite specific attitudes (loosely speaking, this is part of their 'meaning'); note the differences, for example, between beheading a nobleman and hanging a yeoman, burning a heretic and hanging a traitor, hanging an enemy soldier and executing him by firing squad.

It is much easier to show that punishment has a symbolic significance than to state exactly what it is that punishment expresses. At its best, in civilized and democratic countries, punishment surely expresses the community' strong *disapproval* of what the criminal did. Indeed, it can be said that punishment expresses the *judgment* (as distinct from any emotion) of the community that what the criminal did was wrong. I think it is fair to say of our community, however, that punishment generally expresses more than judgments of disapproval; it is also a symbolic way of getting back at the criminal, of expressing a kind of vindictive resentment. To any reader who has in fact spent time in a prison, I venture to say, even Professor Gardner's strong terms—'hatred, fear, or contempt for the convict'—will not seem too strong an account of what imprisonment is universally taken to express. Not only does the criminal feel the naked hostility of his guards and the outside world—that would be fierce enough—but that hostility is self-righteous as well. His punishment bears the aspect of legitimized vengefulness. Hence there is much truth in J. F. Stephen's celebrated remark that 'The criminal law stands to the passion of revenge in much the same relation as marriage to the sexual appetite.'[7]

If we reserve the less dramatic term 'resentment' for the various vengeful attitudes and the term 'reprobation' for the stern judgment of disapproval, then perhaps we can characterize *condemnation* (or denunciation) as a kind of fusing of resentment and reprobation. That these two elements are generally to be found in legal punishment was well understood by the authors of the *Report of the Royal Commission on Capital Punishment*:

> Discussion of the principle of *retribution* is apt to be confused because the word is not always used in the same sense. Sometimes it is intended to mean vengeance, sometimes reprobation. In the first sense the idea is that of satisfaction by the State of a wronged individual's desire to be avenged; in the second it is that of the State's *marking its disapproval* of the breaking of its laws by a punishment proportionate to the gravity of the offense.[8]

II

The relation of the expressive function of punishment to its various central purposes is not always easy to trace. Symbolic public condemnation added to deprivation may help or hinder deterrence, reform, and rehabilitation—the evidence is not clear. On the other hand, there are other functions of punishment, often lost sight of in the preoccupation with deterrence and reform, that presuppose the expressive function and would be difficult or impossible without it.

Authoritative disavowal. Consider the standard international practice of demanding that a nation whose agent has unlawfully violated the complaining nation's rights should punish the offending agent. For example, suppose that an airplane of nation *A* fires on an airplane of nation *B* while the latter is flying over international waters. Very likely high authorities in nation *B* will send a note of protest to their counterparts in nation *A* demanding, among other things, that the transgressive pilot be punished. Punishing the pilot is an emphatic, dramatic, and well-understood way of *condemning* and thereby *disavowing* his act. It tells the world that the pilot had no right to do what he did, that he was on his own in doing it, that his government does not condone that sort of thing. It testifies thereby to government *A*'s recognition of the violated rights of government *B* in the affected area and, therefore, to the wrongfulness of the pilot's act. Failure to punish the pilot tells the world that government *A* does not consider him to have been personally at fault. That in turn is to claim responsibility for the act, which in effect labels that act as an 'instrument of deliberate national policy' and hence an act of war. In that case either formal hostilities or humiliating loss of face by one side or the other almost certainly will follow. None of this scenario makes any sense without the clearly understood reprobative symbolism of punishment. In quite parallel ways punishment enables employers to disavow the acts of their employees (though not civil liability for those acts), and fathers the destructive acts of their sons.

Symbolic nonacquiescence: '*Speaking in the name of the people.*' The symbolic function of punishment also explains why even those sophisticated persons who abjure resentment of criminals and look with small favour generally on the penal law are likely to demand that certain kinds of conduct be punished when or if the law lets them go by. In the state of Texas, so-called paramour killings were regarded by the law as not merely mitigated, but completely justifiable.[9] Many humanitarians, I believe, will feel quite spontaneously that a great injustice is done when such killings are left unpunished. The sense of violated justice, moreover, might be distinct and unaccompanied by any frustrated *Schadenfreude* toward the killer, lust for blood or vengeance, or metaphysical concern lest the universe stay 'out of joint'. The demand for punishment in cases of this sort may instead represent the feeling that paramour killings deserve to be *condemned*, that the law in condoning, even approving of them, speaks for all citizens in expressing a wholly inappropriate attitude toward them. For in effect the law expresses the judgment of the 'people of Texas', in whose name it speaks, that the vindictive satisfaction in the mind of a cuckolded husband is a thing of greater value than the very life of his wife's lover. The demand that paramour killings be punished may simply be the demand that this lopsided value judgment be withdrawn and that the state *go on record* against paramour killings and the law *testify to the recognition* that such killings are wrongful. Punishment no doubt would also help deter killers. This too is a desideratum and a closely related one, but it is not to be identified with reprobation; for deterrence might be achieved by a dozen other techniques, from simple penalties and forfeitures to exhortation and propaganda; but effective public denunciation and, through it, symbolic nonacquiescence in the crime seem virtually to require punishment.

This symbolic function of punishment was given great emphasis by Kant, who, characteristically, proceeded to exaggerate its importance. Even if a desert island community were to disband, Kant argued, its members should first execute the last murderer left in its gaols, 'for otherwise they might all be regarded as participators in the [unpunished] murder'.[10] This Kantian idea that in failing to punish wicked acts society endorses them and thus becomes *particeps criminis* does seem to reflect, however dimly, something embedded in common sense. A similar notion underlies whatever is intelligible in the widespread notion that all citizens share the responsibility for political atrocities. In so far as there is a coherent argument behind the extravagant distributions of guilt made by existentialists and other literary figures, it can be reconstructed in some such way as this: to whatever extent a political act is done 'in one's name', to that extent one is responsible for it; a citizen can avoid responsibility in advance by explicitly disowning the government as his spokesman, or after the fact through open protest, resistance, and so on; otherwise, by 'acquiescing' in what is done in one's name, one incurs the responsibility for it. The root notion here is a kind of 'power of attorney' a government has for its citizens.

Vindication of the law. Sometimes the state goes on record through its statutes, in a way that might well please a conscientious citizen in whose name it speaks, but then owing to official evasion and unreliable enforcement gives rise to doubts that the law really means what it says. It is murder in Mississippi, as elsewhere, for a white man intentionally to kill a Negro; but if grand juries refuse to issue indictments or if trial juries refuse to convict, and this fact is clearly recognized by most citizens, then it is in a purely formal and empty sense indeed that killings of Negroes by whites are illegal in Mississippi. Yet the law stays on the books, to give ever less convincing lip service to a noble moral judgment. A statute honoured mainly in the breach begins to lose its character as law, unless, as we say, it is *vindicated* (emphatically reaffirmed); and clearly the way to do this (indeed the only way) is to punish those who violate it.

Similarly, *punitive damages*, so called, are sometimes awarded the plaintiff in a civil action, as a supplement to compensation for his injuries. What more dramatic way of vindicating his violated right can be imagined than to have a court thus forcibly condemn its violation through the symbolic machinery of punishment?

Absolution of others. When something scandalous has occurred and it is clear that the wrongdoer must be one of a small number of suspects, then the state, by punishing one of these parties, thereby relieves the others of suspicion and informally absolves them of blame. Moreover, quite often the absolution of an accuser hangs as much in the balance at a criminal trial as the inculpation of the accused. A good example of this point can be found in James Gould Cozzens's novel *By Love Possessed*. A young girl, after an evening of illicit sexual activity with her boy friend, is found out by her bullying mother, who then insists that she clear her name by bringing criminal charges against the boy. He used physical force, the girl charges; she freely consented, he replies. If the jury finds him guilty of rape, it will by the same token absolve her from (moral) guilt; and her reputation as well as his rides on the outcome. Could not the state do this job without punishment? Perhaps, but when it speaks by punishing, its message is loud and sure of getting across.

III

A philosophical theory of punishment that, through inadequate definition, leaves out the condemnatory function not only will disappoint the moralist and the traditional moral philosopher; it will seem offensively irrelevant as well to the constitutional lawyer, whose vital concern with punishment is both conceptual, and therefore genuinely philosophical, as well as practically urgent. The distinction between punishment and mere penalties is a familiar one in the criminal law, where theorists have long engaged in what Jerome Hall calls 'dubious dogmatics distinguishing "civil penalties" from punitive sanctions, and "public wrongs" from crimes'.[11] Our courts now regard it as true (by definition) that all criminal statutes are punitive (merely labelling an act a crime does not make it one unless sanctions are specified); but to the converse question whether all statutes specifying sanctions are *criminal* statutes, the courts are reluctant to give an affirmative reply. There are now a great number of statutes that permit 'unpleasant consequences' to be inflicted on persons and yet surely cannot be regarded as criminal statutes—tax bills, for example, are aimed at regulating, nor forbidding, certain types of activity. How to classify borderline cases as either 'regulative' or 'punitive' is not merely an idle conceptual riddle; it very quickly draws the courts into questions of great constitutional import. There are elaborate constitutional safeguards for persons faced with the prospect of punishment; but these do not, or need not, apply when the threatened hard treatment merely 'regulates an activity'.

The 1960 Supreme Court case of *Flemming* v. *Nestor*[12] is a dramatic (and shocking) example of how a man's fate can depend on whether a government-inflicted deprivation is interpreted as a 'regulative' or 'punitive' sanction. Nestor had immigrated to the United States from Bulgaria in 1913 and became eligible in 1955 for old-age benefits under the Social Security Act. In 1956, however, he was deported in accordance with the Immigration and Nationality Act for having been a member of the Communist Party from 1933 to 1939. This was a harsh fate for a man who had been in America for forty-three years and who was no longer a

Communist; but at least he would have his social security benefits to support him in his exiled old age—or so he thought. Section 202 of the amended Social Security Act, however, 'provides for the termination of old-age, survivor, and disability insurance benefits payable to . . . an alien individual who, after September 1, 1954 (the date of enactment of the section) is deported under the Immigration and Nationality Act on any one of certain specified grounds, including past membership in the Communist Party'.[13] Accordingly, Nestor was informed that his benefits would cease.

Nestor then brought suit in a district court for a reversal of the administrative decision. The court found in his favour and held Section 202 of the Social Security Act unconstitutional, on the grounds that 'termination of [Nestor's] benefits amounts to punishing him without a judicial trial, that [it] constitutes the imposition of punishment by legislative act rendering §202 a bill of attainder; and that the punishment exacted is imposed for past conduct not unlawful when engaged in, thereby violating the constitutional prohibition on *ex post facto* laws'.[14] The Secretary of Health, Education, and Welfare, Mr Flemming, then appealed this decision to the Supreme Court.

It was essential to the argument of the district court that the termination of old-age benefits under Section 202 was in fact punishment, for if it were properly classified as non-punitive deprivation, then none of the cited constitutional guarantees was relevant. The Constitution, for example, does not forbid all retroactive laws, but only those providing punishment. (Retroactive tax laws may also be harsh and unfair, but they are not unconstitutional.) The question before the Supreme Court, then, was whether the hardship imposed by Section 202 was punishment. Did this not bring the Court face to face with the properly philosophical question 'What is punishment?' and it is not clear that, under the usual definition that fails to distinguish punishment from mere penalties, this particular judicial problem could not even arise?

The fate of the appellee Nestor can be recounted briefly. The five-man majority of the Court held that he had not been punished—this despite Mr Justice Brennan's eloquent characterization of him in a dissenting opinion as 'an aging man deprived of the means with which to live after being separated from his family and exiled to live among strangers in a land he quit forty-seven years ago'.[15] Mr Justice Harlan, writing for the majority, argued that the termination of benefits, like the deportation itself, was the exercise of the plenary power of Congress incident to the regulation of an activity.

Similarly, the setting by a State of qualifications for the practice of medicine, and their modification from time to time, is an incident of the State's power to protect the health and safety of its citizens, and its decision to bar from practice persons who commit or have committed a felony is taken as evidencing an intent to exercise that regulatory power, and not a purpose to add to the punishment of ex-felons.[16]

Mr Justice Brennan, on the other hand, contended that it is impossible to think of any purpose the provision in question could possibly serve except to 'strike' at 'aliens deported for conduct displeasing to the law-makers'.[17]

Surely, Justice Brennan seems right in finding in the sanction the expression of Congressional reprobation and, therefore, 'punitive intent'; but the sanction itself (in Justice Harlan's words, 'the mere denial of a noncontractual governmental benefit'[18]) was not a conventional vehicle for the expression of censure, being wholly outside the apparatus of the criminal law. It therefore lacked the reprobative symbolism essential to punishment generally and was thus, in its hybrid character, able to generate confusion and judicial disagreement. It was as if Congress had 'condemned' a certain class of persons privately in stage whispers, rather than by pinning the infamous label of criminal on them and letting that symbol do the condemning in an open and public way. Congress without question 'intended' to punish a certain class of aliens and did indeed select sanctions of appropriate severity for that purpose; but the deprivation they chose was not of an appropriate kind to perform the function of public condemnation. A father who 'punishes' his son for a displeasing act the father had not thought to forbid in advance, by sneaking up on him from behind and then throwing him bodily across the room against the wall, would be in much the same position as the legislators of the amended Social Security Act, especially if he then denied to the son that his physical assault on him had had any 'punitive intent', asserting that it was a mere exercise of his paternal prerogative to rearrange the household furnishings and other objects in his own living room. To act in such a fashion would be to tarnish the paternal authority and infect all later genuine punishments with hollow hypocrisy. The same effect is produced when legislators go outside the criminal law to do the criminal law's job.

In 1961 the New York State legislature passed the so-called Subversive Drivers Act requiring 'suspension and revocation of the driver's license of anyone who has been convicted, under the Smith Act, of advocating the overthrow of the Federal government'. The *Reporter* magazine[19] quoted the sponsor of the bill as admitting that it was aimed primarily at one person, Communist Benjamin Davis, who had only recently won a court fight to regain his driver's licence after his five-year term in prison. The *Reporter* estimated that at most a 'few dozen' people would be kept from driving by the new legislation. Was this punishment? Not at all, said the bill's sponsor, Assemblyman Paul Taylor. The legislature was simply exercising its right to regulate automobile traffic in the interest of public safety:

Driving licenses, Assemblyman Taylor explained . . . are not a 'right' but a 'valuable privilege.' The Smith Act Communists, after all, were convicted of advocating the overthrow of the government by force, violence, or assassination. ('They always leave out the assassination,' he remarked. 'I like to put it in.') Anyone who was convicted under such an act had to be 'a person pretty well dedicated to a certain point of view,' the assemblyman continued, and anyone with that particular point of view 'can't be concerned about the rights of others.' Being concerned about the rights of others, he concluded, 'is a prerequisite of being a good driver.'[20]

This example shows how transparent can be the effort to mask punitive intent. The Smith Act ex-convicts were treated with such severity and in such circumstances that no non-punitive legislative purpose could *plausibly* be maintained; yet that *kind* of treatment (quite apart from its severity) lacks the reprobative symbolism essential to clear public denunciation. After all, aged, crippled, and blind persons are also deprived of their licences, so it is not *necessarily* the case that reprobation attaches to that kind of sanction. And so victims of a cruel law understandably claim that they have been punished, and retroactively at that. Yet, strictly speaking, they have not been *punished*; they have been treated much worse.

IV

The distinction between punishments and mere penalties, and the essentially reprobative function of the former, can also help clarify the controversy among writers on the criminal law about the propriety of so-called strict liability offences—offences for the conviction of which there need be no proof of 'fault' or 'culpability' on the part of the accused. If it can be shown that he committed an act proscribed by statute, then he is guilty irrespective of whether he had any justification or excuse for what he did. Perhaps the most familiar examples come from the traffic laws: leaving a car parked beyond the permitted time in a restricted zone is automatically to violate the law, and penalties will be imposed however good the excuse. Many strict liability statutes do not even require an overt act; these proscribe not certain conduct, but certain *results*. Some make mere unconscious possession of contraband, firearms, or narcotics a crime, others the sale of misbranded articles or impure foods. The liability for so-called public welfare offences may seem especially severe:

... with rare exceptions, it became definitely established that *mens rea* is not essential in the public welfare offenses, indeed that even a very high degree of care is irrelevant. Thus a seller of cattle feed was convicted of violating a statute forbidding misrepresentation of the percentage of oil in the product, despite the fact that he had employed a reputable chemist to make the analysis and had even understated the chemist's findings.[21]

The rationale of strict liability in public welfare statutes is that viola-tion of the public interest is more likely to be prevented by unconditional liability than by liability that can be defeated by some kind of excuse; that, even though liability without 'fault' is severe, it is one of the known risks incurred by businessmen; and that, besides, the sanctions are *only fines*, hence not really 'punitive' in character. On the other hand, strict liability to *imprisonment* (or 'punishment proper') 'has been held by many to be incompatible with the basic requirements of our Anglo–American, and indeed, any civilized jurisprudence'.[22] What accounts for this differ-ence in attitude? In both kinds of case, defendants may have sanctions inflicted upon them even though they are acknowledged to be without fault; and the difference cannot be merely that imprisonment is always and necessarily a greater harm than a fine, for this is not always so. Rather, the reason why strict liability to imprisonment (punishment) is so much more repugnant to our sense of justice than is strict liability to fine (penalty) is simply that imprisonment in modern times has taken on the symbolism of public reprobation. In the words of Justice Brandeis, 'It is ... imprisonment in a penitentiary, which now renders a crime infa-mous.'[23] We are familiar with the practice of penalizing persons for 'offences' they could not help. It happens every day in football games, business firms, traffic courts, and the like. But there is something very odd and offensive in *punishing* people for admittedly faultless conduct; for not only is it arbitrary and cruel to *condemn* someone for something he did (admittedly) without fault, it is also self-defeating and irrational.

Although their abundant proliferation[24] is a relatively recent phenome-non, statutory offences with non-punitive sanctions have long been famil-iar to legal commentators, and long a source of uneasiness to them. This discomfort is 'indicated by the persistent search for an appropriate label, such as "public torts," "public welfare offenses," "prohibitory laws," "prohibited acts," "regulatory offenses," "police regulations," "administrative misdemeanors," "quasi-crimes," or "civil offenses." '[25] These represent alternatives to the unacceptable categorization of traffic infractions, inadvertent violations of commercial regulations, and the like, as *crimes*, their perpetrators as *criminals*, and their penalties as *punishments*. The drafters of the new Model Penal Code have defined a class of infractions of penal law forming no part of the substantive criminal law. These they call 'violations', and their sanctions 'civil penalties'.

Section 1.04. Classes of Crimes: Violations
(1) An offense defined by this code or by any other statute of this State, for which a sentence of [death or of] imprisonment is authorized, constitutes a crime. Crimes are classified as felonies, misdemeanors, or petty misdemeanors.

[(2), (3), (4) define felonies, misdemeanors, and petty misdemeanors.]

(5) An offense defined by this Code or by any other statute of this State constitutes a violation if it is so designated in this Code or in the law defining the offense or if no other sentence than a fine, or fine and forfeiture or other civil penalty is authorized upon conviction or if it is defined by a statute other than this Code which now provides that the offense shall not constitute a crime. A violation does not constitute a crime and conviction of a violation shall not give rise to any disability or legal disadvantage based on conviction of a criminal offence.[26]

Since violations, unlike crimes, carry no social stigma, it is often argued that there is no serious injustice if, in the interest of quick and effective law enforcement, violators are held unconditionally liable. This line of argument is persuasive when we consider only parking and minor traffic violations, illegal sales of various kinds, and violations of health and safety codes, where the penalties serve as warnings and the fines are light. But the argument loses all cogency when the 'civil penalties' are severe—heavy fines, forfeitures of property, removal from office, suspension of a licence, withholding of an important 'benefit', and the like. The condemnation of the faultless may be the most flagrant injustice, but the good-natured, non-condemnatory infliction of severe hardship on the innocent is little better. It is useful to distinguish violations and civil penalties from crimes and punishments; yet it does not follow that the safeguards of culpability requirements and due process which justice demands for the latter are always irrelevant encumbrances to the former. Two things are morally wrong: (1) to condemn a faultless man while inflicting pain or deprivation on him however slight (unjust punishment); and (2) to inflict unnecessary and severe suffering on a faultless man even in the absence of condemnation (unjust civil penalty). To exact a two-dollar fine from a hapless violator for overtime parking, however, even though he could not possibly have avoided it, is to do neither of these things.

V

Public condemnation, whether avowed through the stigmatizing symbolism of punishment or unavowed but clearly discernible (mere 'punitive intent'), can greatly magnify the suffering caused by its attendant mode of hard treatment. Samuel Butler keenly appreciated the difference between reprobative hard treatment (punishment) and the same treatment without reprobation:

. . . we should hate a single flogging given in the way of mere punishment more than the amputation of a limb, if it were kindly and courteously performed from a wish to help us out of our difficulty, and with the full consciousness on the part of the doctor that it was only by an accident of constitution that he was not in the like plight himself. So the Erewhonians take a flogging once a week, and a diet of bread and water for two or three months together, whenever their straightener recommends it.[27]

Even floggings and imposed fastings do not constitute punishments, then, where social conventions are such that they do not express public censure (what Butler called 'scouting'); and as therapeutic treatments simply, rather than punishments, they are easier to take.

Yet floggings and fastings do hurt, and far more than is justified by their Erewhonian (therapeutic) objectives. The same is true of our own state mental hospitals where criminal psychopaths are often sent for 'rehabilitation': solitary confinement may not hurt *quite* so much when called 'the quiet room', or the forced support of heavy fire extinguishers when called 'hydrotherapy';[28] but their infliction on patients can be so cruel (whether or not their quasi-medical names mask punitive intent) as to demand justification.

Hard treatment and symbolic condemnation, then, are not only both necessary to an adequate definition of 'punishment'; each also poses a special problem for the justification of punishment. The reprobative symbolism of punishment is subject to attack not only as an independent source of suffering but as the vehicle of undeserved responsive attitudes and unfair judgments of blame. One kind of sceptic, granting that penalties are needed if legal rules are to be enforced, and also that society would be impossible without general and predictable obedience to such rules, might nevertheless question the need to add condemnation to the penalizing of violators. Hard treatment of violators, he might grant, is an unhappy necessity, but reprobation of the offender is offensively self-righteous and cruel; adding gratuitous insult to necessary injury can serve no useful purpose. A partial answer to this kind of sceptic has already been given. The condemnatory aspect of punishment does serve a socially useful purpose: it is precisely the element in punishment that makes possible the performance of such symbolic functions as disavowal, non-acquiescence, vindication, and absolution.

Another kind of sceptic might readily concede that the reprobative symbolism of punishment is necessary to, and justified by, these various derivative functions. Indeed, he may even add deterrence to the list, for condemnation is likely to make it clear, where it would not otherwise be so, that a penalty is not a mere price tag. Granting that point, however, this kind of sceptic would have us consider whether the ends that justify public condemnation of criminal conduct might not be achieved equally well by means of less painful symbolic machinery. There was a time, after all, when the gallows and the rack were the leading clear symbols of shame and ignominy. Now we condemn felons to penal servitude as the way of rendering their crimes infamous. Could not the job be done still more economically? Isn't there a way to stigmatize without inflicting any further (pointless) pain to the body, to family, to creative capacity?

One can imagine an elaborate public ritual, exploiting the most trust-worthy devices of religion and mystery, music and drama, to express in the most solemn way the community's condemnation of a criminal for his dastardly deed. Such a ritual might condemn so very emphatically that there could be no doubt of its genuineness, thus rendering symboli-cally superfluous any further hard physical treatment. Such a device would preserve the condemnatory function of punishment while dispensing with its usual physical media—incarceration and corporal mistreatment. Perhaps this is only idle fantasy; or perhaps there is more to it. The ques-tion is surely open. The only point I wish to make here is one about the nature of the question. The problem of justifying punishment, when it takes this form, may really be that of justifying our particular symbols of infamy.

Whatever the form of sceptical challenge to the institution of punish-ment, however, there is one traditional answer to it that seems to me to be incoherent. I refer to that version of the retributive theory which men-tions neither condemnation nor vengeance but insists instead that the ultimate justifying purpose of punishment is to match off moral gravity and pain, to give each offender exactly that amount of pain the evil of his offence calls for, on the alleged principle of justice that the wicked should suffer pain in exact proportion to their turpitude.

I shall only mention in passing the familiar and potent objections to this view.[29] The innocent presumably deserve *not* to suffer, just as the guilty are supposed to deserve to suffer; yet it is impossible to hurt an evil man without imposing suffering on those who love or depend on him. Deciding the right amount of suffering to inflict in a given case would require an assessment of the character of the offender as manifested throughout his whole life and also his total lifelong balance of pleasure and pain—an obvious impossiblity. Moreover, justice would probably demand the abandonment of general rules in the interests of individuation of punishment since there will inevitably be inequalities of moral guilt in the commission of the same crime and inequalities of suffering from the same punishment. If not dispensed with, however, general rules must list all crimes in the order of their moral gravity, all punishments in the order of their severity, and the matchings between the two scales. But the moral gravity scale would have to list as well motives and purposes, not simply types of overt acts, for a given crime can be committed in any kind of 'mental state', and its 'moral gravity' in a given case surely must depend in part on its accompanying motive. Condign punishment, then, would have to match suffering to motive (desire, belief, or whatever), not to dangerousness or to amount of harm done. Hence some petty larcenies would be punished more severely than some murders. It is not likely that we should wish to give power to judges and juries to make such difficult moral judgements. Worse yet, the judgments required are not merely 'difficult'; they are in principle impossible to make. It may seem 'self-evident' to some moralists that the passionate impulsive killer, for example, deserves less suffering for his wickedness than the scheming deliberate killer; but if the question of comparative *dangerousness* is left out of mind, reasonable men not only can but will disagree in their appraisals of comparative blameworthiness, and there appears to be no rational way of resolving the issue.[30] Certainly, there is no rational way of demonstrating that one criminal deserves exactly twice or three-eights or twelve-ninths as much suffering as another; yet, according to at least some forms of this theory, the amounts of suffering inflicted for any two crimes should stand in exact proportion to the 'amounts' of wickedness in the criminals.

For all that, however, the pain-fitting-wickedness version of the retributive theory does erect its edifice of moral superstition on a foundation in moral common sense, for justice *does* require that in some (other) sense 'the punishment fit the crime'. What justice demands is that the *condemnatory aspect* of the punishment suit the crime, that the crime be of a kind that is truly worthy of reprobation. Further, the degree of disapproval expressed by the punishment should 'fit' the crime only in the unproblematic sense that the more serious crimes should receive stronger disapproval than the less serious ones, the seriousness of the crime being determined by the amount of harm it generally causes and the degree to which people are disposed to commit it. That is quite another thing than requiring that the 'hard treatment' component, considered apart from its symbolic function, should 'fit' the moral quality of a specific criminal act, assessed quite independently of its relation to social harm. Given our conventions, of course, condemnation is expressed by hard treatment, and the degree of harshness of the latter expresses the degree of reprobation of the former. Still, this should not blind us to the fact that it is social disapproval and its appropriate expression that should fit the crime, and not hard treatment (pain) as such. Pain should match guilt only in so far as its infliction is the symbolic vehicle of public condemnation.

Notes

1. See esp. the following: A. G. N. Flew, 'The Justification of Punishment', *Philosophy*, 29 (1954), 291–307; S. I. Benn, 'An Approach to the Problems of Punishment', *Philosophy*, 33 (1958), 325–41; and H. L. A. Hart, 'Prolegomenon to the Principles of Punishment', *Proceedings of the Aristotelian Society*, 60 (1959–60), 1–26.
2. Hart and Benn both borrow Flew's definition. In Hart's paraphrase (op. cit. 4), punishment '(i) . . . must involve pain or other consequences normally considered unpleasant. (ii) It must be for an offense against legal rules. (iii) It must be of an actual or supposed offender for his offense. (iv) It must be intentionally administered by human beings other than the offender. (v) It must be imposed and administered by an authority constituted by a legal system against which the offense is committed.'
3. The distinction between punishments and penalties was first called to my attention by Dr Anita Fritz of the University of Connecticut. Similar distinctions in different terminologies have been made by many. Sir Frederick Pollock and Frederic Maitland speak of 'true afflictive punishments' as opposed to outlawry, private vengeance, fine, and emendation. *The History of English Law before the Time of Edward I* (2nd edn., Cambridge: Cambridge University Press, 1968), ii, 451 ff. The phrase 'afflictive punishment' was invented by Bentham: 'These [corporal] punishments are almost always attended with a portion of ignominy, and this does not always increase with

the organic pain, but principally depends upon the condition [social class] of the offender.' *The Rationale of Punishment* (London: Heward, 1830), 83. Sir James Stephen says of legal punishment that it 'should always connote . . . moral infamy.' *A History of the Criminal Law of England*, 3 vols. (London: Macmillan & Co., 1883), ii, 171. Lasswell and Donnelly distinguish 'condemnation sanctions' and 'other deprivations'. 'The Continuing Debate over Responsibility: An Introduction to Isolating the Condemnation Sanction', *Yale Law Journal*, 68 (1959). The traditional common law distinction is between 'infamous' and 'noninfamous' crimes and punishments. Conviction of an 'infamous crime' rendered a person liable to such postpunitive civil disabilities as incompetence to be a witness.

4. That even punishments proper are to be interpreted as taxes on certain kinds of conduct is a view often associated with O. W. Holmes, Jr. For an excellent discussion of Holmes's fluctuations of this question, see Mark De Wolfe Howe, *Justice Holmes: The Proving Years* (Cambridge: Harvard University Press, 1963), 74–80. See also Lon Fuller, *The Morality of Law* (New Haven, Conn.: Yale University Press, 1964), ch. 2, pt. 7, and H. L. A. Hart, *The Concept of Law* (Oxford: Clarendon Press, 1961), 39, for illuminating comparisons and contrasts of punishment and taxation.

5. Hart, loc. cit.

6. Henry M. Hart, 'The Aims of the Criminal Law', *Law and Contemporary Problems*, 23 (1958), II, A, 4.

7. *General View of the Criminal Law of England* (London: Macmillan & Co., 1863), 99.

8. (London, 1953), 17–18. My italics.

9. The Texas Penal Code (Art. 1220) until recently stated: 'Homicide is justifiable when committed by the husband upon one taken in the act of adultery with the wife, provided the killing takes place before the parties to the act have separated. Such circumstances cannot justify a homicide when it appears that there has been on the part of the husband, any connivance in or assent to the adulterous connection.' New Mexico and Utah have similar statutes. For some striking descriptions of perfectly legal paramour killings in Texas, see John Bainbridge, *The Super-Americans* (Garden City, NY: Doubleday, 1961), 238 ff.

10. *The Philosophy of Law*, trans. W. hastie (Edinburgh: T. & T. Clark, 1887), 198.

11. *General Principles of Criminal Law* (2nd edn., Indianapolis: Bobbs-Merrill Co., 1960), 328.

12. *Flemming* v. *Nestor*, 80 S. Ct. 1367 (1960).

13. Ibid. 1370.

14. Ibid. 1374 (interspersed citations omitted).

15. Ibid. 1385.

16. Ibid. 1375–6.

17. Ibid. 1387.

18. Ibid. 1376.

19. *The Reporter* (11 May 1961), 14.

20. Loc. cit.

21. Hall, op. cit. 329.

22. Richard A. Wasserstrom, 'Strict Liability in the Criminal Law', *Stanford Law Review*, 12 (1960), 730.

23. *United States* v. *Moreland*, 258 US 433, 447–8 (1922). Quoted in Hal, op. cit. 327.

24. 'A depth study of Wisconsin statutes in 1956 revealed that of 1113 statutes creating criminal offenses [punishable by fine, imprisonment, or both] which were in force in 1953, no less than 660 used language in the definitions of the offenses which omitted all reference to a mental element, and which therefore, under the canons of construction which have come to govern these matters, left it open to the courts to impose strict liability if they saw fit.' Colin Howard, 'Not Proven', *Adelaide Law Review*, 1 (1962), 274. The study cited is: Remington, Robinson, and Zick, 'Liability without Fault Criminal Statutes', *Wisconsin Law Review* (1956), 625, 636.

25. Rollin M. Perkins, *Criminal Law* (Brooklyn: The Foundation Press, 1957), 701–2.

26. American Law Institute, *Model Penal Code, Proposed Official Draft* (Philadelphia, 1962).

27. *Erewhon* (new and rev. edn., London: Grant Richards, 1901), ch. 10.

28. These two examples are cited by Francis A. Allen in 'Criminal Justice, Legal Values and the Rehabilitative Ideal', *Journal of Criminal Law, Criminology and Police Science*, 50 (1959), 229.

29. For more convincing statements of these arguments, see *inter alia*: W. D. Ross, *The Right and the Good* (Oxford: Clarendon Press, 1930), 56–65; J. D. Mabbott, 'Punishment', *Mind*, 49 (1939); A. C. Ewing, *The Morality of Punishment* (London: Kegan Paul, Trench, Trubner & Co., 1929), ch. 1; and F. Dostoevski, *The House of the Dead*, trans. H. Sutherland Edwards (New York: E. P. Dutton, 1912).

30. Cf. Jerome Michael and Herbert Wechsler, *Criminal Law and its Administration* (Chicago: Foundation Press, 1940), 'Note on Deliberation and Character', 170–2.

Preface: H. Morris, 'A Paternalistic Theory of Punishment'

In an earlier article (Morris 1968) Morris argued that a proper respect for persons and their integrity as moral agents precluded the coercive 'cures' offered by rehabilitative penal regimes, and that retribution (understood as MURPHY articulated it) was the only proper justification for the practice of punishment. That article was a seminal contribution to the reaction against consequentialism and the revival of retributivism in the 1970s. In the essay presented here, Morris offers a further, deeper development of the paradoxical claim that punishment respects the offender's moral status as a person.

Morris argues that punishment is a 'complex communicative act', which addresses the offender as a moral agent, conveying the message that the offence violated communal values and was therefore wrong. The hope is that, through the process of being punished, offenders will come to see the nature of the good, and freely choose it in future: they will realize the implications of their wrongdoing, see that it threatens their own good as members of a moral community, and accept the appropriateness of their punishment. Legal punishment, like the discipline that good parents impose on their children, is an educative process which (however unwelcome it may be) serves the good of the person punished as well as that of the community at large (see, for similar accounts, Hampton 1984; Duff 1986; for critical discussion, see Deigh 1984; Murphy 1985; Shafer-Landau 1991; von Hirsch 1993: ch. 8; Narayan 1993. CARLEN and ROTMAN offer very different accounts of rehabilitation as the proper aim of a penal system, which can be usefully contrasted with Morris).

Punishment is not, on this account, intended forcibly to 'correct' criminals, or to deter them by fear. The intention is, rather, to teach them a moral lesson which, it is hoped, they will understand and accept for themselves. The aim is to persuade, not to manipulate or coerce. Punishment is thus presented not as the dictate of an austere, unfeeling justice, but as an act of love which recognizes the offender's (flawed) humanity and hopes to persuade him or her to re-embrace the community and its values.

Morris's paternalistic theory shares some of the central features of much contemporary discourse about punishment. Its starting-point is the rejection of rehabilitative or utilitarian approaches which are said to deny the offender's personhood and integrity. It endorses the retributivist principles that punishment must be restricted to the guilty, must be proportionate, and must respect the rights of the offender. It takes very seriously the communicative character of punishment—what is said rather than what is done. But his essay also resonates with more ancient traditions. The narrative of sin, punishment, guilt, and repentance which Morris develops draws upon central themes of the Judaeo–Christian religious tradition, as his language often makes clear. Moreover, by comparing legal punishment to the discipline of the family, Morris grounds his account in an archetypal social situation, so that his arguments, if they ring true, carry the force of familiar practices and experiences.

Analogies illuminate, but they can also conceal, especially if we lose sight of particularities and differences. The penal system does not operate like a happy family, nor even like a church of sinners, and the repentant offender is the exception rather than the rule. Punishment often produces resentment, bitterness, and alienation rather than moral reconciliation. Those who are punished may not share the values of the law-abiding, or live in circumstances in which those values can be easily adhered to. It is not at all clear that our societies constitute the kinds of genuine moral community, united by shared values and mutual concern, within which both crime and punishment could have the moral character that Morris ascribes to them. But one strength of his essay is that he recognizes these problems, and the operative limits of his analogy. His theory thus becomes (as did MURPHY's) an account of what punishment would ideally be, in a just society, with a shared commitment to legal norms (and to each other as fellow members of the community) and equal opportunities to abide by them. To the extent that our societies and their penal practices fall short of that ideal, the theory provides a basis from which to criticize and seek to transform them.

But we must also ask whether Morris offers a plausible ideal of punishment. In particular, should it be the state's job to take such an interest in the moral or spiritual well-being of its citizens? Would we really want the state, even in a better society than our own, to take on the role of parent, or of abbot, seeking to bring (by such coercive means as punishment) its wayward members to repentance and reform? Such a view of the state's proper role is radically at odds with any liberal conception of the state, and presupposes some more communitarian political theory.

References

DEIGH, J. (1984), 'On the Right to be Punished: Some Doubts', *Ethics*, 94: 191–211.

DUFF, R. A. (1986), *Trials and Punishments* (Cambridge).

HAMPTON, J. (1984), 'The Moral Education Theory of Punishment', *Philosophy and Public Affairs*, 13: 208–38.

MORRIS, H. (1968), 'Persons and Punishment', *Monist*, 52: 475–501.

MURPHY, J. G. (1985), 'Retributivism, Moral Education and the Liberal State', *Criminal Justice Ethics*, 4: 3–11.

NARAYAN, U. (1993), 'Appropriate Responses and Preventive Benefits: Justifying Censure and Hard Treatment in Legal Punishment', *Oxford Journal of Legal Studies*, 13: 166–82.

SHAFER-LANDAU, R. (1991), 'Can Punishment Morally Educate?', *Law and Philosophy*, 10: 189–219.

VON HIRSCH, A. (1993), *Censure and Sanctions* (Oxford).

A Paternalistic Theory of Punishment

HERBERT MORRIS

I

Nothing is more necessary to human life, and fortunately nothing more common, than parents' concern for their children. The infant's relatively lengthy period of helplessness requires that others nourish and protect it. And the child's existence as a vital being with an interest in the world, a capacity for eagerness and trust, and a sense of its own worth, all depend upon its receiving loving care, understanding, and attention. With time the normally developing child relinquishes its almost total dependence; it acquires the capacity to conceive of itself as an agent, to set out on its own, and to live in a world less dominated by its bodily needs and by its parents. Inevitably, this growth in competence and strength brings greater potential for self-harm, for the child's fantasies of its power and knowledge stand in marked contrast to the reality of its relative ignorance and vulnerability. In the ordinary course of events, the more powerful and knowledgeable parent often interferes with the child's choices in order to prevent harm and to bring about good and the reason for this is frequently, if the appropriate degree of parental selflessness is present, the child's own best interests, not primarily the interests of the parents or others.

Concern for the child often, of course, is manifested in allowing and encouraging experimentation just as it sometimes is in forceful intrusion. The child's developing individuality and sense of personal responsibility require that others encourage in it a sense of its own power and competence, support its venturing out, and exercise judgment in forbearing from intrusion, permitting it to err and to learn some painful truths from painful consequences suffered. God commanded Adam and Eve but left them free to disobey, thereby providing evidence of both his love and respect. The Devil, preferring for humans a state of permanent infantalism, would, no doubt, have acted differently as Dostoevsky's *Grand Inquisitor* nicely illustrates.[1]

The rational love of parents for their children then guides the parents' conduct so that their children may one day be fortunate enough to say with St Paul, '. . . when I became a man, I put away childish things'. A central drama of many lives is a result of imbalance in the relations between parents and children in this area—of being left too much on one's own or too little, of counting on one's parents too much, or of not being able to count upon them enough, of parental conduct that fosters too great dependence or conduct that imposes upon the child too great a personal responsibility, creating in the child not self-confidence but a sense of being alone and insecure in a threatening world.

Paternalism as a social phenomenon is prefigured in this elemental and universal situation of solicitous parental conduct that has its roots in our common humanity. But paternalism is of philosophic interest, not because of the way parents legitimately relate to their children—indeed there is oddity in describing this conduct as 'paternalistic'—but rather because something like this practice is introduced into relations among adults. If our responses to adults mirror intrusive and solicitous parental responses to children we behave paternalistically.

Contemporary discussions of paternalism, understood in this way, proceed by focusing primarily on specific laws, laws that either prohibit or require certain conduct and that, arguably, have as their principal or sole reason for existence the good of those individuals to whom they are addressed. My focus in this paper is entirely different, for I consider paternalism, its meaning and its possible legitimacy, not in the context of specific laws prohibiting or requiring conduct, but rather with regard to the existence of a system of punitive responses for the violation of any law. I shall consider several issues and make a number of proposals. First, I define my particular version of a paternalistic theory of punishment. Second, I argue for, and consider a variety of objections to, this paternalistic theory. Third, I argue that the paternalistic theory I have constructed implies, in a more natural way than other common justifications for punishment, certain restrictions on the imposition of punishment.

II

Let us turn to the first topic. My aim here is to describe the paternalistic theory of punishment I later defend. I set out a variety of moral paternalism, for the good that is sought is a specific moral good.

First, then, in order to punish paternalistically we must be punishing. I assume that the human institution of punishment presupposes, of course among other things, that certain conduct has been determined to be wrongful, that what are generally recognized as deprivations are imposed in the event of such conduct, that these deprivations are imposed upon the wrongdoer by someone in a position of authority, that wrongdoers are generally made aware that the deprivation is imposed because of the wrongdoing, and that the context makes evident that the deprivation is not a tax on a course of conduct or in some way a compensation to injured individuals but rather a response to the doing of what one was not entitled to do.

I have placed a logical constraint on the concept of punishment that is not customarily explicitly associated with it. I have claimed that in order for a person to be punished there must be an intention—one normally simply taken for granted—to convey to the wrongdoer, and where it is punishment for breach of a community's requirement, to others as well, that the deprivation is imposed because of wrongdoing. A communicative component is a defining characteristic of punishment and in part distinguishes it from mere retaliation or acting out of revenge where the goal of bringing about evil for another may achieve all that one desires. The paternalistic theory I present relies essentially on the idea of punishment as a complex communicative act—the components of which I hope will become clear as I proceed.[2]

A central theme in paternalism is to justify one's conduct out of a concern for the good of another. And so a paternalistic theory of punishment will naturally claim that a principal justification for punishment and a principal justification for restrictions upon it are that the system furthers the good of potential and actual wrongdoers. This contrasts with views—though many of the practices supported may be the same—that it is justice that requires that guilty persons be punished or that it is the utility to society that requires punishment. The theory I put forward emphasizes what retributivist and utilitarian theories largely, if not entirely, ignore, that a principal justification for punishment is the potential and actual wrongdoer's good. The theory should not, however, be confused with 'reform' or 'rehabilitative' theories. First, these theories may be based, not on consideration of what promotes the good of actual and potential wrongdoers, but on what promotes value for society generally. A reform theory, further, may countenance responses ruled out under the paternalistic theory proposed in these pages. And, finally, reform theories usually fail to address the issue of how instituting a practice of punishment, meaning by this both the threat of punishment and its actual infliction, may promote a specific moral good and this is a central feature of the theory I propose.[3]

I also assume that paternalistic measures characteristically involve disregard of, indeed conflict with, a person's desires. Giving a person what they want and being motivated to do so for that person's good is benevolence not paternalism. And so, if a longing for punishment were characteristically the way in which people responded to the prospect of its imposition, there would, I think, be no role for a paternalistic theory regarding the practice, for it would simply be a practice that generally supplied people with what they acknowledged wanting. We may speak meaningfully of a paternalistic theory of punishment for two reasons: first, punishment by its nature characteristically involves a deprivation that individuals seek to avoid, with the implication that there is some conflict between what people want and what they get; second, the practice is such that the desires of a person at the time of the deprivation are not determinative of what they receive. Thus, while there are obviously persons guilty of wrongdoing who desire punishment, this fact will not affect either its being punishment that is meted out to such a person or the punishment being possibly based on paternalistic consideration, for what is customarily viewed as a deprivation is being imposed independently of the individual's desires.

Most importantly, the theory I am proposing requires that the practice of punishment promote a particular kind of good for potential and actual wrongdoers. The good is a moral one, and it is, arguably, one upon which all morality is grounded.

What is the character of this good? It has a number of component parts but it is essentially one's identity as a morally autonomous person attached to the good. This statement obviously needs explanation. First, it is a part of this good that one comes to appreciate the nature of the evil involved for others and for oneself in one's doing wrong. This requires empathy, a putting oneself in another's position; it also requires the imaginative capacity to take in the implications for one's future self of the evil one has done; it further requires an attachment to being a person of a certain kind. The claim is that it is good for the person, and essential to one's status as a moral person, that the evil underlying wrongdoing and the evil radiating from it be comprehended, comprehended not merely, if at all, in the sense of one's being able to articulate what one has done, but rather comprehended in the way remorse implies comprehension of evil caused. A person's blindness about such matters—this view assumes—is that person's loss. The Devil's splendid isolation is his hell.

Of course, this element of the good makes it apparent that for this theory, as with other moral justifications for punishment, that the rules defining wrongdoing, the rules whose violation occasions punishment, themselves meet certain minimal moral conditions. I assume, and do not argue for the view, that attachment to the values underlying these rules partly defines one's identity as a moral being and as a member of a moral community, that it gives one a sense of who one is and provides some meaning to one's life, and that the price paid for unconcern is some rupture in relationships, a separation from others, a feeling ill at ease with oneself, and some inevitable loss of emotional sustenance and sense of identity. I further assume that attachment to these values is a natural by-product of certain early forms of caring, understanding and respect and that the practice of punishment applies to those with such an attachment and not to those who because of some early disasters in primary relationships might value nothing or possess values we might attribute to the Devil.

Second, it is a part of the good that one feel guilt over the wrongdoing, that is, that one be pained at having done wrong, that one be distressed with oneself, that one be disposed to restore what has been damaged, and that one accept the appropriateness of some deprivation, and the making of amends. Not to experience any of this would be to evidence an indifference to separation from others that could only, given the assumptions I have made, diminish one as a person.

Third, it is also part of the good that one reject the disposition to do what is wrong and commit oneself to forbearance in the future. I assume that this makes possible, indeed that it is inextricably bound up with, one's forgiving oneself, one's relinquishing one's guilt, and one's having the capacity fully to enter into life.

Finally, it is part of the good that one possess and vividly retain a conception of oneself as an individual worthy of respect, a conception of oneself as a responsible person, responsible for having done wrong and responsible, through one's own efforts at understanding and reflection, at more clearly coming to see things as they are with a deepened attachment to what is good. This conception of oneself is further nourished by freely accepting the moral conditions placed upon restoring relationships with others and oneself that one has damaged.

It is a moral good, then, that one feel contrite, that one feel the guilt that is appropriate to one's wrongdoing, that one be repentant, that one be self-forgiving and that one have reinforced one's conception of oneself as a responsible being. Ultimately, then, the moral good aimed at by the paternalism I propose is an autonomous individual freely attached to that which is good, those relationships with others that sustain and give meaning to a life.

The theory I propose claims that the potential of punishment to further the realization of this moral good is one principal justification for its existence. From the perspective of this form of paternalism there must be full respect in the design of the practice of punishment for the individual's moral and intellectual capacities. The good places logical and moral constraints on the means that it is permissible to employ to realize it. This is the principal reason that I earlier emphasized the communicative aspect of punishment, for on this theory we seek to achieve a good entirely through the mediation of the wrongdoer's efforts to understand the full significance of the wrongful conduct, the significance of the punishment being imposed, and the significance of acceptance of that punishment. Thus, unacceptable to this theory would be any response that sought the good of a wrongdoer in a manner that bypassed the human capacity for reflection, understanding, and revision of attitude that may result from such efforts. Any punitive response to a fully responsible being, then, and it might be no more than the giving of an evil-tasting pill or some form of conditioning, that directly in some causal way, with or without the agent's consent, sought to bring about a good, say, instantaneous truth or aversion to acting violently, would be incompatible with this constraint. There is, then, a good to be achieved but one cannot, logically or morally, be compelled to obtain it. Throughout there must be complete respect for the moral personality of the wrongdoer; it is a respect also, as I later argue, that must be given despite the wrongdoer's consent to be treated otherwise.

It is evident that this paternalistic goal is not to make people feel less burdened or more content. Once the good is achieved, these may be likely results; they are not, however, what is sought. It is important, too, to recognize that this good differs markedly from those particular goods associated with specific paternalistic legislation. It is not one's health; it is not even one's moral health with respect to any particular matter that is sought to be achieved; it is one's general character as a morally autonomous individual attached to the good.

III

What might be said in favour of such a theory and what might be objections to it? Two major issues will be considered. First, can a plausible case be presented that punishment is connected with the good as I have defined it? Second, is there anything morally offensive or otherwise objectionable, as there often is with particular legislation, in having as one's goal in limiting freedom, the person's own good?

Let us direct attention again to the relationship between parent and child with which I commenced this essay and in which paternalistic-like elements seem clearly and appropriately present. The range of situations here is very great. Sometimes parents coercively interfere to protect the child from hurting itself, sometimes to assure its continued healthy growth, sometimes so that the child will learn to move about comfortably in a world of social conventions. But sometimes, of course, coercion enters in with respect to matters that are moral; certain modes of conduct are required if valued relationships among individuals within the family and outside the family are to come into existence and be maintained.

Slowly such values as obedience, respect, loyalty, and a sense of personal responsibility are integrated into the young person's life. This results to a considerable degree—of course not entirely and in differing degrees in different stages of development—from the child's conduct sometimes meeting with unpleasant responses. Written vividly upon children are lessons associated with some loss or some pain visited upon them by those to whom they are attached. It is important for my purposes that a difference in the significance of the painful responses be noted. The pain experienced by the child subjected to a parent's anger or disapproval only has the significance of punishment if the parent deliberately visits upon the child some pain because of the perceived wrongdoing. The parent's spontaneous anger or disapproval or blame cause the child distress. They may motivate future compliant conduct. They may arouse in the child guilt. They are not, however, by themselves requital for wrongdoing and by themselves do not relieve guilt. My view is that punishment has some special and logical relationship to wrongdoing and to the possibility of a child's acquiring the concept. Because of this relationship, punishment is connected with the good that I have described in a way that blame or disapproval by themselves are not.

First, because of punishment children come to acquire an understanding of the meaning of a limit on conduct. Logically connected with the concept of wrongdoing is the concept of a painful response that another is entitled to inflict because of the wrongful conduct.[4] Second, a punitive response conveys to children the depth of parental attachment to the values underlying the limit. Just as children know from experience that they are disposed to strike out when they or what they care for are injured, so they come to appreciate the seriousness of their parents' attachment to the limit and to the values supported by its existence by the parents' visiting some pain upon them. The degree of punishment, then, conveys to the child the importance parents attach to their child's responding to the limit and promotes in children, not just an appreciation that something is wrong, but how seriously wrong it is. It conveys, too, the significance of different degrees of fault in the doing of what is wrong. Further, particular punishments that are chosen often communicate to children the peculiar character of the evil caused by their disregard of the limit, the evil to others and the evil to themselves. Thus, even young children will find it particularly fitting to penalize a cheater by not permitting, for a time at least, further play, for such punishment conveys the central importance of honesty in the playing of the game and one's placing oneself outside the community of players by dishonesty. 'If you will not abide by what makes this segment of our lives together possible, suffer the consequence of not being here a part of our lives.'

Finally, punishment 'rights the wrong'. It has, in contrast to blame and disapproval, the character of closure, of matters returning to where they were before, of relationships being restored. Just as a limit being placed upon conduct serves to provide a bounded, manageable, world for the child, so the punitive response to a breach defines a limit to separation that is occasioned by wrongdoing. The debt is paid, life can go on.

The young hero in Styron's *Sophie's Choice* gives in to a desire for an exciting ride with a friend and forgets his agreeing to tend the fire before which his invalided mother sits for heat in the freezing weather. The young man is guilty and remorseful. Why, we may wonder, was he grateful to his father for placing him for a period of time in a shed without heat? The answer seems clear. It diminished the young boy's guilt, diminished it in a way that it would not have been were the father merely to have said, 'You did something dreadful; I know you feel bad; don't let it happen again!' The young boy's guilt and remorse were painful; but because they were not deprivations imposed because of wrongdoing, they could not serve to re-establish what had been upset in the relations between parents and child.

What I have described is familiar. What needs emphasizing is that this parental practice of punishing is a complex communication to the child. It aids the child in learning what as a moral person it must know, that some things are not permitted, that some wrongs are more serious than others, that it is sometimes responsible for doing wrong and sometimes not, and that its degree of blameworthiness is not always the same. Further, the child's response to wrongdoing by feeling guilt, its willingness to accept some deprivation, and its commitment to acting differently in the future, all play an indispensable role in its restoring relationships it has damaged, relationships with others and with itself. The claim, then, is that this practice is, in fact, a significant contributing factor in one's development as a moral person.

Now, what more acceptably motivates a parent when it punishes its child than the desire to achieve a goal such as I have described? It would be perverse if the parent were generally to punish primarily from motives of retributive justice or optimal utility for the family. These ends are secondary to, though with retributive ends, to some extent essential to, the child's acquiring the characteristics of a moral person. This much may seem plausible but also quite beside the point. The topic is, after all, punishment in the adult world and there are significant differences between adults and children that may carry fatal implications for a paternalistic theory. I do not believe this is so, but before moving on I want to note a phenomenon that may cast doubt upon the legitimacy of the parental practice itself.

Parents sometimes, when imposing some deprivation upon their children, say, 'I'm only doing this for your own good!' There is, I think, something offensive about this. Does it affect the legitimacy of parental concern primarily for the child's moral development in inflicting punishment?

The answer I think is clearly 'no', for the offensiveness of those words is not limited to situations in which punishment is imposed. Giving some unpleasant medicine or compelling the child to eat some distasteful but allegedly nourishing food, if accompanied by a statement that it is for the child's own good, is equally offensive. The words are customarily uttered in response to some sign of resistance, of some anger, and what they neglect to address is the child's unhappiness. They rather defend the parents before the child, making the child feel guilty because of its failure to be grateful for the good done it. And so imposed upon the child is the burden of getting what it does not want, the burden of checking its understandable anger because of this, and, finally, the burden of having to be grateful for getting what it does not want and, if not grateful, then guilty. It is not the motive of promoting the child's good that is suspect in these cases; it is communicating to the child what one's motive is, with its distressing consequences for the child, and with the still more serious problem, perhaps, that the parent's own guilt is unconsciously sought to be transferred to the child.

IV

One can acknowledge the place of punishment in the moral development of children and acknowledge, too, that it must to some degree be imposed to further this development and wonder what all this has to do with legal punishment of adults. For the law as a means of social control presupposes that the individuals to whom it applies are already responsible persons, responsible both in the sense of having the capacity to govern their actions through an understanding of the meaning of the norms addressed to them and responsible in the sense that they possess a knowledge of and an attachment to the values embodied in the society's laws. There is, nevertheless, a place for punishment in society analogous to its role in the family. I shall briefly sketch what this is.

Through promulgation of laws, through provision of sanctions for their violation, and through the general imposition of sanctions in the event of violation, each citizen learns what is regarded as impermissible by society, the degree of seriousness to be attached to wrongdoing of different kinds, and the particular significance—especially when the punishment is in its severity and character linked to the offence—of the evil underlying offences. Punishment is a forceful reminder of the evil that is done to others and oneself. Were it not present, or were it imposed in circumstances markedly at odds with criteria for its imposition during the process of moral development, only confusion would result. Brandeis, in a quite different context, observed: 'Our government is the potent, the omnipresent teacher. For good or for ill, it teaches the whole people by its example.' My point is that law plays an indispensable role in our knowing what for society is good and evil. Failure to punish serious wrongdoing, punishment of wrongdoing in circumstances where fault is absent, would serve only to baffle our moral understanding and threaten what is so often already precarious.

Further, our punitive responses guide the moral passions as they come into play with respect to interests protected by the law. Punishment, among other things, permits purgation of guilt and ideally restoration of damaged relationships. Punishment, then, communicates what is wrong and in being imposed both rights the wrong and serves, as well, as a reminder of the evil done to others and to oneself in the doing of what is wrong.

Now in addition to making out that punishment may reasonably be thought to play its part, even with adults, in promoting the good of one's moral personality, the paternalist has to have some argument for this as a morally permissible way of proceeding. The paternalist is, I believe, on firm ground here. The guilty wrongdoer is not viewed as damned by his wrongful conduct to a life forever divorced from others. He is viewed as a responsible being, responsible for having done wrong and possessing the capacity for recognizing the wrongfulness of his conduct. Further, the evil—as Socrates long ago pointed out—that he has done himself by his wrongdoing is a moral evil greater than he has done others. His soul is in jeopardy as his victim's is not. What could possibly justify an unconcern with this evil if the person is one of us and, if we sense, rightly I believe, that there but for the grace of God go we? In considering, for example, why we might wish to have a society of laws, of laws associated with sanctions for their violation, of laws that are in fact enforced against others and ourselves, it would be rational, indeed it would be, I think, among the most persuasive of considerations for establishing such a social practice, that it would promote our own good as moral persons. Thinking of ourselves as potential, and thinking of ourselves as actual wrongdoers, and appreciating the connection of punishment with one's attachment to the good, to one's status as a moral person, and to the possibility it provides of closure and resumption of relationships, would we not select such a system, if for no other reason, than that it would promote our own good?

V

We have now to consider certain objections to the theory. First, does it fail to respect one as an autonomous being? The answer is that it does not. One's choices are throughout respected, and it is one's status as a moral person that is sought to be affirmed. But is there not something offensively demeaning in instituting punishment for such a reason? More demeaning, one might ask, than addressing the wrongdoer's sense of fear to which others appeal in their theories of punishment? More demeaning than an indifference to the moral status of the person but totally committed to retributive justice? I am not convinced that this is so either. On the theory I propose one is throughout responded to as a moral person.

But does not a paternalistic theory lead to two unacceptable extremes with respect to punishment, the first that we should always warn before punishing, and wait to see the effects of our warning, the other that we should continue punishing until we achieve the desired effects? The answers here can be brief. First, the announcement of the norm and the provision for punishment in the event of its violation is itself the warning and to allow a person to disobey and threaten that next time there will be punishment is to issue not one but two warnings. Second, the practice of punishment, given the paternalistic goals I have described, cannot permit open-ended punishments, repeated punishments or punishments that are excessively severe. For, first, the goal is not repentance at all costs, if that has meaning, but repentance freely arrived at and not merely a disposition toward conformity with the norms; secondly, the punishment provided for wrongdoing must reflect judgments of the seriousness of the wrong done; such punishment cannot focus on some end state of the person and disregard the potential for moral confusion that would arise from repeated or excessive punishment.

Another criticism might go as follows: 'You have ruled out conditioning a person, even with their consent, so that they might not be disposed to do evil in the future. But surely, while perhaps an unjustifiable practice without consent, it is acceptable with it, for it provides a person what they freely choose and delivers them from an affliction that promotes evil.' Two points need to be made here. First, the theory would not preclude freely chosen forms of conditioning, surgery and the like in those circumstances in which it is acknowledged that the person is not, with respect to the conduct involved, an autonomous agent. There is nothing wrong, for example, in a person choosing surgery to remove a tumour that is causally related to outbursts of violence over which the person has no control. The class of person, then, whose choice would be accorded respect is made up of those we should be disposed to excuse from criminal liability. Second, the theory would regard as morally unacceptable a response, conditioning or otherwise, that had as its goal, not just aversion to doing wrong, but obliteration of one's capacity to choose to do so. What must be aimed at is that the afflicted become autonomous not automatons. There must be freedom to disobey, for the moral price is too high that is paid in purchasing immunity from temptation and guaranteed conformity.

The most troubling objections to the theory are, I think, these: first, it cannot account for the accepted disposition to punish those who are already, as it were, awakened and repentant. And, second, even more seriously, it cannot account for the disposition to punish those who know what the values of society are but who are indifferent to or opposed to them. Someone, for example, may feel inclined to say: 'Look—most serious crimes—and your theory surely most neatly fits such crimes not petty offences—are committed by individuals who are perfectly aware of what they are doing and perfectly aware that society's values are being flouted. These individuals are not going to be instructed about evil or brought to any moral realization about themselves by punishment. Surely, you can't be serious about repentance when considering them, and they certainly do not care a jot about paying off any debt because they do not feel any guilt over what they have done. Your theory fails so to match reality as to be just one more tedious example of a philosopher spinning out fantastic yarns without any genuine relevance to reality.' What can be said in response to these points?

As to the first, I would claim that the guilty and repentant wrongdoers are naturally disposed to accept the appropriateness of the punishment provided, both because this will evidence to them and to others the genuineness of their feelings and because the punishment rights the wrong, brings about closure, and restores relationships that have been damaged. The experience of guilt and remorse, the avowal of repentance do not by themselves achieve this.[5] A general practice of pardoning persons who claimed that they were repentant would destroy the principal means of re-establishing one's membership in the community.

Now for the second major objection. A response here requires that attention be paid to certain general features of the theory that has been put forward. The theory is, of course, not intended as a description of any actual practice of legal punishment or even as realistically workable in a society such as ours. Things are in such a state that it is not. What is proposed is a moral theory of punishment and, as such, it includes at least two conditions that may be only marginally congruent with our social world. The first is that the norms addressed to persons are generally just and that the society is to some substantial extent one in which those who are liable to punishment have roughly equal opportunities to conform to those just norms. The second condition is equally important. The theory presupposes that there is a general commitment among persons to whom the norms apply to the values underlying them. If these two conditions are not met, we do not have what I understand as a practice of punishment for which any moral justification can be forthcoming.

At this point it may be thought, 'fair enough, but then what is the point of the whole exercise?' My response is this: first, the theory is not without applicability to significant segments of our society. Second, it has value, for it provides an important perspective upon actual practices; it throws into relief our society's failures to realize the conditions I have stipulated. And, finally, it assists us in sensitive and intelligent forbearance from putting our moral imprimatur upon practices which the paternalistic model would find unacceptable. Excessively lengthy prison terms and the inhumane conditions under which they are served, for example, can be effectively criticized with a clear conception of the good defined by the paternalistic theory. The theory may serve as a guide in our attempts to adjust present practices so that they more closely accord with moral dictates, to work for precisely that society in which the paternalistic conception provides not just the ring of moral truth but descriptive truth as well.

VI

I want now to shift attention to the issue of restrictions on punishment. The proposed paternalistic theory limits punishment, I believe, in a way that accords more closely with our moral intuitions than a number of alternative theories. First, it follows from the theory that any class of persons incapable of appreciating the significance of the norms addressed to them cannot justifiably be punished. Absence of a free and knowing departure from the norm makes pointless imposition of punishment. Second, it also follows that excuses must be recognized and that mitigating factors be taken into account, including as an excuse, of course, reasonable ignorance or mistake of law.

Perhaps most significantly, a paternalistic orientation implies a position that matches our moral intuitions more closely than other theories on the issue of what kinds of punishment may be inflicted. Punishments that are aimed at degrading or brutalizing a person are not conducive to moral awakening but only to bitterness and resentment. But there is also, I believe, another paternalistic route to limitations upon certain modes of punishment, a limitation that follows from the conception of the moral good.

The wrongdoer has, as we all do, a basic right to be free. How, we may wonder, are we able to justify our imposing our will upon him and limiting his freedom? One answer is that by wrongful conduct he has forfeited his right to freedom. The wrongdoer is in no position to complain if he meets with a response that is similar to what has been visited by him upon another. Such a theory of forfeiture places great weight upon an individual's choice. It holds that rights are forfeitable, waivable, and relinquishable—just so long as the choice involved is informed and free. A person might forfeit his right to life by murdering; a person might relinquish his right to be free by selling himself into slavery. The paternalistic position that I have proposed holds otherwise. It implies that there is a non-waivable, non-forfeitable, non-relinquishable right—the right to one's status as a moral being, a right that is implied in one's being a possessor of any rights at all.

Such a view, when punishment is at issue, makes morally impermissible any response to a person, despite what that person has done, that would be inconsistent with this fundamental right, even though the person were unattached to it, indifferent to its moral value, and eager to forfeit it. A retributivist might respond in kind to any wrong done. A social utilitarian might calculate the effects on people and society in doing so. A paternalist, attached to the good of the wrongdoer, would reject retributive justice and utility as the sole determinative criteria, and would propose a good to be realized that is independent of these values. Punishment will not be permitted that destroys in some substantial way one's character as an autonomous creature. Certain cruel punishments, then, may be ruled out, not merely because they are conducive to hardening the heart but, more importantly, because they destroy a good that can never rightly be destroyed. As I see it, this precludes, on moral grounds, punishment that may be like for like but which nevertheless violates one's humanity by either destroying one's life or destroying one's capacity for rejecting what is evil and again attaching oneself to the good.

Let me be more specific. Suppose that a sadist has cruelly destroyed another human being's capacity for thought while leaving the person alive. Is there a retributivist argument that would bar a like treatment for the sadist? I do not know of it. Certainly, the *lex talionis* would seem to sanction it. Is our inclination to forbear from treating the sadist in a manner that he has treated his victim derived exclusively, then, from social evils that we foresee might flow from such punishment? I do not find this persuasive. Our moral repugnance precedes such calculation and findings inconsistent with this repugnance would be rejected. Is it simply revulsion at the thought of oneself or one's agents deliberately perpetrating such acts? Is it a concern for our own good that motivates us? No doubt, this may play a role, but my conviction is that something else is involved. It is the ingredient to which the moral paternalist draws attention. The wrongdoer possesses something destroyed in another. The wrongdoer may desire to destroy it in himself as well, but that is not his moral prerogative. It is immune from moral transformations brought about by free choice.

VII

I would like, in conclusion, to make somewhat clearer what I am and am not claiming for the theory proposed in these pages and, further, to draw attention to two ironies connected with it.

I have claimed that to have as one's aim in punishing the good of the wrongdoer counts strongly in favor of the moral legitimacy of punishing. I do not claim, of course, that this is the sole justification for punishment, though I do believe that what it seeks to promote is among the most important, if not the most important, of human goods. The practice of punishment is complex and any justification proposed as an exclusive one must, in my judgment, be met with scepticism, if not scorn. There is, too, as I earlier briefly noted, a significant logical overlapping of this theory with retributivism, though at a certain point, when one considers types of punishment, they diverge. A paternalistic theory, given the good as defined, would support principles that are familiar dictates of retributivism—that only the guilty may be punished, that the guilty must be, and that the punishment inflicted reflect the degree of guilt. Failure to comply with the demands of retributivism would preclude realization of the paternalist's goal. I have also, however, suggested that retributivism needs supplementing if it is to meet our intuitions of what is morally permissible punishment. But, of course, this overlapping of justifications for punishment includes as well some form of utilitarianism, for it our goal is as I have defined it, and punishments are threatened and imposed, deterrent values are also furthered. I do not question the rich over-determination of goods promoted by the practice of punishment. I do urge that weight be given, and on the issue of restrictions on punishment, determinative weight, to paternalistic ends.

There are, finally, two ironies to which I wish to draw attention. The first is this. I have selected as the good to be realized by this paternalistic theory of punishment the very good to which philosophers often make appeal in their principled objections to paternalism with regard to specific prohibitions and requirements. Secondly, I have proposed a theory that justifies forceful intrusion into the lives of people. But it is also an atypical paternalistic theory, for it prohibits certain types of intrusion. I reach this conclusion because the good sought does not allow weight to be given to an individual's free choice when the issue is relinquishment of one's status as a moral being. The paternalistic aspect in this derives from the fact that there is a good for the person to which we are attached, though the person might not be, and which we continue to respect in disregard of the usual consequences of a person's free choice. I would guess that something like these thoughts underlies the view that we possess some goods as gifts from God and that it is not within our moral prerogative to dispose of them. It is easy to suppose, but a mistake nevertheless, that because we may be favoured by the gods we are one of them.

Notes

1. What is gained and what is lost by allowing a choice to disobey is also brought out in C. S. Lewis's engaging replay of the Adam and Eve myth in his novel *Pelandra*.
2. See generally Walter Moberly's splendid *The Ethics of Punishment* (London: Faber & Faber, 1968), particularly 201 ff.
3. The reform theories discussed by H. L. A. Hart and found to be unacceptable as answers to the question what could be 'the general justifying aim of punishment' differ, then, from the theory developed in these pages. Hart's change of mind in the notes to his collection of essays is occasioned by consideration of theories that still differ markedly from the one I propose. See *Punishment and Responsibility* (New York and Oxford: Oxford University Press, 1968), 24–7, 240–1.
4. Fingarette, 'Punishment and Suffering', *Proceedings of the American Philosophical Association*, 51 (1977).
5. On the connections of guilt and suffering, see Morris, *On Guilt and Innocence* (Berkeley, Calif.: University of California Press, 1976), 89–110.

Preface: A. von Hirsch, 'Censure and Proportionality'

Since the publication of *Doing Justice* (von Hirsch 1976)—a work which played a central role in the revival of the 'just deserts' approach to punishment—von Hirsch has been a leading advocate of the justice model of corrections, in the USA and in Europe.

That earlier work was founded on a general critique of utilitarian approaches to punishment, and of the welfarist and interventionist state which had been developing in the USA and elsewhere (see above, 8–11). The ambitious aim of 'doing more good' through the penal system was to be replaced by the more modest aim of 'doing justice' (see Cohen 1985: 30–5); and 'doing justice' was understood as a matter of imposing on offenders punishments that were proportionate, and thus retributively appropriate, to their crimes. Only such a retributivist approach, it was argued, would treat offenders as autonomous moral agents, rather than as objects to be manipulated for utilitarian ends. However, the approach of *Doing Justice* was not purely retributivist: penal hard treatment must be deserved, and be proportionate to the seriousness of the crime; but it must also be likely to achieve some social good by helping to prevent crime—most obviously by acting as a deterrent.

In this essay (a chapter from his latest book) von Hirsch founds the principle of proportionality on an account of punishment as censure. Punishment should express the censure which criminals deserve; and if it is to express the appropriate degree of censure, its severity must be proportionate to the seriousness of their offences. But he also tackles the problem of justifying penal 'hard treatment' (see FEINBERG). In a subtle reworking of the idea that hard treatment has a preventive, deterrent function he suggests that it should serve as a prudential *supplement* to the moral reasons for obedience which censure provides (see also Narayan 1993). Censure, which appeals to the offender as a moral agent, is the primary justifying purpose of punishment: but, recognizing that as fallible human beings we are not always sufficiently attentive to the moral appeal of the law, we also give ourselves prudential reasons for obedience. However, such prudential reasons must supplement, rather than replace, the law's moral appeal; and von Hirsch argues (1993: ch. 5) that this account of the proper purposes of punishment sets strict limits on the general severity of punishments. (He suggests that the maximum permitted term of imprisonment, for any crime other than homicide, should be three years). Such a system of punishment would, he thinks, do justice to the consequentialist concern that punishment should prevent crime, whilst still respecting offenders (and potential offenders) as autonomous (but fallible) moral agents.

By giving deterrence this secondary, supplemental role in a system whose primary rationale is censure, von Hirsch hopes to deal with one problem which faced earlier versions of the 'justice model' and the principle of proportionality: that they offered only a principle of 'ordinal' proportionality, requiring that penalties be *relatively* proportionate to the seriousness of the crimes being punished, but setting no absolute limits on the general level of punishment. Thus whilst the early advocates of 'just deserts' were usually liberal reformers hoping to reduce general levels of punishment, the justice model was liable to be hijacked by more conservative forces aiming to increase levels of punishment—especially of imprisonment (see CARLEN: 316–18; Greenberg and Humphries 1980; Hudson 1987; in reply see von Hirsch 1993: ch. 10). Von Hirsch's new account aims to provide a 'cardinal', as well as an 'ordinal', principle which will sharply reduce general levels of punishment by emphasizing the primacy of censure as an enterprise of rational communication. We should note too that he also rejects the more ambitious accounts of punishment as communication offered by theorists like Morris. Whilst it is a proper task for a liberal state to communicate to wrongdoers the censure which they deserve, the state should not try to secure their moral improvement or reform by these coercive means (see Preface to H. MORRIS above; von Hirsch 1993: ch. 8).

One question about this account is whether hard treatment penalties which are modest enough to serve only as supplements to the law's moral appeal will be severe enough to serve as efficient deterrents. Another question concerns the proper role of the principle of proportionality. Should it be the primary principle of sentencing; or should we sometimes allow the demands of strict proportionality to be outweighed by other considerations—for instance by a concern to subject to preventive detention offenders who are manifestly dangerous (see N. MORRIS, and von Hirsch 1985), or by a concern for 'parsimony' in punishment (see TONRY; von Hirsch 1993: chs. 6–7)? We must also ask how far we can in practice hope to achieve a genuine proportionality of punishment to crime (see TONRY and ZIMRING for some of the problems here, and Braithwaite and Pettit 1990: ch. 9); and we must ask again about the possibility of doing penal justice in an unjust society (see Preface to MURPHY above,; von Hirsch 1993: epilogue).

References

BRAITHWAITE, J., and PETTIT, P. (1990), *Not Just Deserts* (Oxford).

COHEN, S. (1985), *Visions of Social Control* (Cambridge).

GREENBERG, D., and HUMPHRIES, D. (1980), 'The Co-optation of Fixed Sentencing Reform', *Crime and Delinquency*, 26: 206–25.

HUDSON, B. (1987), *Justice through Punishment: A Critique of the 'Justice' Model of Corrections* (London).

NARAYAN, U. (1993), 'Appropriate Responses and Preventive Benefits: Justifying Censure and Hard Treatment in Legal Punishment', *Oxford Journal of Legal Studies*, 13: 166–82.

VON HIRSCH, A. (1976), *Doing Justice: The Choice of Punishments* (New York).

—— (1985), *Past or Future Crimes* (Manchester).

—— (1993), *Censure and Sanctions* (Oxford).

Censure and Proportionality

ANDREW VON HIRSCH

The principle of proportionality—that sanctions be proportionate in their severity to the gravity of offences—appears to be a requirement of justice. People have a sense that punishments which comport with the gravity of offences are more equitable than punishments that do not. However, appeals to intuition are not enough: the principle needs to be supported by explicit reasons. What are those reasons?

Although 'Why Punish Proportionately?' is ultimately an ethical question, it has not been explored much by philosophers. Philosophical writing has chiefly confined itself to the general justification for punishment, why the criminal sanction should exist at all. Seldom addressed, however, has been what bearing the justification for punishment's existence has on the question of how much offenders should be penalized.

It is the last question which will be examined in this chapter. Does sentencing theory change, depending on the general justification for punishment? Does one or another such justification provide support for the principle of proportionality, and why is this so? I shall examine two kinds of desert-based general justifications that have attracted recent philosophical attention. One theory sees the institution of punishment as rectifying the 'unfair advantage' which law-breakers obtain by offending. The other focuses on punishment's role as expressing censure or reprobation. With each theory, I shall ask whether it supports proportionate sanctions, and how convincingly it does so.

I begin with the 'unfair advantage' theory. A brief analysis will suggest that the theory, apart from its intrinsic perplexities, provides poor support for the principle of proportionality. I turn, then, to censure. I shall defend an account of the criminal sanction that emphasizes its reprobative features, and then explain why this account supports a requirement of proportionate sanctions. In my account, the institution of punishment has preventive as well as reprobative features. This also will require me to explore the relationship between the criminal sanction's censuring and preventive aspects.

Any desert-based theory of legal punishment assumes that criminal conduct is, in some sense, reprehensible. Censure-based theories clearly have this presupposition, for the conduct is treated as warranting blame. Criminal prohibitions of today have wide scope, however, and include conduct that seems in no plausible way blameworthy. A desert-based theory of punishment, however, need not defend all such prohibitions. It suffices if the core conduct with which the criminal law deals—acts of violence or fraud, for example—can reasonably be described as being reprehensible. At issue here is whether *any* conduct should be legally punishable, and if so, how much punishment that conduct should receive. It is not necessary to defend the criminal law in its full present scope.

Is it so clear, however, that even the core conduct addressed by the criminal law is blameworthy? Conceivably, the State is ill-situated to make authoritative moral judgments at all. Perhaps, the limited life-options of many criminals puts their culpability in doubt. The present chapter, however, is complex enough without introducing these issues, and so I will postpone discussing them until the end of the book (see von Hirsch, *Censure and Sanctions*, epilogue).

1. The 'Unfair-Advantage' Theory

The unfair-advantage (or 'benefits-and-burdens') theory has been attributed to Kant, but whether Kant actually subscribed to it is debatable.[1] The first unequivocal statement of this position appeared two decades ago in the writings of Herbert Morris and Jeffrie Murphy, although both authors have distanced themselves from it recently.[2] A number of other contemporary philosophers, however, continue to defend the theory.[3]*

The unfair-advantage view offers a retributive, retrospectively-oriented account of why offenders should be made to suffer. The account focuses on the criminal law as a jointly beneficial enterprise. The law requires each person to desist from certain kinds of predatory conduct. By so desisting, the person benefits others; but he also benefits from their reciprocal self-restraint. The person who victimizes others while benefiting from their self-restraint thus obtains an unjust advantage. Punishment's function is to impose an offsetting disadvantage.

This theory has various perplexities.[4]† It is arguable (although still

---

* These include John Finnis, Alan Gewirth, George Sher, and Wojciech Sadurski.

† I did endorse the theory in my 1976 book, *Doing Justice*, as a partial justification for the existence of punishment. But I since have been convinced of its deficiencies, and argued against it already in a 1985 volume.

debatable*) that the offender, by benefiting from others' self-restraint, has a reciprocal obligation to restrain himself. It is much more obscure, however, to assert that—if he disregards that obligation and does offend—the unfair advantage he supposedly thereby gains can somehow (in other than a purely metaphorical sense) be eliminated or cancelled by punishing him. In what sense does his being deprived of rights *now* offset the extra freedom he has arrogated to himself *then* by offending? And why is preserving the balance of supposed advantages a reason for invoking the coercive powers of the state?

Even if such queries could be answered, the benefits-and-burdens theory has another difficulty: it provides little or no assistance for determining the quantum of punishment. One problem is that the theory would distort the way that the gravity of crimes is assessed. R. A. Duff has pointed out the artificiality of describing typical victimizing crimes, such as armed robbery, in terms of the advantage the robber gains over uninvolved third parties, rather than in terms of the conduct's intrusion into the rights of victims.[5] Certain types of offence, it is true, might plausibly be explained in terms of unjustified advantage. Tax evasion is an example: it seems to involve taking more than one's share. Although the tax evader refuses to pay his own tax, he gets the benefit of others' payments through the services he receives. Tax evasion, however, is scarcely the paradigm criminal offence, and it is straining to try to explain the heinousness of common crimes such as burglary and robbery in similar fashion.

The theory also provides little or no intelligible guidance on how much punishment an offence of any given degree of seriousness should receive. It is not concerned with literal advantage or disadvantage: what matters, instead, is the additional freedom of action that the offender has unfairly appropriated. But the notion of degrees of freedom is not helpful in making comparisons among crimes. It is one thing to say that the armed robber or the burglar permits himself actions that others refrain from taking, and thereby unfairly gains a liberty that others have relinquished in their (and his) mutual interest. It is different, and much more opaque, to say the robber deserves more punishment than the burglar

---

* A person's receiving benefits from others does not necessarily put him under a duty to reciprocate, unless he accedes to or accepts those benefits. See A. J. Simmons, *Moral Principles and Political Obligation* (1979). Appealing to the benefits received from others' self restraint would also be a rather roundabout way of grounding the duty not to offend. It would seem simpler and more plausible to speak of a direct duty not to infringe the rights of others.

because he somehow has arrogated to himself a greater degree of unwarranted freedom *vis-à-vis* others.[6]*

2. Censure-Based Justifications for Punishment

Reprobative accounts of the institution of the criminal sanction are those that focus on that institution's condemnatory features, that is, its role as conveying censure or blame. The penal sanction clearly does convey blame. Punishing someone consists of visiting a deprivation (hard treatment) on him, because he supposedly has committed a wrong, in a manner that expresses disapprobation of the person for his conduct. Treating the offender as a wrongdoer, Richard Wasserstrom has pointed out,[7] is central to the idea of punishment. The difference between a tax and a fine does not rest in the kind of material deprivation (money in both cases). It consists, rather, in the fact that the fine conveys disapproval or censure, whereas the tax does not.[8]

An account of the criminal sanction which emphasizes its reprobative function has the attraction of being more comprehensible, for blaming is something we do in everyday moral judgements. A censure-based account is also easier to link to proportionality: if punishment conveys blame, it would seem logical that the quantum of punishment should bear a reasonable relation to the degree of blameworthiness of the criminal conduct.

---

* Sadurski has asserted that the extent of the offender's 'benefit' from not having exercised self-restraint varies with the importance of the rights infringed. However, he does not offer a convincing account of why violating a more 'important' prohibition involves taking a greater degree of unwarranted freedom. Why is one more 'free' if one takes another person's life than his property?

Michael Davis claims to have devised a proxy for the offender's 'advantage': the price at which a licence for the behaviour might be had. He asks us to imagine a society in which the government auctioned licences to commit limited numbers of offences of various sorts. Potential offenders would bid, and the size of the bids would reflect the bidder's estimate of the value to himself of having the freedom to engage in the conduct. The rankings of bids resulting would be used to decide the comparative severities of sanctions.

I have criticized Davis's model at some length elsewhere. Suffice it to say here that the licence analogy is misplaced. A licence is permissive: one may legitimately engage in the conduct if one pays the fee. The criminal law, however, is prohibitive and condemnatory: one ought not to engage in the conduct even if one is willing to 'pay the price' by suffering the sanction. It would be surprising if licences illuminated the issue of allocating punishments. Davis's model, moreover, fails to reflect the logic of the unfair-advantage theory. Whereas the theory addresses the additional freedom of action the offender arrogates to himself by offending, the bids at the hypothetical auction would depend on *literal* advantage: if a large theft is more profitable than a killing, it will attract the higher bid.

Why the Censure?

That punishment conveys blame or reprobation is, as just mentioned, evident enough. But why *should* there be a reprobative response to the core conduct with which the criminal law deals? Without an answer to that question, legal punishment might arguably be replaced by some other institution that has no blaming implications—a response akin to a tax meant to discourage certain behaviour.

P. F. Strawson provides the most straightforward account.[9] The capacity to respond to wrongdoing by reprobation or censure, he says, is simply part of a morality that holds people accountable for their conduct. When a person commits a misdeed, others judge him adversely, because his conduct was reprehensible. Censure consists of the expression of that judgment, plus its accompanying sentiment of disapproval. It is addressed to the actor because he or she is the person responsible. One would withhold the expression of blame only if there were special reasons for not confronting the actor: for example, doubts about one's standing to challenge him.

While Strawson's account seems correct as far as it goes—blaming *does* seem part of holding people accountable for their actions—it may be possible to go a bit further and specify some of the positive moral functions of blaming.

Censure addresses the victim. He or she has not only been injured, but *wronged* through someone's culpable act. It thus would not suffice just to acknowledge that the injury has occurred or convey sympathy (as would be appropriate when someone has been hurt by a natural catastrophe). Censure, by directing disapprobation at the person responsible, acknowledges that the victim's hurt occurred through another's fault.[10]

Censure also addresses the act's perpetrator. He is conveyed a certain message concerning his wrongful conduct, namely that he culpably has injured someone, and is disapproved of for having done so. Some kind of moral response is expected on his part—an expression of concern, an acknowledgement of wrongdoing, or an effort at better self-restraint. A reaction of indifference would, if the censure is justified, itself be grounds for criticizing him.*

Censure gives the actor the opportunity for so responding, but it is not a technique for evoking specified sentiments. Were inducing penitent reflection the chief aim, as R. A. Duff has claimed,[11] there would be no

---

* For a useful further analysis of these functions, see Uma Narayan, 'Adequate Responses and Preventive Benefits' (1993).

point in censuring actors who are either repentant or defiant. The repentant actor understands and regrets his wrongdoing already; the defiant actor will not accept the judgement of disapproval which the censure expresses.[12] Yet we would not wish to exempt from blame either the repentant or the seemingly incorrigible actor. Both remain moral agents, capable of understanding others' assessment of their conduct—and censure conveys that assessment. The repentant actor finds his self-evaluation confirmed through the disapproval of others; the defiant actor is made to feel and understand the disapproval of others, whatever he himself may think of his conduct. Such communication of judgement and feeling is the essence of moral discourse among rational agents.

Were the primary aim that of producing actual changes in the actor's moral attitudes, moreover, the condemnor would ordinarily seek information about his personality and outlook, so as better to foster the requisite attitudinal changes. But blaming, in ordinary life as well as in more formal contexts, does not involve such enquiries. One ascribes wrongdoing to the actor and conveys the disapprobation—limiting enquiry about the actor to questions of his capacity for choice. The condemnor's role is not that of the mentor or priest.

The criminal law gives the censure it expresses yet another role: that of addressing third parties, and providing them with reason for desistence. Unlike blame in everyday contexts, the criminal sanction announces in advance that specified categories of conduct are punishable. Because the prescribed sanction is one which expresses blame, this conveys the message that the conduct is reprehensible, and should be eschewed. It is not necessarily a matter of inculcating that the conduct is wrong, for those addressed (or many of them) may well understand that already. Rather, the censure embodied in the prescribed sanction serves to *appeal* to people's sense of the conduct's wrongfulness, as a reason for desistence.[13]*

This normative message expressed in penal statutes is not reducible, as penal utilitarians might suppose, to a mere inducement to compliance—one utilized because the citizenry could be more responsive to moral appeals than bare threats. If persons are called upon to desist because the conduct is wrong, there ought to be good reasons for supposing that it *is* wrong; and the message expressed through the penalty about its degree of wrongfulness ought to reflect how reprehensible the conduct indeed

---

* I thus would not subscribe to views that treat penal censure as primarily a matter of moral education, that is, of inculcating standards. For a fuller critique of such views (including those of Herbert Morris and Jean Hampton), see Narayan, 'Moral Education and Criminal Punishment' (1993).

is. This point will be elaborated upon in the next chapter, where penal censure is contrasted with instrumentalist strategies of 'shaming'.

The foregoing account explains why predatory conduct should not be dealt with through neutral sanctions that convey no disapproval. Such sanctions—even if they were no less effective in discouraging the behaviour—deny the status of the person as an agent capable of moral understanding. A neutral sanction would treat offenders or potential offenders much as tigers might be treated in a circus, as beings that have to be restrained, intimidated, or conditioned into compliance because they are incapable of understanding why biting people (or other tigers) is wrong. A condemnatory sanction treats the actor as a *person* who is capable of such understanding.

A committed utilitarian might insist that treating the actor as a person in this fashion can only be warranted on instrumental grounds. Nigel Walker takes this view: if '. . . the message which expresses blame need have no utility,' he asserts, 'where lies the moral necessity?'[14] This, however, is reductionist. Treating the actor as someone capable of choice, rather than as a tiger, is a matter of acknowledging his dignity as a human being. Is this acknowledgement warranted only if it leads to beneficial social consequences? Those consequences would not necessarily be those of crime prevention—for, as just noted, it might be possible to devise a 'neutral' sanction (one designed to visit material deprivation but convey no blame) that prevents crime at least as well. Might society somehow have better cohesion if actors are treated as being responsible (and hence subject to censure) for their actions? Making such a claim would involve trying to reduce ethical judgments to difficult-to-confirm predictions about social structure. While one can have some confidence in the moral judgement that offenders should be treated as agents capable of choice, it will be difficult to verify that so treating them will lead to a more smoothly-running society.

Why the Hard Treatment?

It is still necessary to address punishment's other constitutive element: deprivation or hard treatment. Some desert theorists (John Kleinig and Igor Primoratz,[15] for example) assert that notions of censure can account also for the hard treatment. They argue that censure (at least in certain social contexts) cannot be expressed adequately in purely verbal or symbolic terms; that hard treatment is needed to show that the disapprobation is meant seriously. For example, an academic department does not show disapproval of a serious lapse by a colleague merely through a verbal admonition; to convey the requisite disapproval, some curtailment of privileges is called for. This justification has plausibility outside legal contexts, where the deprivations involved are modest enough to serve chiefly to underline the intended disapproval. However, I doubt that the argument sustains the criminal sanction.

The criminal law seems to have preventive features in its very design. When the State criminalizes conduct, it issues a legal threat: such conduct is proscribed, and violation will result in the imposition of specified sanctions. The threat appears to be explicitly aimed at discouraging the proscribed conduct.[16] Criminal sanctions also seem too onerous to serve just to give credibility to the censure. Even were penalties substantially scaled down from what they are today, some of them still could involve significant deprivations of liberty or property. In the absence of a preventive purpose, it is hard to conceive of such intrusions as having the sole function of showing that the state's disapproval is seriously intended.

This reasoning led me to suggest, in a 1985 volume,[17] a bifurcated account of punishment. The penal law, I said, performs two interlocking functions. By threatening unpleasant consequences, it seeks to discourage criminal behaviour. Through the censure expressed by such sanctions, the law registers disapprobation of the behaviour. Citizens are thus provided with moral and not just prudential reasons for desistence.

However, the two elements in my account, reprobation and prevention, remained uneasily matched. Whereas the censuring element appeals to the person's moral agency, does not the preventive element play merely on his fear of unpleasant consequences? If the person is capable of being moved by moral appeal, why the threat? If not capable and thus in need of the threat, it appears that he is being treated like a tiger. A clarification of the preventive function—and its relation to the censuring function—is needed.

The preventive function of the sanction should be seen, I think, as supplying a prudential reason that is tied to, and supplements, the normative reason conveyed by penal censure. The criminal law, through the censure embodied in its prescribed sanctions, conveys that the conduct is wrong, and a moral agent thus is given grounds for desistence. He may (given human fallibility) be tempted nevertheless. What the prudential disincentive can do is to provide him a further reason—a prudential one—for resisting the temptation.* Indeed, an agent who has accepted

---

* For a comparable analysis of the relation between censure and prevention, and of prevention as a 'supplementary prudential disincentive', see Narayan, 'Adequate Responses to Preventive Benefits'.

the sanction's message that he ought not offend, and who recognizes his susceptibility to temptation, could favour the existence of such a prudential disincentive, as an aid to carrying out what he himself recognizes as the proper course of conduct.

A certain conception of human nature, of which I spoke in the previous chapter, underlies this idea of the preventive function as a supplementary prudential disincentive. Persons are assumed to be moral agents, capable of taking seriously the message conveyed through the sanction, that the conduct is reprehensible. They are fallible, nevertheless, and thus face temptation. The function of the disincentive is to provide a prudential reason for resisting the temptation. The account would make no sense were human beings much better or worse: an angel would require no appeals to prudence, and a brute could not be appealed to through censure.

Notice that I am speaking here of why prevention might in principle be a legitimate supporting reason for punishment's existence. I have not been speaking of sanctions' severity, where coerciveness could still be a problem. If penalty levels rise too high, the normative reasons for desistence supplied by penal censure could become largely immaterial; and the disincentive become much more than supplementary to the censuring message. If minimal prudence virtually would demand compliance, what difference could the sanction's normative message make? (See von Hirsch, *Censure and Sanctions*, ch. 5, on sanction levels and a penalty scale's anchoring points.)

The Relation Between the Two Elements

What is the relation between the two elements in punishment, the reprobative and preventive? We need to be careful that the latter does not operate independently, or else we may undermine the proportionality requirement.

Prevention, on the account of it that I have just given, cannot stand alone. If the sanction conveys blame, it may also supply the prudential disincentive I have described—the means for overcoming the temptation. But if it *merely* imposes hard treatment, it remains tiger-control. Granted, a morally committed person might find that even a neutral, non-condemnatory sanction makes it easier to resist temptation and thus comply with a moral obligation he himself recognizes. The sanction itself would not be respectful of his agency, however, if it was couched as a naked demand. Whatever the actor's reasons for compliance, the sanctioner would be treating him as a creature to be controlled, not as someone whose normative reasons for acting matter.

The structure of my proposed justification for punishing is also one in which the blaming function has primacy. A condemnatory response to injurious conduct, I have been arguing, can be expressed either in a purely (or primarily) symbolic mode; or else, in one in which the reprobation is expressed through the visitation of hard treatment. The criminal sanction is a response of the latter kind. It is preferred to the purely symbolic response because of its supplementary role as a disincentive. The preventive function thus operates only *within* a censuring framework.

The censure and the hard treatment are intertwined in the way punishment is structured. A penal measure provides that a specified type of conduct is punishable by certain onerous consequences. Those consequences both constitute the hard treatment and express the reprobation. Altering those consequences—by raising or lowering the penalty on the scale—will alter the degree of censure conveyed. This intertwining of punishment's blaming and hard-treatment features is important for the rationale for proportionality, as we will see.

My two-pronged justification would permit the abolition of the institution of punishment were it not needed for preventive purposes. Imagine a jurisdiction in which social and economic conditions improved so much that predatory conduct became quite rare. The criminal sanction—with its armamentarium of courts, correctional agencies, and sanctions—would cease to be required in order to keep such conduct at tolerable levels. Would such a society still have to preserve this institution to deal with the occasional predatory act? I would think not. The society might wish to maintain some form of official censure to convey the requisite disapproval of such acts, but with the need for prevention eliminated, there would no longer be need for so ambitious, intrusive, and burdensome an institution as the criminal sanction.*

---

* The argument for abolition is not quite so simple as the text suggests. Suppose the crime rate has fallen drastically, so that crimes (or at least, those of a substantial nature) become rather rare. Imagine a discussion among a group of citizens about whether punishment should be abolished. Some might argue that such conduct, even if rare, is reprehensible and injurious when it occurs. Even if only a few might be tempted, why not have a sanction that includes a prudential disincentive—to help offset the temptation?

The abolitionists' response would have to be that there are strong countervailing reasons for abolition. The criminal sanction, they might argue, has serious collateral drawbacks: it is prone to errors and abuse and, once established, can lead to unwarranted increases in penalty levels. These drawbacks may have to be tolerated when the criminal sanction assists a significant number of offenders to overcome the temptation to offend. But if such temptation is rare, better let the offender rely on his conscience and whatever form of official censure exists, than create so troublesome an institution as the criminal sanction. (For an analogous argument, see D. Husak, 'Why Punish the Deserving?' (1992).)

3. The Rationale for Proportionality

So much, then, for the general justification for punishment. It is time to move from 'why punish?' to 'how much?'. Assuming a reprobative account of punishment's existence, how can the principle of proportionality be accounted for? The argument will reflect the idea that, if censure conveys blame, its amount should reflect the blameworthiness of the conduct; but it needs to be unpacked more carefully.

Stated schematically, the argument for proportionality involves the following three steps:

1. The State's sanctions against proscribed conduct should take a punitive form; that is, visit deprivations in a manner that expresses censure or blame.
2. The severity of a sanction expresses the stringency of the blame.
3. Hence, punitive sanctions should be arrayed according to the degree of blameworthiness (i.e. seriousness) of the conduct.

Let us examine each of these steps. Step (1) reflects the claim made in the preceding pages: the response to harmful conduct with which the criminal law centrally deals should convey censure. A morally neutral sanction would not merely be a (possibly) less efficient preventive device; it would be objectionable on the ethical ground that it does not recognize the wrongfulness of the conduct, and does not treat the actor as a moral agent answerable for his or her behaviour.

Step (2) has also been touched upon: in punishment, deprivation or hard treatment is the vehicle for expressing condemnation. When a given type of conduct is visited with comparatively more hard treatment, that signifies a greater degree of disapprobation.[18]*

Step (3)—the conclusion—embodies the claim of fairness. When persons are (and should be) dealt with in a manner ascribing demerit, their treatment should reflect how unmeritorious their conduct can reasonably be said to be. By punishing one kind of conduct more severely than another, the punisher conveys the message than it is worse—which is appropriate only if the conduct is indeed worse (i.e. more serious). Were penalties ordered in severity inconsistently with the comparative seriousness of crime, the less reprehensible conduct would, undeservedly, receive the greater reprobation.

---

* A recent work, by John Braithwaite and Phillip Pettit, attempts to question this link between the quantum of the sanction and the degree of blame. See von Hirsch, *Censure and Sanctions* (1993), ch. 3 for a reply to their arguments.

The foregoing case for proportionality holds if my bifurcated justification for the criminal sanction's existence is adopted. It is not necessary to
assert that punishment serves *solely* to express reprobation. In order for
my three-step argument to work, it is necessary merely for its premise
(Step (1)) to obtain: that the sanction should express reprobation. On my
bifurcated view, it should, for I have been arguing why censuring is an
essential (albeit not the exclusive) function of the institution of punishment.[19]*

Does my bifurcated account of punishment, however, create a Trojan
Horse? If punishment's existence is justified even in part on preventive
grounds, might prevention be invoked in deciding comparative severities

---

* Even were the institution of punishment justified wholly on preventive grounds, it still
expresses blame— and hence (for the reasons explained in Steps (2) and (3)) its allocation
criteria should, in fairness, reflect the comparative blameworthiness of offences.

Why, then, not adopt a straightforwardly consequentialist account of a blaming sanction's existence? Such an explanation is readily conceived—indeed, some European theorists
have suggested it. In their view, general prevention operates chiefly through the criminal
sanction's 'moral-educational' effects, stigmatizing predatory conduct and thereby strengthening citizens' moral inhibitions and making them more reluctant to offend. This stigmatizing effect is achieved through the censure which punishment conveys. Why not be satisfied
with such an explanation, if it suffices to support my three-step argument for proportionality? Why bother with all the theorizing of the earlier pages of this chapter concerning the
moral basis for penal censure?

The trouble with such an account is that it leaves open an escape hatch. Perhaps these
European theorists are right that the criminal sanction, as presently constituted, achieves
part of its preventive impact through its 'moral-educational' message. But why not replace
that sanction with a 'neutral' one that visits hard treatment but no censure? Such a response
might also achieve some prevention, through its purely deterrent or incapacitative effects.
Since such a sanction would not express blame, our censure-based argument for proportionality would no longer hold, and the sanction could be distributed without regard to the
blameworthiness of the conduct.

My two-pronged general justification—which treats reprobation as a necessary but not
sufficient reason for punishment's existence—closes off this escape route; and does so as
surely as would wholly reprobative accounts such as Kleinig's or Primoratz's. This is so
because my theory would not permit the creation of a neutral scheme of sanctions that pur-
ports to visit hard treatment only, for such an institution would fail to recognize the repre-
hensibleness of the proscribed behaviour.

† David Dolinko makes this objection in a recent article: if punishment has the twin
objectives of censure and prevention, why not distribute punishments according to the latter aim? He then notes my reply: that reprobation is not merely an aim but an essential
characteristic of punishment—so the comparative severity of the penalty will convey the
degree of reprobation. His response is a strange one: tort liability, he says, in some sense
conveys censure, since the prerequisite of liability is fault on the part of the actor. Yet the
amount of civil recovery depends not on fault but on what is required to make the plaintiff
whole. Why, then, need fault be the measure for the quanta of punishments? The answer to
Dolinko's contention should be obvious: civil remedies are designed to compensate, and do
not have blaming as a central, defining feature. It happens to be that, under existing tort
law, fault is required for liability—because it is thought preferable that the actor bear the
burden of loss, rather than the person he has injured through his carelessness. But it is not

of punishment? Were that permissible, proportionality would be undermined.[20]†

Relying on prevention to decide comparative severities is ruled out by something we have mentioned already: the intertwining of punishment's reprobative and hard-treatment features. It is the threatened penal deprivation that expresses the censure as well as serving as the prudential disincentive. Varying the relative amount of the deprivation thus will vary the degree of censure conveyed. Consider a proposal to increase sanctions for a specified type of conduct (beyond the quantum that would be proportionate) in order to create a stronger inducement not to offend. Could such a step be justified under my theory of punishment— on grounds that prevention is said to be part of the general aim of punishing and that this measure achieves prevention more efficiently? No, it could not; thus:

1. Suppose the increase were accomplished simply by raising the prescribed penalty for this type of crime. That increase in punishment would express increased disapprobation for conduct that, *ex hypothesi*, has become no more reprehensible. The increase thus would be objectionable because it treats the offender as more to blame than his conduct warrants.

2. Alternatively, the increase might be accomplished by visiting the proportionate punishment, and then imposing a separate *non-condemnatory* sanction.[21] Since the additional imposition would not be reprobative in character, it would involve no unjustifiable increase in blame. There is, however, another objection: this separate non-condemnatory sanction clearly falls outside my proposed justification for the hard treatment. We are no longer speaking of a censure-expressing response that, for preventive reasons, also involves material deprivation. Instead, the additional sanction is purely preventive and not reprobative at all. It is of the 'tiger-controlling' kind that does not address the actor as a moral agent.

These scenarios confirm what should be apparent, anyway: that making prevention part of the justification for punishment's existence, in the manner that I have, does not permit it to operate independently as a basis for deciding comparative punishments. Any increase or decrease in the severity-ranking of a penalty on the scale alters how much censure is expressed—and hence needs to be justified by reference to the seriousness of the criminal conduct involved.

part of the point—the very significance—of an ordinary civil recovery to convey disapprobation. Indeed, the fault requirement in civil recoveries could be eliminated, were there a practicable alternative method for distributing the burden of loss: one such method is the no-fault scheme, where those who suffer harm are compensated through State insurance.

4. The Criteria for Proportionality

When we say sanctions should be 'proportionate', what does that mean? Is there any particular quantum of punishment that is the deserved penalty for crimes of a given degree of seriousness? If not, what guidance does the principle give?

To answer such questions, let me advert to the distinction between ordinal and cardinal proportionality.* *Ordinal proportionality* relates to comparative punishments, and its requirements are reasonably specific. Persons convicted of crimes of like gravity should receive punishments of like severity. Persons convicted of crimes of differing gravity should receive punishments correspondingly graded in their degree of severity. These requirements of ordinal proportionality are not mere limits, and they are infringed when persons found guilty of equally reprehensible conduct receive unequal sanctions on ulterior (e.g. crime prevention) grounds. The ordinal proportionality requirements are readily explained on the reprobative conception of punishment just set forth. Since punishing one crime more severely than another expresses greater disapprobation of the former crime, it is justified only to the extent the former is more serious.

Ordinary proportionality involves three sub-requirements, which are worth summarizing briefly.† The first is *parity*: when offenders have been convicted of crimes of similar seriousness they deserve penalties of comparable severity. This requirement does not necessarily call for the same penalty for all acts within a statutory crime category—as significant variations may occur within that category in the conduct's harmfulness or culpability. But it requires that once such within-category variations in crime-seriousness are controlled for, the resulting penalties should be of the same (or substantially the same) degree of onerousness.‡ (This parity requirement has one possible exception, concerning the role of prior convictions.§)

A second sub-requirement is *rank-ordering*. Punishing crime Y more than crime X expresses more disapproval for crime Y, which is warranted only if it is more serious. Punishments should thus be ordered on the penalty scale so that their relative severity reflects the seriousness-ranking of the crimes involved.

* That distinction is outlined in A. von Hirsch, *Past or Future Crimes* (1985), ch. 4.
† For a fuller discussion of these requirements, see ibid., chs. 4–7; and von Hirsch, 'Proportionality in the Philosophy of Punishment' (1992).
‡ For fuller discussion, see von Hirsch, *Censure and Sanctions*, ch. 8.
§ See ibid., ch. 7.

The third sub-requirement concerns *spacing* of penalties. Suppose crimes X, Y, and Z are of ascending order of seriousness; but that Y is considerably more serious than X but only slightly less so than Z. Then, to reflect the conduct's gravity, there should be a larger space between the penalties for X and Y than for Y and Z. Spacing, however, depends on how precisely comparative gravity can be calibrated—and seriousness-gradations are likely to be matters of rather inexact judgment (see von Hirsch, *Censure and Sanctions*, ch. 4).

Scaling penalties calls also for a starting point. If one has decided what the penalty should be for certain crimes, then it is possible to fix the sanction for a given crime, X, by comparing its seriousness with the seriousness of those other crimes. But no quantum of punishment suggests itself as the uniquely appropriate penalty for the crime or crimes with which the scale begins. Why not? Our censure-oriented account again provides the explanation. The amount of disapproval conveyed by penal sanctions is a convention. When a penalty scale has been devised to reflect the comparative gravity of crimes, altering the scale's magnitude by making *pro rata* increases or decreases represents just a change in that convention.

Not all conventions, however, are equally acceptable. There may be limits on the severity of sanction through which a given amount of disapproval may be expressed, and these constitute the limits of *cardinal* or non-relative proportionality. Consider a scale in which penalties are graded to reflect the comparative seriousness of crimes, but in which overall penalty levels have been so much inflated that even the lowest-ranking crimes are visited with prison terms. Such a scale would embody a convention in which even a modest disapproval appropriate to low-ranking crimes is expressed through drastic intrusions on offenders' liberties. If suitable reasons can be established for objecting to this convention (for example, on grounds that it depreciates the importance of the rights of those convicted of such low-ranking crimes*), a cardinal—that is, non-relative—constraint is established.

The cardinal–ordinary distinction explains why one cannot identify a unique 'proportionate' sanction for a given offence. Whether *x* months, *y* months, or somewhere in between is the appropriate penalty for (say) armed robbery depends on how the scale has been anchored and what punishments have been prescribed for other crimes. The distinction explains, however, why proportionality becomes a significant constraint

---

* For fuller discussion, see von Hirsch, *Censure and Sanctions*, ch. 5.

on the ordering of penalties. Once the anchoring points and magnitude of the penalty scale have been fixed, ordinal proportionality will require penalties to be graded and spaced according to their relative seriousness, and require comparably-severe sanctions for equally reprehensible acts.

Notes

1. See e.g. D. E. Scheid, 'Kant's Retributivism' (1983); J. G. Murphy, 'Does Kant Have a Theory of Punishment?' (1987); B. S. Byrd, 'Kant's Theory of Punishment' (1989).

2. Herbert Morris initially advocated the benefits-and-burdens theory, Morris, 'Persons and Punishment' (1968), but subsequently moved away from it, Morris, 'A Paternalistic Theory of Punishment' (1981). Jeffrie Murphy also espoused the benefits-and-burdens view, J. G. Murphy, *Retribution, Justice, and Therapy* (1979), 82–115; however, he, too, subsequently criticized the theory, see J. Murphy, 'Retributivism, Moral Education, and the Liberal State' (1985).

3. For citations in footnote: W. Sadurski, *Giving Desert Its Due* (1985), ch. 8; G. Sher, *Desert* (1987), ch. 5; J. Finnis, *Natural Law and Natural Rights* (1980), 263–4; A. Gewirth, *Reason and Morality* (1978), 294–8.

4. For critiques of the unfair-advantage theory, see, e.g., A. von Hirsch, *Past or Future Crimes* (1985), ch. 5; R. A. Duff, *Trials and Punishments* (1986), ch. 8; H. Bedau, 'Retribution and the Theory of Punishment' (1978); R. Burgh, 'Do the Guilty Deserve Punishment?' (1982). For citations in footnote, A. von Hirsch, *Doing Justice* (1976), ch. 6; von Hirsch, above, n. 4; ch. 5.

5. Duff, above n. 4, 211–16.

6. For references in footnote: Sadurski, above n. 3, 229; M. Davis, 'How to Make the Punishment Fit the Crime' (1983); A. von Hirsch, 'Proportionality in the Philosophy of Punishment: From "Why Punish?" to "How Much?" ' (1990), 265–8. For further criticism of Davis's auction model, see D. Scheid, 'Davis and the Unfair-Advantage Theory of Punishment' (1990).

7. R. Wasserstrom, 'Punishment' (1980).

8. For further discussion of the censuring character of punishment, and a response to some objections by Michael Davis, see von Hirsch, above n. 6, 270–1.

9. P. F. Strawson, 'Freedom and Resentment' (1974).

10. Joel Feinberg speaks of punishment's function in recognizing the wrongfulness of the conduct in his 'Expressive Function of Punishment' (1970). Uma Narayan points out, however, that censure not only recognizes that the conduct is wrong, but confronts the actor as the agent responsible for the wrongdoing. See U. Narayan, 'Adequate Responses and Preventive Benefits' (1993).

11. Duff, above n. 4, ch. 9.

12. For discussion of the defiant-actor case, contrast Duff, above n. 4, 266, with I. Primoratz, 'Punishment as Language' (1989), 195.

13. For citations in footnote see H. Morris, 'A Paternalistic Theory of Punishment' (1981); J. Hampton, 'The Moral Education Theory of Punishment' (1984).
14. N. Walker, *Why Punish?* (1991), 81–2.
15. J. Kleinig, 'Punishment and Moral Seriousness' (1992); Primoratz, above n. 12, 198–202.
16. See N. Jareborg, *Essays in Criminal Law* (1988), 76–8.
17. See von Hirsch, above n. 4, ch. 5.
18. For citations in footnote: J. Braithwaite and P. Pettit, *Not Just Deserts* (1990).
19. For citations in footnote: for a sample of the views of the European theorists, see, K. Mäkelä, 'Om straffets verkningar' (1975), discussed in von Hirsch, above n. 4, 48–51. See also A. C. Ewing, *The Morality of Punishment* (1929), 94–100.
20. For reference in footnote: D. Dolinko, 'Three Mistakes of Retributivism' (1992), 1625; von Hirsch, above n. 4, 35–6.
21. For a comparable suggestion, see D. Wood, 'Dangerous Offenders and the Morality of Protective Sentencing' (1988).

References

BEDAU, H. A. (1978), 'Retribution and the Theory of Punishment', *Journal of Philosophy*, 75: 601–20.

BRAITHWAITE, J. and PETTIT, P. (1990), *Not Just Deserts: A Republican Theory of Justice* (Oxford).

BURGH, R. (1982), 'Do the Guilty Deserve Punishment?' *Journal of Philosophy*, 79: 192–210.

BYRD, B. S. (1989), 'Kant's Theory of Punishment: Deterrence in Its Threat, Retribution in Its Execution', *Law and Philosophy*, 8: 151–200.

DAVIS, M. (1983), 'How to Make the Punishment Fit the Crime', *Ethics*, 93: 726–52.

DOLINKO, D. (1992), 'Three Mistakes of Retributivism', *UCLA Law Review*, 39: 1623–57.

DUFF, R. A. (1986), *Trials and Punishments* (Cambridge).

EWING, A. C. (1929), *The Morality of Punishment* (Monclair, NJ).

FEINBERG, J. (1970), 'The Expressive Function of Punishment', in *Doing and Deserving: Essays in the Theory of Responsibility*, ed. Feinberg, J. (Princeton, NJ), 53–69; this volume, p. 73.

FINNIS, J. (1980), *Natural Law and Natural Rights* (Oxford).

GEWIRTH, A. (1978), *Reason and Morality* (Chicago).

HAMPTON, J. (1984), 'The Moral Education Theory of Punishment', *Philosophy and Public Affairs*, 13: 208–38.

HUSAK, D. (1992), 'Why Punish the Deserving?' *Nous*, 26: 447–64.

JAREBORG, N. (1988), *Essays in Criminal Law* (Uppsala).

KLEINIG, J. (1992), 'Punishment and Moral Seriousness', *Israel Law Review*, 25: 401–21.

MAKELA, K. (1975), 'Om straffets verkningar', *Jurisprudentia*, 6: 237–80.

MORRIS, H. (1968), 'Persons and Punishment', *The Monist*, 52: 475–501.

—— (1981), 'A Paternalistic Theory of Punishment', *American Philosophical Quarterly*, 18: 263–71 this volume, p. 95.

MURPHY, J. G. (1979), *Retribution, Justice, and Therapy* (Dordrecht) this volume, p. 94.

—— (1985), 'Retributivism, Moral Education, and the Liberal State', *Criminal Justice Ethics*, 4(1): 3–11.

—— (1987), 'Does Kant Have a Theory of Punishment?' *Columbia Law Review*, 87: 509–32.

NARAYAN, U. (1993), 'Moral Education and Criminal Punishment', Paper presented at 21st Conference on Value Inquiry, Drew University, NJ, April.

—— (1993), 'Adequate Responses and Preventive Benefits: Justifying Censure and Hard Treatment in Legal Punishment', *Oxford Journal of Legal Studies*, 13: 166–82.

PRIMORATZ, I. (1989), 'Punishment as Language', *Philosophy*, 64: 187–205.

SADURSKI, W. (1985), *Giving Desert Its Due: Social Justice and Legal Theory* (Dordrecht).

SCHEID, D. E. (1983), 'Kant's Retributivism', *Ethics*, 93: 262–82.

—— (1990), 'Davis and the Unfair-Advantage Theory of Punishment', *Philosophical Topics*, 18: 143–70.

SHER, G. (1987), *Desert* (Princeton, NJ).

SIMMONS, A. J. (1979), *Moral Principles and Political Obligation* (Princeton, NJ).

STRAWSON, P. F. (1974) R. Wasserstrom (ed.), 'Freedom and Resentment', in *Freedom and Resentment and Other Essays* (London), 1–25.

VON HIRSCH, A. (1976), *Doing Justice: The Choice of Punishments* (New York).

—— (1985), *Past or Future Crimes: Deservedness and Dangerousness in the Sentencing of Criminals* (New Brunswick, NJ).

—— (1990), 'Proportionality in the Philosophy of Punishment: From "Why Punish?" to "How Much?" ', *Criminal Law Forum*, 1: 259–90.

—— (1992), 'Proportionality in the Philosophy of Punishment', *Crime and Justice: A Review of Research*, M. Tonry (ed.), 55–98.

—— (1993), *Censure and Sanctions* (Oxford).

WALKER, N. (1991), *Why Punish?* (London).

WASSERSTROM, R. (1980) 'Punishment', in R. Wasserstrom (ed.), *Philosophy and Social Issues: Five Studies* (Notre Dame, Ind.), 112–51.

WOOD, D. (1988), 'Dangerous Offenders and the Morality of Protective Sentencing', *Criminal Law Review*, 424–33.

Preface: M. Tonry, 'Proportionality, Parsimony, and Interchangeability of Punishments'

Tonry's essay, like von Hirsch's, situates itself between philosophy and practice. But whilst von Hirsch wants to install proportionality as the fundamental principle of sentencing, Tonry seeks to promote a greater use of 'intermediate punishments' in place of imprisonment, and argues that too rigid an adherence to proportionality will hinder the deployment of such measures.

Intermediate punishments (sanctions such as intensive probation or supervision, substantial fines, and community service, which fall between imprisonment and regular probation) are playing an expanding role in penal policy in the USA and elsewhere (see Morris and Tonry 1990; Home Office 1988, 1990; Gordon 1991). Developed in response to the soaring (financial and human) costs of overcrowded prisons, and the perception that traditional alternatives to imprisonment were insufficiently punitive or controlling, these new sanctions have yet to find a settled place in sentencing practice. Their effective use will depend upon sentencers being willing in appropriate cases to impose intermediate sanctions on offenders who would otherwise receive a custodial sentence; without such a willingness, such sanctions will simply 'widen the net' of penal control. We must therefore, Tonry argues, establish an 'interchangeability' between sentences, and allow sentencers the discretion to decide whether a custodial or a non-custodial sentence is most appropriate for the individual offender. Strict adherence to the principle of proportionality, and the enactment of obligatory sentencing scales which arrange all penalties in a single hierarchy of severity, would be a recipe for the failure of this strategy.

Tonry offers two kinds of argument against any strict principle of proportionality. Both reflect his insistence that the actual world is too complex and messy for any single principle of this kind to be adequate. First, the principle of proportionality cannot actually secure justice. Apart from the problem of trying to achieve 'just deserts in an unjust world' (see Preface to MURPHY above), no system of proportionality-based sentencing guide-lines will actually secure 'equally severe' punishments for 'equally culpable' offenders. Given the individual variations in offenders, in their crimes, and in the impact on them of formally equal sentences, we cannot in practice hope to proportion punishment precisely to criminal desert. Second, we should recognize that punishment, like other human institutions, is a locus of *conflicting* values: in particular, we must recognize that the principle of 'parsimony' (see Morris 1974), favouring the least restrictive sentence which is socially tolerable in the individual case, is in tension with the principle of proportionality.

Tonry seeks a 'middle ground' which will allow due weight to both proportionality and parsimony: a system of 'presumptive sentencing ranges in which the upper bounds are set in accordance with the proportionality principle, and the lower bounds are sufficiently flexible to honour the parsimony principle'. Between those bounds, judges would have discretion to set the sentence most appropriate to the particular case (and see Morris and Tonry 1990). Such a system would avoid imposing unnecessarily harsh penalties for the sake of proportionality; it would also, Tonry argues, do less injustice, since it would be more sensitive to offenders' individual circumstances, and the various kinds of social deprivation which may have led them into crime (for critical responses to this argument, see Brownlee 1994; von Hirsch 1993: ch. 7 and epilogue).

Now those, like von Hirsch, who argue for a strong principle of proportionality are also concerned with parsimony: sentences should be no more severe than is strictly necessary. One question then is how can we reconcile these two principles? Should we, as Tonry urges, allow parsimony to override the demands of proportionality in individual cases—so that one offender might, for reasons of parsimony, receive a significantly lighter sentence than another whose culpability is no greater? Or should we, as von Hirsch urges, apply the principle of parsimony to the sentencing system as a whole rather than to individual cases, and seek a general lowering of sentencing levels? Another question is whether the impossibility of achieving a *perfect* proportion between crime and punishment should lead us to downgrade the principle of proportionality. Or should we instead still seek to do such justice as we can within the practical constraints which will admittedly ensure that any actual sentencing system is imperfect? A third question concerns the likely practical effects of a system of the kind favoured by Tonry. The initial drive for more determinate sentencing systems in the 1970s derived in part from a perception that judicial and executive sentencing discretion was being used to the advantage of well-to-do offenders, and to the unjust disadvantage of poor or minority offenders (American Friends Service Committee 1971, Greenberg and Humphries 1980). How confident can we be that a similar bias against the underprivileged would not infect the kind of judicial discretion which Tonry favours?

References

American Friends Service Committee (1971), *Struggle for Justice* (New York).
BROWNLEE, I. (1994), 'Hanging Judges and Wayward Mechanics', in R. A. Duff, S. E. Marshall, R. E. Dobash, and R. P. Dobash (eds.), *Penal Theory and Practice* (Manchester), 85–92.

GORDON, D. R. (1991), *The Justice Juggernaut: Fighting Street Crime, Controlling Citizens* (New Brunswick, NJ).

GREENBERG, D., and HUMPHRIES, D. (1980), 'The Co-optation of Fixed Sentence Reform', *Crime and Delinquency*, 26: 206–25.

Home Office (1988), *Punishment, Custody and the Community* (London).

—— (1990), *Crime, Justice and Protecting the Public* (London).

MORRIS, N. (1974), *The Future of Imprisonment* (Chicago).

—— and TONRY, M. (1990), *Between Prison and Probation: Intermediate Punishments in a Rational Sentencing System* (New York).

VON HIRSCH, A. (1993), *Censure and Sanctions* (Oxford).

Proportionality, Parsimony, and Interchangeability of Punishments

MICHAEL TONRY

If intermediate punishments are to be used more widely, procedures and principles governing their use must be developed. Although new intermediate punishments are often conceived in large part for use in lieu of incarceration, experience on three continents shows that many judges prefer to impose such penalties on offenders who would not otherwise be bound for prison. Working out procedures governing intermediate punishments will be hard enough. Working out principles governing imposition of penalties in individual cases may be harder and will require consideration of finer-grained issues than writing on the philosophy of punishment traditionally addresses. Most philosophical writing on punishment deals with broad issues of justification. In so far as questions of distribution are considered, attention focuses on prison sentences. Because prison sentences can be expressed in seemingly objective units of months or years, and since 'disparity' in prison terms looks prima facie to be a bad thing, recent writing on the distribution of punishment celebrates what Andrew von Hirsch (1992) calls 'the principle of proportionality'.

The theses of this essay are that strong proportionality constraints in the distribution of punishments generally are likely to cause more injustice than they prevent, and that application of strong proportionality constraints to intermediate sanctions will stifle their development, circumscribe their use, and produce avoidable injustices.

There are three fundamental problems with a strong proportionality principle. First, by celebrating equality in suffering for 'like-situated' offenders, it often requires imposition of more severe and intrusive punishments than are required by prevailing social norms and political values. Second, it misleadingly objectifies punishment, by allocating punishments in terms of 'like-situated offenders' and generic penalties. Third, it ignores the problem of 'just deserts in an unjust society'. Most offenders committing common law crimes come from disadvantaged backgrounds, and disproportionately they come from minority groups.

Arguments for a highly proportional system of deserved punishments evade the question of whether offenders from deeply deprived backgrounds deserve the same penalties as do other, less deprived, offenders.

A punishment system permitting interchangeability of roughly equivalent penalties is likely, overall, to be more just, less harsh, and more sensitive to problems of social injustice than a punishment system predicated on desert-based proportionality. 'Like-situated offenders' convicted of comparable crimes can justly receive quite different sentences including financial penalties for some, incarceration for others, and community-based sanctions for still others.

This essay attempts to demonstrate and defend the preceding observations. Part I describes policy developments that make consideration of the applied philosophy of intermediate sanctions timely. Part II reviews philosophical writings on punishment and argues that principles of proportionality and parsimony are in stark conflict in general and in many specific cases. Part III examines in some detail Andrew von Hirsch's arguments for a strong principle of proportionality and his proposals for devising a punishment scheme premissed on proportionality concerns. Part IV offers a critique of von Hirsch's proposals and Part V sketches a counterproposal that reconciles concerns for proportionality and parsimony.

Why Intermediate Punishments?

Policy-makers in the United Kingdom and the United States are considering how to incorporate intermediate punishments into comprehensive sentencing policies.[1] Passage in the UK of the Criminal Justice Act 1991 with its increased emphasis on non-custodial penalties has drawn attention to the subject.

In the United States, historically high and growing prison populations, severe pressures on public budgets, and the evolution of the American sentencing reform movement have combined to focus interest on non-custodial (or partly custodial) penalties, and on the integration of non-custodial penalties into comprehensive systems of sentencing guide-lines.

American incarceration rates have risen steadily since 1970 but startlingly since 1980, when the number of sentenced offenders held in state prisons (that is, disregarding those in county gaols serving sentences of one year or less) stood at 330,000. By 30 June 1992, that number had increased to 856,000. The combined prison and gaol incarceration rate in 1990 was 455 per 100,000 population, a level five to ten times that of most developed countries. On 31 December 1991, state prisons were on average operating at 131 per cent of rated capacity and federal prisons at 146 per cent.

Competition for scarce public funds, coupled with a continuing federal commitment to a 'war on drugs' and an ever-toughening crime control strategy, produced great interest in the 1980s in a wide range of intermediate punishments, including house arrest, intensive (sometimes fifteen to twenty-five contacts per month) probation, day-reporting centres, restitution, community service, electronic monitoring, residential drug treatment, day fines, and boot camps.

Many intermediate punishment programmes have failed to achieve their objectives. Initiated in hopes of reducing prison crowding (by diverting less serious offenders from prison), reducing recidivism (by enhancing surveillance and some services), and reducing costs (by shifting offenders from more-expensive prisons to less-expensive community programmes), in many programmes none of these goals are being realized. When tested, these programmes generally achieve no worse, but no better, recidivism rates than do prisons when comparable groups of offenders are compared. Many judges order intermediate punishments for offenders who otherwise would receive probation. This increases costs. Moreover, because intermediate sanctions are more intensive and structured than probation, more condition violations and new offences are observed and acted upon; in many programmes 40 to 50 per cent of offenders are ejected for misconduct and sent to prison or gaol as punishment. Since many of these offenders would in past years have received probation, they are in effect shifted twice upwards, first to an intermediate sanction and then to prison. This also increases costs. If intermediate punishments are to achieve their goals, it has become clear that standards are needed both for assigning offenders to particular penalties and for setting 'back-up' penalties for violations of programme conditions.

A few states have taken tentative steps toward standards for use of intermediate sanctions. Washington allows for modest interchangeability of punishments (e.g. day-for-day substitution of community service days for up to thirty days confinement). Oregon, in addition to setting presumptive sentencing ranges in months, specifies 'punishment units' for each cell in its guide-lines grid, to provide a generic coin to permit (an as yet uncompleted task) convertibility of sanctions. Pennsylvania includes the words 'intermediate punishments' in the lower levels of its guide-lines, although no other guidance is offered. Many Minnesota counties, and some individual judges across the country, use local guide-lines for non-custodial penalties.

There are, however, no well-established models for devising comprehensive systems of structured sentencing discretion that incorporate intermediate punishments. Both mechanics and normative rationales need development. Unusually, policy-makers are interested in learning what theorists and philosophers can tell them, and, if the advice makes sense, policy-makers are likely to pay attention.

Two broad, albeit not fully developed, approaches have been proposed. One, associated with Andrew von Hirsch, Martin Wasik, and Andrew Ashworth, among others, calls for stacking of punishments: prison terms scaled to offence severity for the most serious crimes, restrictive community sanctions for the next-most-serious, large financial penalties for the next-most-serious, and so on, allowing relatively little latitude for imposition of different kinds of punishment on like-situated offenders (Wasik and von Hirsch 1988; Ashworth 1992). A second, proposed by Norval Morris and me, allows for much greater substitution and interchangeability of punishments and proportions maximum penal vulnerability to offence severity but allows substantial discretion to impose less severe sentences (Morris and Tonry 1990).

Increased interest in intermediate sanctions has sharply posed the conflict between principles of proportionality and parsimony. Concern for proportionality calls for like treatment of like-situated offenders. Concern for parsimony, a Hippocratic criminal justice prescription to do least harm, calls for imposing the least severe punishment that meets legitimate social purposes.

The tension between proportionality and parsimony has always existed below the surface in indeterminate sentencing systems, and is likely to survive silently in recent Swedish and English schemes that rely on principles rather than numbers for guidance to judges. Without guide-lines, judges can balance concerns for deserved punishments and parsimony in individual cases. Lip service can be paid to concern for horizontal equity, avoiding disparity, and treating like cases alike. Without concrete criteria of proportionate sentencing, individual sentences cannot easily be assessed for their consistency with proportionality principles.

The tension between proportionality and parsimony, however, became apparent when American jurisdictions began to develop sentencing guide-lines for prison sentences and it became acute when policy-makers began to work on standards for non-custodial penalties. American sentencing guide-lines to date mostly set standards for prison sentences calibrated to measures of current and past criminality. Proportionality is a prominent feature. Guidelines derive in part from concern to alleviate sentencing disparities; once offences are scaled for severity, some proportionality between penalties for different offences inexorably follows. In effect, sentencing guide-lines for prison sentences prefer proportionality over parsimony. If some sentences are harsher than judges believe appropriate, the harshness is said to be justifiable because the punishment is no more or less severe than that suffered by 'like-situated' offenders.

Justification and Distribution

The tension between proportionality and parsimony and the problem of just deserts in an unjust world are the fundamental problems facing an applied philosophy of punishment concerning intermediate sanctions. This section attempts to frame these issues by considering how Bentham and Kant might address proportionality in distribution and then looking at how modern writers have addressed it.

Proportionality based on justification

Neither classical utilitarian punishment theories in principle nor classical retributive theories in practice provide convincing explanations of why punishment should (or can) observe strict proportionality conditions.

Proportionality is presumably a value for utilitarians only to the extent that its non-observance produces net dissatisfaction. For utilitarians, invoking Bentham, punishment itself is an evil and should be used as sparingly as possible: 'upon the principle of utility, if [punishment] ought at all to be admitted, it ought only to be admitted in as far as it promises to exclude some greater evil' (Bentham 1948 [1789]: 281, quoted in Pincoffs 1966: 20).

No doubt utilitarian concerns require some observance of proportionality in punishment. Punishments completely divorced from community notions of fairness (in our time, perhaps, to refuse to punish child abusers, or to sentence two of three equally culpable participants in a crime to five years imprisonment and the third to a $50 fine) would produce unacceptable levels of dissatisfaction and indicate, on utility grounds, that some greater acknowledgement of the importance of violated community values is required; however, that imposes at most only a weak proportionality condition, relating punishment not to notions of desert but to notions of social consequences.

Thoroughgoing retributivists, for whom a retributive justification of punishment entails retribution in distribution, might prefer a system of perfectly proportioned punishments, but in practice such a system is unrealizable. Kant's principle of equality, the Right of Retaliation, 'the mode and measure of punishment which public justice takes as its principle and standard', has practical limits. It may be that 'the principle of equality . . . may be rendered by saying that the undeserved evil which anyone commits on another is to be regarded as perpetrated on himself' (Kant 1887 [1797]: 195–7), but it is far from clear what that means. Capital punishment for murder, a $500 penalty for a $500 theft, perhaps (squeamishly) a beating for an assault; these crimes and punishments satisfy the test. But how to punish an attempted murder, a rape, emotional abuse of the elderly, securities fraud, environmental crimes? No doubt systems of scaled punishment can be devised, but only with formidable working out of details. Does Kant's principle of equality require punishment scaled to the offender's culpability, to the offender's benefit, to the victim's harm? What of villainous attempts that serendipitously produce no harm? What of venial crimes that unforeseeably produce great harm? Is the offender's evil-doing to be assessed as the Recording Angel would, taking account of his weaknesses, the pressures to which he was subject, his motives, or primarily as measured by the objective evil his offence embodies?

Proportionality in distribution

The normative conflict concerning proportionality in distribution is between those (e.g. Ashworth 1992; von Hirsch 1992) who believe that equality and proportion in distribution are overridingly important and those (Hart 1968, Honderich 1989: 237–41; Morris and Tonry 1990: ch. 4; Walker 1991: ch. 15) who do not.

There are at least three major categories of writers on punishment who argue for weak proportionality conditions. First, writing in a utilitarian framework, and positing that punishment has principally preventive purposes, H. L. A. Hart writes of 'the somewhat hazy requirement that "like cases be treated alike" ' (1968: 24). Hart's argument for this modest recognition of proportionality is, however, not retributively premissed but derives from concern for the adverse social effects of divorcing punishment too greatly from common morality: 'for where the legal gradation of crime expressed in the relative severity of penalties diverges sharply from this rough scale, there is a risk of confusing common morality or flouting it and bringing the law into contempt' (p. 25).

Second, proponents of hybrid theories, including Morris (1974) and Honderich (1989), argue that principled systems of punishment must take account of both preventive and retributive considerations. Honderich, for example, argues that retribution, in James Fitzjames Stephens's sense of revenge and satisfaction of grievance, and deterrence, each have roles to play (1989: 233–7). Morris (1974) argues for a system of limiting retributivism in which punishment's primary purposes are preventive but subject to the desert constraint that punishments be 'not undeserved' and, within the range of not undeserved punishments, the parsimonious constraint that no punishment be imposed that is more severe than is necessary to achieve legitimate social purposes.

Third, proponents of a variety of ideal punishment theories reject their policy implications on 'just deserts in an unjust world' grounds but presumably would allow room for distributive echoes of their ideal rationales. R. A. Duff (1986), for example, rejects his own retributive/ expressive ideal theory in favour of deterrent approaches for social injustice reasons. This is my own view as well: in the abstract I have some sympathy for a retributive scheme with strong proportionality conditions; in practice, observing that the vast preponderance of common law offenders are poor, ill educated, often mentally subnormal, and often from minority groups, I believe that punishment strongly committed to proportionality will exacerbate social injustice and further disadvantage the already disadvantaged.

The Principle of Proportionality

Andrew von Hirsch has, over the last fifteen years (e.g. 1976, 1985, 1992), shown how a punishment system can be devised and justified that has equality and proportionality as central elements. For many people, there is strong intuitive appeal in a punishment system that attaches high value to equality and proportionality. Public opinion surveys have repeatedly demonstrated strong public support for the maxim 'treat like cases alike and different cases differently' (e.g. Doble, Immerwahr, and Richardson 1991).

Von Hirsch acknowledges both the limits of Kant's 'principle of equality' and human incapacity to specify the single ideally appropriate punishment for any individual offender who has committed a particular offence, but none the less offers a comprehensive scheme for assuring proportionality. He distinguishes between ordinal and cardinal magnitudes of punishments (1985: ch. 4). The cardinal magnitude is the unknowable, single deserved penalty. Ordinal magnitude indicates a crime's seriousness relative to other crimes. In von Hirsch's scheme, cardinal magnitude can be approximated or negotiated for use in setting the 'anchoring points' of a punishment scale, the most and (possibly) the least severe punishments that can appropriately be imposed on offenders. Within these anchoring points, punishments can be scaled in terms of relative severity of offences. Assuming, for example, that crimes were divided into fifteen severity categories, level 8 offences should, all else being equal, be punished more severely than level 7 offences and less severely than level 9 offences. Thus, the combination of cardinal anchors with ordinal rankings celebrates equality (all level 8 offences receive similar punishments) and proportionality (less serious offences receive less severe punishments, more serious offences receive more severe punishments). Some subsidiary issues remain a bit vague, including specification of anchoring points, the step problem (how many severity categories), and the interval problem (are the severity differences between offence levels the same throughout the scale, or may it be that, for example, level 10 offences are only 10 per cent more serious than level 9 offences while level 5 offences are twice as serious as those at level 4?). In a work in progress, von Hirsch is addressing these and other questions.

Rationale

The overall premiss of von Hirsch's argument is that punishment is an exercise in blaming, and proportionality is a necessary implication. Persons committing relatively more severe offences are relatively more blameworthy and deserve relatively more severe punishments.

Prior record

Von Hirsch's punishment scheme is based principally on *offences*, with only minor adjustments to take account of prior criminality. Some writers on just deserts (Fletcher 1978; Singer 1979) argue that prior criminality should have no effect on punishment for a new crime; prior penalties have 'paid for' prior crimes.

Von Hirsch allows some increases of penalty for past crimes on the rationale that penalties for a first offence should be somewhat less than is deserved. Because a first offence may be out of character and result from extenuating situational conditions, first offenders may be less blameworthy than it appears and should be given the benefit of the doubt. For some number of subsequent offences, a gradually disappearing discount may be appropriate. Thereafter each offence should receive its full, deserved, proportionate punishment.

Measure of offence

Although von Hirsch has written about concepts of scaling crime sever-ity, his proportionality analysis takes criminal codes more or less as given. Thus, answers to classical, substantive law harm-versus-culpability argu-ments—whether attempts should be punished as seriously as completed crimes, whether fortuitous harm (the picked pocket containing the unex-pected thousand-dollar coin, the assault that unforeseeably results in death) is relevant to punishment, whether there should be a general defence of necessity—do not shape the scale.

Measure of culpability

Von Hirsch's scheme is premissed on legal, rather than moral, assess-ments of blameworthiness (although the rationale for leniency for first offenders shades into character assessment). The offender is to be blamed for the *offence*, not for the moral culpability it expresses. If Jean Valjean and Leona Helmsley are both convicted of stealing bread, they are to be blamed for stealing bread and identically punished accordingly. Although von Hirsch coined the phrase 'just deserts in an unjust society' in *Doing Justice* (1976), he argues that, on balance, disadvantaged offenders will be better served under a desert scheme than under a utilitarian scheme: they will be punished no more severely than others for a given offence (as they might under predictive (more likely to reoffend) or deterrent (more likely to be tempted) systems). And if they are stigmatized by conviction and punishment, at least the resulting 'disabilities are the consequence of the person's own actions in having violated the law' (1976: 148).

Standard punishments

Just as offences are considered generically for purposes of scaling and punishment, punishments are designed to deal with 'standard cases' and the 'characteristic onerousness of various sanctions' (von Hirsch 1990: 10). One contrary view, as with the contrary view of offender culpability, would be to consider the subjective impact of the sanction on the offender. Another would be to take account of the objective conditions of different kinds of institutions, different probation regimes, and so on.

Von Hirsch notes these possibilities but responds in three ways. First, the 'law generally works with standard cases', and why not here? Second, in special (limited) circumstances, such as illness or advanced age, there might be deviations from the standard case. Third, although sanction severity depends in part on subjective painfulness, it also depends on 'the moral importance of the rights taken away' (1990: 10) and prison deprives crucial liberty rights of free movement and association.

Von Hirsch's scheme could provide a comprehensive desert-based system of punishment. The question is whether such a system offers a just and practicable system for punishing convicted offenders.

Critique of Principle of Proportionality

Efforts to apply philosophers' distinctions to policy-makers' decisions necessarily raise different concerns than do disagreements among philosophers. Current initiatives to increase use of 'non-custodial' penalties in the United Kingdom and 'intermediate' sanctions in the United States necessarily require translation of theorists' distinctions into practitioners' realities.

It is at this point of translation that the case for strong proportionality conditions breaks down. There are at least five major difficulties. First, strong proportionality conditions require objectification of categories of offenders and offences that are oversimplified and overinclusive. Second, proportionality arguments are often premissed on objective legal measures of desert, typically current and past crimes, rather than on the subjective degree of moral culpability expressed by the offender, under particular circumstances and conditions. Third, strong proportionality conditions run head-on into 'just deserts in an unjust society'. Fourth, strong proportionality conditions violate notions of parsimony by requiring imposition of unnecessarily severe punishments in individual cases in order to assure formal equivalence of suffering. Fifth, strong proportionality conditions presuppose that imposition of offenders' deserved punishments is an overriding moral imperative rather than one of several competing ethical considerations.

The illusion of 'like-situated offenders'

If recent efforts in the United Kingdom and the United States to increase use of intermediate sanctions are to succeed, the appropriateness of different punishments for 'like-situated offenders' must be recognized.

'Like-situated offender' is nested in quotation marks to express the artificiality of notions of like-situated offenders, comparable crimes, and generic punishments. A strong proportionality-in-punishment argument insists on equal treatment of like-situated offenders and proportionately different treatment of differently situated offenders. A fundamental difficulty is that this assumes that offenders can conveniently and justly be placed into a manageable number of more-or-less desert categories and that standard punishments can be prescribed for each category. Unfortunately, neither side of the desert–punishment equation lends itself to standardization.

Neither offenders nor punishments come in standard cases. The practice of dividing offenders and punishments into generic categories produces much unnecessary suffering and provides only illusory proportionality. A look at Minnesota's sentencing guide-lines shows why.

Fig. 1 sets out the original 1980 Minnesota sentencing guide-lines grid, which was expressly premissed on 'modified just deserts'.[2] Offences are divided on the vertical axis into ten categories and on the horizontal axis into seven categories of criminal history. An offender's presumptive sentence is determined by consulting the cell at which the row containing his conviction offence meets the column expressing his criminal history. Cases falling in cells below the bold black line are presumed bound for state prison for a term of months within the narrow range specified. Cases falling above the line are presumed not bound for prison (the number in the above-the-line cells represents the prison sentence to be imposed if the offender fails satisfactorily to complete a non-prison sentence).

Because the guide-lines attach high value to proportionality, 'departures' are discouraged. Either party may appeal a departure which, to be upheld, must be found to have been based on 'substantial and compelling' reasons. Rules set out illustrative bases for departures and forbid some. For example, the original rules prohibited departures based on offenders' educational, vocational, family, or marital circumstances and also forbade departures based on predictions of dangerousness or 'amenability' to treatment.[3] The reasons behind these prohibitions are not unattractive—to prevent judges from favouring more advantaged, often white, offenders over more disadvantaged, often black or Indian, offenders, to prevent imposition or prolongation of prison sentences on rehabilitative or incapacitative grounds, and to prevent judges from departing from presumptive prison sentences for middle-class offenders because they are especially amenable to non-incarcerative sentences.

Minnesota's tidy system, whatever its abstract merits, overaggregates offenders in at least four ways. First, consider Table 1, which shows the offences that fall within offence severity levels five and six, and Table 2, which shows the rudiments of the scheme for calculating criminal histories. Persons convicted of solicitation of some forms of prostitution are

Figure 1. Minnesota sentencing guidelines grid (in months)

Severity Levels of Conviction Offence		Criminal History Score						
		0	1	2	3	4	5	6
Unauthorized Use of Motor Vehicle Possession of Marijuana	I	12*	12*	12*	15	18	21	24
Theft-related Crimes ($150–2,500) Sale of Marijuana	II	12*	12*	14	17	20	23	27 / 25–29
Theft Crimes ($150–2,5000)	III	12*	13	16	19	22 / 21–23	27 / 25–29	32 / 30–34
Burglary—Felony intent Receiving Stolen Goods ($150–2,500)	IV	12*	15	18	21	25 / 24–26	32 / 30–34	41 / 37–45
Simple Robbery	V	18	23	27	30 / 29–31	38 / 36–40	46 / 43–49	54 / 50–58
Assault, 2nd Degree	VI	21	26	30	34 / 33–35	44 / 42–46	54 / 50–58	65 / 60–70
Aggravated Robbery	VII	24 / 23–25	32 / 30–34	41 / 38–44	49 / 45–53	65 / 60–70	81 / 75–87	97 / 90–104
Assault, 1st Degree Criminal Sexual Conduct, 1st Degree	VIII	43 / 41–45	54 / 50–58	65 / 60–70	76 / 71–81	95 / 89–101	113 / 106–120	132 / 124–140
Murder, 3rd Degree	IX	97 / 94–100	119 / 116–122	127 / 124–130	149 / 143–155	176 / 168–184	205 / 195–215	230 / 218–242
Murder, 2nd Degree	X	116 / 111–121	140 / 133–147	162 / 153–171	203 / 192–214	243 / 231–255	284 / 270–298	324 / 309–339

Source: Minnesota Sentencing Guidelines Commission (1980).

Notes:

* One year and one day.

Italicized numbers within the grid denote the range within which a judge may sentence without the sentence being deemed a departure.

Table 1. *Offence levels V and VI, Minnesota Sentencing Guidelines* (1 January 1980 version)

Level V
Vehicular homicide
Criminal sexual conduct (3rd degree)—statutory rape, offender more than 2 years older
Manslaughter (2nd degree)
Perjury—in felony trial or firearms permit application
Possession of incendiary device
Robbery
Solicitation of prostitution
Tampering with a witness

Level VI
Arson (2nd degree)—with over $2,500 loss
Assault (2nd degree)—with a deadly weapon
Burglary of a dwelling while armed
Criminal sexual conduct (2nd degree)—statutory rape
Criminal sexual conduct (4th degree)—forcible rape or incompetent victim
Escape—with violence or threat
Kidnapping—victim released unharmed
Receipt of stolen goods—over $2,500
Sale of hallucinogens
Sale of heroin
Sale of other narcotics

Source: Minnesota Sentencing Guidelines Commission (1980).

Table 2. *Criminal history score, Minnesota Sentencing Guidelines* (1 January 1980 version)

Each previous felony conviction	1 point
Current offence committed while on probation or parole, in gaol or prison, or released pending sentencing for prior crime	1 point
Four prior misdemeanour convictions	1 point
Two prior gross misdemeanour convictions	1 point

Source: Minnesota Sentencing Guidelines Commission (1980).

considered equally as culpable as people convicted of robbery or second degree manslaughter, and persons convicted of four minor property misdemeanours are considered as culpable as people convicted of a violent felony. A person convicted of solicitation with four prior misdemeanour convictions is thus, for Minnesota sentencing purposes, like-situated to a person convicted of manslaughter or robbery with a prior robbery conviction. Similarly, a person convicted of sale of marijuana with four misdemeanour convictions is like-situated to a person convicted of forcible rape with a prior rape conviction. There are plausible arguments for why offenders were grouped and criminal history scores calibrated as they were. The Minnesota commission was serious and idealistic in making these decisions. None the less, at day's end, offenders classified by Minnesota as like-situated will in many peoples' eyes look very unlike indeed.

Second, Minnesota's guide-lines are based on *conviction offences*,[4] which are at best imperfect and inconsistent measures of culpability. Because of ubiquitous plea bargaining in the United States, one of two equal participants in a robbery may be convicted of robbery and the other of aggravated robbery. Similarly, one may plead guilty to the reduced charge of robbery while the other is convicted at trial of aggravated robbery. Of two otherwise comparable robbers, one might be charged in a rural county where prosecutorial policy requires guilty pleas to the full offence (aggravated robbery), whilst another is allowed to plead to robbery in an urban county where aggravated robberies are common and office policy routinely permits acceptance of pleas to lesser offences. For reasons of local prosecution priorities, or limited manpower, or concern with evidentiary problems, one offender may be convicted of a greatly reduced offence while another comparable offender not affected by those considerations will be convicted of the full offence. The point is not to challenge the legitimacy of the considerations that lead to convictions of particular crimes in particular cases, but to point out that offenders convicted of the same offence may have committed very different acts reflecting very different culpability and, conversely, that offenders convicted of different crimes may have committed comparable acts with similar culpability.

Third, looking behind the grid, Minnesota allows little play for non-criminal-record factors to influence penalties. Consider a minority offender who grew up in a single-parent, welfare-supported household, who has several siblings in prison, and who was formerly drug-dependent but who has been living in a common law marriage for five years, has two children whom he supports, and has worked steadily for three years at a service station—first as an attendant, then an assistant mechanic, and now a mechanic. In Minnesota, none of these personal characteristics are supposed to influence the sentencing decision, and certainly not to justify imposition of a non-custodial sentence on a presumed prison-bound offender. For people who believe in individualized sentences, on either utilitarian or retributive grounds, Minnesota's refusal to consider my hypothetical offender's promising features will seem regrettable. For people concerned by the gross over-representation in courts, gaols, and prisons of deeply disadvantaged people, Minnesota's refusal to consider evidence that my hypothetical offender is overcoming the odds will seem deeply regrettable.

Fourth, Minnesota attaches no significance to the collateral effects of a prison sentence on the offender, or on the offender's family or children, what Nigel Walker (1991: 106–8) calls incidental (on the offender) and obiter (on the offender's dependants and associates) effects of punishment. Incarceration for a drug crime for a woman raising children by herself may result in the break-up of her family and placement of her children in foster homes or institutions, or in homes of relatives who will not be responsible care-providers. Incarceration of an employed father and husband may mean loss of the family's home and car, perhaps the break-up of a marriage, perhaps the creation of welfare dependency by the wife and children. To ignore that incidental and obiter effects of punishments vary widely among seemingly like-situated offenders is to ignore things that most people find important.

Thus, for a wide diversity of reasons, offenders whom Minnesota's sentencing guide-lines treat as like-situated often are not. A similar analysis could be offered of the punishment side of the crime and punishment equation. Objectively, punishments valued in the generic coin of imprisonment can be very different. In most American jurisdictions, a prison sentence means 'placed in the custody of the department of corrections', which in turn can mean anything from placement in a fear-ridden, gang-dominated maximum security prison under lock-up twenty-three hours a day, through placement in a minimum security camp or campus, to home confinement. Objectively, a sentence to twenty-four months probation can mean anything from living normally and mailing a bi-monthly post-card to the probation office to being contacted ten to twenty-five times a month, reporting to the probation office three times a week, observing a curfew, and being subject to frequent unannounced urinalyses.

Subjectively, three years' imprisonment may mean very different things to a 23-year-old gang member, for whom it is a rite of passage; a 40-year-old employed husband and father, for whom it will likely destroy the material conditions of his and his family's lives; a frightened, effeminate 20-year-old middle-class student, for whom it may result in sexual victimization; or a 70-year-old, for whom it may be life imprisonment.

Problems of objectification of crimes, offenders, and punishments are especially stark in a numerical guide-lines system. In systems that feature written policy guide-lines, they lurk beneath the surface. The Minnesota illustration is generally relevant to analysis of proportionality in punishment, however, because it makes real world implications of strong proportionality conditions starkly apparent. If proportionality is an, or the, overriding principle in the distribution of punishment in practice, then the imperfections of objectification that I describe are presumably regrettable but acceptable costs to be paid for a principled punishment system. If they appear unacceptable, the problem may be that the principle of proportionality offers less helpful guidance than its proponents urge.

Objective measures of responsibility

Von Hirsch's proportionality argument relies on objective measures of penal deservedness. This is curious. Desert theories, especially blaming theories, are premissed on notions of individual blameworthiness, which seem inexorably linked to particularized judgments about moral responsibility. Objective measures of harm are seldom sufficient for conviction in the criminal law: that is why doctrines of competency, *mens rea*, and affirmative defence exist and why doctrines like strict liability and felony-murder are disfavoured. If individualized moral judgments are germane to conviction, it is not obvious why they are not also germane to punishment.

If punishment is principally about blaming, surely it is relevant whether the offender was mentally impaired, socially disadvantaged, a reluctant participant, or moved by humane motives. Surely it is morally relevant, whatever the path to conviction, what the offender did, with what *mens rea*, and under what circumstances. Surely it is morally relevant whether a particular punishment will be more intensely experienced by one person than by another. In other words, the three subjective considerations that Minnesota's guide-lines ignore—what did he really do, what will the conditions of his sanction really be, will he suffer more intensely than others—are relevant to moral judgments of blameworthiness and proportionate punishments. Nigel Walker expresses this when he observes: 'Retributive reasoning would lead instead to a "personal price list" which would take into account not only gradations of harm but offenders' culpability and sensibility' (1991: 103).[5]

The failure of von Hirsch's arguments to take account of individualized differences in culpability and individual effects of punishment looks strange when we recall that von Hirsch's is a retributive theory. Utilitarian theories reject interpersonal comparisons of utility, as Lionel Robbins's classic essay (1938) explains, either on measurement grounds (variable intensity of satisfactions, utility monsters, and so on), or on normative grounds (no individual's satisfactions *should* count for more). However, utilitarian theories are concerned with general policies and aggregate social measures and not with fine-tuned moral judgments.

An unjust society

Punishment schemes that attach high value to proportionality necessarily ignore the differing material conditions of life, including poverty, social disadvantage, and bias, in which human personalities and characters take form. The substantive criminal law rejects motive for intention and in the English-speaking countries allows no formal excusing or mitigating defence of social disadvantage. Yet, in both the United Kingdom and the United States, most common law offenders are products of disadvantaged and deprived backgrounds and in both countries vastly disproportionate numbers of alleged, convicted, and imprisoned offenders are members of racial and ethnic minorities. The likelihood, for example, that a black American male is in prison today is eight times greater than that a white American male is in prison.

The problem of 'just deserts in an unjust world' is a fundamental problem for a strong proportionality constraint. Whether retributive theories are rationalized in terms of benefits and burdens, or equilibrium, or blaming, or condemnation, or penance, they must presume equal opportunities for all to participate in society. When some are disabled from full participation by discrimination, disability, or exclusion, by denial of access to public goods, by the burdens of social and economic disadvantage, it is difficult to claim that they enjoy the benefits of autonomy that produce obligation. To take just one example, proponents of benefits and burdens theories are hard pressed to explain how a person who is denied society's benefits deserves to be burdened by social obligation.

Many writers on the philosophy of punishment from both retributive and utilitarian premises recognize this problem. R. A. Duff, after developing an ideal theory of expressive punishment based on social condemnation and individual penance, rejects his own proposals in favour of a deterrence-premissed system because: 'punishment is not justifiable within our present legal system; it will not be justifiable unless and until we have brought about deep and far-reaching social, political, legal, and moral changes in ourselves and our society' (1986: 294).

Jeffrie Murphy, after developing an ideal punishment theory deriving from a Rawlsian original-position analysis of benefits and burdens, rejects it on grounds that it will not serve justice until 'we have restructured society in such a way that criminals genuinely do correspond to the only model that will render punishment permissible—i.e., make sure that they are autonomous and that they do benefit in the requisite sense' (1973: 110).

Even Andrew von Hirsch, arguing that a desert-based system of distribution will achieve less additional disadvantage to the disadvantaged than a utilitarian system, concludes none the less: 'as long as a substantial segment of the population is denied adequate opportunities for a livelihood, any scheme for punishing must be morally flawed' (1986: 149).

Not surprisingly, proponents of utilitarian and mixed punishment theories acknowledge the same problem. H. L. A. Hart, for example, in explaining the role of excuses in the substantive criminal law, notes in respect of deeply disadvantaged people, 'The admission that the excusing condition may be of no value to those who are below a minimum level of economic prosperity may mean, of course, that we should incorporate as a further excusing condition the pressure of gross forms of economic necessity' (1968: 51).

Ted Honderich, who argues for a hybrid punishment theory, observes: 'there is nothing that can be called the question of [punishment's] moral justification which is left to be considered if one puts aside the great question of the distribution of goods in society' (1989: 238–9).

In the United States, giving lip service to concern for offenders from disadvantaged backgrounds, most sentencing commissions have forbidden judges to 'depart' from sentencing guide-lines on grounds of offenders' personal circumstances. The putative rationale for such policies is that judges would favour middle-class offenders in mitigating sentences. This rationale is empirically misconceived and perverse; only an insignificant proportion of common law offenders are from middle- and upperclass backgrounds. The normal range of socio-economic backgrounds of common law offenders ranges from the deeply disadvantaged to the merely deprived. The chimerical middle-class offender is conspicuous by his absence. The perversity of such policies is that they forbid special treatment of offenders from deprived backgrounds who have achieved some personal successes. The minority offender from a broken home and a devastated neighbourhood who has none the less managed a reasonably stable domestic life, achieved some educational success, and found secure employment is as unentitled to a mitigated sentence as a middleclass offender. Thus, policies designed to prevent unfair treatment of disadvantaged offenders as a class have the likely effect of unfair treatment of disadvantaged offenders as individuals.

A proponent of proportionality might respond by noting that loosening proportionality conditions to permit mitigation of sentences for 'deserving' disadvantaged offenders also permits aggravation of sentences for the 'undeserving', especially those who appear likeliest to offend again. This is a different problem and one that can be addressed by placing strict proportionate limits on maximum sentences and by establishing stringent standards to guide decisions to aggravate punishments.

Parsimony

Proponents of strong proportionality conditions necessarily prefer equality over minimization of suffering. For nearly two decades in the United States, Andrew von Hirsch and Norval Morris have been disagreeing over the role of parsimony in punishment. Von Hirsch (1985) has argued for strong desert limits on punishment and high priority to pursuit of equality and proportionality in punishment. Morris (1974) has argued that desert is a limiting, not a defining, principle of punishment and that policy should prescribe imposition of the least severe 'not undeserved' sanction that meets legitimate policy ends. Within these outer bounds of 'not undeserved' punishments Morris has consistently argued for observance of a principle of parsimony.

To some extent Morris and von Hirsch have argued past each other. Morris argues that a desert approach is unnecessarily harsh and von Hirsch responds by noting that he personally favours relatively modest punishments and, in any case, desert schemes are not inherently more severe than other schemes. In turn, von Hirsch argues that Morris's 'not undeserved' proportionality constraints are vague, the breadth of allowable ranges of sentencing discretion is never specified, and Morris responds by noting that absolute measures of deserved punishment are unknowable and that his aim is to minimize imposition of penal suffering within bounds that any given community finds tolerable.

The problem is that they start from different major premisses—von Hirsch's is the 'principle of proportionality', Morris's the 'principle of parsimony'. The difference between them can be seen by imagining a comprehensive punishment scheme, perhaps resembling Minnesota's (see Fig. 1). Imagine that policy-makers have conscientiously classified all offenders into ten categories and, using von Hirsch's ordinal/cardinal magnitude and anchoring points approach, have decided that all offences at level VII deserve twenty-three- to twenty-five-month prison terms. Imagine further that reliable public opinion surveys have shown that 90 per cent of the general public would find a restrictive non-custodial punishment 'not unduly lenient' and a thirty-six month prison term 'not unduly severe' for level VII offences.

Von Hirsch would, I presume, argue that for non-exceptional cases concern for proportionality requires that persons convicted of level VII crimes receive at least a twenty-three-month prison term, even though public opinion would support much less severe punishments. To achieve greater proportionality, von Hirsch would punish some offenders much more severely than is socially or politically required.

Morris, by contrast, would presumably argue that imposing twenty-three-month terms on all level VII cases would be unjust because it would constitute imposition of punishment that is not required by public attitudes or preventive considerations. Morris would argue that, barring exceptional circumstances, no level VII offender should receive more than twenty-five months' incarceration but that many should receive less than twenty-three months. To achieve less aggregate suffering, Morris would punish some offenders much less severely than concern for proportionality would suggest.

The preceding hypothetical is overstated. Von Hirsch would, at least for exceptional cases, approve departures from the twenty-three- to twenty-five-month range or perhaps approve a wider range (for example, eighteen to twenty-eight months). Morris would almost certainly want to establish a normal upper bound lower than thirty-six months and would want to devise some system for assuring that level VII offenders receive roughly equivalent punishments.

Sorting out principles

Disagreements about just punishments, like disagreements about the death penalty or abortion, are often in the end disagreements about powerful intuitions or deeply embedded values. It may be that differences in view between those who give primacy to proportionality and those who give primacy to parsimony cannot be bridged.

The burden of persuasion should rest, however, it seems to me on those who reject Isaiah Berlin's observations that 'not all good things are compatible, still less all the ideals of mankind' (1969: 167) and that 'the necessity of choosing between absolute claims is then an inescapable characteristic of the human condition' (1969: 169).

Punishment raises at least two important conflicts between ideals—between the principles of proportionality and parsimony, between the quests for criminal justice and social justice.

Punishment is not unique in this respect. *Justice, Equal Opportunity, and the Family* (1983) by James Fishkin shows similar irreconcilable conflicts in ideals that are posed by family policy. Even in ideal theory, he argues, values inherent in support for equal opportunity conflict with values inherent in support for family autonomy. Notions of equal opportunity, he argues, must include a 'principle of merit', that 'there should be a fair competition among individuals for unequal positions in society' (p. 19), and a 'principle of equal life chances specifying roughly equal expectations for everyone regardless of the conditions into which they are born' (p. 20). Without equal life chances, both common experience and modern sociology instruct, scarce social goods will not be distributed according to merit. As Fishkin observes, 'if I can predict the outcomes achieved by an individual merely by knowing his or her race, sex, ethnic origin, or family background, then equality of life chances has not been realised' (p. 34).

If we were single-mindedly devoted to equal opportunity, then, we should view equalization of life chances as an overriding goal of social policy. However, Fishkin argues, efforts to equalize life chances run head on into another powerful principle, that the value of autonomy in a private sphere of liberty encompasses a principle of family autonomy, of non-intrusion by the state into the family's sphere of private liberty.

In other words, equal opportunity and family autonomy conflict fundamentally. Full respect for equal opportunity would involve intrusion into the family that would widely be seen as objectionably intrusive. Full respect for family autonomy would widely be seen as cruel disregard for children's basic needs.

And so it may be with punishment. Principles of proportionality and parsimony may simply conflict, with resolutions between them necessarily partial and provisional.

Reconciling Proportionality and Parsimony

A middle ground exists on which a punishment scheme can be built that honours both proportionality and parsimony—development of sentencing guide-lines that establish presumptive sentencing ranges in which the upper bounds are set in accordance with the proportionality principle and the lower bounds are sufficiently flexible to honour the parsimony principle. This would discourage disparately severe punishments, including aggravation of sentences on predictive or rehabilitative grounds beyond what would otherwise be deemed appropriate. If von Hirsch is correct as a social psychologist of punishment when he insists that desert schemes are not necessarily more severe than other schemes, use of proportionality constraints to set upper bounds (within higher statutory maxima) should result in upper-bound penalties that are no harsher than would occur in a scheme with narrow ranges. Below those upper bounds, however, judges could set sentences not premissed on 'standard cases' or 'standard punishments'.

The challenge is not to decide between proportionality and parsimony, but to balance them in ways that preserve important elements of each. This is not the place to discuss mechanics at length. A reconciliation can be sketched.[6]

Use proportionality to establish presumptive maximum sentences

Much of von Hirsch's proportionality analysis can be used in setting maximum bounds of sentencing authority for ordinary cases. By using standardized measures of offence severity, proportionate maximum sentences can be specified, the gap between those upper bounds and statutory maxima to be reserved for extraordinary cases subject to the provision of reasons and the possibility of appellate sentence review. The Advisory Council on the Penal System (1978) proposed such a scheme, albeit not in the vocabulary of guide-lines. The worst injustices in sentencing and the worst disparities are those suffered by people who receive aberrantly long or severe penalties. Presumptive guide-lines for maximum sentences scaled to proportionality could both lessen the likelihood of aberrantly severe penalties and achieve proportionality among those offenders receiving the most severe presumptive sentences.

Parsimony presumption

Within the authorized bounds, judges should be directed to impose the least severe sentence consistent with the governing purposes *at* sentencing (e.g., Morris and Tonry 1990: 90–2). Within, for example, any category of offences encompassed in an offence severity level in Minnesota's sentencing guide-lines grid, judges should be directed to consider monetary penalties or their equivalents (e.g., community service) when retribution or deterrence is the governing purpose, stringent community controls when incapacitation is at issue, and community controls with treatment conditions when sex or drug or alcohol treatment is called for, reserving incarcerative sentences only for cases when deterrence, public attitudes, or incapacitation seem to dictate. If the parsimony presumption favoured the least restrictive alternative, judges would have to devise particularized reasons for doing otherwise—including imposition of sentences for incapacitative or deterrent reasons.

Rough equivalence

Efforts to devise ways to make punishments interchangeable have foundered on proportionality's shoals. If prison is used as the norm, and all other penalties must be converted to carceral coin, interchangeability soon collapses. Almost inexorably, one day in prison equals two or more days of house arrest equals two or more days of community service. Something about the process seems to force literal thinking. If sentences must be proportionate in incarceration time, the scope for use of non-custodial penalties necessarily is limited.

Thinking about equivalences becomes easier if proportionality constraints are loosened. If any prison sentence up to twenty-four months can be imposed in a given case, then the range for substitution is broadened immensely.

Thinking about equivalences also becomes easier if prison is replaced by money, say a day's net pay, as the basic unit from and to which sanctions are converted.

Thinking about equivalences becomes easier if we think about different purposes to be served *at* sentencing in a given case. If the goals are retribution and deterrence, then prison and financial penalties ought to be fully interchangeable as might also, for the indigent, a combination of residential controls, community service, restitution, and supervision.

If, for normative reasons, sentencing guide-lines and guidance are to be scaled proportionately to the severity of crime, objectively measured, and expressed in standardized units of incarceration, objectively characterized, the scope for non-custodial penalties will necessarily be slight. It is not easy to devise non-custodial penalties that are objectively equivalent to twenty-three months' incarceration.

If non-custodial penalties are to be widely adopted and used, proportionality constraints must be loosened to take account of the almost infinite variety of offender circumstances, offence contexts, and punishment dimensions. If ways can be devised to institutionalize principles of both proportionality and parsimony in punishment, we are likely to do less injustice than if we establish systems that seek an illusion of equality of suffering for offenders in whose lives equality in most other things has been conspicuously absent.

Notes

1. Citations of sources for empirical assertions in this section can be found in Morris and Tonry (1990).
2. Since the guide-lines took effect in 1980, law-and-order political pressures have influenced statutory changes and policy decisions by the commission that have selectively but substantially increased penalties for controversial crimes and made the system's claims for principled scaling and proportionality weaker (Frase 1991).
3. Appellate decisions have since recognized limited 'amenability to probation' and 'non-amenability to prison' criteria for departures (see Frase 1991).
4. The US Sentencing Commission, to avoid problems described in this paragraph, based its guide-lines on 'relevant conduct', by which it refers to the defendant's actual behaviour and its consequences. In practice, prosecutors manipulate the federal guide-lines extensively but use more ingenious subterfuges (Federal Courts Study Committee 1990).
5. Walker defines 'sensibility': 'the intensity of the suffering, hardship, or inconvenience which a given penalty will inflict depends on the individual: on sex, age, social position, and so on' (Walker 1991: 99).
6. Among the issues that might be discussed: the strengths and weaknesses of the punishment units approach; whether sentencing grids should have two, three, four, or more 'bands' representing different presumptions concerning the appropriate type of sentence; at what offence severity level the normal offence is so serious that only incarceration sentences should be authorized; the widths of bands of authorized sentences for categories of cases; whether equivalences should be conceptualized in terms of suffering, intrusiveness, or some other measure. There is little literature on any of these subjects and this essay does not add to it.

References

Advisory Council on the Penal System (1978), *Sentences of Imprisonment: A Review of Maximum Penalties* (HM Stationery Office, London).

ASHWORTH, ANDREW (1992), 'Non-custodial Sentences', *Criminal Law Review*, 242–51.

BENTHAM, JEREMY (1948), *Introduction to the Principles of Morals and Legislation* (1789), ed. Wilfred Harrison (Oxford University Press, Oxford).

BERLIN, ISAIAH (1969), *Four Essays on Liberty* (Oxford University Press, Oxford).

DOBLE, JOHN, IMMERWAHR, STEPHEN, and RICHARDSON, AMY (1991), *Punishing Criminals: The People of Delaware Consider the Options* (The Public Agenda Foundation, New York).

DUFF, R. A. (1986), *Trials and Punishments* (Cambridge University Press, Cambridge).

160 *M. Tonry*

Federal Courts Study Committee (1990), *Report* (Administrative Office of the US Courts, Washington, DC).

FISHKIN, JAMES S. (1983), *Justice, Equal Opportunity, and the Family* (Yale University Press, New Haven, Conn.).

FLETCHER, GEORGE (1978), *Rethinking Criminal Law* (Little Brown, Boston).

FRASE, RICHARD (1991), 'Sentencing Reform in Minnesota: Ten Years After', *Minnesota Law Review*, 75: 727–54.

HART, H. L. A. (1968), *Punishment and Responsibility: Essays in the Philosophy of Law* (Oxford University Press, Oxford).

HONDERICH, TED (1989), *Punishment: The Supposed Justifications* (Polity, Cambridge).

KANT, IMMANUEL (1887), *Rechtslehre* (1797), pt. II, 49, trans. W. Hastie (T. & T. Clark, Edinburgh).

Minnesota Sentencing Guidelines Commission (1980), *Report to the Legislature: January 1, 1980* (Minnesota Sentencing Guidelines Commission, St Paul).

MORRIS, NORVAL (1974), *The Future of Imprisonment* (University of Chicago Press, Chicago).

—— and TONRY, MICHAEL (1990), *Between Prison and Probation: Intermediate Punishments in a Rational Sentencing System* (Oxford University Press, New York).

MURPHY, J. G. (1973), 'Marxism and Retribution', *Philosophy and Public Affairs*, 2: 217–43; as repr. in J. G. Murphy, *Retribution, Justice and Therapy* (Dordrecht, 1979), 93–115; this volume, p. 44.

PINCOFFS, EDMUND L. (1966), *The Rationale of Legal Punishment* (Humanities Press, New York).

ROBBINS, LIONEL (1938), 'Interpersonal Comparisons of Utility: A Comment', *Economic Journal*, 48: 635–41.

SINGER, RICHARD G. (1979), *Just Deserts: Sentencing Based on Equality and Desert* (Ballinger, Cambridge, Mass.).

VON HIRSCH, ANDREW (1976), *Doing Justice: The Choice of Punishments* (Hill & Wang, New York; rev. edn. 1986, Northeastern University Press, Boston).

—— (1985), *Past or Future Crimes: Deservedness and Dangerousness in the Sentencing of Criminals* (Rutgers University Press, New Brunswick, NJ).

—— (1990), 'Scaling Intermediate Punishments: A Comparison of Two Models', unpublished MS, Rutgers University Department of Criminal Justice, Rutgers, NJ.

—— (1992), 'Proportionality in the Philosophy of Punishment', in Michael Tonry (ed.), *Crime and Justice: A Review of Research* (University of Chicago Press, Chicago), 16: 55–98.

WALKER, NIGEL (1991), *Why Punish?* (Oxford University Press, Oxford).

WASIK, MARTIN, and VON HIRSCH, ANDREW (1988), 'Noncustodial Penalties and the Principles of Desert', *Criminal Law Review*, 555–72.

Preface: F. Zimring, 'Making the Punishment Fit the Crime: A Consumer's Guide to Sentencing Reform'

Zimring's essay was published in 1977, at the beginning of what was to be a major wave of sentencing reform in the USA (see Tonry 1988; von Hirsch and Ashworth 1992: ch. 5; and Preface to VON HIRSCH above). Responding to calls for a system of determinate sentencing, based on 'just deserts' and designed to eliminate discretion and disparity, Zimring highlights the difficulties which such programmes are liable to encounter, and the underlying political and cultural conflicts which make criminal justice so resistant to rational reform.

In the years since the essay was written, Zimring's scepticism has come to seem powerfully prescient. During that time the determinate sentencing movement has ceased to be a reforming crusade against an entrenched rehabilitative system, and has itself become the guiding philosophy in many jurisdictions. Many US states, as well as the federal court system, now have determinate sentencing statutes of one form or another (see Tonry 1987), as do some European states such as Sweden (see von Hirsch and Jareborg 1989). And although the Scottish and English judiciary have resisted any significant statutory constraints on 'judicial independence' in sentencing, penal theorists have been arguing for a more determinate, less discretionary sentencing system in Britain (see for instance Ashworth 1992; Wasik and Pease 1987). Increasingly, therefore, it is the pathologies of determinate sentencing which draw critical attention, rather than the problems which it initially sought to overcome.

Like TONRY's essay, Zimring's is sceptical about the prospects for achieving genuinely just and proportionate punishments through any statutory system of sentencing; but whilst TONRY focuses on problems internal to the process of judicial sentencing, Zimring reminds us that the penal fate of offenders depends crucially on the decisions made, and the discretions exercised, outside the particular context of judicial sentencing. We should be concerned not only about the dangers of injustice which may flow from fixed sentences unadjusted to individual cases (a point emphasized by TONRY), but also about the strengthening of prosecutorial discretion (which is largely invisible and thus uncontrolled), and about the 'legislative law and order syndrome'.

Zimring's description of criminal justice as a system of multiple discretions, with sentencing power distributed between legislature, prosecutors, judges, and parole authorities, is an important reminder that sentencing is not the monopoly of the trial judge (see also Bottomley 1973). Indeed, one might add to this list a fifth locus of sentencing power: prison officials, whose power to grant remission ('good time') can reduce a prison term by as much as 50 per cent (see Jacobs 1982). All too often the formal distinction between the courts, where justice is supposedly done, and the 'administration' that supposedly serves them, has prevented normative theories from addressing the real sources of penal power in modern systems (see Braithwaite and Pettit 1990 for an attempt to sketch a comprehensive theory of criminal justice; see also Foucault 1977 on the historical rise of executive power in the penal system).

Zimring suggests an alternative perspective on the issue of 'discretion' from that normally adopted in the contemporary literature. Evidence of systematic bias and discrimination in the use of discretion led many critics of rehabilitation to demand the abolition of discretionary decision-making, and a renewed emphasis on the strict rule of law. Zimring's account suggests that, because the rule of law cannot be self-enforcing, discretionary judgments will always be a feature of criminal justice: if they are curtailed at one point in the system, they are liable to re-emerge somewhere up or down the line, given the multiple pressures and values that operate in this field. But he also suggests that the distribution of discretionary powers between, for instance, prosecution, judge, and parole board, might allow a process of checking and balancing to take place, which will lead to more rather than fewer just and consistent outcomes. The aim should be to ensure that such discretionary powers are used justly and responsibly, not to attempt to abolish them altogether.

But, as Zimring also points out, hopes for the 'just' or 'rational' administration of justice run up against the problem that these very notions are chronically contested in our societies. The injustices, inconsistency, and discrimination which mar criminal justice may not after all be caused by failures of design or by maladministration. Rather, they may express underlying conflicts of value and principle—disagreements about the roots of crime and the worth of criminals; contradictions between the desire to do justice and the desire to reduce crime; schizoid wishes to deal with social problems without transforming mainstream social institutions; demands that action be taken but reluctance to will the necessary means. These are the echoes of larger political and cultural struggles, which will not be resolved merely through the reform of criminal justice.

References

ASHWORTH, A. J. (1992), *Sentencing and Criminal Justice* (London).
BOTTOMLEY, A. K. (1973), *Decisions in the Penal Process* (London).
BRAITHWAITE, J., and PETTIT, P. (1990), *Not Just Deserts* (Oxford).
FOUCAULT, M. (1977), *Discipline and Punish* (London).

JACOBS, J. B. (1982), 'Sentencing by Prison Personnel: Good Time', *UCLA Law Review*, 30/2: 217–20.

TONRY, M. (1987), *Sentencing Reform Impacts* (Washington, DC).

—— (1988), 'Structuring Sentencing', *Crime and Justice*, 12: 267–337.

VON HIRSCH, A., and ASHWORTH, A. J. (1992) (eds.), *Principled Sentencing* (Boston, Edinburgh).

—— and JAREBORG, N. (1989), 'Sweden's Sentencing Statute Enacted', *Criminal Law Review*, 275–81.

WASIK, M., and PEASE, K. (1987), *Sentencing Reform: Guidance or Guidelines* (Manchester).

Making the Punishment Fit the Crime: A Consumer's Guide to Sentencing Reform

FRANKLIN E. ZIMRING

In its current crisis the American system of criminal justice has no friends. Overcrowded, unprincipled, and ill-coordinated, the institutions in our society that determine whether and to what extent a criminal defendant should be punished are detested in equal measure by prison wardens and prisoners, cab drivers and college professors. What is more surprising (and perhaps more dangerous), a consensus seems to be emerging on the shape of desirable reform—reducing discretion and the widespread disparity that is its shadow, abolishing parole decisions based on whether a prisoner can convince a parole board he has been 'reformed', and creating a system in which punishment depends much more importantly than at present on the seriousness of the particular offence.

A number of books and committee reports that have endorsed these goals and proposed various structural reforms to achieve them are the stimulus for this essay. While diverse in style, vocabulary, and emphasis, at least six books in the past two years have proposed eroding the arenas of discretion in the system.[1] Some authors, such as James Q. Wilson and Ernst van den Haag, see reform as a path to enhancing crime control. Others, such as Andrew von Hirsch, the Twentieth Century Fund Committee and David Fogel, advocate reform for less utilitarian reasons, with titles or subtitles such as 'Doing Justice', 'A Justice Model of Corrections', and 'Fair and Certain Punishment'.

This note cannot comprehensively review such a rich collection of literature, nor is it politic for me to oppose justice, fairness, or certainty. Rather, I propose to summarize the present allocation of sentencing power in the criminal justice system and discuss some of the implications of the 'structural reforms' advocated in some current literature.

First published as number 12 of *Occasional Papers*, published by the Law School of the University of Chicago (1977).

Multiple Discretions in Sentencing

The best single phrase to describe the allocation of sentencing power in state and federal criminal justice is multiple discretion. Putting aside the enormous power of the police to decide whether to arrest, and to select initial charges, there are four separate institutions that have the power to determine criminal sentences—the legislature, the prosecutor, the judge, and the parole board or its equivalent.

The *legislature* sets the range of sentences legally authorized after conviction for a particular criminal charge. Criminal law in the United States is noted for extremely wide ranges of sentencing power, delegated by legislation to discretionary agents, with extremely high maximum penalties and very few limits on how much less than the maximum can be imposed. In practice, then, most legislatures delegate their sentencing powers to other institutions. For example, second degree murder in Pennsylvania, prior to 1973, was punishable by 'not more than 20 years' in the state penitentiary.[2] Any sentence above 20 years could not be imposed: any sentence below 20 years—including probation—was within the power of the sentencing judge.

The *prosecutor* is not normally thought of as an official who has, or exercises, the power to determine punishment. In practice, however, the prosecutor is the most important institutional determinant of a criminal sentence. He has the legal authority to drop criminal charges, thus ending the possibility of punishment. He has the legal authority in most systems to determine the specific offence for which a person is to be prosecuted, and this ability to select a charge can also broaden or narrow the range of sentences that can be imposed upon conviction. In congested urban court systems (and elsewhere) he has the absolute power to reduce charges in exchange for guilty pleas and to recommend particular sentences to the court as part of a 'plea bargain'; rarely will his recommendation for a lenient sentence be refused in an adversary system in which he is supposed to represent the punitive interests of the state.

The *judge* has the power to select a sentence from the wide range made available by the legislature for any charge that produces a conviction. His powers are discretionary—within this range of legally authorized sanctions his selection cannot be appealed, and is not reviewed. Thus, under the Pennsylvania system we studied, a defendant convicted of second degree murder can be sentenced to probation, one year in the penitentiary, or 20 years. On occasion, the legislature will provide a mandatory minimum sentence, such as life imprisonment for first degree murder, that reduces the judge's options once a defendant has been convicted of that particular offence. In such cases the prosecutor and judge retain the option to charge or convict a defendant for a lesser offence in order to retain their discretionary power.[3] More often the judge has a wide range of sentencing choices and, influenced by the prosecutor's recommendation, will select either a single sentence (e.g., two years) or a minimum and maximum sentence (e.g., not less than two nor more than five years) for a particular offender.

The *parole* or *correctional authority* normally has the power to modify judicial sentences to a considerable degree. When the judge pronounces a single sentence, such as two years, usually legislation authorizes release from prison to parole after a specified proportion of the sentence has been served. When the judge has provided for a minimum and maximum sentence, such as two to five years, the relative power of the correctional or parole authority is increased, because it has the responsibility to determine at what point in a prison sentence the offender is to be released. The parole board's decision is a discretionary one, traditionally made without guidelines or principles of decision.

This outline of our present sentencing system necessarily misses the range of variation among jurisdictions in the fifty states and the federal system, and oversimplifies the complex interplay among institutions in each system. It is useful, however, as a context in which to consider specific proposed reforms; it also helps to explain why the labyrinthine status quo has few articulate defenders. With all our emphasis on due process in the determination of guilt, our machinery for setting punishment lacks any principle except unguided discretion. Plea bargaining, disparity of treatment, and uncertainty are all symptoms of a larger malaise—the absence of rules or even guide-lines in determining the distribution of punishments. Other societies, less committed to the rule of law, or less infested with crime, might suffer such a system. Powerful voices are beginning to tell us we cannot.

Parole Under Attack

Of all the institutions that comprise the present system, parole is the most vulnerable—a practice that appears to be based on a now-discredited theoretical foundation of rehabilitation and individual predictability. The theory was that penal facilities rehabilitate prisoners and that parole authorities could select which inmates were ready, and when they were ready, to re-enter the community. The high-water mark of such thinking is the indeterminate sentence—a term of one-year-to-life at the discretion of the correctional authority for any adult imprisoned after conviction for a felony. Ironically, while this theory was under sustained (and ultimately successful) attack in California, New York was passing a set of drug laws that used the one-year-to-life sentence as its primary dispositive device. Yet we know (or think we know) that prison rehabilitation programmes 'don't work', and our capacities to make individual predictions of future behaviour are minimal.

So why not abolish parole in favour of a system where the sentence pronounced by the judge is that which is served by the offender? The costs of post-imprisonment sentence adjustments are many: they turn our prisons into 'acting schools', promote disparity, enrage inmates, and undermine both justice and certainty.[4]

There are, however, a number of functions performed by parole that have little to do with the theory of rehabilitation or individual predictability. A parole system allows us to advertise heavy criminal sanctions loudly at the time of sentencing and later reduce sentences quietly. This 'discounting' function is evidently of some practical importance, because David Fogel's plan to substitute 'flat time' sentences for parole is designed so that the advertised 'determinate sentences' for each offence are twice as long as the time the offender will actually serve (since each prisoner gets a month off his sentence for every month he serves without a major disciplinary infraction). In a system that seems addicted to barking louder than it really wants to bite, parole (and 'good time' as well) can help protect us from harsh sentences while allowing the legislature and judiciary the posture of law and order.

It is also useful to view the abolition of parole in terms of its impact on the distribution of sentencing power in the system. Reducing the power of the parole board increases the power of the legislature, prosecutor, and judge. If the abolition of parole is not coupled with more concrete legislative directions on sentencing, the amount of discretion in a system will not decrease; instead, discretionary power will be concentrated in two institutions (judge and prosecutor) rather than three. The impact of this reallocation is hard to predict. Yet parole is usually a statewide function, while judges and prosecutors are local officials in most states. One function of parole may be to even out disparities in sentencing behaviour among different localities. Abolishing parole, by decentralizing discretion, may increase sentencing disparity, at least as to prison sentences, because the same crime is treated differently by different judges and prosecutors. Three discretions may be better than two!

There are two methods available to avoid these problems. Norval Morris argues for retaining a parole function but divorcing it from rehabilitation and individual prediction by providing that a release date be set in the early stages of an offender's prison career. This would continue the parole functions of 'discounting' and disparity reduction, while reducing uncertainty and the incentive for prisoners to 'act reformed'. It is a modest, sensible proposal, but it is not meant to address the larger problems of discretion and disparity in the rest of the system.[5]

Fixed Price Sentencing

A more heroic reform is to reallocate most of the powers now held by judges and parole authorities back to the legislature. Crimes would be defined with precision and specific offences would carry specified sentences, along with lists of aggravating and mitigating circumstances that could modify the penalty. The three books with 'justice' or 'fairness' in their titles advocate this 'price list' approach, albeit for different reasons and with different degrees of sophistication. The Twentieth Century Fund study goes beyond advocating this approach and sets out sections of a sample penal code, although all members of the committee do not agree on the specific 'presumptive sentences' provided in the draft.

There is much appeal in the simple notion that a democratically elected legislature should be capable of fixing sentences for crimes against the community. Yet this is precisely what American criminal justice has failed to do, and the barriers to a fair and just system of fixed sentences are imposing. The Twentieth Century Fund scheme of 'presumptive sentences', because it is the most sophisticated attempt to date, will serve as an illustration of the formidable collection of problems that confront a system of 'Fair and Certain' legislatively determined punishments. In brief, the proposal outlines a scale of punishments for those first convicted that ranges (excluding murder) from six years in prison (aggravated assault) to probation (shoplifting). Premeditated murder is punished with ten years' imprisonment. Burglary of an empty house by an unarmed offender has a presumptive sentence of six months; burglary of an abandoned dwelling yields a presumptive sentence of six months' probation. The sample code clearly aims at singling out violent crimes such as armed robbery for heavier penalties, while the scale for nonviolent offenders led two of the eleven Task Force members to argue that the 'range . . . appears to be unrealistically low in terms of obtaining public or legislative support'.[6] Repeat offenders receive higher presumptive sentences, under specific guide-lines.

The Task Force proposal produces in me an unhappily schizophrenic response. I agree with the aims and priorities of the report, at the same time that I suspect the introduction of this (or many other) reform proposals into the legislative process might do more harm than good.

Why so sceptical? Consider a few of the obstacles to making the punishment fit the crime:

1. *The incoherence of the criminal law.*[7] Any system of punishment that attaches a single sanction to a particular offence must define offences with a morally persuasive precision that present laws do not possess. In my home state of Illinois, burglary is defined so that an armed housebreaker is guilty of the same offence as an 18-year-old who opens the locked glove compartment of my unlocked stationwagon. Obviously, no single punishment can be assigned to crime defined in such sweeping terms. But can we be precise? The Task Force tried, providing illustrative definitions of five different kinds of night-time housebreaking with presumptive sentences from two years (for armed burglary, where the defendant menaces an occupant) to six months' probation. The Task Force did not attempt to deal with daylight or non-residential burglary.

The problem is not simply that any such penal code will make our present statutes look like Reader's Digest Condensed Books: we lack the capacity to define into formal law the nuances of situation, intent, and social harm that condition the seriousness of particular criminal acts. For example, the sample code provides six years in prison for 'premeditated assault' in which serious harm was intended by the offender, and one-third that sentence where 'serious harm was not intended'. While there may be some conceptual distinction between these two mental states, one cannot confidently divide hundreds of thousands of gun and knife attacks into these categories to determine whether a 'Fair and Certain Punishment' is six years or two.

Rape, an offence that encompasses a huge variety of behaviours, is graded into three punishments: six years (when accompanied by an assault that causes bodily injury); three years (when there is no additional bodily harm); and six months (when committed on a previous sex partner, with no additional bodily harm). Two further aggravating conditions are also specified.[8] Put aside for a moment the fact that prior consensual sex reduces the punishment by a factor of six and the problem that rape with bodily harm has a 'presumptive sentence' one year longer than intentional killing. Have we really defined the offence into its penologically significant categories? Can we rigorously patrol the border between forcible rape without additional bodily harm and that with further harm—when that distinction can mean the difference between six months and six years in the penitentiary?

I am not suggesting that these are problems of sloppy drafting. Rather, we may simply lack the ability to comprehensively define in advance those elements of an offence that should be considered in fixing a criminal sentence.

2. *The paradox of prosecutorial power.* A system of determinate sentences reallocates the sentencing power shared by the judge and parole authorities to the legislature and the prosecutor. While the judge can no longer select from a wide variety of sanctions after conviction, the prosecutor's powers to select charges and to plea-bargain remain. Indeed, a criminal code like that proposed by the Twentieth Century Fund Task Force will enhance the relative power of the prosecutor by removing parole and restricting the power of judges. The long list of different offences proposed in the report provides the basis for the exercise of prosecutorial discretion: the selection of initial charges and the offer to reduce charges (charge-bargaining) are more important in a fixed-price system precisely because the charge at conviction determines the sentence. The prosecutor files a charge of 'premeditated' killing (10 years) and offers to reduce the charge to 'intentional' killing (5 years) in exchange for a guilty plea. In most of the major crimes defined by the Task Force—homicide, rape, burglary, larceny, and robbery—a factual nuance separates two grades of the offence where the presumptive sentence for the higher grade is twice that of the lower grade.[9]

This means that the disparity between sentences following a guilty plea and those following jury trial is almost certain to remain. Similarly, disparity between different areas and different prosecutors will remain, because one man's 'premeditation' can always be another's 'intention'. It is unclear whether total disparity will decrease, remain stable, or increase under a regime of determinate sentences. It is certain that disparities will remain.

The paradox of prosecutorial power under determinate sentencing is that exorcising discretion from two of the three discretionary agencies in criminal sentencing does not necessarily reduce either the role of discretion in sentence determination or the total amount of sentence disparity. Logically, three discretions may be better than one. The practical lesson is that no serious programme to create a rule of law in determining punishment can ignore the pivotal role of the American prosecutor.

3. *The legislative law-and-order syndrome.* Two members of the Twentieth Century Fund Task Force express doubts that a legislature will endorse six-month sentences for burglary, even if it could be shown that six months is above or equal to the present sentence served. I share their scepticism. When the legislature determines sentencing ranges, it is operating at a level of abstraction far removed from individual case dispositions, or even the allocation of resources to courts and correctional agencies. At that level of abstraction the symbolic quality of the criminal sanction is of great importance. The penalty provisions in most of our criminal codes are symbolic denunciations of particular behaviour patterns, rather than decisions about just sentences. This practice has been supported by the multiple ameliorating discretions in the present system.

It is the hope of most of the advocates of determinate sentencing that the responsibilities thrust on the legislature by their reforms will educate democratically elected officials to view their function with realism and responsibility—to recognize the need for priorities and moderation in fixing punishment. This is a hope, not firmly supported by the history of penal policy and not encouraged by a close look at the operation and personnel of state legislatures.

Yet reallocating power to the legislature means gambling on our ability to make major changes in the way elected officials think, talk, and act about crime. Once a determinate sentencing bill is before a legislative body, it takes no more than an eraser to make a one-year 'presumptive sentence' into a six-year sentence for the same offence. The delicate scheme of priorities in any well-conceived sentencing proposal can be torpedoed by amendment with ease and political appeal. In recent history, those who have followed the moral career of the sentencing scheme proposed by Governor Brown's Commission on Law Reform through the Senate Subcommittee on Crime can testify to the enormous impact of apparently minor structural changes on the relative bite of the sentencing system.[10]

If the legislative response to determinate sentencing proposals is penal inflation, this will not necessarily lead to a reign of terror. The same powerful prosecutorial discretions that limit the legislature's ability to work reform also prevent the legislature from doing too much harm. High fixed sentences could be reduced: discretion and disparity could remain.

4. *The lack of consensus and principle.* But what if we could trade disparity for high mandatory sentences beyond those merited by utilitarian or retributive demands of justice? Would it be a fair trade? It could be

argued that a system which treats some offenders unjustly is preferable to one in which all are treated unjustly. Equality is only one, not the exclusive, criterion for fairness.

This last point leads to a more fundamental concern about the link between structural reform and achieving justice. The Task Force asks the question with eloquent simplicity: 'How long is too long? How short is too short?'[11] The question is never answered in absolute terms: indeed, it is unanswerable. We lack coherent principles on which to base judgments of relative social harm. Current titles of respectable books on this subject range from 'Punishing Criminals' to 'The End of Imprisonment', and the reader can rest assured that the contents vary as much as the labels. Yet how can we mete out fair punishment without agreeing on what is fair? How can we do justice before we define it?

Determinate sentencing may do more good than harm; the same can be said for sharp curtailment of judicial and parole discretion. Such reforms will, however, be difficult to implement, measure, and judge. Predicting the impact of any of the current crop of reform proposals with any degree of certainty is a hazardous if not foolhardy occupation.

Not the least of the vices of our present lawless structures of criminal sentencing is that they mask a deeper moral and intellectual bankruptcy in the criminal law and the society it is supposed to serve. The paramount value of these books and reform proposals is not the 'structural reforms' that each proposes or opposes. It is the challenge implicit in all current debate: no matter what the problems with particular reforms, the present system is intolerable. The problems are deeper than overcrowding or lack of co-ordination, more profound than the structure of the sentencing system. These problems are as closely tied to our culture as to our criminal law. They are problems of principle that have been obscured by the tactical inadequacies of the present system.

Notes

1. Norval Morris, *The Future of Imprisonment* (University of Chicago Press, 1974); James Q. Wilson, *Thinking about Crime* (Basic Books, 1975); Ernst van den Haag, *Punishing Criminals* (Basic Books, 1975); Andrew von Hirsch, *Doing Justice: The Choice of Punishments: The Report of the Committee for the Study of Incarceration* (Hill & Wang, 1976); David Fogel, *We Are the Living Proof: The Justice Model of Corrections* (W. H. Anderson, 1975); Task Force on Criminal Sentencing, *Fair and Certain Punishment: Report of the Twentieth Century Task Force on Criminal Sentencing* (McGraw-Hill, 1976).

2. The old Pennsylvania statute is used as an example because we have recently studied the old distribution of punishment for criminal homicide in Philadelphia. See Zimring, Eigen, and O'Malley, 'Punishing Homicide in Philadelphia: Perspectives on the Death Penalty', 43 *University of Chicago Law Review* 227 (1976).

3. See Zimring *et al.*, *supra* n. 2, at 229–41.

4. Fogel, *supra* n. 1, at 196–9.

5. Morris, *supra* n. 1, at 47–50.

6. Task Force Report, *supra* n. 1, at 55–6.

7. The phrase is borrowed from my colleague James White, who is preparing a book with this title.

8. The aggravating factors are (1) 'the victim was under 15 or over 70 years of age' and (2) the victim was held captive for over two hours. Task Force Report at 59.

9. The presumptive sentence for rape doubles with an assault causing bodily injury. The penalty for armed robbery where the offender discharges a firearm is three years if the offender did not intend to injure and five years if intent can be established. The presumptive sentence is two years if the weapon is discharged but the prosecutor cannot or does not establish that 'the likelihood of personal injury is high'. The penalty for armed burglary doubles when the dwelling is occupied. An armed burglar who 'brandishes a weapon' in an occupied dwelling receives 24 months while a non-brandishing armed burglar receives 18. Assault is punished with 6 years when 'premeditated' and committed with intent to cause harm. Without intent, the presumptive sentence is two years. See *Fair and Certain Punishment* at 38–9, 56–9. Threat of force in larceny means the difference between six and twenty-four months. As I read the robbery and larceny statutes, armed taking of property by threat to use force is punished with a presumptive sentence of six months on p. 40 of the report while the same behaviour receives 24 months on pp. 60–1.

10. Compare the *Final Report of the National Commission on Reforms of Federal Criminals Laws* (Government Printing Office, 1971) with Senate Bill 1, 94th Cong., 1st Session (1975). Among other things, the Senate Bill changes a presumption in favour of probation to a presumption against probation, increases the number of felonies in the proposed code and increases the length of authorized sentences by a considerable margin. See Schwartz, 'The Proposed Federal Criminal Code', *Criminal Law Reporter*, 17 (1975), 3203.

11. Task Force Report *supra* n. 1, at 4.

Preface: J. Q. Wilson, 'Penalties and Opportunities'

Philosophical discourse may have become increasingly retributivist in recent years, but utilitarian thinking retains a powerful hold on penal policy. General deterrence policies have flourished alongside the revival of retributivist theorizing; so too has talk of the cost–benefit advantages of selectively incapacitating high-rate offenders (see N. MORRIS, and the Preface to his essay). Wilson has been a leading proponent of such policies, and an influential figure in the politics of crime control (see Stenson and Cowell 1991).

Wilson characterizes his work as 'policy analysis', rather than 'criminology' or 'social science'. His concern is not to understand crime in all its dimensions, nor to build an ideal theory of justice. Instead he focuses on the problem of crime control: what can in fact be done to improve the cost-effectiveness of crime-control policies? He argues (see Wilson 1983) that social-psychological explanations which attribute criminal behaviour to defective socialization or to the strains caused by social inequalities might be intellectually persuasive, but are of little practical use, because it is not politically feasible for governments to try to change the way families rear their children, or the way the economy distributes wealth. Useful knowledge in this sphere is, for Wilson, knowledge that indicates how the policy instruments which governments do control (laws, taxes, subsidies, criminal justice agencies) can be put to better use within the limits imposed by current political arrangements.

One major impact of Wilson's work has been on official conceptions of the individual offender ('the criminal' as he or she is often termed). Implicit in much post-war crime-control policy was a conception of offenders as maladjusted or undersocialized, and so unresponsive to the law's threats and penalties. Hence the supposed need for individualized rehabilitative treatment, and for social programmes to transform ghetto cultures and open paths for upward mobility (see Clarke and Cornish 1983 for a critical discussion). Hence the supposed inefficiency of deterrent punishments. Against this older orthodoxy, Wilson claims that there is no need for in-depth accounts of delinquent cultures and personalities, or for policies to deal with deep rooted problems. Offenders can (for purposes of penal policy) be seen as rational calculators, who will adjust their conduct to avoid penalties and to pursue opportunities (see Clarke and Felson 1993; Cornish and Clarke 1986; Mayhew et al. 1976). Economics, not sociology, is the appropriate framework for thinking about crime; and crime rates, like other economic phenomena, will respond to costs in a predictable way (see Posner 1985). This view fits happily with the broader shift from welfarism to neo-liberalism which has marked social policy in the 1980s, but contrasts with the conceptions of offenders embodied in other theories of punishment. MURPHY, for instance, presupposes a society of free and rational agents who are not simply utility-calculators, but have a sense of justice. VON HIRSCH presupposes agents who are prudentially rational (and thus deterrable), but who are also (albeit imperfectly) moral. H. MORRIS's 'paternalistic' theory, on the other hand, rests on a very different conception of the offender as someone who has lost touch with 'the Good', and with their own good. We must ask not only what conception of offenders is plausible, but also what conception should inform penal policy. How should the state see its citizens?

Wilson reviews the large body of research on deterrence, to seek indications of what works and what does not. Although the evidence is inconclusive, he argues that changes in penalty levels are less likely to be effective than are changes in the probability of being apprehended and convicted. We should therefore attend more to police and prosecution practices than to levels of punishment (see also Walker 1980: ch. 4). He also considers the benefits which might be made available for non-criminal behaviour, and here he discusses the research on the crime-reducing effects of job-creation schemes, and shows it to be no more conclusive than that on penal deterrence (but see Pawson and Tilley (forthcoming) on the methodological inadequacies of much research in this area). In cost–benefit terms, he argues, it is better to increase penalties than to try to increase opportunities: for increased penalties only heighten the risks faced by criminals, whereas a failure to try such deterrent measures heightens the risks of victimization for the innocent (contrast Braithwaite and Pettit 1990: 140–5, for a consequentialist argument for a 'decremental strategy' of progressively reducing levels of punishment).

Wilson's consequentialist account will of course face retributivist objections. Even if deterrent punishments secure the social good of crime prevention (but see MATHIESEN for doubts on this); even if we assume that only the guilty may be punished (though this restriction cannot be justified in consequentialist terms; see Hart 1968; Walker 1991: ch. 11): we must also ask whether the state has the right to use such means to secure that good (see MURPHY), and whether a system of deterrent punishments respects the moral standing of the citizen (see VON HIRSCH: xx–x; Duff 1986; 178–86).

Furthermore, can we simply ignore the social determinants of crime (whose explanatory importance Wilson admits)? Should we disregard as irrelevant the ways in which our social, political, and economic structures may help produce crime as normal outcomes of their operation (see MURPHY, MATHIESEN, CARLEN; Felman 1994)? Instead of taking 'rational economic actors' as a given, and seeking to manipulate their marginal incentives, should we not ask how law-abiding sociable actors are formed, and how we can reform our basic institutions to foster more solidarity and civility (see Currie 1986; Hudson 1987: ch. 6)? We should not assume that, just because we have developed a penal system, penality is (morally or practically) the best way to deal with crime. Nor should we take it for granted that 'crime', the criminal conduct of individual agents, is 'the problem' to be addressed when we concern ourselves with those social harms which are currently dealt with through the criminal law (see BIANCHI; Hulsman 1986). If we are unwilling, or find it politically unfeasible, to change our basic institutions in order to alleviate 'the crime problem', we should recognize that this too is a policy choice, and face the charge that we are choosing to punish and scapegoat individual offenders rather than address the processes which recruit them.

References

BRAITHWAITE, J., and PETTIT, P. (1990), *Not Just Deserts* (Oxford).

CLARKE, R. V. G., and CORNISH, D. B. (1983), *Crime Control in Britain: A Review of Policy Research* (Albany, NY).

—— and FELSON, M. (1993) (eds.), *Routine Activity and Rational Choice* (New Brunswick, NJ).

CORNISH, D. B., and CLARKE, R. V. G. (1986) (eds.), *The Reasoning Criminal* (New York).

CURRIE, E. (1986), *Confronting Crime* (New York).

DUFF, R. A. (1986), *Trials and Punishments* (Cambridge).

FELMAN, M. (1994), *Crime and Everyday Life* (New York).

HART, H. L. A. (1968), 'Prolegomenon to the Principles of Punishment', in H. L. A. Hart, *Punishment and Responsiblity* (Oxford), 1–27.

HUDSON, B. (1987), *Justice through Punishment? A Critique of the 'Justice' Model of Corrections* (London).

HULSMAN, L. (1986), 'Critical Criminology and the Concept of Crime', *Contemporary Crises*, 10: 63–80.

MAYHEW, P., CLARKE, R. V. G., STURMAN, A., and HOUGH, M. (1976), *Crime as Opportunity* (London).

PAWSON, R. and TILLEY, N. (forthcoming), 'What Works in Evaluation Research?', *British Journal of Criminology*.

POSNER, R. A. (1985), 'An Economic Theory of the Criminal Law', *Columbia Law Review*, 85: 1193–231.

STENSON, K., and COWELL, D. (1991) (eds.), *The Politics of Crime Control* (London).

WALKER, N. (1980), *Punishment, Danger and Stigma* (Oxford).

—— (1991), *Why Punish?* (Oxford).

WILSON, J. Q. (1983), 'Thinking about Crime', in J. Q. Wilson, *Thinking about Crime* (2nd edn., New York), ch. 3.

Penalties and Opportunities

J. Q. WILSON

The average citizen hardly needs to be persuaded of the view that crime will be more frequently committed if, other things being equal, crime becomes more profitable compared to other ways of spending one's time. Accordingly, the average citizen thinks it obvious that one major reason why crime has gone up is that people have discovered it is easier to get away with it; by the same token, the average citizen thinks a good way to reduce crime is to make the consequences of crime to the would-be offender more costly (by making penalties swifter, more certain, or more severe), or to make the value of alternatives to crime more attractive (by increasing the availability and pay of legitimate jobs), or both. Such opinions spring naturally to mind among persons who notice, as a fact of everyday life, that people take their hands off hot stoves, shop around to find the best buy, smack their children to teach them not to run out into a busy street, and change jobs when the opportunity arises to earn more money for the same amount of effort.

These citizens may be surprised to learn that social scientists who study crime are deeply divided over the correctness of such views. To some scholars, especially economists, the popular view is also the scientifically correct one—becoming a criminal can be explained in much the same way we explain becoming a carpenter or buying a car. To other scholars, especially sociologists, the popular view is wrong—crime rates do not go up because people discover they can get away with it and will not come down just because society decides to get tough on criminals.

The debate over the effect on crime rates of changing the costs and benefits of crime is usually referred to as a debate over deterrence—a debate, that is, over the efficacy (and perhaps even the propriety) of trying to prevent crime by making would-be offenders more fearful of committing crime. But that is something of a misnomer, because the theory of human nature on which is erected the idea of deterrence (the theory that people respond to the penalties associated with crime) is also the theory of human nature that supports the idea that people will take jobs in preference to crime if the jobs are more attractive. In both cases, we are saying that would-be offenders are reasonably rational and respond to their perception of the costs and benefits attached to alternative courses of action. When we use the word 'deterrence', we are calling attention only to the cost side of the equation. There is no word in common scientific usage to call attention to the benefit side of the equation; perhaps 'inducement' might serve. To a psychologist, deterring persons from committing crimes or inducing persons to engage in non-criminal activities are but special cases of using 'reinforcements' (or rewards) to alter behaviour.

The reason there is a debate among scholars about deterrence is that the socially imposed consequences of committing a crime, unlike the market consequences of shopping around for the best price, are characterized by delay, uncertainty, and ignorance. In addition, some scholars contend that a large fraction of crime is committed by persons who are so impulsive, irrational, or abnormal that, even if there were no delay, uncertainty, or ignorance attached to the consequences of criminality, we would still have a lot of crime.

Imagine a young man walking down the street at night with nothing on his mind but a desire for good times and high living. Suddenly he sees a little old lady standing alone on a dark corner stuffing the proceeds of her recently cashed social security check into her purse. There is nobody else in view. If the boy steals the purse, he gets the money immediately. That is a powerful incentive, and it is available immediately and without doubt. The costs of taking it are uncertain; the odds are at least fourteen to one that the police will not catch a given robber, and even if he is caught the odds are very good that he will not go to prison, unless he has a long record. On the average, no more than three felonies out of one hundred result in the imprisonment of the offender. In addition to this uncertainty, whatever penalty may come his way will come only after a long delay; in some jurisdictions, it might take a year or more to complete the court disposition of the offender, assuming he is caught in the first place. Moreover, this young man may, in his ignorance of how the world works, think the odds in his favour at even greater and that the delay will be even longer.

Compounding the problems of delay and uncertainty is the fact that society cannot feasibly reduce the uncertainty attached to the chances of being arrested by more than a modest amount (see J. Q. Wilson *Thinking about Crime*, Ch. 4 (rev. edn., New York, 1983), and though it can to some degree increase the probability and severity of a prison sentence for those who are caught, it cannot do so drastically by, for example, summarily executing all convicted robbers or even by sending all robbers to twenty-year prison terms (see ibid., ch. 8). Some scholars add a further complication: the young man may be incapable of assessing the risks of crime. How, they ask, is he to know his chances of being caught and punished? And even if he does know, is he perhaps 'driven' by uncontrollable impulses to snatch purses whatever the risks?

As if all this were not bad enough, the principal method by which scholars have attempted to measure the effect on crime of differences in the probability and severity of punishment has involved using data about aggregates of people (entire cities, counties, states, and even nations) rather than about individuals. In a typical study, of which there have been several dozen, the rate at which, say, robbery is committed in each state is 'explained' by means of a statistical procedure in which the analyst takes into account both the socioeconomic features of each state that might affect the supply of robbers (for example, the percentage of persons with low incomes, the unemployment rate, or the population density of the big cities) and the operation of the criminal justice system of each state as it attempts to cope with robbery (for example, the probability of being caught and imprisoned for a given robbery and the length of the average prison term for robbery). Most such studies find, after controlling for socioeconomic differences among the states, that the higher the probability of being imprisoned, the lower the robbery rate. Isaac Ehrlich, an economist, produced the best known of such analyses using data on crime in the United States in 1940, 1950, and 1960. To simplify a complex analysis, he found, after controlling for such factors as the income level and age distribution of the population, that the higher the probability of imprisonment for those convicted of robbery, the lower the robbery rate. Thus, differences in the certainty of punishment seem to make a difference in the level of crime. At the same time, Ehrlich did not find that the severity of punishment (the average time served in prison for robbery) had, independently of certainty, an effect on robbery rates in two of the three time periods (1940 and 1960).[1]

But there are some problems associated with studying the effect of sanctions on crime rates using aggregate data of this sort. One is that many of the most important factors are not known with any accuracy. For example, we are dependent on police reports for our measure of the robbery rate, and these undoubtedly vary in accuracy from place to place. If all police departments were inaccurate to the same degree, this would not be important; unfortunately, some departments are probably much less accurate than others, and this variable error can introduce a serious bias into the statistical estimates of the effect of the criminal justice system.

Moreover, if one omits from the equation some factor that affects the crime rate, then the estimated effect of the factors that are in the equation may be in error because some of the causal power belonging to the omitted factor will be falsely attributed to the included factors. For example, suppose we want to find out whether differences in the number of policemen on patrol among American cities are associated with differences in the rate at which robberies take place in those cities. If we fail to include in our equation a measure of the population density of the city, we may wrongly conclude that the more police there are on the streets, the *higher* the robbery rate and thus give support to the absurd policy proposition that the way to reduce robberies is to fire police officers. Since robberies are more likely to occur in larger, densely settled cities (which also tend to have a higher proportion of police), it would be a grave error to omit such measures of population from the equation. Since we are not certain what causes crime, we always run the risk of inadvertently omitting a key factor from our efforts to see if deterrence works.

Even if we manage to overcome these problems, a final difficulty lies in wait. The observed fact (and it has been observed many times) that states in which the probability of going to prison for robbery is low are also states which have high rates of robbery can be interpreted in one of two ways. It can mean *either* that the higher robbery rates are the results of the lower imprisonment rates (and thus evidence that deterrence works) *or* that the lower imprisonment rates are caused by the higher robbery rates. To see how the latter might be true, imagine a state that is experiencing, for some reason, a rapidly rising robbery rate. It arrests, convicts, and imprisons more and more robbers as more and more robberies are committed, but it cannot quite keep up. The robberies are increasing so fast that they 'swamp' the criminal justice system; prosecutors and judges respond by letting more robbers off without a prison sentence, or perhaps without even a trial, in order to keep the system from becoming hopelessly clogged. As a result, the proportion of arrested robbers who go to prison goes down while the robbery rate goes up. In this case, we ought to conclude, not that prison deters robbers, but that high robbery rates 'deter' prosecutors and judges.

The best analysis of these problems in statistical studies of deterrence is to be found in a report of the Panel on Research on Deterrent and

Incapacitative Effects, set up by the National Research Council (an arm of the National Academy of Sciences). That panel, chaired by Alfred Blumstein of Carnegie-Mellon University, concluded that the available statistical evidence (as of 1978) did not warrant reaching any strong conclusions about the deterrent effect of existing differences among states or cities in the probability of punishment. The panel (of which I was a member) noted that 'the evidence certainly favors a proposition supporting deterrence more than it favors one asserting that deterrence is absent' but urged 'scientific caution' in interpreting this evidence.[2]

Subsequently, other criticisms of deterrence research, generally along the same lines as those of the panel, were published by Colin Loftin[3] and by Stephen S. Brier and Stephen E. Feinberg.[4]

Some commentators believe that these criticisms have proved that 'deterrence doesn't work' and thus the decks have now been cleared to get on with the task of investing in those programmes, such as job creation and income maintenance, that *will* have an effect on crime. Such a conclusion is, to put it mildly, a bit premature.

Rehabilitating Deterrence

People are governed in their daily lives by rewards and penalties of every sort. We shop for bargain prices, praise our children for good behaviour and scold them for bad, expect lower interest rates to stimulate home building and fear that higher ones will depress it and conduct ourselves in public in ways that lead our friends and neighbours to form good opinions of us. To assert that 'deterrence doesn't work' is tantamount to either denying the plainest facts of everyday life or claiming that would-be criminals are utterly different from the rest of us. They may well be different to some degree—they most likely have a weaker conscience, worry less about their reputation in polite society, and find it harder to postpone gratifying their urges—but these differences of degree do not make them indifferent to the risks and gains of crime. If they were truly indifferent, they would scarcely be able to function at all, for their willingness to take risks would be offset by their indifference to loot. Their lives would consist of little more than the erratic display of animal instincts and fleeting impulses.

The question before us is whether feasible changes in the deferred and uncertain penalties of crime (and, as we shall see, in the deferred and uncertain opportunities for employment) will affect crime rates in ways that can be detected by the data and statistical methods at our disposal.

Though the unreliability of crime data and the limitations of statistical analysis are real enough and are accurately portrayed by the Panel of the National Research Council, there are remedies and rejoinders that, on balance, strengthen the case for the claim that not only does deterrence work (the panel never denied that), it probably works in ways that can be measured, even in the aggregate.

The errors in official statistics about crime rates have been addressed by employing other measures of crime, in particular reports gathered by Census Bureau interviewers from citizens who have been victims of crime. While these victim surveys have problems of their own (such as the forgetfulness of citizens), they are not the same problems as those that affect police reports of crime. Thus, if we obtain essentially the same findings about the effect of sanctions on crime from studies that use victim data as we do from studies using police data, our confidence in these findings is strengthened. Studies of this sort have been done by Itzhak Goldberg at Stanford and by Barbara Boland and myself, and the results are quite consistent with those from research based on police reports.[5] As sanctions become more likely, crime becomes less common.

There is a danger that important factors will be omitted from any statistical study of crime in ways that bias the results, but this problem is no greater in studies of penalties than it is in studies of unemployment rates, voting behaviour, or any of a hundred other socially significant topics. Since we can never know with certainty everything that may affect crime (or unemployment, or voting), we must base our conclusions not on any single piece of research, but on the general thrust of a variety of studies analysing many different causal factors. The Panel of the National Research Council took exactly this position. While noting that 'there is the possibility that as yet unknown and so untested' factors may be affecting crime, 'this is not a sufficient basis for dismissing' the common finding that crime goes up as sanctions become less certain because 'many of the analyses have included some of the more obvious possible third causes and they still find negative associations between sanctions and crimes'.[6]

It is possible that rising crime rates 'swamp' the criminal justice system so that a negative statistical association between, say, rates of theft and the chances of going to prison for theft may mean not that a decline in imprisonment is causing theft to increase, but rather that a rise in theft is causing imprisonment to become less likely. This might occur particularly with respect to less serious crimes, such as shoplifting or petty larceny; indeed, the proportion of prisoners who are shoplifters or petty thieves has gone down over the last two decades. But it is hard to imagine that the criminal justice system would respond to an increase in murder or armed robbery by letting some murderers or armed robbers off with no punishment. There is no evidence that convicted murderers are any less likely to go to prison today than they were twenty years ago. Moreover, the apparent deterrent effect of prison on serious crimes, such as murder and robbery, was apparently as great in 1940 or 1950, when these crimes were much less common, as it is today, suggesting that swamping has not occurred.[7]

The best studies of deterrence that manage to overcome many of these problems provide evidence that deterrence works. Alfred Blumstein and Daniel Nagin studied the relationship between draft evasion and the penalties imposed for evading the draft. After controlling for the socioeconomic characteristics of the states, they found that the higher the probability of conviction for draft evasion, the lower the evasion rates. This is an especially strong finding because it is largely immune to some of the problems of other research. Draft evasion is more accurately measured than street crime, hence errors arising from poor data are not a problem. And draft evasion cases did not swamp the federal courts in which they were tried, in part because such cases (like murder in state courts) make up only a small fraction of the courts' workload (7 per cent in the case of draft evasion) and in part because the attorney general had instructed federal prosecutors to give high priority to these cases. Blumstein and Nagin concluded that draft evasion is deterrable.[8]

Another way of testing whether deterrence works is to look, not at differences among states at one point in time, but at changes in the nation as a whole over a long period of time. Historical data on the criminal justice system in America is so spotty that such research is difficult to do here, but it is not at all difficult in England where the data are excellent. Kenneth I. Wolpin analysed changes in crime rates and in various parts of the criminal justice system (the chances of being arrested, convicted, and punished) for the period 1894 to 1967, and concluded that changes in the probability of being punished seemed to cause changes in the crime rate. He offers reasons for believing that this causal connection cannot be explained away by the argument that the criminal justice system was being swamped.[9]

Given what we are trying to measure—changes in the behaviour of a small number of hard-to-observe persons who are responding to delayed and uncertain penalties—we will never be entirely sure that our statistical manipulations have proved that deterrence works. What is impressive is that so many (but not all) studies using such different methods come to similar conclusions. (In Wilson, *Thinking about Crime*, ch. 10, I set out more evidence, which suggests that, though the evidence as to whether capital punishment deters crime is quite ambiguous, most of the studies find that the chances of being imprisoned for murder do seem to affect the murder rate.) Even after wading through all this, the sceptical reader may remain unconvinced. Given the difficulties of any aggregate statistical analysis, that is understandable. But if unconvinced, the reader cannot conclude that criticisms of the statistical claims for deterrence have by implication enhanced the statistical claims for job creation. This is one time when, if you throw out the bath water, you will have to throw out the baby as well.

Evaluating Employment

Deterrence and job-creation are not different crime-fighting strategies; they are two sides of the same strategy. The former emphasizes (and tries to increase) the costs of crime; the latter emphasizes (and tries to increase) the benefits of non-crime. Both depend on the assumption that we are dealing with reasonably rational persons who respond to incentives. The principal means used to estimate the effect on crime rates of changes in the benefits of non-crime have been exactly the same as the ones used to evaluate the effect of changes in the costs of crime—the statistical techniques reviewed by the National Research Council Panel.

To make this clear, let us return to our original example. The young man who was trying to decide whether to mug a little old lady is still yearning for the money necessary to enjoy some high living. Let us assume that he considers, as a way of getting money, finding a job. He knows he will have to look for one, and this will take time. Even if he gets a job, he will have to wait to obtain his first paycheck. Moreover, he knows that young men have difficulty finding their first jobs, especially in inner-city neighbourhoods such as his, and there is a great deal of uncertainty attached to even the delayed benefits of legitimate employment. Thus, he cannot be certain that the job he might get would provide benefits that exceed the costs. Working forty hours a week as a messenger, a dishwasher, or a busboy might not be worth the sacrifice in time, effort, and reputation on the street corner that it entails. The young man may be wrong about all this, but if he is ignorant of the true risks of crime, he is probably just as ignorant of the true benefits of non-crime.

In addition to the problems of delay, uncertainty, and ignorance is the fact that society cannot make more than modest changes in the employment prospects of young men. Job creation takes a long time when it can be done at all, and many of the jobs created will go to the 'wrong' (that is, not criminally inclined) persons; thus, youth unemployment rates will not vary greatly among states and will change only slowly over time. And if we are to detect the effects of existing differences in unemployment rates (or income levels) on crime, we must estimate those effects by exactly the same statistical techniques that are used to estimate the effects of criminal justice sanctions. Indeed, they involve the very same equations (remember, to measure the effects of sanctions, we first had to hold constant the effects of socioeconomic variables; now, to measure the effects of the latter, we must first hold constant the former).

The problem of measurement error arises because we do not know with much accuracy the teenage or youthful unemployment rate by city or state. Much depends on who is looking for work and how hard, how we count students who are looking for only part-time jobs, and whether we can distinguish between people out of work for long periods and those who happen to be between jobs at the moment. Again, since inaccuracies in these data vary from place to place, we will obtain biased results.

The problem of omitted factors is also real, as is evident in a frequently cited study done in 1976 by Harvey Brenner of Johns Hopkins University.[10] He claimed to find that, between 1940 and 1973, increases in the unemployment rate led to increases in the homicide rate. But he omitted from his analysis any measures of changes in the certainty or the severity of sentences for murder, factors that other scholars have found to have a strong effect on homicide.[11]

Finally, there is probably a complex, not a simple, relationship between crime and unemployment (or poverty), just as there may be a complex relationship between imprisonment and crime. For example, suppose, in a statistical study that managed to overcome the problems already mentioned, we discover that, as unemployment rates go up, crime rates go up. One's natural instinct is to interpret this as meaning that rising unemployment causes rising crime. It is just as possible that rising crime causes rising unemployment. This could be the case if young men examining the world about them concluded that crime pays more than jobs (for instance, that stealing cars is more profitable than washing them). They might then leave their jobs in favour of crime. That this happens is no mere conjecture; it lies at the heart of some unknown but probably large fraction of the growing 'underground economy'.[12] Some young men find dealing in drugs or other rackets much more attractive than nine-to-five jobs, but technically they are 'unemployed'. Or it may be the case that both crime and unemployment are the results of some common underlying cause. In 1964, the unemployment rate for black men aged twenty to twenty-four was 10 per cent; by 1978 it was 23 per cent. During the same period, crime rates, in particular those involving young black men, went up. Among the several possible explanations are the changes that have occurred in the inner parts of large cities where so many young blacks live. There has been a movement out of the inner cities of both jobs and the social infrastructure that is manned by adult members of the middle class (see Wilson, *Thinking about Crime*, ch. 2). The departure of the jobs led to increased unemployment, the departure of the middle class to lessened social control and hence to more crime. If we knew more than we now know, we would probably discover that all three relationships are working simultaneously—for some persons, unemployment leads to crime, for others crime leads to unemployment, and for still others social disintegration or personal inadequacies leads to both crime and unemployment.

That several of these relationships are in fact at work is suggested by the previously mentioned study of Brenner's. Even if the effect of unemployment on homicide persisted after taking into account changes in penalties (which it probably does not), Brenner himself noted that the murder rate also went up with increases in per capita income and (sometimes) inflation as well as with a rise in joblessness.[13] But if the stress of joblessness leads to more murders, what is it about increases in average income (or in inflation) that also lead to more murders? And if society attempts to reduce the murder rate by reducing unemployment, how can it do this without at the same time increasing the murder rate because, as a result of lessened unemployment, it has managed to increase per capita incomes or stimulate inflation?

I do not say this to explain away the studies purporting to show that unemployment or poverty causes crime, for in fact (contrary to what many people assert) there are very few decent pieces of research that in fact show a relationship between economic factors and crime. Robert W. Gillespie reviewed studies available as of 1975 and was able to find three that asserted the existence of a significant relationship between unemployment and crime but seven which did not.[14] Thomas Orsagh and Ann Dryden Witte in 1981 reviewed the studies that had appeared since 1975 and found very little statistically strong or consistent evidence to support the existence of a connection. The evidence linking income (or poverty) and crime is similarly inconclusive, and probably for the same reasons: there are grave methodological problems confronting anyone trying to find the relationship, and the relationship, to the extent it exists, is probably quite complex (some people may turn to crime because they are poor, some people may be poor because they have turned to crime but are not very good at it, and still other persons may have been made both poor and criminal because of some common underlying factor). To quote Orsagh and Witte: 'Research using aggregate data provides only weak support for the simple proposition that unemployment causes crime . . . [and] does not provide convincing tests of the relationship between low income and crime.'[15]

Back to Square One: Studying Individuals

We seem to be at a dead end. But we are not. Whenever we are trying to discover a relationship between hard-to-measure factors that operate deep inside a complex social structure, we are well advised not to rely on any single method of analysis and particularly well advised not to rely on statistical studies using aggregate data. We should attack the same problem from a number of angles, using different kinds of data and various methodologies. Above all, we should look at what happens to individuals (rather than to cities or states) and what happens when a new programme is tried (rather than measuring the natural variation found in the world as it is).

Ideally, we would like to know how the probability or severity of a possible punishment will affect the behaviour of persons who *might* commit a serious crime. Such persons constitute only a small fraction of the total population, but they are an important fraction. Most of us would not commit a serious crime because of the operation of internal controls on our behaviour, reinforced by the fear or embarrassment should our misconduct be detected. A few of us may commit serious crimes with only small regard to the risks, unless those risks can be made great and immediate. For example, most men would never dream of killing their wives, and a few men might kill them (perhaps in an alcoholic rage) unless a police officer were standing right next to them. But for a certain fraction of men, the idea of doing away with their wives is strongly conditioned by their perception of the risks. Wives, and in particular feminist organizations, concede this when they demand, as they have with increasing vigour, the strict enforcement of laws against wife-abuse. (Not long ago, the New York Police Department was obliged to promise in writing to arrest and prosecute wife-beating men who previously had been handled in a more conciliatory fashion.)

I mention wife-abuse and murder because some people think of such actions as inevitably the result of a deranged or irrational mind, and thus of one insensitive to the risks attendant on such actions. Sometimes this may be so, but more often it is not, as is evident by the fact that the arrival of a police officer usually results in the end of the fight, at least in its physical phase. Even when no officer is there, people pay attention to some costs when engaged in even the most emotional behaviour. As my colleague Richard Herrnstein likes to point out, when husbands and wives start throwing dishes at each other, they are more likely to throw the everyday crockery rather than the fine china. I can imagine getting drunk enough or mad enough to challenge somebody in a bar to a fight, but I cannot imagine getting drunk or mad enough to challenge that somebody if his name happens to be Sugar Ray Leonard or Mean Joe Greene.

If the consequences of even emotional and impulsive acts are given some weight by most people, then the consequences of less emotional acts (such as shoplifting, auto theft, robbery, and burglary) are likely to play an even larger role in affecting the willingness of people to engage in them. What we would like to know is how changes in the prospective costs of crime and the prospective benefits of pursuing legitimate alternatives to crime affect, at the margin, the behaviour of those individuals who are 'at risk'.

Persons who are 'at risk' are those who lack strong, internalized inhibitions against misconduct, who value highly the excitement and thrills of breaking the law, who have a low stake in conformity, who are willing to take greater chances than the rest of us, and who greatly value quick access to ready cash. Such persons tend, disproportionately, to be young males. As Philip J. Cook has argued, it is not necessary for those would-be offenders to be entirely rational or fully informed for the criminal justice system (or the legitimate labour market) to have an effect on them.[16] It is only necessary that they attach some value to the consequences of their actions (since we know they attach a positive value to the loot, it is reasonable to suppose they also attach some value—a negative one, that is— to the chances of being caught) and that they operate on the basis of at least a crude rule of thumb about how great or small those risks are, a rule of thumb that can be affected by society.

Most of us are probably not very well informed about the true costs of crime; being law-abiding, we probably imagine that the chances of being caught are higher than in fact they are and that the severity of the sentence (measured in years in prison) is greater than it really is. But most of us depend for our information on newspaper stories, detective programmes on television, and our own deep fear of being exposed as a disreputable person. But persons at risk (young men hanging around on street corners and thieves who associate with other thieves) have quite different sources of information. These are the accounts of other young men and other thieves who have had a run-in with the police or the courts and who therefore can supply to their colleagues a crudely accurate rule of thumb: 'the heat is on' or 'the heat is off', Judge Bruce MacDonald* is either 'Maximum Mac' or 'Turn'Em Loose Bruce', the prosecutor will let you 'cop out' to a burglary charge so that it gets marked down to a misdemeanour larceny or will 'throw the book at you' and demand 'felony time'.

It is the behaviour of these persons, thus informed, that we wish to observe. But how? As we have seen, we cannot easily do it with aggregate statistical studies in which the behaviour of these persons is often buried in the 'noise' generated by the behaviour of the majority of people who do not commit crimes whatever the advantages. There have in fact been only a few efforts to measure the deterrent effect of the sanctions of the criminal justice system on individuals, as opposed to cities or states (though some of the studies of rehabilitation can be reinterpreted as studies of deterrence; see Wilson, *Thinking about Crime*, ch. 9). One such effort was made by Ann Witte, who followed for about three years the activities of 641 men released from prison in North Carolina. She gathered information not only about their subsequent brushes with the law (80 per cent were rearrested) but also about their experiences with the law before being imprisoned (their prior risk of being arrested, convicted, and imprisoned), the time it took them to find a job after release and the amount it paid in wages, and such aspects of their life-style as their involvement with alcohol and drugs.

Witte could not find out directly how these ex-convicts evaluated their chances of being caught if they broke the law in the future, but she could observe how frequently in the past (that is, before being imprisoned the last time) their arrests had led to a conviction and their convictions had led to imprisonment. Her assumption was that these men might be influenced in their future conduct by their past experience with the criminal justice system. The results of her analysis based on this assumption were

---

* A fictional name.

complex and not entirely consistent, but in general she found that 'deterrence works'—the higher the probability of being punished in the past, the lower the number of arrests per month free on the street in the future. She also found that deterrence works differently for different kinds of offenders. For persons who engaged in violent offences or drug use, the severity of the prior sentence seemed to have the greatest effect, whereas for persons who engaged in less serious property offences the certainty of imprisonment seemed to be most significant. Deterrence may not work, judging from her data, for thieves who were also drug addicts. The availability of jobs had no consistent effect on subsequent criminality.[17]

There are some obvious limitations to this study. One is that, as Witte notes, it is a study of 'losers'—older men (the average age was thirty-two) who had already been in prison, often many times. What we would prefer knowing is whether differences in sanctions or job availability affect the behaviour of persons not yet involved in crime or young men involved for the first time. Because her group consisted of older, ex-cons, it is quite possible her findings understate the true effect of either sanctions or jobs.

A comparable study was carried out in Cook County, Illinois, and this was aimed at the young offender. Charles A. Murray and Louis A. Cox, Jr., followed the criminal careers (measured by the number of times they were arrested per month free on the street) of 317 Chicago boys who had been incarcerated for the first time by the Illinois Department of Corrections. Though young (their average age was sixteen), they were scarcely novices at crime: they had been arrested an average of thirteen times each before receiving this, their first prison sentence. Nor were their offences trivial: as a group, they had been charged with fourteen homicides, twenty-three rapes, over three hundred assaults and a like number of auto thefts, nearly two hundred armed robberies, and over seven hundred burglaries. The patience of the court finally exhausted, they were sent off to a correctional institution, where they served an average sentence of ten months. Murray and Cox followed them for (on the average) seventeen months after their release. During this period, the frequency with which they were arrested (that is, arrests per month per one hundred boys) declined by about two-thirds. To be exact, the members of this group of hard-core delinquents were arrested 6.3 times each during the year before being sent away but only 2.9 times each during the seventeen months on the street after release.[18]

Murray and Cox refer to this as the 'suppression effect'; namely, the tendency of the first exposure to prison to suppress the rate at which delinquents are arrested and, presumably, the rate at which they actually were committing crimes.* (See Wilson, *Thinking about Crime*, ch. 9, for discussion of some of the implications of this study and of some of the objections that have been raised to it.)

The Murray and Cox study, one of the few of its kind that has been carried out, adds some support to the deterrence theory. But it still focuses on persons who have already committed crimes; we remain uncertain about the effect of changes in the criminal justice system on would-be offenders. It is almost impossible to study behaviour that does not occur except to ask, as some scholars have done, various persons, often students, whether they would commit or have committed a crime when they perceived the penalties to be of a given severity and a given probability. One such study was done among students at an eastern college,[19] and another among high school students in Arizona.[20] Both found that the students who believed there was a high probability of being punished for a particular criminal act were less likely to report (anonymously) having committed the act than were students who thought there was a low probability of being punished. Both studies are broadly consistent with the view that deterrence works, but both are also difficult to interpret. It is hard to be confident that the number of offences the students reported bears any relationship to the number they actually committed. More important, the studies raise the possibility that what actually deters these students (very few of whom commit any serious acts with any frequency) is not what they guess to be the chances of being caught, but the moral opprobrium with which such acts are viewed. For most people in most circumstances, the moral nature of the act and the internalized inhibitions on misconduct arising out of that moral code are probably the major deterrents to crime (see Wilson, *Thinking about Crime*, ch. 12). Interviewing students may highlight that fact, but it cannot tell us what happens, at the margin, when society alters

---

* Another study of individual responses to sanctions was carried out among shoplifters caught by store detectives in a large California department store. Of the 371 individuals caught shoplifting during one year only three were caught again during the year in any of the department stores in that region, even though the majority who were caught were not taken to court. The authors interpret this as evidence of the deterrent effect of apprehension, though the lack of any control group (persons shoplifting but not caught) render this conclusion somewhat speculative. Lawrence E. Cohen and Rodney Stark, 'Discriminatory Labeling and the Five-Finger Discount: An Empirical Analysis of Differential Shoplifting Dispositions', *Journal of Research in Crime and Delinquency*, 11 (1974), 25–39. For a similar conclusion, see also Mary Owen Cameron, *The Booster and the Snitch* (New York: Free Press, 1964), 159–70.

the certainty or severity of punishment for a given offence. And for purposes of public policy, that is exactly what we want to know.

Experimenting with Changing the Costs of Crime

The best way to find out the circumstances under which punishing or helping people will affect the likelihood of such persons committing crimes is to try it. Unfortunately, learning from experience is harder than acquiring experience, because many things that are tried as ways of reducing crime, including both alterations in the penalties for crime and in the opportunities for avoiding crime, are never evaluated in any serious way. As a result, the study of public policy toward crime is cluttered with unsupported assertions and reinvented wheels.

There have been some efforts to make changes under conditions permitting a serious and competent evaluation, and we can report the results. A few were designed from the first as true experiments (one of them, the Kansas City Preventive Patrol project, is described in Wilson, *Thinking about Crime*, ch. 4), others have been 'quasi-experiments'— changes in policy that were accompanied by efforts to find out what happened (one of these, involving the assignment of more officers to the New York City subways, is also described in ibid.).

Most experiments in deterrence have involved changes in police behaviour rather than changes in the behaviour of judges and prosecutors. As I argued (ibid.), the result of those changes seems to indicate that the more focused and aggressive the police effort, the greater the chance of it making a difference. Changes in the level of random preventive patrol in marked cars seemed to make little difference in crime rates in Kansas City, but changes in the number of officers riding New York subway cars and changes in the aggressiveness with which San Diego police stopped and interrogated persons on the streets did seem to make a difference.* Comparable results come from a study of drunk driving in

---

* A study by Barbara Boland and myself involving a complex statistical analysis of the relationship between police behaviour and robbery rates in thirty-five large American cities seems to confirm these experimental findings. The number of police officers on the street and the aggressiveness with which they patrolled had, independently, effects on the reported rate of robberies. The study employed methods (estimating simultaneous equations using two-stage least squares) and assumptions designed to eliminate the risk that the finding of a deterrent effect would be spurious owing to the reciprocal relationship between crime and the number and behaviour of police officers. In particular, it was designed to overcome the problems mentioned earlier in this chapter and in the report of the National Research Council Panel on Deterrence arising from the fact that the number of robberies may affect the number of police and the rate at which they make arrests just as the number

Great Britain. The police began a programme to use a breathalyser to catch inebriated motorists in hopes of reducing traffic accidents, especially fatal ones. A careful study by H. Laurence Ross clearly indicates that these hopes were borne out: 'the Road Safety Act caused a reduction in casualties' by as much as two-thirds during weekend evenings when drunk driving is likely to be most common.[21] Unhappily, the police did not like to enforce this law, which could lead to the mandatory revocation of the driving licence of a motorist whose blood alcohol level exceeded 0.08 per cent. In time, the authorities made a highly publicized effort to get the police to make random stops and administer breathalyser tests, and once again accidents declined.[22]

Perhaps the most dramatic evidence of the operation of deterrence—dramatic because it involved a true experiment on individuals in the real world—comes from an effort in Minneapolis to find out how the police can best handle incidents of spouse assault. The conventional wisdom had been that if one or both parties to such an assault were handled by the officer informally—by mediation or referral to a social work agency—the parties would be better off than if the assaulter were arrested. And the police themselves often preferred not to make an arrest because it took time and effort and often led to no prosecution when the victim refused to press charges. With the advice of the Police Foundation, a group of Minneapolis officers began handling their misdemeanour spouse-assault cases by randomly assigning the assaulter to one of three dispositions: arresting him, advising him, or sending him out of the house to cool off. Over 250 cases were treated in this experimental fashion and followed up for six months. The assaulters who were arrested were less likely to be reported to the police for a subsequent assault than were those advised and much less likely than those sent out of the house. And this was true even though the arrested person, in the vast majority of cases, spent no more than a week in gaol.[23]

These police experiments and quasi-experiments support the concept of deterrence, but they are not an especially hard test of it. The police are the persons closest to a potential offender, and if they suddenly act in a more conspicuous or aggressive manner, these changes are often quickly noticed by would-be offenders who then alter their behaviour accordingly. Moreover, the kinds of offences most worrisome to citizens are

of police and the arrest rate may affect the number of robberies. James Q. Wilson and Barbara Boland, 'The Effect of the Police on Crime', *Law and Society Review*, 12 (Spring 1978), 367–90, and 'The Effects of the Police on Crime: A Rejoinder', *Law and Society Review*, 16 (1981–2), 163–9.

often those, such as burglary, street robbery, and assault, that are difficult for the police to detect or intercept. The deterrent effect of policing is likely to be greatest when the police can act in a visible way in a closed system (such as a subway or in a school building) or when they can take action on their own initiative without first waiting for a report that a crime has occurred (as in stopping motorists and administering breathalyser tests or questioning suspicious teenagers on a street corner). The deterrent value of the police is likely to be least when the crime to be deterred involves stealth (such as burglary).

A tougher and, for policy purposes, more useful test of deterrence would be to alter the sentences a person gets without altering police conduct. We have surprisingly few careful studies of the results of doing that even though sentences are regularly altered. Many states have passed mandatory minimum sentences for certain offences and some have tried to eliminate plea bargaining or, at least, to insure that serious offenders cannot have the charges against them reduced simply to induce a guilty plea. Unfortunately, most of these changes were made under circumstances that rendered any serious evaluation of their effect difficult, if not impossible.

The two best-known changes in sentencing practices that have been studied were the so-called Rockefeller drug laws in New York and the Bartley-Fox gun law in Massachusetts. In 1973, New York State revised its criminal statutes relating to drug trafficking in an attempt to make more severe and more certain the penalties for the sale and possession of heroin (the law affecting other drugs was changed as well, but the focus of the effort, and the most severe penalties, were reserved for heroin). The major pushers—those who sold an ounce or more of heroin—would be liable for a minimum prison term of at least fifteen years and the possibility of life imprisonment. There were some loopholes. An ounce dealer could plea bargain the charges against him down, but to no lower a charge than would entail a mandatory one-year minimum prison sentence. Police informants could get probation instead of prison, and persons under the age of sixteen were exempt from the mandatory sentences. Persons ages sixteen to eighteen might be exempted from the law, a provision that was made explicit by amendments passed in 1975. A group was formed to evaluate the effect of this law. Its report, issued in 1977, concluded that there was no evidence the law had reduced either the availability of heroin on the streets of New York City or the kinds of property crime often committed by drug users. Of course, it is almost impossible to measure directly the amount of an illegal drug in circulation or to observe the illicit transactions between dealers and users, but a good deal of circumstantial evidence, gathered by the study group, suggests that no large changes occurred. There were no marked shifts in deaths from narcotics overdoses, in admissions to drug treatment programmes, in the incidence of serum hepatitis (a disease frequently contracted by junkies who use dirty needles), or in the price and purity of heroin available for sale on the street (as inferred from undercover buys of heroin made by narcotics agents).

The explanation for this disappointing experience, in the opinion of the study group, was that difficulties in administering the law weakened its deterrent power, with the result that most offenders and would-be offenders did not experience a significantly higher risk of apprehension and punishment. There was no increase (or decrease, for that matter) in the number of arrests, no increase in the number of indictments, and a slight decline in the proportion of indictments resulting in conviction. Offsetting this was a higher probability that a person convicted would go to prison. The net effect of these offsetting trends—fewer indictments but a higher risk of imprisonment if indicted and convicted—was that the probability of imprisonment for arrested drug dealers did not change as a result of the law: it was about one imprisonment per nine arrests before the law, and about one in nine afterward. On the other hand, the sentences received by those who did go to prison became more severe. Before the law was passed, only 3 per cent of persons imprisoned for drug offences received a sentence of three years or more. After the law went into effect, 22 per cent received such sentences. Perhaps because sentences became more severe, more accused persons demanded trials instead of pleading guilty and, as a result, the time it took to dispose of the average drug case nearly doubled.

Does the experience under the Rockefeller law disprove the claim that deterrence works? Not at all. If we mean by 'deterrence' changing behaviour by increasing either the certainty or the swiftness of punishment, then the Rockefeller law, as it was administered, could not have deterred behaviour because it made no change in the certainty of punishment and actually reduced the swiftness of it. If, on the other hand, we define 'deterrence' as changing behaviour by increasing the severity of punishment, then deterrence did not work in this case. What we would like to know is whether heroin trafficking would have been reduced *if* the penalties associated with it could have been made swifter or more certain.

It is possible that severity is the enemy of certainty and speed. As penalties get tougher, defendants and their lawyers have a greater incentive to slow down the process, and those prosecutors and judges who oppose heavy sentences for drug dealing may use their discretionary powers to decline indictment, accept plea bargains, grant continuances, and modify penalties in ways that reduce the certainty and the celerity of punishment. The group that evaluated the Rockefeller law suggests that reducing severity in favour of certainty might create the only real possibility of testing the deterrent effect of changes in sentences.[24]

The Bartley-Fox gun law in Massachusetts was administered and evaluated in ways that avoided some of the problems of interpreting the results of the Rockefeller drug laws. In 1974, the Massachusetts legislature amended the law that had long required persons carrying a handgun to have a licence by stipulating that a violation of this law would now entail a mandatory penalty of one year in prison, which may not be reduced by probation, parole, or judicial finagling. When the law went into effect in April 1975, various efforts were made to evaluate both the compliance of the criminal justice system with it and the law's impact on crimes involving handguns. James A. Beha traced the application of the law for two years and concluded that, despite widespread predictions to the contrary, the police, prosecutors, and judges were not evading the law. As in New York, more persons asked for trials, and delays in disposition apparently increased, but unlike in New York the probability of punishment increased for those arrested. Beha estimated in 1977 (at a time when not all the early arrests had yet worked their way through the system) that prison sentences were being imposed four times more frequently on persons arrested for illegally carrying firearms than had been true before the law was passed. Owing to some combination of the heavy publicity given to the Bartley-Fox law and to the real increase in the risk of imprisonment facing persons arrested while carrying a firearm without a licence, the casual carrying of firearms in Massachusetts seems to have decreased. This was the view expressed to interviewers by participants in the system, including persons being held in gaol, and it was buttressed by the fact that there was a sharp drop in the proportion of drug dealers arrested by the Boston police who, at the time of their arrest, were found to be carrying firearms.[25]

Three studies were made of the impact of the law on serious crime. They used slightly different methods, but in general came to the same conclusion; namely, that there was a measurable decline in the kinds of crimes that involve the casual use of firearms. More exactly, there appeared to be a decline in the proportion of assaults, robberies, and homicides in which a gun was used even though the total number of assaults and robberies in Boston was going up and the number of murders was constant. Moreover, the proportion of assaults and robberies in which guns were used did not go down in other large cities in the United States during this time.[26] In sum, the Bartley-Fox law, as applied, seems, at least during the years in which its effect was studied, to have increased the risk associated with carrying a gun, reduced the frequency with which guns were casually carried, and thereby reduced the rate at which certain gun-related crimes were committed.

An effort to achieve the same results in Michigan did not work out as well, in large measure because the judges there (in particular the judges in Wayne County, which includes Detroit) refused to apply the law. The Michigan Felony Firearm Law, which went into effect in 1977, required the imposition of a two-year prison sentence for possessing a firearm while committing a felony, and the two-year firearm sentence was to be added on to whatever sentence was imposed for the other felony. There was no general change in either the certainty or the severity of sentences issued to gun-carrying felons. To avoid adding on the two-year term required by the Felony firearm Law, many judges would reduce the sentence given for the original felony (say, assault or robbery) in order to compensate for the add-on. In other cases, the judge would dismiss the gun count or the defendant would be allowed to plea to a less serious charge.[27] Given this evasion, it is not surprising to learn that there was little effect of the law on the rate at which gun-related crimes were committed.[28]

Several states have recently altered the legal minimum drinking age; because of the effect of teenage drinking on highway fatalities, these changes have been closely studied. Between 1970 and 1973, twenty-five states lowered their legal drinking age. Shortly thereafter, Allan F. Williams and his associates examined the effect of these age reductions on highway accidents and concluded that the changes in the laws had contributed to an increase in fatal motor vehicle accidents.[29] Reacting to the implications of such findings, at least fourteen states, beginning in 1976, raised their minimum drinking ages from eighteen or nineteen to twenty or twenty-one. Williams and associates studied these changes in nine states and concluded that making it illegal for young persons (typically, those eighteen and under) to buy alcoholic beverages led to a reduction in fatal auto accidents occurring at night (when most drink-related accidents take place).[30] Alexander C. Wagenaar looked closely at one state, Michigan, and came to the same conclusion. When the legal drinking age there was lowered to eighteen, the number of persons aged eighteen to twenty involved in accidents who reportedly had been drinking began to rise; when the drinking age was raised to twenty-one, the number of such persons in crashes began to decrease.[31] Comparable conclusions were reached from a study of the consequences of altering the legal drinking age in Maine.[32] In his evaluation of laws governing drunk driving around the world, H. Laurence Ross concluded that increasing the certainty of punishment reduces the level of drunk driving.[33] By contrast, decriminalizing abortions in Hawaii did not seem to affect the estimated number of abortions performed.[34]

In sum, the evidence from these quasi-experiments is that changes in the probability of being punished can lead to changes in behaviour, though this may not happen when the legal changes exist only on paper and not in practice or when the benefits to be had from violating the law are so great as to make would-be perpetrators indifferent to the slight alteration in the risks facing them. For example, when the prospective gains from heroin trafficking or obtaining (and supplying) illegal abortions are very large, these gains can swamp the effect of modest changes in the costs of these actions, especially when (as with the New York drug law and the Michigan firearms law) the criminal justice system does not in practice impose greater risks. When the prospective benefits from violating the law are small (as with teenage drinking or perhaps with carrying an unlicensed gun), small changes in the risks can have significant effects on behaviour.

All this means that it is difficult, but not impossible, to achieve increased deterrent effects through changes in the law. To obtain these effects, society must walk a narrow line—the penalties to be imposed must be sufficiently great to offset, at the margin, the benefits of the illegal act but not so great as to generate resistance in the criminal justice system to their prompt imposition.

Experiments with Changing the Benefits of Non-crime

The hope, widespread in the 1960s, that job-creation and job-training programmes would solve many social problems, including crime, led to countless efforts both to prevent crime by supplying jobs to crime-prone youth and to reduce crime among convicted offenders by supplying them with better job opportunities after their release from prison. One preventive programme was the Neighborhood Youth Corps that gave jobs to poor young persons during the afternoons and evenings and all days during the summer. Gerald D. Robins evaluated the results of such programmes among poor blacks in Cincinnati and Detroit. He found no evi-

dence that participation in the Youth Corps had any effect on the proportion of enrollees who came into contact with the police.[35] Essentially the
same gloomy conclusion was reached by the authors of a survey of some
ninety-six delinquency prevention programmes, though there were a few
glimmers of hope that certain programmes might provide some benefits
to some persons.[36] For example, persons who had gone through a Job
Corps programme that featured intensive remedial education and job
training in a residential camp were apparently less likely to be arrested six
months after finishing their training than a control group.[37]

Though preventing crime and delinquency by job programmes of the
sort developed by the 'Great Society' seemed a lost hope, there was, initially at least, more success reported from efforts to reduce crime among
ex-offenders. Philip Cook followed 325 men who had been released from
Massachusetts prisons in 1959 and found that those parolees who were
able to find 'satisfactory' jobs (not just any job) were less likely to have
their parole revoked because they committed a new crime during an
eighteen-month follow-up period. This was true even after controlling
for the personal attributes of the parolees, such as race, intelligence, marital status, education, prior occupation, and military service.[38]

Findings such as Cook's may have reinforced the belief of policy-
makers that if only we could reintegrate the ex-offender into the labour
market, we could cut crime and at the same time save money through
reduced prison populations. By the early 1970s, forty-two states had
adopted some variety of 'work-release' programmes for prisoners by
which convicts nearing the end of their prison terms were released into
the community in order to work at various jobs during the day, returning
to prison at night or on weekends. Gordon P. Waldo and Theodore G.
Chiricos evaluated the results of work-release in Florida, and did so on
the basis of a particularly sophisticated research design. Eligible inmates
were *randomly* assigned to either a work-release or a non-release group,
to insure that there were no differences between those enrolled in the
programme and those not enrolled. And many different measures of
recidivism were calculated, not just whether the offender was later
arrested (this is a common flaw in most experiments on rehabilitation;
see Wilson, *Thinking about Crime*, ch. 9), but also the *rate* of arrests per
month free. Waldo and Chiricos found no differences whatsoever in the
rearrest rate (or in any measure of recidivism) between persons in work-
release and persons not.[39] An equally unpromising result was found by
Ann Witte in North Carolina, though there work-release may have led
offenders to commit somewhat less serious offences.[40]

If work-release seems not to reduce crime rates, perhaps it is because it focuses on work rather than wealth. Perhaps if ex-offenders had more money, especially during the crucial few months after their release, they would not need to steal in order to support themselves. Some preliminary evidence gives credence to this view. In Baltimore, about four hundred ex-convicts had been randomly assigned to one of four groups: those receiving nothing, those receiving employment assistance, those receiving financial aid, and those receiving both job placement services and financial aid. After two years, it was clear that getting employment counselling made no difference in the chances of being rearrested but that getting financial aid ($60 a week for thirteen weeks) did make a small difference (about 8 per cent). There were a host of problems with this finding, however. For one thing, recidivism was defined as whether or not the person was rearrested, not the *rate* at which he was rearrested (thus possibly obscuring changes in the frequency with which persons committed crimes). Moreover, the study excluded first offenders, alcoholics, heroin users, and persons who had not committed property offences.[41]

A fuller test of the combined effects of employment and wealth on criminal behaviour was made in Georgia and Texas. Called TARP (Transitional Aid Research Program), it involved randomly assigning about two thousand ex-convicts in each state to groups that on release from prison received financial aid, job placement services, or nothing. This experiment was not only much larger than the one in Baltimore, it did not exclude certain categories of offenders, and it used the number of arrests (and not simply whether or not arrested even once) as the measure of the outcome. It also arranged for the financial aid that ex-convicts received to be reduced, dollar for dollar, by any income they received from jobs—a more realistic assumption than operated in Baltimore, where the ex-convicts got to keep their financial aid whether or not they worked.

The ex-convicts receiving financial aid and/or employment counselling had about the same arrest rate after release as did the group not receiving the aid or the counselling. Moreover, individuals receiving TARP financial aid worked less than those who did not, so the money could be said to have discouraged, rather than encouraged, employment. The authors of the evaluation, however, were not discouraged by these findings. A complex statistical analysis led them to claim that *if* the financial aid had not induced the ex-convicts to reduce the amount of time they worked, then the payments might have reduced the ex-cons' tendency to commit crimes. That speculation, weak at best, has been challenged by critics. What is not in dispute is that, as administered, the TARP payments did not reduce crime.[42]

The reader who has followed this far a somewhat confusing array of findings should conclude, I think, something like this: there is some experimental evidence (the Cook study, TARP) that unemployment among ex-convicts tends to contribute to crime, but it is by no means easy to find ways of decreasing that unemployment (the work-release evaluation), and unemployment can be artificially increased by paying people not to work (TARP).

The best and most recent effort to master the link between employment and crime was the 'supported work' programme of the Manpower Demonstration Research Corporation (MDRC). In ten locations around the country, MDRC randomly assigned four kinds of people with employment problems to special workshops or to control groups. The four kinds of problem persons were long-term welfare (Aid to Families of Dependent Children) recipients, youthful school dropouts, former drug addicts, and ex-convicts. The workshops provided employment in unskilled jobs supplemented by training in job-related personal skills. The unique feature of the programme was that all the participants in a given work setting were drawn from the people with problems so as to minimize the usual difficulties experienced by persons with chronic unemployment problems when they find themselves competing with persons who are successful job seekers and job holders. Moreover, the workshops were led by sympathetic supervisors (often themselves ex-addicts or ex-convicts) who gradually increased the level of expected performance until, after a year or so, the trainees were able to go out into the regular job market on their own. This government-subsidized work in a supportive environment, coupled with training in personal skills, was the most ambitious effort of all we have examined to get persons with chronic problems into the labour force. Unlike vocational training in prison, supported work provided real jobs in the civilian world and training directly related to what the recipient was paid to do. Unlike work-release programmes, supported work did not leave the ex-convict to sink or swim on his own in the competitive civilian job market.

Welfare recipients and ex-addicts benefited from supported work, but ex-convicts and youthful school dropouts did not. Over a twenty-seven-month observation period, the school dropouts in the project were arrested as frequently as the similar dropouts in the control group, and the ex-offenders in the project actually were arrested more frequently (seventeen more arrests per hundred persons) than the ex-offenders in the control group.[43]

Some individuals did benefit, and they are exactly the ones we would predict would have benefited given what we know about the criminal career. School dropouts who had not been arrested before they joined the programme were less likely to be arrested later on than similar dropouts in the control group; on the other hand, youths with a prior arrest record did not benefit at all from the programme. This is consistent with what we have learned from various efforts at rehabilitation; namely, young persons inexperienced in crime are much easier to change than young persons who have committed several crimes (see Wilson, *Thinking about Crime*, ch. 9). By the same token, the older (over age thirty-five) ex-convicts seemed to benefit more from the programme than the younger ex-offenders.[44] This is consistent with the well-known tendency of many persons to 'mature out of crime' in their thirties; the supported work programme probably gave these people a little extra push in this direction.

The clear implication, I think, of the supported work project—and of all the studies to which I have referred—is that unemployment and other economic factors may well be connected with criminality, but the connection is not a simple one. If, as some persons often assume, 'unemployment causes crime', then simply providing jobs to would-be criminals or to convicted criminals would reduce their crime rates. There is very little evidence that this is true, at least for the kinds of persons helped by MDRC. Whether the crime rate would go down if dropouts and ex-convicts held on to their jobs, we cannot say, because, as the supported work project clearly showed, within a year-and-a-half after entering the programme, the dropouts and ex-convicts were no more likely to be employed than those who had never entered the programme at all, despite the great and compassionate efforts made on their behalf.[45] There are some persons for whom help, training, and jobs will make a difference—the young and criminally inexperienced dropout, the older 'burned-out' ex-addict, the more mature (over age thirty-five) ex-convict. But ex-addicts, middle-aged ex-cons, and inexperienced youths do not commit most of the crimes that worry us. These are committed by the young, chronic offender.

Marvin Wolfgang and his colleagues at the University of Pennsylvania followed the criminal careers of about ten thousand boys born in Philadelphia in 1945 (see Wilson, *Thinking about Crime*, ch. 1): they found that about one-third of the boys were arrested, but for about half of these their criminal 'careers' stopped with their first arrest. However, once a juvenile had been arrested three times, the chances that he would be arrested again were over 70 per cent.[46] These findings are consistent with the view that, for novice offenders (to say nothing of non-offenders), some combination of informal social control, the deterrent effect of punishment, and the desire for normal entry into the world of work served to restrain the growth of criminality. It is among this group that we should look for evidence of the effects of changes in the probability and severity of punishment and of changes in job availability. At the other end of the scale, 6 per cent of the Philadelphia boys committed five or more crimes before they were eighteen, accounting for over half of all the recorded delinquencies of the entire ten thousand boys and about two-thirds of all the violent crimes committed by the entire cohort.[47] The evidence from MDRC is consistent with the view that job programmes are not likely to be effective with these repeat offenders. Since we have only a few studies of the effect of deterrence on individuals (as opposed to large aggregates of people), we cannot be confident that increasing the certainty or severity of punishment would affect this group of hard-core, high-rate offenders, but there is some evidence in the Witte and Murray and Cox studies that it may.

Conclusions

The relationship between crime on the one hand and the rewards and penalties at the disposal of society on the other is complicated. It is not complicated, however, in the way some people imagine. It is not the case (except for a tiny handful of pathological personalities) that criminals are so unlike the rest of us as to be indifferent to the costs and benefits of the opportunities open to them. Nor is it the case that criminals have no opportunities. In the TARP study, for example, about half the convicts were employed just prior to being imprisoned. And in the Cook study, it was clear that ex-convicts can find jobs of a sort, though often not very attractive ones.

It is better to think of both people and social controls as arrayed on a continuum. People differ by degrees in the extent to which they are governed by internal restraints on criminal behaviour and in the stake they have in conformity;[48] they also differ by degrees in the extent to which they can find, hold, and benefit from a job. Similarly, sanctions and opportunities are changeable only within modest limits. We want to find out to what extent feasible changes in the certainty, swiftness, or severity of penalties will make a difference in the behaviour of those 'at the margin'—those, that is, who are neither so innocent nor so depraved as to be prepared to ignore small changes (which are, in fact, the only feasible changes) in the prospects of punishment. By the same token, we want to know what feasible (and again, inevitably small) changes in the availability of jobs will affect those at the margin of the labour market—those, that is, who are neither so eager for a good job nor so contemptuous of 'jerks' who take 'straight jobs' as to ignore modest changes in job opportunities. I am aware of no evidence supporting the conventional liberal view that while the number of persons who will be affected by changing penalties is very small, the number who will be affected by increasing jobs is very large; nor am I aware of any evidence supporting the conventional conservative view, which is the opposite of this.

I believe that the weight of the evidence—aggregate statistical analyses, evaluations of experiments and quasi-experiments, and studies of individual behaviour—supports the view that the rate of crime is influenced by its costs. This influence is greater—or easier to observe—for some crimes and persons than for others. It is possible to lower the crime rate by increasing the certainty of sanctions, but inducing the criminal justice system to make those changes is difficult, especially if committing the offence confers substantial benefits on the perpetrator, if apprehending and punishing the offender does not provide substantial rewards to members of the criminal justice system, or if the crime itself lacks the strong moral condemnation of society. In theory, the rate of crime should also be sensitive to the benefits of non-crime—for example, the value and availability of jobs—but thus far efforts to show that relationship have led to inconclusive results.[49] Moreover, the nature of the connection between crime and legitimate opportunities is complex: unemployment (and prosperity!) can cause crime, crime can cause unemployment (but probably not prosperity), and both crime and unemployment may be caused by common third factors. Economic factors probably have the greatest influence on the behaviour of low-rate, novice offenders and the least on high-rate, experienced ones. Despite the uncertainty that attaches to the connection between the economy and crime, I believe the wisest course of action for society is to try simultaneously to increase both the benefits of non-crime and the costs of crime, all the while bearing in mind that no feasible change in either part of the equation is likely to produce big changes in crime rates.

Some may grant my argument that it makes sense to continue to try to make those marginal gains that are possible by simultaneously changing in desirable directions both the costs of crime and benefits of non-crime, but they may still feel that it is better to spend more heavily on one side or the other of the cost–benefit equation. I have attended numerous scholarly gatherings where I have heard learned persons subject to the most searching scrutiny any evidence purporting to show the deterrent effect of sanctions but accept with scarcely a blink the theory that crime is caused by a 'lack of opportunities'.[50] Perhaps what they mean is that, since the evidence on both propositions is equivocal, then it does less harm to believe in—and invest in—the 'benign' (that is, job-creation) programme. If so, they are surely wrong. If we try to make the penalties for crime swifter and more certain, and it should turn out that deterrence does not work, then all we have done is increase the risks facing persons who commit a crime. If we fail to increase the certainty and swiftness of penalties, and it should turn out that deterrence *does* work, then we have needlessly increased the risk of innocent persons being victimized.

There is one objection to this line of analysis with which I do agree. If we try to improve on deterrence by sharply increasing the severity of sentences, and we are wrong, then we may spend a great deal of money and unnecessarily blight the lives of offenders who could safely be punished for much shorter periods of time. Reaching a sound judgment about how severe penalties should be is a much more difficult matter than deciding how certain they should be; indeed, one cannot reach such a judgment at all on purely empirical grounds. The problem of severity is inextricably bound up with the problem of justice.

Notes

1. Isaac Ehrlich, 'Participation in Illegitimate Activities: A Theoretical and Empirical Investigation', *Journal of Political Economy*, 81 (1973), 521–65.
2. Alfred Blumstein, Jacqueline Cohen, and Daniel Nagin (eds), *Deterrence and Incapacitation: Estimating the Effects of Criminal Sanctions on Crime Rates* (Washington, DC: National Academy of Sciences, 1978). Isaac Ehrlich responds to this report and its criticisms of his work in Ehrlich and Mark Randall, 'Fear of Deterrence', *Journal of Legal Studies*, 6 (1977), 293–316.
3. Colin Loftin, 'Alternative Estimates of the Impact of Certainty and Severity of Punishment on Levels of Homicide in American States', in Stephen E. Feinberg and Albert J. Reiss (eds.), *Indicators of Crime and Criminal Justice: Quantitative Studies*, report number NCJ-62349 of the Bureau of Justice Statistics (Washington, DC: US Department of Justice, 1980), 75–81.
4. Stephen S. Brier and Stephen E. Feinberg, 'Recent Econometric Modeling of Crime and Punishment: Support for the Deterrence Hypothesis?', in Feinberg and Reiss, *Indicators of Crime and Criminal Justice*, 82–97.

5. Itzhak Goldberg, 'A Note on Using Victimization Rates to Test Deterrence', Technical Report CERDCR-5-78, Center for Econometric Studies of the Justice System, Stanford University (Dec. 1978); James Q. Wilson and Barbara Boland, 'Crime', in William Gorham and Nathan Glazer (eds.), *The Urban Predicament* (Washington, DC: Urban Institute, 1976).

6. Blumstein *et al.*, *Deterrence and Incapacitation*, 23.

7. Isaac Ehrlich and Mark Randall, 'Fear of Deterrence', *Journal of Legal Studies*, 6 (1977), 304–7.

8. Alfred Blumstein and Daniel Nagin, 'The Deterrent Effect of Legal Sanctions on Draft Evasion', *Stanford Law Review*, 28 (1977), 241–75.

9. Kenneth I. Wolpin, 'An Economic Analysis of Crime and Punishment in England and Wales, 1894–1967', *Journal of Political Economy*, 86 (1978), 815–40.

10. Harvey Brenner, 'Estimating the Social Costs of National Economic Policy', vol. i, paper number 5 of *Achieving the Goals of the Employment Act of 1946*, a study prepared for the Joint Economic Committee, US Congress (94th Cong., 2d Sess.), 26 Oct. 1976.

11. Michael Block and Fred Nold, 'A Review of Some of the Results in Estimating the Social Cost of National Economic Policy', unpub. paper, Center for Econometric Studies of the Justice System, Stanford University, 1979.

12. Carl P. Simon and Ann D. Witte, *Beating the System: The Underground Economy* (Boston: Auburn House, 1982).

13. Brenner, 'Estimating the Social Costs of National Economic Policy', 70–1, 76–7, 141–6.

14. Robert W. Gillespie, *Economic Factors in Crime and Delinquency* (Washington, DC: National Institute of Law Enforcement and Criminal Justice, 1975).

15. Thomas Orsagh and Ann Dryden Witte, 'Economic Status and Crime: Implications for Offender Rehabilitation', *Journal of Criminal Law and Criminology*, 72 (1981), 1055–71.

16. Philip J. Cook, 'Research in Criminal Deterrence: Laying the Groundwork for the Second Decade', in Norval Morris and Michael Tonry, *Crime and Justice*, ii (Chicago: University of Chicago Press, 1980), 219.

17. Ann Dryden Witte, 'Estimating the Economic Model of Crime with Individual Data', *Quarterly Journal of Economics*, 94 (1980), 57–84.

18. Charles A. Murray and Louis A. Cox, Jr., *Beyond Probation: Juvenile Correlations and the Chronic Delinquent* (Beverly Hills, Calif.: Sage Publications, 1979).

19. Matthew Silberman, 'Toward a Theory of Criminal Deterrence', *American Sociological Review*, 41 (1976), 442–61.

20. Maynard L. Erickson, Jack P. Gibbs, and Gary F. Jensen, 'The Deterrence Doctrine and the Perceived Certainty of Legal Punishment', *American Sociological Review*, 42 (1977), 305–17. See also Charles R. Tittle, *Sanctions and Social Deviance: The Question of Deterrence* (New York: Praeger, 1980).

21. H. Laurence Ross, 'Law, Science, and Accidents: The British Road Safety Act of 1967', *Journal of Legal Studies*, 2 (1973), 1–78.

22. H. Laurence Ross, 'Deterrence Regained: The Cheshire Constabulary's "Breathalyzer Blitz" ', *Journal of Legal Studies*, 6 (1977), 241–9.
23. Lawrence W. Sherman and Richard A. Berk, 'The Specific Deterrent Effects of Arrest for Domestic Assault: Preliminary Findings,' unpub. paper, Police Foundation, Washington, DC, 28 Mar. 1983.
24. Joint Committee on New York Drug Law Evaluation, *The Nation's Toughest Drug Law: Evaluating the New York Experience* (New York: Association of the Bar of the City of New York, 1977), part 1, esp. pp. 13–18.
25. James A. Beha II, 'And Nobody Can Get You Out: The Impact of a Mandatory Prison Sentence for the Illegal Carrying of a Firearm on the Use of Firearms and the Administration of Criminal Justice in Boston', *Boston University Law Review*, 57 (1977), 98–146, 289–333.
26. Glenn I. Pierce and William J. Bowers, 'The Bartley–Fox Gun Law's Short-term Impact on Crime in Boston', *Annals*, 455 (1981), 120–37; Stuart Jay Deutsch and Francis B. Alt, 'The Effect of Massachusetts' Gun Control Law on Gun-Related Crimes in the City of Boston,' *Evaluation Quarterly*, 1 (1977), 543–68; Philip J. Cook, 'The Role of Firearms in Violent Crime', unpub. paper, Institute of Policy Sciences, Duke University (May 1981); Beha, 'And Nobody Can Get You Out'.
27. Milton Heumann and Colin Loftin, 'Mandatory Sentencing and the Abolition of Plea Bargaining: The Michigan Felony Firearm Statute', *Law and Society Review*, 13 (1979), 393–430.
28. Colin Lofton, Milton Heumann, and David McDowall, 'Mandatory Sentencing and Firearms Violence: Evaluating an Alternative to Gun Control', *Law and Society Review*, 17 (1983), 287–318.
29. Allan F. Williams *et al.*, 'The Legal Minimum Drinking Age and Fatal Motor Vehicle Crasher', *Journal of Legal Studies*, 4 (1975), 219–39.
30. Allan F. Williams *et al.*, 'The Effect of Raising the Legal Minimum Drinking Age on Fatal Crash Involvement', *Journal of Legal Studies*, forthcoming.
31. Alexander C. Wagenaar, 'Effects of the Raised Legal Drinking Age on Motor Vehicle Accidents in Michigan', *HSRI Research Review* (Jan.–Feb. 1981).
32. Terry M. Klein, 'The Effect of Raising the Minimum Legal Drinking Age on Traffic Accidents in the State of Maine', National Highway Traffic Safety Administration Technical Report (Dec. 1981).
33. H. Laurence Ross, *Deterring the Drunk Driver* (Lexington, Mass.: Lexington Books–D. C. Heath, 1982), 102–15. Ross notes that the deterrent effect decays over time unless reinforced by periodic and well-publicized enforcement efforts. He speculates that this decay occurs because the actual risk of apprehension for drunk driving is so slight that deterrence can only work when people form an exaggerated opinion of the risk they face.
34. Franklin E. Zimring, 'Of Doctors, Deterrence, and the Dark Figure of Crime: A Note on Abortions in Hawaii', *University of Chicago Law Review*, 39 (1972), 699–721.

35. Gerald D. Robin, 'Anti-Poverty Programs and Delinquency,' *Journal of Criminal Law and Criminology*, 60 (1969), 323–31.

36. William E. Wright and Michael C. Dixon, 'Community Prevention and Treatment of Juvenile Delinquency', *Journal of Research in Crime and Delinquency*, 14 (1977), 35–67.

37. Evaluation of the Job Corps cited in Orsagh and Witte, 'Economic Status and Crime', 1066 n. 71.

38. Philip J. Cook, 'The Correctional Carrot: Better Jobs for Parolees', *Policy Analysis*, 1 (1975), 11–54.

39. Gordon R. Waldo and Theodore G. Chiricos, 'Work Release and Recidivism', *Evaluation Quarterly*, 1 (1977), 87–107. An earlier evaluation of a California work-release program found a crime-reduction effect, but it was methodologically inferior to the Waldo–Chiricos evaluation because it did not randomly assign the inmates to experimental and control groups. Robert Jeffrey and Stephen Woolpert, 'Work Furlough as an Alternative to Incarceration', *Journal of Criminal Law and Criminology*, 65 (1974), 405–15.

40. Ann Witte, *Work Release in North Carolina: An Evaluation of its Post-Release Effects* (Chapel Hill, NC: Institute for Research in Social Science, 1975).

41. *Unlocking the Second Gate: The Role of Financial Assistance in Reducing Recidivism among Ex-Prisoners*, R. & D. Monograph no. 45 (Washington, DC: US Department of Labor, Employment and Training Administration, 1977); Charles D. Mallar and Craig V. D. Thornton, 'Transitional Aid for Released Prisoners: Evidence From the LIFE Experiment', *Journal of Human Resources*, 13 (1978), 208–36.

42. Richard A. Berk, Kenneth J. Lenihan, and Peter H. Rossi, 'Crime and Poverty: Some Experimental Evidence From Ex-Offenders', *American Sociological Review*, 45 (1980), 76–86; Peter H. Rossi, Richard A. Berk, and Kenneth J. Lenihan, *Money, Work, and Crime: Experimental Evidence* (New York: Academic Press, 1980). The claim that there was any crime-reduction effect from the financial aid is disputed in Hans Zeisel, 'Disagreement over the Evaluation of a Controlled Experiment', *American Journal of Sociology*, 88 (1982), 378–89. There is a rejoinder by Rossi, Berk, and Lenihan in the same journal (pp. 390–3) and a surrejoinder by Zeisel (pp. 394–6). I think Zeisel gets the better of the argument.

43. Peter Kemper *et al.*, *The Supported Work Evaluation: Final Benefit–Cost Analysis*, vol. v of the Final Report of the National Supported Work Demonstration (New York: Manpower Demonstration Research Corp., 1981), 69–77.

44. Irving Piliavin and Rosemary Gartner, *The Impact of Supported Work on Ex-Offenders*, vol. ii of the Final Report of the Supported Work Evaluation (New York: Manpower Demonstration Research Corp., 1981), 88–92.

45. Ibid. 43–52; Rebecca Maynard, *The Impact of Supported Work on Young School Dropouts*, vol. i of the Final Report of the Supported Work Evaluation (New York: Manpower Demonstration Research Corp., 1980), 62–6.

46. Marvin Wolfgang, Robert M. Figlio, and Thorsten Sellin, *Delinquency in a Birth Cohort* (Chicago: University of Chicago Press, 1972), 54, 65, 162.

47. Ibid., ch. 6.

48. The concept of a 'stake in conformity' is from Jackson Toby, 'Social Disorganization and Stake in Conformity', *Journal of Criminal Law and Criminology*, 48 (1957), 12–17.

49. Cf. Richard B. Freeman, 'Crime and Unemployment', in James Q. Wilson (ed.), *Crime and Public Policy* (San Francisco: Institute for Contemporary Studies, 1983), ch. 6.

50. An egregious example of the double standard at work is Charles Silberman, *Criminal Violence, Criminal Justice* (New York: Random House, 1978), wherein the studies on deterrence are closely criticized (pp. 182–95) in a way that leads the author to conclude that 'more punishment is not the answer' (p. 197) but 'community development programs' are found (on the basis of virtually no data whatsoever) to lead to 'community regeneration' and a virtual absence of criminal violence (pp. 430–66).

Preface: N. Walker, 'Reductivism and Deterrence'

As we noted in our Preface to WILSON's essay, the retributivist revival by no means silenced utilitarian or consequentialist voices in penal theory and practice. Nigel Walker is one of those who have held out most firmly against any form of retributivism, though he allows that a justifiable penal system must include a non-consequentialist (but not retributivist) constraint against the deliberate punishment of the innocent (1991: ch. 11). In these excerpts from his 1980 book *Punishment, Danger and Stigma* he sketches a utilitarian—or, as he more accurately labels it, 'reductive'—perspective on punishment, and defends the deterrent justification of punishment against some familiar objections. In the part of chapter 4 not reproduced here, he discusses the evidence as to whether punishment is effective as a deterrent, and concludes that 'the few fairly sound experiments so far reported are consistent with the common sense expectation that compliance will increase in frequency with a recent increase in some people's estimate of the probability of being detected and penalised if they do not comply' (p. 80; and see WILSON). But his concern in the passages reproduced here is with certain moral objections to the use of punishment as a deterrent.

Walker mentions and rejects, the argument that deterrents are used only to maintain the political status quo. In fact, whatever the merits of such an argument, it is not levelled against deterrence as a particular penal aim, but rather against any system of state punishment. Walker's main focus, however, is on the Kantian objection that deterrent punishments wrongly use those punished 'as means' to the social good of crime prevention, thus denying their proper moral status as 'ends' (see MURPHY: xx; VON HIRSCH: xx; Duff 1986: 178–86). He argues, first, that in other contexts we are willing to sacrifice the interests of some for the sake of a general good. Quarantine is an obvious example: if we are prepared to detain the non-culpable carrier of a dangerous disease in order to prevent harm to others, why should we not be equally willing to imprison a culpable criminal in order to prevent harm to others (for a response to this argument see Duff 1986: 172–8)? Second, he argues that a system of deterrent punishment can satisfy any plausible version of the Kantian demand that we treat people 'as ends', and never 'merely as means', so long it punishes only those who voluntarily break the law, and respects humanitarian limitations on excessively cruel or harmful penalties (for other arguments aiming to show that a system of deterrent punishments is consistent with the Kantian demand, see Lucas 1968; Nino 1983; Farrell 1985; Baker 1992).

Walker's account faces the same kinds of objection as Wilson's (see above, pp. 174, 209). First, can punishment be a cost-effective system of deterrence, bearing in mind that for consequentialists punishment can be justified only if its crime-preventive or other benefits do outweigh its costs, including the suffering caused to those punished and their families or friends? Second, even if we do, on humanitarian grounds, forbid grossly cruel penalties, might we not for the sake of efficient deterrence have to inflict penalties which are out of all proportion to the seriousness of the crime? It is hard to see how the 'reductive' aim of preventing crime could by itself generate a firm requirement of proportionality between seriousness of crime and severity of punishment (see Hart 1968; Goldman 1979, who argues that a system of deterrent punishments could be effective only if it imposed disproportionately harsh penalties). Finally, we must ask again whether the deterrent threat of punishment against potential offenders (and not just the actual imposition of punishment on actual offenders) does not fail to treat them with the moral respect that is their due.

References

BAKER, B. M. (1992), 'Consequentialism, Punishment, and Autonomy', in W. Cragg (ed.), *Retributivism and its Critics* (Stuttgart), 149–61.

DUFF, R. A. (1986), *Trials and Punishments* (Cambridge).

FARRELL, D. M. (1985), 'The Justification of General Deterrence', *Philosophical Review*, 94: 367–94.

GOLDMAN, A. H. (1979), 'The Paradox of Punishment', *Philosophy and Public Affairs*, 9: 42–58.

HART, H. L. A. (1968), 'Prolegomenon to the Principles of Punishment', in H. L. A. Hart, *Punishment and Responsibility* (Oxford), 1–27.

LUCAS, J. R. (1968), 'Or Else', *Proceedings of the Aristotelian Society*, 69: 207–22.

NINO, C. S. (1983), 'A Consensual Theory of Punishment', *Philosophy and Public Affairs*, 12: 289–306.

WALKER, N. (1991), *Why Punish?* (Oxford).

Reductivism and Deterrence

N. WALKER

The Utilitarian (Reductive) Justification

This holds that the justification for penalizing offences is that this reduces their frequency. It is therefore more precise to call this the 'reductive' point of view, since utilitarians are really concerned with maximizing the sum of human happiness, and could conceivably argue that penalties severe enough to make a real impact on the frequency of, say, motoring offences would generate more unhappiness than they would prevent. 'Reducers' believe that penalties reduce the frequency of offences in one or more of the following ways:

   (i) deterring the offender (i.e. inducing him to refrain from further law-breaking—or at least law-breaking of the same sort—by means of the memory of the penalty);

  (ii) deterring potential imitators (i.e. discouraging them from following the offender's example through fear of the penalty which he incurred);

 (iii) reforming the offender (i.e. improving his character so that he is less often inclined to commit offences even when he can do so without fear of the penalty);

 (iv) educating the public to take a more serious view of such offences (thus indirectly reducing their frequency);

  (v) protecting the public (or specific potential victims such as wives) by incapacitating offenders (e.g. by long prison sentences).

Reducers can compromise with limiting retributivists by accepting maximum penalties, although these will occasionally interfere to some extent with their aims: for example by setting a limit to the length of protective custody. They can also compromise with the retributive principle of 'no penalty without culpability'. They are probably making a sacrifice by doing so, since it is generally believed that the efficacy of general deterrents would be maximized by ensuring that *someone* is penalized for every known crime, even if those who penalized were secretly aware that they were sometimes penalizing the innocent. But by conceding that the innocent should not be knowingly penalized the reducer is not surrendering his position.

Deterring

Why is deterrence, one of the oldest techniques of social control, nowadays so discreditable? Partly because it is associated in people's minds with inhumane kinds of penalty, and especially capital punishment. Deterrence is, after all, the *deliberate* threat of harm with the purpose of discouraging specified types of conduct: a threat which, if it is to be credible, has to be carried out. In a non-sadistic culture the deliberate infliction of death, pain, or other harm is seen as requiring a very strong justification if it is not to be condemned. Dentists and surgeons, who knowingly cause pain, are tolerated only because they are believed to be conferring a benefit which outweighs the pain. If the benefit is doubtful or non-existent, toleration very quickly turns into censure. Or if the benefit excludes the person harmed, this too is nowadays regarded by many people as morally unacceptable. It is all right, even praiseworthy, if someone decides to die for his country; but no longer all right to compel him to do so against his will.

Both these arguments are well-known objections to deterrents. More recently I have heard a political argument. Although I cannot find it in the literature, it was put forward in discussion at the Stockholm Symposium on deterrence in 1975. It is that deterrents are used only to maintain the political status quo. This implies of course that the status quo is bound to be worse than the changes which deterrents prevent or delay: a naïvely sweeping assumption. Naïvety apart, however, it is demonstrably untrue that deterrents are never used in political innovation. New regimes often enforce change by executions or other harsh penalties. Nor will it do to shift ground slightly and say that even if deterrents are used in this way it emphasizes that they are always instruments of the faction in power. For they are also used by terrorists, as the very name suggests.

A fourth argument is also latent rather than explicit in the literature. It is that to be effective deterrents must exceed the limits of what is acceptable, limits which can be defined either in retributive or in humanitarian terms. This argument can be considered after the two main objections have been discussed.

[In the section of Walker 1980, ch. 4 not reprinted here, Walker deals with 'the argument that deterrents are immoral because they involve the

deliberate infliction of suffering for a purpose which they cannot achieve':
he argues that '[t]he few fairly sound experiments so far reported are consistent with the commonsense expectation that compliance will increase in
frequency with a recent increase in some people's estimate of the probability of being detected and penalized if they do not comply' (p. 80).]

Deterrence as Human Sacrifice

This does not, however, answer the moralist who concedes that deterrence benefits those who would otherwise be victims of crime, but points
out that it does not benefit the criminals who suffer the deterrent penalties.[1] He might argue that we no longer regard it as right to compel people to sacrifice themselves unwillingly for the benefit of the societies to
which they belong. Sacrifices must be voluntary. Vaccination and inoculation are no longer compulsory for Britons in spite of the death and
impairment which they would save. Conscientious objectors to service in
the armed forces are no longer conscripted even in wars.

This is probably an oversimplification. Vaccination and inoculation are
no longer compulsory, but quarantine can be; and typhoid carriers in
catering jobs can be compelled to find other occupations. Conscientious
objectors may be excused from killing but required to perform other
tasks which help an embattled society, such as ambulance work. It is
expediency rather than morality which has prompted these concessions.
Conscientious objectors are a nuisance in the armed services.
Compulsory vaccination was unpopular, troublesome, and eventually
unnecessary. We do not think it immoral to require many minor and
some not so minor acts of self-sacrifice: examples are jury service, cur-
rency restrictions, food rationing, or the compulsory purchase of homes
as part of replanning operations.

Is there something special about the involuntary sacrifices involved in
deterrents which makes them morally objectionable? Kant is often
quoted in support of the view that there is:

... Punishment can never be administered merely as a means for promoting
another Good, either with regard to the Criminal himself or to Civil Society, but
must in all cases be imposed only because the individual on whom it is inflicted
has committed a Crime. For one man ought never to be dealt with merely as a
means subservient to the purpose of another, nor be mixed up with the subjects
of Real Right [i.e. goods or property]. Against such treatment his Inborn
Personality has a Right to protect him, even although he may be condemned to
lose his Civil Personality. He must first be found guilty and punishable, before

there can be any thought of drawing from his punishment any benefit for himself or his fellow citizens.[2]

It should be noticed, however, that what Kant is condemning is the use of punishment *merely* as a means of promoting, say, the good of society. He seems to concede that once a person has been found guilty and punishable it is not reprehensible to think of 'drawing from his punishment ... benefit for himself or his fellow citizens'. As Hart says '... Kant never made the mistake of saying that we must never treat men as means. He insisted that we should never treat them *only* as means, "but in every case as ends also".'[3]

Persons as Ends

If so, deterrents are morally objectionable *only if their use is incompatible with treating men as ends*. This raises the question 'What did Kant mean by treating a person as an end?'; or rather, since Kant is dead but his viewpoint survives, however imprecisely, 'What sensible meaning can now be attached to these words?' For Kant almost certainly meant 'punishing them retributively as morally responsible agents'.[4] Since it would be a pity to beg the whole question by assuming the primacy of the retributive justification of punishment, let us consider non-Kantian versions:

(i) that penal systems should deal with people as if they were rational actors cognizant of (if not necessarily subscribing to) the laws of the society in which they live.

But this version would not merely be compatible with the use of penalties as deterrents; it would tend to support it. If people act rationally, and know the laws and the penalties for breaking them, it is arguable that we acknowledge and honour this by deterrents, and certainly more so than by attempts at reform: that we are in effect treating offenders as having voluntarily chosen to risk penalties as the price of disobedience.

Obviously it is fictional to proceed as if all law-breakers voluntarily choose this risk. The impulsive and compulsive do not; nor do those who fail to realize that they are breaking the law. Officially the law presumes that people know what is prohibited and intend the natural consequences of their acts; but sentencers are usually more realistic, and mitigate penalties in cases of pardonable ignorance of the law or thoughtless actions. This is not inconsistent with a policy of penalizing intentional law-breakers in deterrent ways; and it does not mean that interpretation (i) rules this out: merely that to impose deterrents on *all* law-breakers would be going too far.

The second non-Kantian interpretation of 'treating a person as an end' is:

> (ii) that penal measures should have regard to the welfare of the people subjected to them.

This could either have a strong or a weak meaning. In its strong form it would in effect be saying that no penalty should operate to the detriment of the offender himself. Only penalties which conferred benefits on him, whether spiritual or material, should be used. This would allow reformative measures but not the deliberate infliction of loss or hardship in order to deter others. If it were intended to deter the offender himself from further law-breaking it would have to be shown to be likely that the deterrent penalty was less injurious than the non-penal consequences of future law-breaking to the offender. This would limit individual deterrents to cases in which the penalized behaviour was likely to damage the offender's health, finances, or social relations.[5]

Retributive or Humanitarian Limits

Even if the strong version seems to go too far, interpretation (ii) does seem to express a feeling which a lot of people have about deterrents, a feeling that in order to be effective they must often exceed the limits of what is morally acceptable. I referred to this earlier as the fourth moral argument against deterrence, and it seems to be concerned, as interpretation (ii) is, with the offender's own welfare. It implies that, if the limits of what is acceptable by way of imposed loss, suffering, or hardship could be defined, some intended deterrents might be found to fall within them, some beyond them.

But how and where are the limits set? If by retributive considerations, proportionality[6] will merely dictate that the deterrent penalty for illegal parking should be less severe than that for reckless driving, and so on. In extreme cases it will also dictate that the harm done to the offender should not exceed the harm which he intended or consciously risked.

More often, the limits which are envisaged seem to be humanitarian rather than retributive. Do they involve any principles that can be put into general terms? If we list the kinds or aspects of deterrent penalties to which humane objections are most often raised, they seem to be

a. death, mutilation, and other corporal punishments;

b. permanently stigmatizing penalties;

c. penalties which impose hardship on innocent dependants or associates as well as on the defender.

Deterrents such as fines, which have no permanent or stigmatizing effects, do not seem to arouse moral objections. It seems possible to define the target of humanitarian objections as harm which is bodily, life-long, or spread to non-offenders.

This would rule out capital punishment, flogging, the amputation of hands, the deliberate penalizing of, say, offenders' families, and detention for periods or under conditions which are likely to have permanent ill-effects. It would not rule out fines fixed with due regard to offenders' situations, short periods of detention in decent conditions, compulsory service to the community, disqualification from driving,[7] or other common deterrents.

The weak form of interpretation (ii) would also involve a duty to do what is possible to ensure that the harm done by deterrents is limited, as far as is practicable, to the offender himself and to a tolerable period.[8]

Notes

1. Except to the extent that some of them are saved from being the victims of others' crimes.
2. *Rechtslehre* (1797).
3. (1968).
4. See T. Honderich's discussion of what he meant (1976).
5. e.g. misuse of alcohol or drugs. But individual deterrents are not very effective in such cases.
6. See Sir Rupert Cross (1975: 117–18).
7. It may be pointed out that disqualification from driving was intended by the legislature as a means of protection, not as a deterrent. That does not mean, however, that it does not operate as a deterrent.
8. This has implications for the control of stigma; see Walker (1980: ch. 7).

References

CROSS, R. (1975), *The English Sentencing System* (2nd edn., Butterworths, London; 1st edn. 1971).

HART, H. L. A. (1968), *Punishment and Responsibility: Essays in the Philosophy of Law* (Oxford University Press, London).

HONDERICH, T. (1976), *Punishment: The Supposed Justifications* (2nd edn., Penguin, Harmondswroth; 1st edn. 1969).

KANT, I. (1797), *Rechtslehre* (Voss, Leipzig; translated as *The Philosophy of Law* by W. Hastie, Clarke, Edinburgh, 1887).

WALKER, N (1980), *Punishment, Danger and Stigma* (Oxford).

Preface: T. Mathiesen, 'General Prevention as Communication'

One of the most interesting features of contemporary penal discourse is the extent to which communication is seen as a central feature of punishment. Philosophers claim that an essential characteristic of punishment is the moral message which it seeks to convey, whether to express community feelings (see FEINBERG), to communicate censure to the criminal (VON HIRSCH), or to teach the wrongdoer a moral lesson (H. MORRIS). Proponents of deterrence (see WILSON, WALKER) also rely on the communicative dimension of punishment, although the message that punishment conveys is, on this account, very different: what the law now says to potential criminals is 'Obey, or else'; and such a strategy can be effective only if they understand that message, and accordingly resist the temptation to offend. Mathiesen here analyses this process of penal communication, and argues that it is much more complex and problematic than is usually assumed.

As part of a wider critique of the prison and its various supposed rationales, Mathiesen addresses the 'general prevention paradigm'. 'General prevention' refers to the various processes of deterrence, moral education, and habit formation through which penal measures aim to influence the conduct of those who might otherwise be tempted to commit crimes. This way of thinking about punishment's effects is, Mathiesen argues, so deeply ingrained in our common-sense thinking that it has become an almost unassailable mental 'paradigm'. Instead of questioning whether punishments do indeed have the intended kinds of preventive effect, we take it for granted that they do. Negative research findings do little to erode the deep-rooted assumption that punishment is an effective general deterrent, and advocates of deterrent policies frequently appeal to common sense experience rather than to empirical research results, as evidence that agents can be deterred by disincentives. However, Mathiesen argues, the fallacy in such appeals lies in the fact that while 'the average citizen' (see WILSON: 177) might indeed view the risk of criminal conviction and punishment as an effective disincentive, this might not be how differently placed individuals assess their position. It might well be that 'general prevention functions in relation to those who do not "need" it. In relation to those who "need" it, it does not function (below, p. 231).'

Deterrent theorists (see WILSON, WALKER) will argue against this that there is empirical evidence to support the 'common-sense' view that punishment can deter. But Mathiesen offers a deeper analysis of the process of general prevention as a communicative process, and of the central (but largely unexplored) mechanisms of action which this process involves. He argues that the process is subject to all the vicissitudes which threaten *any* process of communication. Drawing on contemporary work in semiotics and communication studies, he breaks the penal communication down into its component parts, and makes explicit the assumptions which must hold, and the conditions which must obtain, if the process is effectively to convey its intended message to its intended audience. One such condition is that the message must be transmitted clearly and faithfully; another is that the signs and symbols which carry the intended message must be read and understood in the same way by sender and receiver. But neither of these conditions, Mathiesen argues, in fact obtains.

Contemporary penality relies on the mass media to carry its message to the public; punishment is no longer a public spectacle, directly viewed by the citizenry (for descriptions of earlier penal spectacles, see Spierenburg 1984; van Dulmen 1990; Linebaugh 1992). Consequently, the filtering and focusing effects of the media—which pursue their own conceptions of what is newsworthy—distort the penal communication and give an inaccurate depiction of the realities of crime and punishment (see Ericson *et al.* 1991). Furthermore, the 'public' is not a homogenous population which reads and interprets meanings in the same way. Instead, it consists of differentiated groups, with different social positions, different experiences, and different orientations to the law and its meaning. Instead of interpreting penal messages as morally authoritative statements, or warnings of imminent capture and conviction, the most criminally active groups may read them as merely the empty threats of a repressive authority.

Mathiesen's analysis raises important questions about the intended audience for penal communications. While many theorists (including deterrence theorists) have assumed that punishment's message is primarily for the criminal or potential criminal (but see FEINBERG for other possible addressees), one might suggest that the intended audience for much penal symbolism is actually the law-abiding, respectable public, who are being reassured that 'something is being done' about crime (see also Durkheim 1984 for the view that punishment's symbols are primarily directed towards the law-abiding). If this is indeed so (and much recent law and order politics fits this posture), it raises in a new way the moral problem of using the offender as a means of serving the ends of others.

Mathiesen himself goes on to raise moral objections to the use of punishment (particularly imprisonment) as a deterrent: it involves improperly sacrificing some for the sake of others (but see WALKER); and the pains of punishment fall with disproportionate severity on the disadvantaged (see also MURPHY; CARLEN; and Hudson 1987). His conclusion is not that we must therefore find some other rationale for imprisonment: rather, we should seek to abolish its use.

But is there no truth in the 'common-sense' view that punishment can (to some extent and in some cases) serve as a deterrent; that at least some offenders have voluntarily and culpably broken laws that justifiably claimed their obedience; and that they are not treated unjustly if they are then punished in order to deter them and others from crime? Furthermore, if we are to abolish prisons (if not all kinds of punishment), what should replace them? Mathiesen argues that abolitionists should not try to offer determinate alternatives to imprisonment (see Mathiesen 1974: 11–36; 1986, on 'the unfinished') and this may indeed be a useful tactic in respect of particular campaigns for change. But questions remain about the alternative routes which might be explored, where they might lead, and at what cost (see Downes 1980). We must ask too whether we can plausibly hope to abolish imprisonment as such—a goal which is quite distinct from other, less utopian aims, such as reducing rates of imprisonment, shortening prison terms, humanizing the regimes in which prisoners serve their sentences, and creating a more 'porous' prison which is less completely cut off from the community outside (see Wood 1992; also see CARLEN and BIANCHI on abolitionist modes of detention).

References

DOWNES, D. (1980), 'Abolition: Possibilities and Pitfalls', in A. E. Bottoms and R. H. Preston (eds.), *The Coming Penal Crisis* (Edinburgh), 71–83.

DURKHEIM, E. (1984), *The Division of Labour in Society* (1893), trans. W. D. Halls (London).

ERICSON, R. V., BARANEK, P. M., and CHAN, J. B. L. (1991), *Representing Order: Crime, Law, and Justice in the News Media* (Toronto).

HUDSON, B. (1987), *Justice through Punishment? A Critique of the 'Justice' Model of Corrections* (London).

LINEBAUGH, P. (1992), *The London Hanged* (London).

MATHIESEN, T. (1974), *The Politics of Abolition* (London).

—— (1986), 'The Politics of Abolition', *Contemporary Crises*, 10: 81–94.

SPIERENBURG, P. (1984), *The Spectacle of Suffering* (Cambridge).

VAN DULMEN, R. (1990), *Theatre of Horror: Crime and Punishment in Early Modern Germany* (Cambridge).

WOOD, C. (1992), *The End of Punishment* (Edinburgh).

General Prevention as Communication

T. MATHIESEN

The serious uncertainty and lack of clarity which at best may be said to exist concerning the effects of general prevention will be taken as the point of departure below. The discussion will run through the following steps.

First, we shall try to explain why the results show such uncertainty, lack of clarity, and at best such modest or marginal associations. In order to do so, we shall utilize some basic notions from communications sociology.

Next, we shall discuss the moral problems which reasoning in terms of general prevention raises. General prevention does not only raise questions of efficacy, but also questions of morality. In particular, we shall emphasize the moral problem inherent in exposing a few, usually impoverished and stigmatized people, to particular pain in order to prevent others from committing similar acts. . . .

General Prevention as Communication

In the context of general prevention, punishment may be viewed as a *message* from the state. First, punishment is a message which intends to say that crime does not pay (deterrence). Secondly, it is a message which intends to say that you should avoid certain acts because they are morally improper or incorrect (moral education). Thirdly, it is a message which intends to say that you should get into the habit of avoiding certain acts (habit formation). The criminal justice system, comprising the prosecuting authorities, the police, the courts, and the sanctioning apparatus which includes the prison system, may be seen as a large machine having the purpose of communicating this message to the people. The machinery constitutes one of the state's most important mechanisms for 'talking' to the people about the people's own doings.

The fact that punishment is an attempt to communicate a message, or a set of messages, is acknowledged by the analysts and proponents of general prevention. For example, Andenæs says that 'The communication process from the legislator and the law enforcement agencies to the public is therefore a central link in the operating of general prevention' (Andenæs 1977: 216–17). Andenæs also states that in 'older penal theory there was not much emphasis on this. It seems as if a correspondence between the objective realities and the comprehension of the individual was tacitly assumed' (Andenæs 1977: 217).

But even if the communication process today presumably is seen as 'a central link', there is not much emphasis on it. What is emphasized, if anything, is the rather simplistic question of people's knowledge of the law and legal regulations, for example their knowledge of maximum penalties. However, the communication process is a complex process of interaction between sender and receiver, which raises far broader and more complicated questions than just 'knowledge' of the law. Legal and penal theory of general prevention has hardly, if at all, approached these questions.

The questions go to the core of the issue 'does prison have a defence— in general prevention?'

The politics of signification

First of all, what do we understand by 'communication'? The concept is complex. In extremely few words, communication stands for *the transfer of meaning* between interacting parties. Transfer of meaning may take place between individuals, groups, classes, or whole societies, or between the state and the members of a society. When transfer of meaning takes place between the state and the members of society, which is the assumption of general prevention theory, particular state institutions are responsible for the transmission, and the transmission is usually very predominantly a one-way process—from the state institutions to the people.

But meaning cannot be transferred directly. As the Norwegian sociologists Hjemdal and Risan (1985) have formulated it, we need what may be called 'carriers of meaning' to accomplish the transfer. Carriers of meaning may be words, pictures, bodily postures, facial expressions, etc. Language is of course a crucial carrier of meaning. It is, then, *the carriers of meaning which are transferred*: the receivers must recreate the meaning from the carriers which they receive. This particular point is very significant. The recreation of meaning from the carriers which are received presupposes a common context of symbolic understanding. When such a context is not there, or is insufficient, the recreation of meaning becomes correspondingly broken or deficient. The function of the carriers of meaning in the communication process may be elaborated as follows.

The meaning which people assign to events and objects is not only dependent on how the events and objects 'are'. The meaning which people assign to events, such as new legislation or sentences proclaimed by the courts, or to objects, such as police uniforms of police roadblocks, is not only dependent on how these events and objects 'are' in an external sense. The meaning is also to a great extent dependent on how the events and objects are signified. Without the signs which signify, the events and objects alone would be meaningless. 'Sign' here is used as a synonym for 'carrier of meaning'. The signs 'carry' the meaning. Language is a particularly important set of signs carrying meaning. Other material expressions which may be perceived through our senses may also function as signs carrying meaning.

The signs, whether they are language or other expressions which may be perceived, 'carry' the meaning to the other party, thus creating meaning, only when they function within a context of understanding which is given in advance. The signs, then, become creative of meaning when they function in relation to a background of other signs which provide a pre-understanding; the meaning carried by the signs comes forth and becomes 'understandable' when the sign is seen in relation to the sign system or structure of signs which it enters into. This pre-understanding or structure of signs must be common to sender and receiver if the meaning which is created in the receiver is to be a meaning common to the two parties.

Thus, in a very brief and sketchy way we may say that 'meaning' is produced through the relationship between an external reality (what we here have called events and objects), signs (whether they are language or other expressions which may be perceived), and interpretation (the process by which the sign is seen in relation to the structure of signs which it enters into).

We have here touched on and interpreted some features of the school of thought within linguistics called 'semiology' or 'semiotics'. (Central contributors are Ferdinand de Saussure, C. S. Peirce, Roland Barthes and Umberto Eco; see for example Barthes 1972; for a general presentation, see Fiske 1982.) Semiology comes from the Greek *semion* which stands for 'sign', and *logos* which stands for 'teaching' or 'science'. Semiology, then, is 'the general science of signs'.

Thus, it may be said that the state's communication with members of the society, its attempt at communicative transfer of meaning, constitutes a *politics of signification* (to paraphrase Hall *et al.* 1978). The state's politics of signification are exercised in a long string of institutional contexts, such as the school, church institutions, and in the so-called criminal justice system. And signs which are seemingly small and insignificant may be of crucial importance.

The *school*, in other words, is not just an institution for the inculcation of knowledge, but also an institution which in decisive ways brings signs to bear on reality, or signifies reality, for generation after generation. The designations 'curriculum', 'lesson', 'test', and 'examination' are a few of the very large number of designations of reality which enter into a structure of signs relevant to the school, and which give definite and general associations in the direction of ascetic duty and discipline.

The *church* is not just an institution which satisfies people's religious beliefs and needs, but also an institution which—historically in at least as decisive a way as the school—has signified reality for generation after generation. The designations 'sin', 'damnation', 'belief', and 'forgiveness' are some of the many designations which comprise a churchly structure of signs, and which give associations in the direction of divine omnipotence and churchly wisdom.

The same applies to the system which—not accidentally—is designated *the criminal justice system*: this system is not just a system which prosecutes and punishes offenders against the law, but is also an institution which, precisely while prosecuting and punishing, very strongly emphasizes a whole series of designations of reality. The designations 'guilty', 'sentence', 'legal procedure', and 'criminal justice system' are some of the many designations used by the 'criminal justice system' which jointly comprise a structure of legal signs giving associations in the direction of thorough, carefully prepared, and reasonable treatment of offenders. In the context of this book, the example of the 'criminal justice system' is particularly interesting: it shows how the soothing designations of the system are so ingrained that it is difficult to avoid them even here.

The question of the preventive effect of punishment, and of prison as punishment, may now be considered within the framework of the politics of signification.

Punishment and signification

Above we emphasized that meaning is produced through the relationship between an external reality—what we called events and objects; signs—language and other perceivable expressions; and interpretation—the process of placing the sign in relation to a wider structure of signs.

Meaning, then, is produced through an interaction between these three aspects or elements.

As a method of implementing general prevention, state-produced punishment is confronted by problems in all three respects. In more detail, state punishment with a view to general prevention fails to the extent that the factual events and objects in question (the legislative measures, the sentencing practice, and so on), the designations used, and the sign structure within which the signification is received and interpreted deviate from what it takes to make general prevention work.

The general point is that the failure of punishment as the state's communicative practice contributes significantly to explain the unclarity and uncertainty which prevails with respect to the preventive effect of prison.

The factual: sentencing practice, legislation, and detection risk Some star examples exist to which proponents of general prevention frequently refer in support of the theory. The high risk of detection and the severe punishments against breaking the rules (concerning the blackout during World War II, for instance) is one of them. In the Scandinavian context, a particular period without any police in Denmark, also during World War II, is another.

The example of the blackout is referred to by Johs. Andenæs in an article from 1950:

As an example of rules which are close to 100% effective because the actor must count on every rule violation being detected and consequential, the rules concerning blackout in wartime may be mentioned. Here the purely deterrent effect is sufficient, even without any support from the moral authority which the law normally has. (Andenæs 1950/1962: 116–17, translated from the Norwegian by the present author.)

In the same article he has the following to say about the period without police in Copenhagen:

In September 1944, the Germans arrested the whole Danish police force. During the rest of the occupation, the police service was performed by an improvised and unarmed team of guards, who were almost completely unable to do anything unless the perpetrator was caught in the very act . . . Crime immediately proved to increase very significantly . . . (Andenæs 1950/162: 121.)

The high detection risk and the severe punishments in connection with the blackout probably did create conformity. And the sudden and complete dissolution of the whole police force probably did increase the crime rate. (Though it should be mentioned that blackout during wartime is obviously also very much in one's own interest, and that doubts have been raised concerning the effect of the dissolution of the police force in Denmark: it has been argued that the crime figures during this particular period were to be expected simply by extrapolating from the figures prior to the period—see Wolf 1967; discussed in Balvig 1984a.) However, as Nils Christie (1971) has pointed out in an important article, such drastic changes in the sanctioning system are certainly not a part of the daily round. On the contrary, they are very unusual, atypical, and extreme events within the criminal justice system. Christie formulates it as follows, in connection with court decisions:

The point here is that almost all of the star examples concerning the effects of general prevention are relevant *to a situation which is completely different from that which confronts the judge* when he is to select the concrete reaction. Normally, the judge must choose between sanctions which are rather close to each other— three or six months imprisonment, or at most between conditional and unconditional sentence—while the examples of general prevention concern dramatic differences between stimuli, such as police control against no police control. (Christie 1971: 55, translated from the Norwegian by the present author.)

The same point is also important in connection with the legislative process. Because the legislative process is complex and slow, the legal rules—for example the punishment limits for given types of offence—are largely changed gradually and/or in terms of details. To be sure, in situations of moral and social panic, change may occur suddenly, and it may be extensive (see Mathiesen 1990: ch. 5). But despite the existence of important examples of moral panics, which do say much about instability of the moral standards in society, they (fortunately) do not constitute the everyday life of the legislation process. Furthermore, we have no theoretical or empirical grounds for assuming that legal change based on a panic is particularly effective in terms of general prevention. If anything, the irrationality, frenzy, and brushing aside of elementary principles of due process which tend to characterize moral panics, probably produce the reverse of the desired effect in the relevant groups where the panic strikes.

From a communicative point of view, what we have pointed to above is of decisive importance. It is unreasonable to expect the choices between sanctions or sanctioning levels which are close to each other, and which constitute the everyday routine of criminal policy, to be picked up and received by the receivers with a meaning corresponding to that of the senders. Disregarding for a minute the mediating links in the communication process, which make communication selective (and which we will return to shortly), *reality* in the message structure is in other words such that the process of picking up the message is difficult: the relatively fine nuances which exist in sentencing practice are based on complex conditions relevant to the particular individuals who are brought to trial. And, in much the same way, complex arguments concerning obedience to the law and the effects of legislation constitute the background for the gradual and/or small changes which occur in criminal law.

The following should be noted clearly. Taken together, and over time, small changes in sentencing practice and legislation may lead to larger-scale changes in criminal policy. Indeed, this is happening today. The criminal policy of a number of Western countries is currently being tightened up, with an increased punishment level (see Mathiesen 1990: ch. 1). This is an important part of the background for the congested prisons. The point is that the changes which occur *at a given point in time* are usually relatively small, and based on complex reasoning.

The fact that large-scale changes to a significant extent occur over time through an accrual of small changes may be generalized to other parts of criminal policy. The development of the Norwegian police constitutes an interesting case in point. In 1970 a general plan advocating major changes in the organization of the police as well as greatly increased resources to the police was presented (Aulie Report 1970). Precisely because it was presented as a major plan, it was possible to discuss and criticize it publicly, and the plan was in fact abandoned in the mid-1970s. After the shelving of the plan, however, the police have changed in ways which are very reminiscent of the original proposal. But the changes have occurred gradually, in a cumulative fashion from year to year (Lorentzen 1977). The gradual changes have not caused any sensation or debate, and today the Norwegian police are completely reorganized and greatly strengthened in terms of power and authority. The significant lesson for us is that a political message structure consisting of small, cumulative steps is more difficult to perceive, pick up, and react to—much like the small steps in a cumulative penal development.

Before concluding this section, let me add that a very low detection risk (see Mathiesen 1990: 55–7) is also an integral part of what we have called the reality of the message structure. In an industrialized, urbanized, and anonymized society increased police resources will only change the detection risk in a marginal way. This is a basic feature of modern social reality, which has become a part of the message structure. A detection risk like the one we had during the blackouts of World War II is entirely atypical.

Signification: filtration and focusing   Above (p. 223) we emphasized that 'reality'—the events and objects which form a part of the message structure—not only constitute actual events and objects, but also simultaneously designations which carry (or fail to carry) meaning. In other words, the actual events or objects cannot be separated from their designations: they simultaneously signify (or fail to signify) a meaning which the senders wish to transmit to the receivers. The signification aspect of events and objects was actually with us in the preceding discussion: the conditions which sentencing practice is based on, and the arguments concerning obedience to the law and the effects of legislation which constitute the basis of new penal legislation, do not find adequate designations through the factual aspects of sentencing practice and legislation.

But the signification process may also be discussed in more direct terms, and with an emphasis on some further aspects. Through which media is information about the law communicated in our society? Primarily through the large mass media, which are complex organizations with internal tensions, conflicts, and modes of co-operation, and which, above all, represent interests quite different from that of communicating information about the law. The interests in question may be summarized as a combination of news and sales interests: a combined emphasis on striking news and news that sells. This distorts the information in general which is transmitted, and it certainly distorts the communication of information about crime in the direction of the highly deviant, the violent, and the sexual (Aarsnes *et al.* 1974; Simonsen 1976; From 1976; Hjemdal 1987; summarized in Mathiesen 1986: 154–7). And the more or less refined details in legislation and sentencing practice have a very hard time penetrating and becoming recognizable. The process has two related features. First, what may be called *filtration*.

'Filtration' means that the details of legislation and sentencing practice, the choices between sanctions which are close to each other and which constitute the everyday routine of criminal policy, are systematically if not totally left out. Filtration takes place in a number of concrete nodal points in media organizations: in the relationship between the journalist and his or her source, at the internal meetings where long-range priorities concerning news are decided, at the desk where the quick and short-range decisions about priorities are made.

Secondly, what may be called *focusing*. 'Focusing' means that, after filtration has taken place, specific attention is paid to what is considered really newsworthy. A magnifying glass, so to speak, is put on the newsworthy. Focusing takes place through decisions about priorities concerning the front page, the selection of pictures, decisions about layout, the use of vignettes calling the reader's or viewer's attention to the story, as well as dramaturgic treatment of the material through the use of serials, the selection of background material, and so on (on the dramaturgy of the media, see Hernes 1984; Mathiesen and Hjemdal 1986).

The difference as well as the relationship between filtration and focusing is important. Through filtration, unsensational and undramatic material is taken *out*, while through focusing, sensational and dramatic material is moved *forward*. This is the main difference between the two. But, as mentioned already, focusing on the sensational and dramatic at the same time takes place *with the background of* filtration; with the background, you might say, of the first preliminary sorting. This is the main relationship between the two. The unsensational and undramatic material which survives filtration remains in the news. But focusing gives it only a relegated position.

There are variations between the media in terms of degree of filtration and focusing. There are, in this respect, differences between the radio, television, and newspapers, as well as for example between various newspapers. But the literature on media sociology gives us reason to emphasize that the two processes are accelerating, and that a development is taking place in the direction of uniformity with respect to content. It would lead us too far from our topic to detail the indications and background of this development (for a discussion of it, see Mathiesen 1986: chs. IV, VI). Here the point is that the acceleration of the two processes, and the increasing uniformity of media content, provides a background for the generalizations concerning the communication process presented above.

The main point may also be formulated in this way. Due to filtration and focusing, it is primarily the sensational and dramatic 'legal news' which is transmitted through the media, thus reaching the larger population—dramatic changes in legislation, particularly sensational or titillating cases, and so on. The small differences, and the way in which the criminal justice system handles mass crime, which constitute the large bulk of grey, everyday attempts to provide messages with a preventive effect, are only to a very small extent transmitted. Communication of 'legal news' is fundamentally distorted.

The sign structure: context for interpretation   We shall now say something about the third point, the sign structure which the designations enter into and are interpreted through.

By way of introduction: towards the end of his article from 1977/1982, Andenæs makes the following statement: 'I believe very many can testify, on the basis of personal experience, that the risk of detection and negative sanctions play a role in connection with crimes such as tax evasion, smuggling, drunken driving, and traffic violations' (Andenæs 1977/1982: 229). Andenæs's point of departure, then, is 'personal experience'. It should be emphasized that he clearly restricts the types of crime which his personal experience supposedly throws light on. And he also points out that 'there is of course a danger in generalizing from oneself. Knowledge of other groups and their attitudes is important' (Andenæs 1977/1982: 229). Nevertheless, personal experience is basic, and equivalent to common-sense reasoning: 'In my opinion, there has been a tendency among criminologists to underestimate the significance of common-sense reasoning about general prevention, based on ordinary psychological facts and the experience of everyday life' (Andenæs 1977/1982: 229).

The question is, however, whether 'personal experience' is such a fruitful point of departure. What is 'common-sense reasoning'? Phenomenological sociology gives us a hint. 'Common-sense reasoning' is the world of everyday experiences which are so prevalent, so ingrained in our lives, that they are taken for granted. 'Common-sense reasoning' is built on knowledge which is so much a part of us that we do not question it. What we are particularly prone not to question is *precisely the generalization of our own experience to others*. We take for granted that others experience the world as we do. We are psychologically unable to pull ourselves out of this pre-understanding and genuinely take a different perspective, seeing the world from the point of view of others.

But if we are to understand the preventive effect, or, rather, the lack of preventive effect, of punishment, this is precisely what we have to do. Lawyers are usually not so skilful at doing it, because their reasoning about facts is so unempirical, and based precisely on 'common sense' (Graver 1986).

There is a fairly good basis for the following generalization: the higher the crime rate in a given group, the less effective will punishment be as a preventive measure. You could also put it this way: for those who—for other reasons— are safely placed on the 'right' side of the line, the thought of a penal sanction perhaps functions as an added obstacle. For those who—again for other reasons—are squarely placed on the 'wrong' side, the penal sanction is neutralized as such an obstacle.

This generalization has a good deal of empirical support, even if it probably requires further specification. As a point of departure, we know that a large part of an average Norwegian population has committed criminal acts, and not just trifling acts at that (Stangeland and Hauge 1974). In this sense, crime is an everyday thing. However, we also know that those who *remain* criminally active, and who recidivate frequently and end up with long-term sentences in our prisons, show an accumulation of indices of social and personal problems—alcohol use, poor education, family disruption, etc. (Bødal 1962, 1969; Christie 1982). And we know that a relatively small group of youths with a wide range of serious problems are responsible for a large part of the more serious juvenile delinquency (Balvig 1984b). The point here is that, when facing people with such a complex and problematic background, a background which, as a life context, increases the probability of criminal behaviour, the preventive effect of punishment is also neutralized. Put briefly and in bold relief: general prevention functions in relation to those who do not 'need' it. In relation to those who do 'need' it, it does not function.

This main point may be placed within our communicative frame of reference. The sign structure which the preventive message lands in and is interpreted within, the context of interpretation within which the signal is picked up and understood, is such that the signal is not effective, and the message not understood as the sender has meant it. With a background in complex problems related to alcohol, family life, work situation, and educational situation, which together constitute the relevant sign structure or context of interpretation, the signal is not interpreted as a (threat of a) deterrent sanction or an educational message. Rather, it is for example interpreted as more oppression, more moralizing, and more rejection.

Above we have talked about what may broadly be called 'traditional' crime—the usual types of property crime, violent street crime, drug-related crime. A corresponding line of argument may be offered for modern economic crime. That part of the business community which largely keeps away from grey or black [i.e. semi-legal or illegal] economic activity on normative grounds, lives in a normative sign structure or moral context of interpretation which at the same time makes the threat of punishment appear as a deterrent sanction or a sensible educational message. Those who are not kept back on normative grounds, however, live within a normative sign structure which neutralizes the deterrent effect of punishment. Again in bold relief: general prevention functions in relation to those who do not 'need' it. In relation to those who 'need' it, it does not function.

Communication process and research results

In view of what we have said about the factual aspects of messages, the designations that messages are given, and the sign structures within which they are received and interpreted, we may return to the uncertainty and lack of clarity of the research results in the area (see Mathiesen 1990: 51–8).

The main features of the communication process go a long way towards explaining this uncertainty and lack of clarity. In a communication situation where the factual aspects of the messages are such that the messages are unclear, in a situation where the designations which are provided increase this lack of clarity significantly, and in a situation where the sign structure, the context of interpretation, *among those who are criminally active* is such that the deterrent, educative, and habit-forming effect of the messages is neutralized, lack of clarity and uncertainty of research results—and only modest or marginal correlations—is simply to be *expected*.

Lack of clarity and uncertainty as something to be *expected* is overlooked in general prevention research. Rather, these are viewed as regrettable characteristics of the research situation, or characteristics which may be overcome through better research techniques and increased knowledge. In this way, general prevention research adjusts to general prevention as a paradigm, and also to an underlying main view in research in general, which implies that uncertain and unclear results are a function of imperfect research instruments, and that *reality is 'actually' certain and clear*. The expectation of reaching a final result which is certain and clear is deeply rooted in science, and reflected for example in the many statistical tests developed within the social sciences to ascertain certain and clear differences. As far as general prevention goes, the communication process necessarily makes the results uncertain and unclear and the correlations weak at best. This is, you might say, 'preventive reality'.

Thus, the communication process itself becomes a very important background for having far greater doubts about the notion of the preventive effect of punishment than is usually entertained.

General Prevention and Morality

The notion of general prevention does not only raise questions about the effectiveness of punishment. It also raises a basic moral question, and this contains two parts. First, what is the moral basis for punishing someone, perhaps hard, in order to prevent entirely different people from committing equivalent acts?

Here the question is formulated in general terms, and is relevant regardless of what is being punished—whether the person is rich or poor, strong or weak. Quite generally: can we sacrifice one person to make another go free?

The question is raised in penal theory, but its bluntness is frequently softened by an emphasis on various other considerations. Various circumstances, it is claimed, such as the seriousness of the crime we try to prevent in others, the consideration of retribution in relation to the offender we punish, and so on, enter into a kind of aggregated conclusion. At times it seems as if considerations are added to save the final conclusion—the consideration of general prevention. But the moral question nevertheless remains, troublesome and unanswered, however masked.

Secondly, and as a further sharpening of the first problem: what is the moral basis for punishing someone, perhaps hard, in order to prevent entirely different people from committing equivalent acts, when those we punish to a large extent are poor and highly stigmatized people in need of assistance rather than punishment?

There are solid grounds for posing the moral question in the latter, sharper form. Today we know that the penal system strikes at the 'bottom' rather than at the 'top' of society. Largely, the harder the punishment, the poorer and more stigmatized are those exposed to it.

Part of the reason for this lies in a fact we mentioned in the discussion of sign structures. Those who remain criminally active, and wind up with long prison sentences, show an accumulation of social and personal problems (see again for example Balvig 1984b). Another part of the reason, however, has to do with the functioning of the penal system, notably its systemic tendency to create social inequality.

The prisons are above all filled by people from the lower strata of the working class who have committed theft and other 'traditional' crimes (for the Norwegian situation, see Stortingsmelding Government White Paper 104, 1977–8: 188; Christie 1982: 117; Mathiesen 1982: 31–2). The class character of the penal system may be explained as the result of a process through which the formal equality of the law, with systematic exclusion of any reference to class, actually does not function as a brake on inequality.

The first step in the process lies in *the definition of criminal behaviour provided by the law*. The law is equal for everybody, but to 'the extent that our society is a class society, the law will also have this characteristic. The law threatens neither private capital nor international exploitation of weak nations' (Christie 1982: 118, translated from the Norwegian by the present author). The law threatens, on the other hand, theft and related acts, typically committed by people from the lowest strata of the working class. While the socially damaging transactions and acts of the ship-owner are typically legal or semi-legal, the equivalent acts of the alcoholic vagrant (if they may be viewed as equivalent) are typically illegal.

The second step in the process is *detection risk*. Even if penal law is constructed as suggested above, people from higher strata obviously also commit acts which are punishable. But their illegal acts are usually 'less visible, by taking place within a complex organizational framework and with methods which are extremely difficult to uncover. Breaking-and-entering is so simple in terms of form. The reception of money, or other favours—kept outside the company accounts in return for letting company A rather than company B do a particular job—takes place more quietly and exists in the unclear borderland between gifts and deception' (Christie 1982: 118–19). The same holds for fraud in connection with grants, companies operating with fictitious accounts, planned bankruptcies, fraudulent investments, manipulation with company capital, environmental crime, etc. These are acts which take place 'within a complex organizational framework and with methods which are extremely difficult to uncover'.

The third step concerns *the unequal ability to settle the matter*, and get it over and done with, if detection and suspicion nevertheless follow. The detected tax evader or VAT embezzler is more easily able to settle the matter than is the burglar or the vagrant. This inequality probably permeates the finest details of the class and stratification system. A Norwegian study of cases of VAT embezzlement reported to the police provides an interesting example. The study showed that the cases of VAT embezzlement reported to the police by the taxation authorities were systematically *small* companies and business people (Hedlund 1982). There is little reason to believe that large and wealthy companies do not attempt to evade VAT, and never come under suspicion for it by the taxation authorities. The small companies were probably reported because they had a weak economy, thus being unable to come to agreement with the taxation authorities concerning postponement of payment, payment in instalments, and the like.

The fourth step in the process consists of a series of *other selective mechanisms* contained in the operations of the police and the criminal justice system. For example, largely, policy activity and resources are geared towards catching the small fry who have committed traditional crimes. Only a minor part of police resources are 'oriented upwards'. And if those who commit 'modern' economic crimes are in fact detected and caught, they are able to pay for a good defence.

This is a summary of some of the most important steps in the process. What, finally, about the courts? Is there also inequality before the courts? Empirically, it is difficult to find out, because we are so rarely presented with similar cases which may be compared. And when we try to 'create' equal cases by traditional sociological methodology, holding various background factors constant, our figures soon become too small for comparisons. A comprehensive study by Wilhelm Aubert (1972: ch. 8) suggested that low status people were more often given harder sentences when various other factors were controlled. But the numbers soon became small, and one difficulty in the study was that the offences in question were characterized by the legal regulations applying to them, a fact which might hide important differences.

In other words, the answer to the question of whether the courts handle similar cases unequally does not have an entirely easy answer. But I am not so sure that this question is all that vital. The main point is that the judge *is so rarely confronted by similar cases from different social classes*. Through the process described above, those who are brought before the courts are largely going to be the more or less poverty-stricken performers of traditional crimes. Regardless of whether there is equality before the courts, they are the ones who end up in our prisons.

This brings us back to the question of morality. The systematic process whereby the formal equality of penal law does not function as an effective brake on inequality (but, rather, masks actual inequality), puts the moral question on its sharp edge: if we punish people on the grounds of general prevention, we actually to a very large extent sacrifice poor and stigmatized people in order to keep others on the narrow path.

The point may be elaborated. In part, the legislator's and the judge's use of the argument of general prevention is directed towards other poor and stigmatized people. This is for example the case with respect to drug-related crimes: some poor people are sacrificed in order to keep other poor people on the narrow path. One might have tried to do something fundamental with the general situation of the poor, which might have abolished the criminal offence as such a likely solution. Instead, an attempt is made to discipline the many poor by sanctioning some of them.

In part, however, the argument of general prevention has a rather diffuse direction—in its most general form, the aim is to improve people's general tendency to be law-abiding. This means that quite different categories of people, far outside the range of the poor and stigmatized, are also included as target groups for the message of general prevention, and seen as groups to be kept in line by pain infliction on the poor.

I am not sure which of the two directions of the argument is the more questionable from a moral point of view.

References

AARSNES, S. G., FUGLEVIK, TOR, HESSTVEDT, OLA, JOHANSEN, VIGGO, and MYKLEBUST, GUNNAR (1974), *Kriminalitet til salgs: En rapport om presse og kriminalitet* ('Crime for sale: a report on the press and crime'), (Oslo: Institutt for kriminologi og strafferett, Universitetet i Oslo, Institute Series no. 28).

ANDENÆS, JOHS (1950), 'Almenprevensjon—illusjon eller realitet?' ('General prevention—illusion or reality?'), *Nordisk Tidsskrift for Kriminalvidenskab*, 38: 103–33; also published in Johs Andenæs, *Avhandlinger og foredrag* (Oslo: Universitetsforlaget, 1962), 109–32.

—— (1977), 'Nyere forskning om almenprevensjonen—status og kommentar' ('Recent research on general prevention—status and comments'), *Nordisk Tidsskrift for Kriminalvidenskab*, 65: 61–101; also published in Andenæs (1982), 196–239).

—— (1982), 'Straffeutmåling i promillesaker' ('Sentencing in drunk-driving cases"), *Lov og Rett*: 115–37.

AUBERT, VILHELM (1972), *Likhet og rett* ('Equality and law') (Oslo: Pax).

AULIE REPORT (1970), 'Innstilling om den sentrale politiadministrasjon', from a committee appointed 9 Sept. 1966 with Andreas Aulie as chairman. Printed in *Innstillinger og betenkninger* (Oslo), part 2.

BALVIG, FLEMMING (1984a), *Kriminalitetens udvikling i Danmark før 1950* ('The development of crime in Denmark before 1950') (Copenhagen: Kriminalistisk Institut, Københavns Universitet).

—— (1984b), *Ungdomskriminalitet i en forstadskommune* ('Juvenile delinquency in a suburban community') (Copenhagen: Det kriminalpræventive råd).

BARTHES, ROLAND (1972), *Mythologies* (New York: Hill & Wang).

BØDAL, KÅRE (1962), *Arbeidsskolen og dens behandlingsresultater* ('The Borstal and its treatment results) (Oslo: Universitetsforlaget).

—— (1969), *Fra arbeidsskole til ungdomsfengsel—klientel og resultater* ('From Borstal to youth prison—clientele and results') (Oslo: Universitetsforlaget).

CHRISTIE, NILS (1971), 'Forskning om individualprevensjon kontra almenprevensjon' ('Research on individual prevention as opposed to general prevention'), *Lov og Rett*: 49–60.

—— (1982), *Hvor tett et samfunn?* ('How dense a society?') (rev. edn., Oslo: Universitetsforlaget; 1st pub. 1975).

FISKE, JOHN (1982), *Introduction to Communication Studies* (New York: Methuen).

FROM, CHRISTINA (1976), *Antonsensaken til salgs* ('The Antonsen case for sale') (Oslo: Institutt for rettssosiologi, Universitetet i Oslo, Institute Series no. 14).

GRAVER, HANS PETTER (1986), *Den juristskapte virkelighet* ('The legal construction of reality') (Oslo: Tano).

HALL, STUART, CRITCHER, CHAS, JEFFERSON, TONY, CLARKE, JOHN, and ROBERTS, BRIAN (1978), *Policing the Crisis. Mugging, the State, and Law and Order* (London: Macmillan).

HEDLUND, MARY ANN (1982), *Politianmeldt momskriminalitet: En undersøkelse av de anmeldelsene som ble ferdig etterforsket i 1977* ('VAT offences reported to the police: a study of the reports invested by the police in 1977') (Oslo: Universitetsforlaget).

HERNES, GUDMUND (1984), 'Media—Struktur, vridning, drama' ('Media—structure, twisting, drama'), *Nytt Norsk Tidskrift*, 1: 38–58.

HJEMDAL, OLE KRISTIAN (1987), 'Kriminalreportasjen—Myter til salgs, prosjektbeskrivelse' ('Write-ups about crime—myths for sale, project description') (Oslo: Institutt for rettssosiologi, Universitetet i Oslo).

—— and RISAN, LEIDULV (1985), *Infromasjonsvirksomhet* ('Informational activity') (Oslo: Kommunal og arbeidsdepartementet).

LORENTZEN, HÅKON (1977), 'Politiopprustning—aktører, interesser og strategier', *Rætferd*, 5: 7–26.

MATHIESEN, THOMAS (1982), *Kriminalitet, straff og samfunn* ('Crime, punishment and society') (3rd rev. edn., Oslo: Aschehoug).

—— (1986), *Makt og medier: En innføring i mediesosiologi* ('Power and media: an introduction to media sociology') (Oslo: Pax).

—— (1990), *Prison on Trial: A Critical Assessment* (London).

—— and HJEMDAL, OLE KRISTIAN (1986), *Treholt-saken i offentligheten—et grunnlag for forhåndsdømming* ('The Treholt case in the public sphere—a basis for prejudgement') (Oslo: Universitetsforlaget).

SIMONSEN, GUNNAR (1976), *Pressen og virkeligheten* ('The Press and reality') (Oslo: Institutt for rettssosiologi, Universitetet i Oslo, Institute Series no. 14).

STANGELAND, PER, and HAUGE, RAGNAR (1974), *Nyanser i grått: En undersøkelse av selvrapportert kriminalitet blant norsk ungdom* ('Nuances in grey: A study of self-reported crime among Norwegian youth') (Oslo: Universitetsforlaget).

Stortingsmelding, *Om kriminalpolitikken* (1977–8), no. 104 (Norwegian Government White Paper on the Criminal Policy, 1977–8, no. 104) (Oslo: Justisdepartementet).

WOLF, PREBEN (1967), 'Innlegg i diskusjon om politieffektivitet og allmennprevensjon' ('Statement in discussion on police efficiency and general prevention'), in *Nordisk kontakt-seminar om politiet og kriminologien*, Brabrand, Denmark, p. 94 (Stockholm: Nordisk Samarbeidsråd for Kriminologi).

Preface: N. Morris, '"Dangerousness" and Incapacitation'

A central theme in contemporary philosophy of punishment is that offenders must be treated as moral agents. Those human beings who break the law have not thereby lost their status as autonomous, responsible agents and punishment must respect the rights which flow from that status. Utilitarian approaches to punishment are therefore morally suspect, as failing to take the rights of offenders seriously (see Introduction: 10–12; and MURPHY).

However, a central concern of penal practice has always been to calculate the risks of future crimes which individual offenders pose, and to try to tailor penal controls to prevent those future crimes. Such 'preventive' or 'incapacitative' measures, which aim to disable the individual offender from further offending, take a variety of forms, and have a long and undistinguished history in Western penality. The death penalty is the most obvious and effective mode of incapacitation, and more limited modes (transportation abroad, the maiming of thieves, the castration of sex offenders) have been utilized at various times. Nowadays, however, 'incapacitation' typically refers to the placing of offenders in custody, usually for long periods of time, in order to protect the public. The 'preventive detention' of habitual criminals formed an explicit aspect of penal policy in England and elsewhere from the beginning of the twentieth century (see Morris 1951 on the operation of the Prevention of Crime Act 1908). The scope of such provisions has been gradually reduced in English law (for a recent debate, see Floud and Young 1981; Bottoms and Brownsword 1982; Lacey 1983; Honderich 1982), but the Criminal Justice Act 1991, whilst abolishing existing provisions for extended prison sentences for persistent offenders (s. 5 (2)), still makes provision for extended sentences 'to protect the public from serious harm' from violent or sexual offenders (ss. 1 (2) (*b*), 2 (2) (b)).

It is perhaps not surprising that incapacitation should continue to be seen as a proper goal of punishment. Many would argue that society must be entitled to defend itself against dangerous criminals, even if this necessitates detaining them for longer than their past offences would otherwise deserve. And whatever doubts might exist about imprisonment's reformative or deterrent efficacy, incapacitation presents itself a strategy which 'works' (whatever its financial and moral costs). Furthermore, research by criminologists (see Wolfgang, Figlio, and Sellin 1972; Greenwood and Abrahamse 1982; but see Greenberg 1975 for doubts about these findings) claims to show that certain offenders commit crimes at a very high rate: consequently, a policy of selective incapacitation aimed at such 'career criminals' promises to produce a high yield of crime prevention for a low investment of resources (see Wilson 1983: ch. 8). It is against this background of debate about the selective incapacitation of offenders who are deemed to be 'dangerous' or 'high rate', or 'career criminals' that Norval Morris argues in this lecture that we should recognize a proper, but limited, role for selective incapacitation (he focuses on violent offenders, rather than on 'career criminals', who are typically burglars or property-offenders; but his argument could apply to the latter category too).

Any policy of selective incapacitation faces two kinds of objection (see von Hirsch 1985; von Hirsch and Ashworth 1992: ch. 3). First, our predictive diagnoses of criminal dangerousness are often inaccurate. Any policy which captures a significant number of those who would otherwise have committed serious future crimes will also capture a significant number of 'false positives' who would not have committed further crimes if left free. Second, even if accuracy were possible, it is wrong, in principle, to punish offenders for their predicted future conduct: they should be punished for what they *have* done, not in respect of what they *will* or *might* do. We should treat individuals (unless they are insane) as moral agents who can choose whether or not to desist from future crimes. To treat them as 'unexploded bombs', as Morris puts it, is not to treat them as responsible moral agents.

Morris recognizes the current limitations of prediction, and argues that incapacitative sentences should be permitted only when reliable information indicates a high probability of future offending. But in such cases an incapacitative sentence is, he argues, justifiable, as 'shifting the risk' of future offending from the community on to the offender. Against the in-principle objection, he argues that diagnoses of dangerousness should be thought of as statements about the offender's present condition, rather than as predictions of future conduct. He thus posits a view of the individual radically at odds with that assumed by incapacitation's moral critics. Instead of seeing offenders as free moral agents who choose their conduct anew on each occasion, Morris portrays them as being governed by psychological dispositions which pattern their conduct. This conception of the individual may indeed be empirically more accurate, or it may even be that such a conception is a more useful fiction by which to guide our institutional practices. But whatever the facts of the matter, it is none the less true that on Morris's approach the offender is being treated on the basis of status (what he or she *is*) rather than on the basis of conduct (what he or she has *done*).

Another important aspect of Morris's position is his insistence that incapacitative sentences should not exceed the maximum which *desert* considerations would set as appropriate for the crime(s) that the offender has actually committed. Since he thinks (see also TONRY) that desert criteria can generate only broad sentencing ranges, rather than uniquely deserved sentences, there is room on his account for considerations of incapacitation to be used within those ranges (see the 1991 Criminal Justice Act s. 2 (2) (b)). This raises again the question of whether the demands of proportionality should be thus qualified (see VON HIRSCH against TONRY): but another possible difficulty for this approach is whether maximum sentences which are high enough for effective incapacitation might not exceed the bounds of any plausible notion of desert (see von Hirsch 1993: ch. 6). Incapacitative sentences which respected Morris's restrictive guide-lines might thus be infrequent, and of little real effect—in which case his argument amounts to a critical tool for restricting incapacitation, rather than an endorsement of it.

References

BOTTOMS, A. E., and BROWNSWORD, R. (1982), 'The Dangerousness Debate after the Floud Report', *British Journal of Criminology*, 22: 229–54.

FLOUD, J., and YOUNG, W. (1981), *Dangerousness and Criminal Justice* (London).

GREENBERG, D. (1975), 'The Incapacitative Effect of Imprisonment: Some Estimates', *Law and Society Review*, 9: 541–80.

GREENWOOD, P., and ABRAHAMSE, A. (1982), *Selective Incapacitation* (Santa Monica, Calif.).

HONDERICH, T. (1982), 'On Justifying Protective Punishment', *British Journal of Criminology*, 22: 268–75.

LACEY, N. (1983), 'Dangerousness and Criminal Justice: The Justification of Preventive Detention', *Current Legal Problems*, 36: 31–49.

MORRIS, N. (1951) *The Habitual Criminal* (London).

VON HIRSCH, A. (1985), *Past or Future Crimes* (Manchester).

—— (1993), *Censure and Sanctions* (Oxford).

—— and ASHWORTH, A. J. (1992) (ed.), *Principled Sentencing* (Boston, Edinburgh).

WILSON, J. Q. (1983), *Thinking about Crime* (rev. edn., New York).

WOLFGANG, M., FIGLIO, R., and SELLIN, T. (1972), *Delinquency in a Birth Cohort* (Chicago).

handwritten annotations at top of page:

- moral agency
- clinical prediction
- positive/negative measurement errors
- utilitarianism
- pre-emtive crime control
- civil com.

'Dangerousness' and Incapacitation

NORVAL MORRIS

I want to focus your attention on definitional, moral, and evidentiary problems in the application of the concept of 'dangerousness' in the judicial process, particularly in criminal law matters but also occasionally in problems of the commitment of the mentally ill.

In the criminal law, if not in international relations, the pre-emptive strike has great attraction; to capture the criminal before the crime is surely an alluring idea. In a variety of ways, implicit and expressed, that idea has been pursued for centuries and is being more vigorously pursued today—and, of course, it is also at the foundation of the civil commitment of those mentally ill or retarded persons who are thought likely to be a danger to themselves or others.

My purpose is not at all to attack the idea of the pre-emptive strike. I think one could easily attack it—it is far from invulnerable—but my effort is different, and is clearly more difficult. I will try to enunciate those principles under which such pre-emptive strikes would be jurisprudentially acceptable.

I decided on this topic before I received the great advantage of two decisions of the United States Supreme Court at the end of last term, *Jones* v. *United States*, 103 S. Ct. 3043 (1983), and *Barefoot* v. *Estelle*, 103 S. Ct. 3383 (1983), in both of which aspects of this topic were dealt with by the same five-member majority. And it seemed to me that majority was wrong—wrong not in the sense of a judgment on policy, but wrong in the sense that the justices had not faced up to a series of important issues that were unavoidable if they were responsibly to dispose of the cases.

Very briefly, in the *Jones* case the question was whether Michael Jones, who had pleaded not guilty by reason of insanity to attempted petit larceny, a misdemeanour, and had then been committed to St Elizabeth's Hospital, should be under the same standards for detention or release from mental hospital at the end of a year as any other civilly committed patient. A year was the maximum term that he could have served had he been convicted of the crime with which he was charged.

In the *Barefoot* case the Court addressed the distasteful question of whether the state of Texas had, within constitutionally acceptable processes of proof, established that Barefoot was more dangerous than other murderers, and therefore an appropriate subject for capital punishment. The Court did not satisfactorily dispose of the question of the standards that should be pursued to test his higher dangerousness.

I have reduced my argument to the following seven submissions, which I shall try to defend in this lecture. here they are:

Some Submissions

1. Clinical predictions of dangerousness unsupported by actuarial studies should not be relied on for other than short-term intervention.
2. The autonomy of the individual should sometimes be restricted because of his predicted dangerousness. The relevant considerations are:
   - the extent of the harm that may occur,
   - the likelihood of its occurrence,
   - the extent of individual autonomy to be limited to avoid the harm.
3. A prediction of dangerousness is a statement of a present condition, not the prediction of a particular result.
4. It is a mistake to confuse the sufficiency of proof of dangerousness with the decision on whether to require proof beyond a reasonable doubt, or by clear and convincing evidence, or on a balance of probability. The decision of the Supreme Court in *Addington* v. *Texas*, 491 US 418 (1979), has entrenched this error.
5. Punishment should not be imposed, nor the term of punishment extended, by virtue of a prediction of dangerousness, beyond that which would be justified as a deserved punishment independently of that prediction.
6. Provided the previous limitation is respected, predictions of dangerousness may properly influence sentencing decisions (and other decisions under the criminal law).
7. The base expectancy rate of criminal violence for the criminal predicted as dangerous must be shown by reliable evidence to be substantially higher than the base expectancy rate for another criminal, with a closely similar criminal record and convicted of a closely similar crime, but not predicted as unusually dangerous, before the

greater dangerousness of the former may be relied on to intensify or extend his punishment.

Nostradamus was not the only one involved in predictions. We all live by predictions of the future behaviour of others. Many of these predictions are predictions of dangerousness. You can't cross a city street without making life-protecting predictions of how others will behave. I find this particularly so in new York. I walked about here all day today and it's quite clear that you cannot rely upon the green light. You have to make assumptions about the misbehaviour of others on yellow and indeed on red. Such assumptions are all too frequently accurate. We are all constantly involved in predicting the behaviour of others.

In the operation of the criminal law and the law relating to mental illness, it is convenient to divide these predictions of future dangerous behaviour into those that are *implicit* and those that are *explicit*.

Implicit predictions of dangerousness percolate many justiciable issues, both in criminal law and in mental health law. They influence bail decisions by judges, sentencing and release decisions, parole and work-release decisions, as well as decisions about the compulsory and emergency commitment of the mentally ill. Indeed, whenever discretion is exercised to invoke or not to invoke the criminal law, whether by a victim or a relative, a policeman, a psychiatrist or a social worker, a prosecutor or a judge, it is likely that predictions of the offender's dangerousness, or of the dangerousness of the mentally ill person, are central to the decision. They are implicit, intuitive decisions that form part of our sense of fear that is generated by criminality.

But there is also a lengthy history of attempts in the criminal law and in mental health law to apply *express* predictions of dangerousness, often statutorily authorized. The best-known example is the rash of sexual psychopath laws which disgraced our jurisprudence, grossly misapplying what little knowledge we have about the sexual offender; but the same principle of the pre-emptive strike, the express pre-emptive strike against threatened harm, is to be found in habitual-criminal legislation, vagrancy laws, special dangerous-offender sentencing provisions, and many similar efforts to base punishment on expected future criminality. I suppose this principle lies at the heart of the question of bail you are now addressing in New York, as well as the problem of your crowded gaols and the prediction of those who are safe to let out, or perhaps it is better to say safer to let out than others. The pre-emptive strike is a very common legislative and judicial process. Recently the stakes of these types of predictions have been raised in the criminal law, with the application of career criminal projects at the prosecutorial level and policies of selective incapacitation at the sentencing level, under the apparent belief that legislatures, prosecutors, judges, and juries are able to select the more dangerous criminals for swifter and more determined prosecution and for more protracted incarceration—or, in the extreme case of Texas and some other states, for capital punishment instead of life imprisonment because, as it is phrased in the Texas Code, 'there is a probability that the defendant would commit criminal acts of violence that would constitute a continuing threat to society' (Texas Code Crim. proc. Ann. ss. 37.071).

Policy recommendations move even further. A precise example is Professor James Q. Wilson's summary of the essays he edited in the recently published *Crime and Public Policy*, as follows: 'Prosecutors would screen all arrested persons . . . and give priority to those who, whatever their crime, were predicted to be high-rate offenders . . . If found guilty, the offender's sentence would be shaped . . . by an informed judgment as to whether he committed crimes at a high or low rate when free on the street. . . . Scarce prison space would be conserved by keeping the terms of low-rate offenders very short and by reserving the longer terms for the minority of violent predators' (*Crime and Public Policy* (ICS Press, San Francisco 1983), 286–7). There is no doubt of the increasing pressure for the exercise of the pre-emptive strike in the criminal law.

For these explicit predictions of dangerousness, which seem to be increasingly relied upon in the evolution of our jurisprudence of punishment, the psychiatrist is being pressed into service despite the vigorous opposition of the discipline of psychiatry as expressed in public statements of the American Psychiatric Association. The courts, including the Supreme Court in the depressing *Jones* and *Barefoot* decisions at the conclusion of its last term, allow much greater reliance to be placed on psychiatric predictions of dangerousness than does the organized profession of psychiatry. It is a paradoxical situation: the psychiatric literature and the official statements of the organized profession of psychiatry stress the unreliability of psychiatric predictions while the courts increasingly rely on those same predictions by individual psychiatrists despite their admittedly prejudicial impact—an impact certainly greater than is justified by their validity.

I am confining analysis in this lecture to the prediction of behaviour that is dangerous to the person or threatens the person, in effect, to assaultive criminality. I do not mean to deprecate the significance of the threats of predatory theft, or of many other crimes, to social welfare; I have narrowed my focus primarily to assist analysis and in the belief that if I can struggle toward principle here the task will be easier in relation to other criminal conduct. I am also excluding considerations of self-injury as a ground for civil commitment of the mentally ill, the danger to others from a patient, as distinct from the danger to the patient, providing the analogy to the criminal's threat to the physical safety of others. But this at least should be noted about predictions of other forms of dangerousness: it seems clear that predictions of suicidal attempts can for some disturbed persons be made with higher likelihoods than any predictions of violence to others; similarly, predictions of predatory theft can often be made with higher likelihoods than can predictions of criminal violence.

The problem then is: suppose we knew with some precision how well we could predict future violent behaviour, how and to what extent should we in justice apply that knowledge?

I must make one self-protective comment at this point.

To discuss the definition and application of concepts of dangerousness in the criminal law, and in the law relating to mental health, may give the impression that I favour the widespread application of this concept. I certainly do not. My submission is different. It is that a jurisprudence that pretends to exclude such concepts is self-deceptive; they will frequently figure prominently in decision-making, whether or not they are spelled out in jurisprudence. One can pretend to ignore such predictions, but it will be a pretence. My view is that it is better to recognize the reality of such predictions and try to put them into their proper jurisprudential place, difficult though that may be.

But that is not the only reason for pursuing this topic of reliance on predictions of dangerousness. If such predictions are in fact made and relied on and cannot be banished from the criminal law, that circumstance may be one reason for studying them, for trying to improve their validity and stability over time, and even for making speeches about them (though you may already begin to doubt that). But there is a larger justification. Suppose our present weak predictive capacity proves to be the best we can do for decades, which I think quite likely. Suppose for a high risk of a crime of violence the best we can do at present is to predict one in three, in the sense that to be sure of preventing one crime we would have to lock up three people. My submission is, and it is a difficult one, that it is still ethically appropriate and socially desirable to take such predictions into account in many police, prosecutorial, judicial, correctional, and legislative decisions. The justification is positive, not merely negative; indeed, it is compelled if we are, with appreciation of our modest store of knowledge, justly to allocate our properly limited punitive powers under the criminal law.

That is an unfashionable position. It may well be a wrong position. So let me approach its defence with caution, starting with the obvious question of how well we can predict violent behaviour. I shall skim over the literature—you will either take it as truth from me or you will pursue it somewhere else. Current research supports the working hypothesis that we can predict about one in three crimes of violence in a high risk group. The literature is extensive—if you want to get at it there are two books that cover it comprehensively: John Monahan's recent book *The Clinical Prediction of Violent Behavior* (London, 1981) and Jean Floud and Warren Young's *Dangerousness and Criminal Justice* (London, 1981). They both conclude that of the highest group of offenders we can now select as most likely to commit an offence of violence, if they are free for the next two years in the community, two out of three will not be arrested for such an offence if released.

I am anxious not to be trapped in extensive discussion of these empirical materials, because I want to assume the truth of this limited predictive capacity, but I must drive it home a little further. Let me put it most cautiously. Social science research on this topic in this country and in Western Europe, and I don't know of any elsewhere, makes no claim for a capacity to select a group of persons, no matter what their criminal records, who have a 50 per cent base expectancy rate of serious violence or of a threat of violence to the person over the next five years they are at large. The Supreme Court in *Barefoot*, both the majority and the minority, accepted that proposition. I'll be careful and read what they accepted. 'The "best" clinical research currently in existence indicates that *psychiatrists and psychologists are accurate in no more than one out of three predictions of violent behaviour over a several year period among institutionalized populations that had both committed violence in the past . . . and who are diagnosed as mentally ill*' (103 S. Ct. 3398 n. 7 (citing Monahan at 47–9) (emphasis in original)). I hope you will accept that as sufficient discussion of our present weak capacity to predict violent behaviour so that we can discuss its implications.

Prediction and Risk Shifting

Classifications are often arbitrary, and the classification that follows is not necessarily compelling, but for me there are only three paths to the prediction of a person's future behaviour.

First: this is how he behaved in the past when circumstances were similar. It is likely that he will behave in the same way now. Let me call this an *anamnestic* prediction.

Second: this is how people like him, situated as he is, behaved in the past. It is likely that he will behave as they did. This, of course, is an *actuarial* prediction. It is the basis of all insurance, of a great deal of our efforts to share and shift risk in the community.

And the third type of prediction, which is harder to state, is this: from my experience of the world, from my professional training, from what I know about mental illness and mental health, from my observations of this patient and efforts to diagnose him, I think he will behave in the following fashion in the future. This is a *clinical* prediction; it has elements of the first two in it but it includes professional judgmental elements that the psychiatric literature treats as distinct from the others.

Anamnestic and actuarial predictions are linear in the sense that the relevant historical facts to justify the prediction can be produced and adduced, weighed and added. Clinical predictions are not like that. They are immune from evidentiary examination except in relation to the reputation, experience, and past success or failure of the predictor.

Anamnestic predictions are often very reliable. Indeed, they reach the highest levels of validity. He has taken out the old raincoat and exposed his rampant self to the young girls in the park every Friday for the past year. Here he is, this Friday, wearing his raincoat though the weather be fine and he is heading again for the park. Who says a prediction of only one in three is all you can make?—of course you can make a higher prediction in that situation. But that does not controvert what I said earlier; it is a short-term prediction and it does not concern a crime of violence.

Actuarial predictions also are often very reliable—the insurance industry lives by them. The economic affairs of everyone in this room are to a substantial extent influenced by them, and you look a prosperous lot to me.

Clinical predictions are of a different order. They are intuitive rather than verifiable, except in the result. At first blush it would seem that the best predictions of human behaviour would be based on a combination of all three of these types of prediction, that is to say, would take in the pattern of behaviour of the person under consideration, would be advised by how others like him behaved in the past, and would also be guided by a total clinical consideration of his case, which would improve on the prediction from the first two categories by taking into account what was distinctive in him—that is to say, would individualize the prediction to his particular circumstances. And that is correct for the prediction of certain types of human behaviour—how someone will hit a tennis ball, whether he will be late to work one day next week, and so on. But it is not true for the prediction of violent behaviour at the present level of our knowledge. It has not been demonstrated, and psychiatrists have not claimed, that clinical predictions can improve upon actuarial and anamnestic predictions—certainly not on actuarial predictions. That leads me to my first formal submission to you: clinical predictions of dangerousness unsupported by actuarial studies should not be relied on for other than short-term intervention.

As lawyers, we should insist on testing psychiatric predictions by probing the actuarial and anamnestic bases for such prediction. And the organized profession of psychiatry is pressing us to do just that. What I am submitting is not a heretical suggestion. In many other areas of medical practice we do it. Mortality and morbidity rates are calculated for many medical interventions and are relied on by the best clinical practitioners in deciding what to do in a given case. Indeed, it would often be malpractice for a surgeon to operate without such knowledge and without sharing it with the patient to allow for his informed consent. But in relation to psychiatric predictions of dangerousness we follow different patterns of thought. We should not.

Let me offer as an example of those erroneous patterns of thought the Supreme Court case of *Jones* v. *United States*, 103 S. Ct. 3043 (1983). The issue was the greater dangerousness of Michael Jones, given the record I told you—an attempted petit larceny and a plea of not guilty by reason of insanity a year later—than persons who were civilly committed to mental hospital. Here is Mr Justice Powell speaking for the Court: 'It comports with common sense to concluded that someone whose mental illness was sufficient to lead him to commit a criminal act is likely to remain ill and in need in treatment' (103 S. Ct. at 3050). The response of Mr Justice Brennan in dissent is compelling: 'None of the available evidence that criminal behavior by the mentally ill is likely to repeat itself distinguishes between behaviors that were "the product" of mental illness and those that were not. It is completely unlikely that persons acquitted by reason of insanity display a rate of future "dangerous" activity higher than civil committees with a similar arrest records, or than persons convicted of crimes who were later found to be mentally ill' (103 S. Ct. at 3058).

It is sometimes suggested that it is improper to restrict liberty on the basis of those types of weak predictions of future risk. In my view, that is not so, however the prediction be reached. Confining ourselves to predictions of dangerousness as I am trying to use the phrase—that is, to predictions of future violence to the person—let me suggest situations where it would be entirely proper to exercise state power to restrict individual autonomy on the basis of such a prediction. And here I am trying to give more precise meaning to my second submission to you.

An example occurred earlier this year which you may have seen in the press. It is a somewhat frivolous one, but it may make my point. You will recall that this year's annual meeting of the National Rifle Association was addressed by President Reagan. As was widely reported, all those attending that meeting, when the President undertook the heavy burden of persuading the NRA membership of the virtues of the handgun, had to pass through metal detectors as they entered the auditorium to insure that they were not entering the President's presence in their usual heavily armed condition. The authorities responsible for the President's security had properly formed the view that the audience presented a higher base expectancy rate of an assassination attempt than another audience of similar size—since not all the President's audiences are so tested (though it would not matter to the thrust of my example if they were). I do not know what the base expectancy rate of an assassination attempt is; let me guess—one in a hundred million. Is it reasonable to impose the obligation of passing through a metal detector on the basis of such a low prediction? Of course it is. And if you match the risk profile when you are about to board an airplane and are asked to step aside and be searched and perhaps to answer some questions, those procedures are probably an appropriate interference with your freedom. Always the base expectancy rate—the relationship between the true positive predictions (one in a hundred million) and false positive predictions—must be balanced by two further considerations: how serious is the interference with liberty involved in preventing the possibility of that prediction coming true, and how serious will the injury be if it does come true?

Take the hypothetical another step. Should anyone with a past record of threatening the President be excluded from the auditorium? Of course he should! You don't have to know much about prediction to reach that result. A very slight risk of a most serious injury without any grave interference is a justification in my view for invocation of state authority. So my second submission to you is: dangerousness is to be balanced in relation to the extent of the harm risked, the likelihood of its occurrence, and the extent of individual autonomy to be invaded to avoid the harm. And this is true, I believe, throughout criminal law and the law relating to mental health.

The next proposition that I want to make—my third submission—may be thought to be only linguistic, but I think it is necessary in order to develop several major points. A statement of a prediction of dangerousness is a statement of a present condition, not the prediction of a particular result. The belief that it is the prediction of a result is an error that is constantly made and leads many astray. An analogy to a dangerous object rather than to a dangerous person may help clarify my point.

I remember the drab postwar days in London. The bombing had stopped but the scars of war were pervasive. And on occasion the risks of war returned in their earlier force. An unexploded bomb would be found and would have to be moved and rendered safe. Death and severe injuries were very rare; the base expectancy rate was very low; there were large numbers of 'false positives' for every 'true positive'—bombs that didn't go off, as distinguished form those that did. The area would be cleared, the bomb disposal crew would begin their delicate work, and in all but a few instances manage it successfully. When the talk resumed that night in the neighbouring pub, would anyone say the bomb was not dangerous because it did not go off? Would anyone say that because it proved to be a 'false positive' it was not dangerous? Of course not; that is not how words are used when the focus is on dangerous things as distinct from dangerous people. Yet the similarities of risk and analysis are great. Why the difference of usage? In part, I think, because we tend to think of dangerous people as those who intend harm—yet that view conceals the psychological reality.

In sum, that the person predicted as dangerous does no future injury does not mean that the classification was erroneous.

Let me take you along another definitional path to the same result. I think the journey is worthwhile, giving a different perspective on the contours of the country that has to be crossed.

Assume that in every instance the question is: who shall bear the risk of harm, the individual or the community? This assumption presupposes, of course, that the risk can be quantified as a base expectancy rate and the harm defined with some precision, and further, that it can substantially be shifted from the community, the cost of the shift being paid by the individual by his being controlled in one or another fashion, usually by detaining him in custody.

Consider the case of a sixteen-year-old black youth who has just dropped out of school and who has no employment, whose mother was herself a child on welfare when he was born, who does not know his father, who runs with a street gang, and who lives in a destroyed inner-city neighbourhood. How should we assess the risk of his being involved in the next six months in a crime of personal violence? Since we own the numbers, let us give him a base expectancy rate of, say, to be conservative, one in twenty. That risk now rests on the community in which he lives. May we, without further justification, at this one-in-twenty level, shift that risk from the community and make him bear the cost of the shift in the coinage of institutional detention until we can do something to reduce the risk, by retraining him or by allowing time to pass while the threat he presents diminishes? Clearly no. But let him be involved in a non-violent crime, say, shoplifting, and even if that conviction makes no difference to his base expectancy rate of a crime of violence, there is no doubt that in practice we would then take into account the risk of a crime of violence in deciding what to do about him and for how long. Within our sentencing discretions we would take into account the risk of violence he presents. How should it be taken into account?

The Burden of Proof of Dangerousness

The discussion of sentencing that young criminal was in large part only a restatement of the position earlier advanced, but it allows me to bring out one point that I think important. What elements of the 'dangerousness' sentencing of that hypothetical young man are capable of proof and at what level of persuasiveness? His personal circumstances, the historical facts of his mother and his absent father, his truancy, his school and employment records, his gang membership are all capable of what I might call absolute proof. It makes very little difference whether the burden of their proof is on a balance of probabilities, or has to be by clear and convincing evidence, or has to be beyond reasonable doubt. And is that not also true of his base expectancy rate of violence? The scientific work to define a group and to assess its base expectancy rate of criminal violence within a given period has been done or it has not been done. Its stability over time and in different regions has either been tested or has not been tested. If the facts of the future criminal behaviour of the group to which he is said to belong have been found actuarially, then the question of his risk to the community is not properly related to the different burdens of proof of those actuarial facts. The difficulty of proof of the base expectancy rate is not in any inherent sense more difficult than proof of the historical facts on which the rate was calculated. Hence my fourth formal submission to you: it is a mistake to confuse the sufficiency of proof of dangerousness with the decision to require proof beyond a reasonable doubt, or by clear and convincing evidence, or on a balance of probability. The decision by the Supreme Court in *Addington* v. *Texas*, 441 US 418 (1979), has entrenched this error and has impeded rational analysis.

Addington figures prominently in *Jones*, and less prominently in *Barefoot*. In *Addington* the Supreme Court held, without dissent, that the due process clause of the Fourteenth Amendment requires, in a civil commitment hearing, a standard of proof on the issues of the patient's mental illness and of his danger to himself or to others equal to or greater than 'clear and convincing' evidence. The Court recognized the difficulty of quantifying, even of clearly stating, the differences between the usual three standards of proof—balance of probabilities, beyond reasonable doubt, and an intermediate standard of clear and convincing evidence— but saw the distinction between them as 'more than an empty semantic exercise' (ibid. at 425), being rather an expression of 'the degree of confidence our society thinks . . . [the fact-finder] should have in the correctness of factual conclusions for a particular type of adjudication' (ibid. at 423).

One of the reasons the Court was satisfied by the 'clear and convincing' standard in an issue involving deprivation of liberty, and rejected the need, as a constitutional matter, for proof beyond reasonable doubt (though many state civil commitment statutes continue to require proof beyond reasonable doubt in this context), was this: 'Given the lack of certainty and the fallibility of psychiatric diagnosis there is a serious question as to whether a state could ever prove beyond a reasonable doubt that an individual is both mentally ill and likely to be dangerous' (ibid at 429).

Well, I think that is just error. That he is 'likely to be dangerous' can be proved at any level required, provided 'likely to be dangerous' is given careful construction. If that phrase is defined as 'belonging to a group with a risk of dangerous behaviour unacceptable in relation to its gravity, if the harm occurs, and outweighing the reduction of individual freedom involved in its avoidance', then the existence of the likelihood of injury can be proved at the same level as many other facts. It is a fact in the same sense that a broken bone is a fact. By contrast, if that phrase, 'likely to be dangerous', is defined as requiring proof on a balance of probability that *this* patient will injure himself or others, or that *he* is more likely than not to so act, then it can be proved at *no* level of confidence. In the latter perspective, in practice, it can never be proved, since at present our best predictive capacities fall far below that level.

The confusion lies in the admixture of ideas of probability of future events and the degrees of confidence in facts required by the usual three standards of proof. The odds question, which is what we are dealing with if relative and not absolute probability is what properly triggers a civil commitment, is not a problem of the weight of the burden of proof to be placed on the affirmant of a risk, and it is a mistake to decide the balance between the risk to the community and the restrictions on the individual as a problem of the burden of proof. It is a policy question to be deduced from interpretation of the statute, the answer not being capable of expression solely as a problem of evidence. Once the risk is defined, the elements that go to prove the existence of that risk can be made subject to different burdens of proof, but not the risk itself.

Two quite separate issues emerge: the weight of the burden of proof and the degree of probability of the injurious event sought to be avoided by the statute. Blending the two, as if they were susceptible to a single conclusion, has caused confusion.

Of course, the decision in *Addington* is well justified by other considerations—I do not for a moment doubt that it expresses sound policy—but it is not justified by the impossibility of proving risk beyond a reasonable doubt.

I want to drive this point even further home because it helps at the next stage of the argument. Assume, following *Addington*, that the risk of serious injury to another person, if the patient is not civilly committed, is one in three. That is to say, the patient belongs to a defined group, one in three of whom in the past who were not committed, soon after they were diagnosed as falling with that group, seriously injured someone else. The personal history, relevant environmental circumstances, and psychopathology of this patient match in all predictive material those of the previously defined group. Does *Addington's* constitutional requirement of clear and convincing evidence of his dangerousness preclude the civil commitment of this patient? Clearly not. If it did, few indeed could be constitutionally committed in any state of the Union. What *Addington* requires is a larger degree of confidence by the trier of facts, judge or jury, in the definition of the group, and in its base expectancy rate of violence, which one hopes has been validly assessed and shown to be relatively stable, and in the inclusion of this patient within that group. You may find all this relatively unhelpful because it suggests the existence of a body of established research far in excess of what there is, and in truth, I know of only eight serious prospective predictive studies. There are, of course, other studies, retrospective studies, looking at past records of people who have been involved in violence, or looking at prison populations and finding their criminal records, or looking at our parole prediction capacity. But in this area of the prediction of dangerous personal violence there really are only eight. (For an incisive summary of these eight, see John Monahan, 'The Prediction of Violent Criminal Behavior: A Methodological Critique and Prospectus' in *Deterrence and Incapacitation: Estimating the Effects of Criminal Sanctions on Crime Roles* (National Research Council, 1978), 244–69.)

My insistence on an assumption of a capacity to predict is nevertheless important since it forces confrontation with issues that our current verbal manipulations of imprecise burdens of proof and unquantified articulations of risk allow us to finesse. And when that confrontation occurs, the problem shifts from one of language and statutory interpretation to one of morality, of the proper balance between state authority and personal autonomy.

False Positives and the Conviction of the Innocent

Under this heading I want to defend three submissions that complete the argument in this lecture. The three submissions are:

5. Punishment should not be imposed, nor the term of punishment extended, by virtue of a prediction of dangerousness, beyond that which would be justified as a deserved punishment independently of that prediction.
6. Provided the previous limitation is respected, predictions of dangerousness may properly influence sentencing decisions (and other decisions under the criminal law).
7. The base expectancy rate for the criminal predicted as dangerous must be shown by reliable evidence to be substantially higher than the base expectancy rate of another criminal, with a closely similar criminal record and convicted of a closely similar crime, but not so predicated as unusually dangerous, before any distinction based on his higher dangerousness may be relied on to intensify or extend his punishment.

These three submissions form an effort to state a jurisprudence of predictions of dangerousness for punishment purposes that would achieve both individual justice and better community protection.

The opinion of the Supreme Court in *Barefoot* v. *Estelle*, 103 S. Ct. 3383 (1983), delivered by Mr Justice White, opened forcefully the question of the admissibility of psychiatric testimony of dangerousness. 'The suggestion that no psychiatrist's testimony may be presented with respect to a defendant's future dangerousness is somewhat like asking us to disinvent the wheel' (103 S. Ct. at 3396). The Court then expressly approved Mr Justice Stevens's statement in *Jurek* that 'Any sentencing authority must predict a convicted person's probable future conduct when it engages in the process of determining what punishment to impose' (103 S. Ct. at 3396).

Given that reality, it would seem futile to deny the relevance and propriety of such predictions to a wide range of discretions exercised under the aegis of the criminal law, and in particular to decisions whether to imprison and for how long. Yet, if moral issues are to be taken seriously, the fact of approved use is not compelling and the morality of applying predictions based on group behaviour to predict the likely behaviour of the individual requires justification.

Thought has been led astray here, by equating the assumption of power (or of extra power) over the individual on a basis of a prediction of dangerousness to reluctance to risk convicting the innocent. The model of the criminal trial has confused analysis.

If it is true that it is better that nine guilty men be acquitted rather than one innocent man be convicted, why does not a similar though more compelling equation apply to the prediction of dangerousness—so that it is better that two men who would not in fact injure or threaten others (two false positives) should be released rather than one who would (one true positive) be detained? If one to nine is unacceptable in one case, how can two to one be acceptable in the other?

This line of reasoning, though it has persuaded many commentators and some judges, seems to me deeply flawed. The equation with the proof of guilt misses the point. Let us assume a properly convicted criminal, Criminal X, with a one in three base expectancy rate of violence (as we have defined it), and another criminal, Criminal Y, also properly convicted of the identical offence, but who has a very much lower base expectancy rate—same record, same offence. Unlike X, Y was not a school dropout; he has a job to which he may return and a supportive family who will take him back if he is not imprisoned, or after his release from prison. May Criminal X be sent to prison while Criminal Y is not? Or may Criminal X be sent to prison for a longer term than Criminal Y, despite the same record and the same gravity of offence, the longer sentence being justified by the utilitarian advantages of selective incapacitation? My answer to both questions is in the affirmative; he may. But since this appears to be the advocacy of locking up two 'innocent' men to prevent crime by a third, I must offer a brief defence of my view.

The central idea that moves me in defending submissions 5, 6, and 7 and the conclusion about Criminal X is recognition of the imprecision of our moral callipers. In no exact sense can one say of punishment: 'That was a just punishment.' St Peter is reputed to be informed on those matters and I am prepared to yield that he can make a statement like that; but I cannot, and I have never met anyone who can. All I have ever been able to say about the justice of a particular sentence on a convicted criminal, and all I have ever thought people sensibly said was: 'As we know our community and its values, that does not seem to be an unjust punishment.' Retributive sentiments properly limit but do not define a just punishment.

The injustice of a punishment, assuming proper proof of guilt, is thus defined in part deontologically, in limited retributivist terms and not solely in utilitarian terms. The upper and lower limits of 'deserved' punishment set the range in which utilitarian values, including values of mercy and human understanding, may properly fix the punishment to be imposed. There is always a range of a 'not unjust' punishment, measured in relation to the gravity of an offence and the offender's criminal record. And when punishment systems fail to appreciate that, as ours occasionally does, and set up mandatory sentencing, they always get into trouble. Such rigid systems are either circumvented or achieve gross injustice—or both.

The philosophy of punishment I am offering is that of a limiting retributivist, and I suggest that punishments, and a just scale of punishment, should always allow for discretion to be exercised, under proper legislative guidance, by the judicial officer of the state. I have developed that argument at excessive length elsewhere and I am not going to inflict it again on you now. The key to the argument that I am advancing is submission 7; let me illustrate its operation by an example or two.

Submission 7—that the base expectancy rate for the criminal predicted as dangerous must be shown by reliable evidence to be substantially higher than the base expectancy rate for another criminal, with a closely similar criminal record and convicted of a closely similar crime, but not so predicted as unusually dangerous, before any distinction based on his higher dangerousness may be relied on to intensify or extend his punishment—may seem a pallid and toothless proposition, but if accepted it would have a dramatically restrictive effect on the acceptability of predictions of dangerousness in the criminal law. Rightly or wrongly, prior record and severity of the last offence are seen in all legal systems as defining the retributive range of punishment. Once criminal record and severity of the last offence are included, the definition of groups with higher base expectancy rates than those with similar crimes and similar criminal records becomes very much more difficult of proof.

Let me test my submission in relation to my criminals X and Y and show you one real defect in what I am offering, and then let me try to illustrate how my thesis might apply to the *Barefoot* case. Criminals X and Y had identical criminal records and had committed identical crimes, but X was not a school dropout, X had a job to which he could return if not sent to prison, and X had a supportive family who would take him back if allowed to do so, while the unfortunate Y was a school dropout, was unemployed, and lacked a supportive family. And let us suppose that past studies reveal that criminals with Y's criminal record and with his environmental circumstances have a base expectancy rate of 1 in 10 of being involved in a crime of personal violence. While no such calculations have been made for criminals like X, it is quite clear that they have a much lower base expectancy rate of future violent criminality. I suggest that Y should be held longer than X based on these predictions.

In fairness I must note that I have lured myself on to some very unpleasant terrain, for the reality in this country at this time will be that my apparently aseptic principles will grossly favour the wealthy to the detriment of the poor, and will be used to justify even more imprisonment of blacks and other underclass minorities than at present obtains— as will the whole 'selective incapacitation' process. Put curtly, without knowing more about our hypothetical criminals, we already confidently guess the pigmentation of X and Y. As a matter of statistical likelihood, X is white and Y is black.

I do not take lightly this line of criticism of the thesis I have offered tonight. I do not enjoy advancing principles which if accepted would have those effects. So let me offer one or two comments by way of explanation—not really apology—for my thesis. The sad fact is that in our society predictors of violence are not racially neutral. How could they be racially neutral, when at this moment one of every twenty black males in their twenties is either in prison or in gaol. And that really underestimates the difference between blacks and whites in prisons and gaols, since when black youths move into the middle class their crime rates are just the same as those of white youths. It is the black underclass, left behind, which have these enormously high rates of imprisonment and gaoling and very much higher rates of violence. Predicting violence in the inner-city slum is grossly easier than predicting it in the dormitory suburb. And what else is characteristic of the inner-city ghetto? Much else that distinguishes our Criminal X from our Criminal Y—school absenteeism, unemployment, functional illiteracy, generations on welfare, no supportive families. Blackness and a higher base expectancy rate of violence overlap. And that is the problem of all these pre-emptive sentencing processes.

What, then, is the conclusion properly to be drawn from these sad realities? Some would say: 'Don't base decisions in the criminal justice system at all on predictions of dangerousness; they are racially skewed, and we already lock up too many members of our minorities.' I sympathize with the reason, but reject the conclusion. The criminal justice system cannot rectify racial inequalities and social injustices; it will do well if it does not exacerbate them. It is proper that predictions of violence should figure in many decisions in applying the criminal law, and if they are applied within principles that I am seeking to tease out that is all that can be expected. My submissions may be in error, but if they are then anyone seeking to apply predictions should offer alternative predictions. We cannot properly close our eyes to the different threats that Criminal X and Criminal Y pose to the community. But it is of first importance that we base our decisions about their respective dangerousness on validated knowledge and not on prejudice, particularly racial prejudice, and hence that we insist on the most careful validation of such stereotypes of dangerousness; my submissions are an effort to define what is required to achieve such validation. We must insist, if predictions are to be used, that they be reliable.

Let me give an example of the application of this thesis, this time in relation to *Barefoot*. In that case we find a psychiatrist saying that this prisoner, Barefoot, is a psychopath (a meaningless though pejorative diagnosis), that he is highly likely to be a danger to the community if released, or if maintained in prison, and that because of his higher dangerousness he should be executed. Now I think it is true that the witness grossly exaggerated his capacities to predict, and that the Court's suggestion that the jury is capable of distinguishing the wheat from the chaff in his testimony—the good prediction from the bad prediction—is at best ingenuous. (The Court also agrees that there isn't any wheat there, it's all chaff; and the suggestion that the jury should be able to do what the court cannot guide them how to do—because nobody could so guide them—is I think bordering on the improper.) But, however that may be, what would be the proper proof? What would have been properly acceptable evidence? If my principles are right, here is what would be proper proof. The psychiatrist would be asked: 'If Barefoot's murder is compared with a murder of similar gravity by a man with a similar record to Barefoot's, does the fact that you diagnose him as a psychopath mean, and the other diagnostic information about him also mean, that he has a higher likelihood of being injurious to people if not executed?' It is not that he has a high likelihood—we know that. The point is that he must have a *higher* likelihood than those with whom we are comparing him, otherwise we have to execute them all—or none. If we are with justice to select him, we must have a comparison group. Who should constitute the comparison group? The comparison group must be murderers with the same record and the same severity of offence whom you do *not* call psychopaths and do not otherwise selectively diagnose. Very well, Doctor, give us the evidence on which you have based your findings that this diagnostic category 'psychopath' has a higher base expectancy rate, seriously higher, than others?

Of course, there is no such evidence. But that, I submit, is how the question ought to be posed. That is a pattern of thought which could justify a selection under which one might be able with justice to increase punishment by virtue of a prediction of future violent behaviour—but not otherwise.

To conclude. As is so often the case with issues of justice, procedural and evidentiary issues become of central importance. Let me put the point curtly and again. Clinical predictions of dangerousness unsupported by actuarial studies should never be relied on. It is shocking that the Supreme Court relies on such statements without validated statistical support. Clinical judgements firmly grounded on well-established base expectancy rates are a precondition, rarely fulfilled, to the just invocation of prediction of dangerousness as a ground for intensifying punishment. My conclusions then are my seven submissions—I know that they are unrealistic, but I affirm they provide a rational process by which one can think of the just use of predictions. Unless they or something like them are fulfilled the present movement to the overuse of predictions of dangerousness is a threat to justice.

I must admit that, if my submissions are accepted, I doubt the availability of sufficient knowledge to meet the necessary preconditions of just sentencing based on express predictions of violence. Further, that gap in our knowledge should make us sceptical about our present widespread reliance on implicit and intuitive predictions of dangerousness in exercising discretion—in situations where we do not declare that usage as we do in the situations I have been discussing.

Developing a coherent and practical jurisprudence of dangerousness will not be an easy task. I know I have not done so; but I hope I have enunciated some principles that may be useful to that task. Courts have long hidden behind the wall of standards of proof and behind the white coats of psychiatrists and psychologists, so that difficult issues have been avoided. Yet predictions of dangerousness have been applied implicitly and explicitly by judges and parole boards, hospital administrators and psychiatrists, police and correctional officers, victims of crime and prosecutors of criminals. Scholarship and legal analysis have failed sufficiently to recognize the danger of this untested and intuitive use of our poor capacity accurately to predict future violent behaviour. There is a danger both to liberty and to effective crime control in the concept of dangerousness, yet we cannot and should not do without it. It is a sin against the light to extend the application of the concept of dangerousness in the criminal law and in the law of mental health without more careful evaluation of our predictive capacities than those eight prospective studies which seem to make up our limited present knowledge, and with such scant efforts at jurisprudential analysis of the concept's proper role in those systems of social control.

Preface: P. Hirst, 'The Concept of Punishment'

Paul Hirst's discussion of punishment is part of his broader sociological analysis of law as a regulatory institution (see Hirst 1986). A characteristic of 'law' (or the legal order) is that its norms claim to be obligatory, and to prevail over all competing norms. To sustain this claim, legal rules—particularly those of the criminal law—are backed by sanctions of various kinds. Punishment is a major form of legal sanction (others include revocation of licence, civil penalties, rendering agreements null and void), and, Hirst argues, this institutional function makes punishment a necessary part of any legal system. Individuals may comply with legal norms for all sorts of reasons, but, where non-compliance occurs, forceable sanctions are crucial to upholding law's claim to be the dominant normative order. It does not follow from this that punishment can effectively prevent deviance; nor that punishment is always the most appropriate way of sanctioning violations of the criminal law; nor that current forms and levels of penal sanction are the most appropriate or desirable. But it *does* suggest that punishment is not an institution that could ever be abolished. It has a 'last resort' necessity which renders it indispensible to social organization. (Abolitionists might reply that we can, and should, seek to replace punishment by *non-punitive* sanctions; see BIANCHI.)

Hirst's concern here is to analyse punishment as a social institution, outlining its function within the wider processes of social regulation, investigating the ways in which particular penal practices have historically come into existence, and identifying what punishments can and cannot achieve. He notes the contemporary popularity of expressivist justifications of punishment, and of policies such as incapacitation and just deserts. Such approaches, he thinks, have a dangerously reactionary cast, being more attuned to the symbolic politics of law and order than to the objectives of a rational penology. Instead of reducing the punitiveness of penal institutions or ensuring that they are properly regulated by law, these approaches are liable to transform penal measures into occasions for ritualistic vengeance or methods of raising the morale of the law-abiding.

The current popularity of 'punishment for its own sake' reflects in part the perceived failure of penal policies which espoused more utilitarian objectives. But, Hirst argues, this perceived failure is a result not of misguided policies, but of unrealistic expectations. A realistic assessment of the institution will show that punishment always has some measure of failure built into it: even expressive penalties can convey the wrong message (see MATHIESEN); and retributive measures can fail to inflict the suffering they intend (see TONRY; and generally Abel 1991). This acknowl-edgement that punishment is to some degree necessary and yet of very limited pos-itive utility (see Garland 1990 on punishment's 'tragic' character) leads Hirst to suggest that our goal should be to explore the minimum necessary extent of its use. 'How and how much we punish is a political issue, and should not be dictated by misplaced concern with the degree to which punishments "work".'

If punishments rarely succeed in their official objectives, penal practices and institutions cannot be adequately understood merely in instrumental terms—as means designed to achieve a particular end. We must rather, Hirst argues, under-stand specific penal measures, such as the prison, the gallows, the fine, or the community service order, as 'artefacts of social organization'; as historical prod-ucts which have been constructed over time within complex configurations of social circumstances. Penal measures have evolved as consequences of the inter-action of numerous forces which have been extensively described by historians; Hirst gives a flavour of these analyses in his discussion of the development of the prison and the modern fine. While instrumental considerations no doubt have some impact on penal forms, punishments also have a particular cultural style, and embody a certain sensibility, which in turn depend upon the 'institutional, technical and discursive conditions' that Hirst sketches. What is true of particular penal methods can also be expected to be true of movements in penal theory: a sociologist of penal thought will trace the development of different normative theories through the changing social and political conditions from which they emerge, and will argue that these cannot be understood purely in their own terms, as exercises in socially detached or a priori theorizing (see Garland 1985, 1990; Norrie 1991).

Hirst thus reminds us that penal reform depends more upon political forces and struggles than on shifts in normative theory or on the exigencies of crime control. His analysis presents a challenge to the kinds of normative theorizing in which earlier essays in this volume have been engaged. For whether a normative theory can apply to 'the actual social world in which we live' (MURPHY: 57) depends not only on whether the theory's preconditions for justified punishment are satisfied in that actual world, but also on whether the theory can in fact influ-ence our penal practices. If practice is shaped by wider social and political forces, rather than by normative theorizing about the justifying aims of punishment, then we must think again about the importance of such theorizing. However, Hirst himself engages in normative argument about the proper uses and extent of punishment; and, whilst some theorists will argue that punishment can and must still be justified by some normative theory, others argue—as we will see in the following three essays—that we should engage in more radical normative theo-rizing about the proper role of punishment in our societies.

References

ABEL, R. (1991), 'The Failure of Punishment as Social Control', *Israel Law Review*, 25: 740–52.

GARLAND, D. (1985), *Punishment and Welfare: A History of Penal Strategies* (Aldershot).

—— (1990), *Punishment and Modern Society: A Study in Social Theory* (Oxford).

HIRST, P. Q. (1986), *Law, Socialism and Democracy* (London).

NORRIE, A. W. (1991), *Law, Ideology and Punishment* (Dordrecht).

The Concept of Punishment

P. Q. HIRST

'Punishment' has become an increasingly problematic and controversial category in the last forty years or so. Particular punishments such as the death penalty have become symbolic of wider political divisions, as the recent controversy in the United Kingdom demonstrated. The opposing forces have fought their symbolic battles over the utility of hanging as a means to an end. Abolitionists argue that it cannot function as a deterrent. Restorationists argue that it would so function and, moreover, in some cases also argue that certain criminals justly deserve to be executed, whatever the deterrent effect of the penalty. In like manner, prisons have become a focus of controversy, which centres on whether or not they 'work'. A substantial libertarian lobby argues that prisons have 'failed'; they serve no purpose but to degrade inmates and to breed hardened criminals and, therefore, should be abolished. A more cautious and conservative economy-minded lobby calls for shorter sentences and more non-custodial sentences for less serious criminals, reserving prison for the most serious cases. By no means incompatible with the latter view is the stridently expressed current of opinion that demands longer sentences for serious crimes, mandatory sentences, and more prisons—prisons here being perceived as the most effective means of checking a supposed slide into lawlessness.

It is only apparently paradoxical that both the forces that criticize particular forms of punishment from a libertarian and reformist stance and the forces that berate the present penal regime from a 'law and order' stance help to create a climate of opinion in which modern means of punishment have 'failed'. This climate in large measure derives from viewing particular means of punishment as means to some definite end—a state of affairs that should prevail among the recipients of such means, such as deterrence or reform.[1] One consequence of this 'climate of failure'— given that the vast majority of citizens intuitively sense that some form of penal sanction is necessary—is to give credence to those justifications of punishment and those views of the purpose of punishment that are least concerned with success or failure. I refer here to justifications in terms of 'just deserts', victim satisfaction, and 'social defence'.[2] These justifications of and purposes for punishment are the very ones that anybody concerned to minimize the punitiveness of sanctions and who favours the most thorough legal regulation of punishment should fear. Deterrence and reform have been the goals in terms of which reformers have sought to reduce the severity of punishments. The failure to achieve these goals makes it possible to argue for punishments that appear less likely to fail precisely to the degree they approach the ritualistic ends of vengeance and the raising of the morale of the law-abiding.

It is, therefore, far from paradoxical that those who favour the greatest legal protection for those subject to punishment under the law and the least punitive means to stand for sanctions need to know *why* we punish and what the use of penal sanctions can and cannot accomplish. Libertarians who aim for a utopia in which there are no punitive sanctions and ultra-conservatives satisfied with ritualistic vengeance can dispense with the question. Knowing that penal sanctions are necessary to a legal order and that we can accomplish little by means of them—if, that is, the standard of measure of means is some outcome in terms of the behaviour of those to whom they are applied or the community at large—provides a powerful rationale for seeking to reduce to the minimum the coerciveness and suffering entailed in punishments. Educating people not to expect punishment to 'succeed' ought to be a primary liberal goal.

In this chapter I shall try to provide some of the elements of a knowledge of why we punish and what punishment can and cannot accomplish. I shall argue:

1. that every regime of punishment has always 'failed'—punishment is always in crisis if it is viewed as a means to some typical outcome in respect of the mass of offenders subject to it;
2. that the punishments that are commonly available at any given time mainly prevail not because they are chosen as the most efficacious means to an end, but because they are consequences of the prevailing mode of social organization;
3. that we have probably 'invented' all the possible modes of punishment; novel means to provide sanction to laws lie in the areas of surveillance and supervision, treatment and behaviour modification, but such means tend to undercut our dominant conception of punishment as a legally specified penalty consequent on a particular criminal act—they tend to lead to the policing of categories of 'dangerous' individuals and they tend to give discretion to agencies other than specifically legal ones;

4. that where possible we should seek non-punitive means to give
   sanction to legal norms, but that there is an ultimate and inevitable
   element of coercion underlying any legal order—that is, legal regulation differentiates itself from other rules for conduct by its claim
   to be dominant and obligatory. In modern states that claim depends
   ultimately on the legally justified use of force to sustain it.

I shall discuss sanctions and punishment only in so far as they form
part of the regulation of the conduct of social agents within a legal order.
Other uses of punishment and practices of punishing are subject to legal
sanction and regulation: thus parents and teachers may 'punish' children,
but certain actions and consequences constitute unlawful harm. It should
be clear that the legal regulation of conduct takes a number of forms and
does not consist purely in prohibitive norms; for example, law regulates
conduct through specifying the statuses and defining the capacities of
social agents. Law is in essence a regulatory activity, and all regulation,
however 'creative', involves an element of sanction. The claim entailed
in a legal order to be both the dominant and an obligatory mode of patterning conduct means that compliance with legal norms is not a matter
of 'ought', as in a moral injunction; rather it has the compelling and overriding force of a 'must'. Sanction follows from this claim to dominance
and obligatoriness; it is the element of compulsion that gives whatever
substance the claim has. All legal orders have a limited capacity to
substantiate their claims and compel through sanctions, but most compliance of social agents is as the result of rationales and inducements other
than sanctions.

A sanction may be defined as any legally recognized means whereby
an attempt is made to ensure conformity with norms. Sanctions and punishments are not co-extensive. A sanction may be the threat of loss of
status and, therefore, of some capacity that stems from legal recognition;
loss of corporate personality, withdrawal of a licence, etc., are examples
of such sanctions. Punishment must therefore be viewed as one means of
sanctioning. As such it supposes not just the attempt to ensure conformity with legal norms but the use of some punitive means to ensure such
compliance—'punitive' meaning the imposition of some loss or suffering
on the agent. The idea of a penalty cannot escape some utilitarian calcu-
lus, however vague and imprecise, of pleasure and pain. Punishments
suppose the recipient is an agent, that is, an entity whose behaviour is the
result of some capacity for decision and who will exercise that capacity in
the appropriate way given a specific pressure to desist from an action.

The idea of a penalty does not necessarily imply any moral connotation. We speak of guilt in certain cases and suppose punishment a justified consequence, but other offences that attract penalties are objective and the penalty is a formal consequence and not a 'just desert' in the sense of being merited by a criminal intention of the agent. For example, traffic fines are penalties: they are aimed at reducing regular illegal parking by imposing a cost that is hopefully unacceptable to the motorist. However, they and other punishments often actually function as a 'tariff', which instead of acting as a means to ensure compliance becomes a fee for tolerated illegality, and thus ceases properly speaking to be a penalty.

The notion of punishment supposes some particular method of punishment used to a certain extent. The reason that persons are sentenced to *a* punishment, even if this be an indeterminate period in prison, rather than to whatever amalgam of means happen to prove effective in their case to ensure a commitment to future conformity with norms, is because all forms of legal order regulate not merely the acts of social agents but also the mode in which attempts are made to control or compensate for such acts. Legal regulation does not end with the determination of guilt or fault, but also extends to the consequences that follow from such judgments. 'Punishments' as means to sanction are claimed to be part of the legal order and not some realm of purely administrative and unregulated means exterior to it. Our prisons often appear to be a private empire outside the law, but they are not *claimed* to be so. Were that the case the legal order's claim to dominance and obligatoriness in all spheres would be forfeit. It is the legal regulation of punishment that sets limits to possible punitive means, that specifies a method and extent. Regulation is a process, and it need not be effective—indeed regulation has built in to it the possibility of evasion and failure.

My analysis of the concepts of sanction and punishment (not as 'ideas' but as working social categories) indicates that particular penal means must to some degree be viewed instrumentally in that they represent the means used to sanction and are part of an attempt to ensure conformity with norms. But the predominantly teleological views of punishment go beyond this minimal instrumentalism in that particular penalties are evaluated in terms of whether or not they lead to certain outcomes or states of affairs, for example, deterrence or providing the preconditions for reform. This teleological view of punishment and the consequent standard of evaluation in terms of whether particular penal means 'work' or not is shared by philosophers seeking justifications for the right to punish, by pragmatic penal reformers and by social scientists. The problem here is that these teleological views of punishment as instruments tend to roll up a number of distinct issues:

1. Penalties are means to sanction conformity with norms. Some such means are inescapable if we are to have a legal order and the claims it makes, but the degree to which any such set of penalties actually does produce the degree of conformity we observe is virtually incalculable. Many factors other than the use of sanctions or the anticipation by actors of their use induce conformity. This point is widely recognized but it tends to be dismissed when viewing punishments instrumentally because it undercuts arguments against a given penalty in terms of its ineffectiveness or in favour of some new or restored penalty because of its greater effectiveness.

2. The question of whether punishments 'work' tends to be evaluated in terms of consequent states of affairs, such as deterrence and crime rates. Less attention is devoted to the question of whether given penalties are actually *penal*; that is, whether they lead to a sufficient measure of loss or suffering to be compelling in attaining the particular end supposed. If this question is raised it is usually in the manner that such penalties would be so compelling if they were properly applied and to an appropriate extent.

Philosophical discussions of punishment tend to be instrumentalist and seek a justification in terms of the states of affairs the application of a punishment is intended to bring about. The great bulk of justificatory argument tends to be conducted in utilitarian terms, with 'just deserts' views forming a definite minority. This has recently changed with the 'new retributionism'. Instrumentalism tends to prevail in that:

1. Liberal accounts of punishment in general raise the question of individual 'rights'. Punishment is thus considered justified if the act punished involves the commensurate violation of the rights of others and if it is no more than sufficient to prevent such violation and is effective in doing so. 'Excessive' punishments and 'ineffective' punishments should therefore be abandoned.

2. The notions of 'effectiveness' and 'excess' here suppose that punishment is a means–end relation in which some actual state of affairs is attained. Thus punishment may legitimately be conceived as acting as a deterrent, as a basis for reform, etc. Punishments as a mere 'tariff' on conduct or as vengeance are generally condemned by liberals. Tariff, disassociated from deterrence, implies a 'price' for certain acts and, like vengeance, is regarded as irrational. Tariff as deter-

rence involves the notion that the law serves as a guide to action, that it prevents actions by setting a minimum sufficient level of unacceptable cost. This is the view advanced in Cesare Beccaria's *Dei delitti e delle pene* (1764). It involves the notion of a rational calculating subject, who faced with certain and definite sanctions will weigh the costs and benefits and desist from certain acts. It is also one definite form of stating the lawfulness of punishment—that it involves a known and certain ratio between crimes and offences and sanctions.

Such a 'liberal' justification of punishment is a clear form of the teleological approach to punishment. In a sense, however, *all* legal punishments are conceived to some degree teleologically. Thus to give an example from a non-liberal or pre-liberal conception of punishment, we may consider the *Ancien Régime* conception of *supplice* outlined by Foucault in *Discipline and Punish* (1977). Here the *end* of punishment was the symbolic affirmation of the power of the Sovereign. Punishment served to affirm the priority of the Crown by the spectacular destruction of the offender. Its end was symbolic and its means expressive—the measured destruction of the body of the offender. But the symbolic-expressive conception of punishment as a means–ends relation was neither limitless nor arbitrary, contrary to the later claims of Enlightenment critics. Definite acts were specified to be done to a regicide, a parricide, a common murderer, etc.; these and no others were deemed appropriate. The Enlightenment critics regarded these punishments as irrational and arbitrary precisely because they could no longer countenance the end towards which such inhumane and barbarous forms of punishment served as means. Punishment, for the Enlightenment reformer, should govern conduct in a differently purposive way: it should reform or deter the offender, and/or deter others from committing similar offences. The spectacular is rejected because it is considered inefficacious for *those* ends.

The modern regime of punishment is generally recognized to have 'failed' in terms of the two dominant ends that governments, prison officials, and penologists have claimed for it—deterrence and reform. Rising crime rates and recidivism are widely cited as evidence for this, and in addition many critics and reformers regard prisoners' conditions as offensive to a civilized society. The result is the crisis of confidence in penal means on the part of those who regard them as instruments to attain certain states of affairs. It has to be accepted, however, in a broader sense that 'punishment'—a particular method used to a certain extent—has a degree of failure built into it. This broader sense is that the application of penal means may fail to be 'punitive'; that is, the persons to whom such means are applied may not suffer pain or loss in the manner prescribed or indeed at all. This may seem odd, but I give some examples below—like the not so apocryphal case of the tramp who commits an offence in the *hope* of being sent to prison. Even those who conceive reform and rehabilitation as the end of a penal sentence must nevertheless suppose its application sufficiently compelling that the convicted person sees such an objective as a reasonable alternative to their previous course of action.

Such ironic lack of success does not, however, exhaust punishments' intrinsic capacity for failure. Punishment, in the sense of a particular method used to a particular extent, *stands for* the general requirement of law that its norms be sanctioned. Sanctioning is represented by the action of certain penal means. We may say that penal means are the 'sign' of sanction—they represent it as specific means of compulsion. In this sense the general requirement of legal norms that they be sanctioned is met by some prescribed and definite means. A legal order cannot therefore adjust its means of sanction precisely to each state of affairs and offender in such a way that they are actually compelling; it must use a set of definite penal means. The result is a greater or lesser rate of failure depending upon how far actual states of affairs and offenders differ from the ones supposed in the means available to be applied.

Punishment may fail to sanction because it takes a definite form relative to offences and involves definite penal means. This relation punishment–offence and these penal means always entail and suppose a 'typical' subject or individual in receipt of punishment and to whom the action of these means is punitive. Punishment often fails to produce a punitive effect because the object of the legally specified means is a 'representative individual', i.e. one to whom the means would be necessarily punitive and who would therefore actually suffer those means as sanction. Particular punishments in their legal form, because they are specified and regulated, must make suppositions about the calculation, motives, and feelings that individuals 'typically' have. Such typical subjects are presupposed in the particular penal means, but the actual individuals who commit offences are diverse and may not actually suffer in this postulated way when the means are applied to them. The following are examples of this discrepancy between means and supposed effect, between the 'representative individual' and the actual agent responsible for an offence:

- The imprisonment of the desperately poor and homeless, who may actually *commit* offences to get a bed and some food. Prison regimes, however harsh, suppose minimum standards in any system where detention is more than mere incarceration, i.e. where detention is for reform, and/or where social agents are supposed to have certain minimum rights, involving some regard to health and nutrition. Hence in a society where prison conditions are regulated but individuals' 'private' circumstances are less so, certain individuals such as vagrants may actually live in conditions inferior to those of prison populations.[3]

- Fining both the desperately poor or those in receipt of minimum state benefits and the very rich on a fixed scale related to the offence.
- Even execution may not be effectively 'punitive', not merely in the sense that it fails to deter other offenders but in that certain subjects, like political terrorists or members of resistance movements, may actually *seek* execution as a means of martyrdom and propaganda by act.

In each of the above cases, the offence and the conception of the typical subject define the extent and manner of punishment and not the conditions that would be effectively punitive to the actual individuals who commit offences. To be actually punitive to all given individuals, punishments would have to be adjusted precisely to individuals' circumstances. However, this individuated process of making punishments punitive would actually disrupt the notion of an 'end' as the objective of punishment. This is because a genuinely 'punitive' individuated sanction, which really did make an individual suffer, might have to take a form that did not attain the broader end—neither reforming nor deterring. The punitiveness of punishment is designed to *do* something or to serve as a precondition *for* something else—to humiliate, to predispose to rehabilitation, to deter, etc.; it is never an end in itself. Even 'just deserts' or vengeance theories of punishment suppose that the penal means convey a judgment of value or in some way measure the crime; they can fail too.

Furthermore, the adjustment of punishments to individual circumstances would undercut the rule-governed and procedural nature of legal punishment. Notions of a definite 'tariff', of the rights of subject in law, and of the certainty of the legal process would no longer apply. Rules and forms would pertain to procedures to determine guilt but not to subsequent dispositions. Hence the certainty of the expectations of subjects under law, the comparability of treatment for analogous offences, etc., would be further undercut. This does not apply merely to 'liberal' expectations about the certainty and calculability of law. It applied equally well where, for example, status governed the means of punishment and nobles regarded it as a right and a mark of rank to be beheaded rather than hanged. Limits related to offences and to the status of offenders are no peculiar mark of post-Enlightenment justice but are necessary in any system of procedure where punishments are seen as themselves law governed and applied according to rules.

Hence views such as Barbara Wootton's (1959), which seek to individuate corrective dispositions in the interests of social control, threaten to move correction outside of a specifically *legal* sphere. Attempts to make the sanctioning of conduct certain in its application to individuals therefore also undercut the very means–ends relation within law that is already made problematic in the use of definite means of punishment related to offences and the status of offenders. The 'punitive' nature of the means used to sanction is therefore always to a degree 'hypothetical'; it involves an hypothesis about the persons who are the objects of punishment and in doing so supposes a 'typical individual' who is being punished. Hence the conditions of 'punishment' as an attainable state of affairs for all individuals are not given in the means that can be legally used. Punishments cannot be wholly individuated *and* remain part of 'legal order'.

Punishment is therefore always to a degree inadequate and any given penal means cannot merely be evaluated in terms of a means–ends relation. Thus to point out that hanging does not 'work' because it does not deter and that imprisonment does not 'work' because it does not deter or reform (these failures being evidenced by rising rates of capital crimes or rising rates of recidivism) is not to argue against the use of these punishments *per se*. It is to do so only if we accept that such punishments are to be considered *only* as means to those ends. Indeed, such arguments play into the hands of retributionists. Those who are willing to use punishment as a ritual, as a symbol of resolve, or as a sop to victims or those frightened about law and order need to be challenged by arguments other than that punishments do not 'work', because they are willing to forgo the aim of reform and willing to accept that deterrence effects may be weak. Indeed, if they are told that prevailing penal methods do not punish, that merely reinforces their case for a stronger dose of the same or a search for some new method. There are other arguments against hanging—that the process of determining guilt is too fraught with errors and no restitution can be made to the innocent; that the law should not use violent means to prevent violent acts—which do not fall into the retributionist trap. Likewise there are arguments against imprisonment as a general method of punishment—that it is expensive; that it is so destructive of many individuals' capacities that they become unfitted for any kind of normal social life—which escape the same consequence.

Punishment may be 'hypothetical' in its supposed conditions of application but it always takes a definite social form as certain means applied
to social agents. These means do not arise simply because of the agitation
of reformers or by a policy process that seeks the rational determination
of means to ends. Rather, means of punishment are *artefacts of social organization*, the products of definite institutional, technical and discursive
conditions in the same way as other artefacts like technologies or built
environments. Artefacts can be explained not by their individual 'purpose' alone but by the ensemble of conditions under which such con-
structions or forms become possible. First, forms of punishment are
related to conditions of social and political organization. Thus imprisonment as a form of punishment in itself rather than detention prior to punishment supposes certain capacities on the part of the state to levy taxes
and to administer complex organizations. Fines suppose certain social
relations of production, i.e. a fairly high level of generalized commodity
production and exchange and the mass monetary circulation coincident
upon it. Secondly, the procedural forms in law that specify and limit the
forms of punishment have complex conditions of existence. Thus John
Langbein (1974, 1977) has shown that the inquisitorial procedure that utilized torture to obtain confessions to prove guilt arose because courts
and jurists at that time lacked the autonomy to determine the result of a
case by the forms of evidence modern courts now find sufficient. A full
confession or a complete proof were necessary because state power and
its judges were as yet insufficiently insulated from the pressures of the
remaining feudal powers, kin groups and confraternities, and the mob.
Torture was part judicial procedure and part punishment because substantial partial proofs and evidence were necessary in order that it be
applied; the criminal accused was thus already in part presumed 'guilty'
in order for torture to be applied. Likewise, *supplice* as a form of punishment under the *Ancient Régime* involved a conception of the Sovereign as
a *person* whose majesty and whose peace were threatened directly by
crime. Crime was a personal offence to the Sovereign because of the
form sovereignty took: public power was embodied in the person of the
monarch and the claims of law implicated in the personal attributes and
dignity of the monarch. *Lèse majesté* was the ultimate form of offence
because the person of the Sovereign was central to the claims of the law
to be a dominant and obligatory order of regulation of conduct.

Thus forms of procedure and punishment both have definite conditions of existence outside of any reformer or official's conception of a
means–ends relation. Likewise limits set by procedure on punishment

can arise from conditions quite different from those in modern liberal assumptions. Beccaria's *Dei delitti e delle pene* (1764) is a key reference point for the liberal myth of rational sentencing replacing arbitrary injustice, of punishments fitted to the gravity of the crime. Beccaria's teleological 'political geometry', with its stress on *results*, i.e. the certainty and calculability of the law in its action, exemplifies the instrumentalist way of viewing punishment. In contradistinction to Beccaria, we can say that *there never can be* certain and calculable punishments, and that such certainty and calculability in punishment would undercut precisely the forms of procedural certainty Beccaria wished to introduce for punishment, i.e. law as a guide to action and a calculable tariff-deterrent. Beccaria perceives torture and *supplice* as inherently arbitrary and unlimited, signs of the arbitrary power of the *Ancien Régime*. He mistakes the forms of procedural limitation he proposes with the possibilities of limitation *per se*. The procedural limitations of pre-Enlightenment justice appear absurd to him and non-existent. This is evidenced by the remarks of Beccaria's patron, Pietro Verri, who took the trial of the *untori* in seventeenth-century Milan as a classic example of the arbitrariness inherent in any procedure that worked through torture. However, as the novelist and grandson of Beccaria, Alessandro Manzoni (1964), pointed out, the case Verri chose did not prove his point. The confessions of those accused of smearing the poison on the walls of houses in the city were in fact obtained by violating the procedural limits set down by Renaissance jurisconsults for the use of torture. Leading questions, the use of threats and inducements, etc., were expressly forbidden in the guides for procedure written by jurists (see Ruthven 1978: 16–17). One might as well say that the Smith Act trials in the USA proved the inherent arbitrariness of liberal constitutionalism. On the contrary, both periods of 'clear and present danger' merely prove that any system of procedural limits can be violated or cast aside if legal personnel deem certain political objectives or needs of the social order paramount.

Procedural limitations and legally specified means of punishment are thus not specifically post-Enlightenment and 'liberal' phenomena; they existed in Renaissance and *Ancien Régime* legal systems and they involved just the same problematicity in regarding particular forms of punishment as a means to an end. Thus *supplice*, far from necessarily upholding the majesty of the Sovereign and through him the law, actually often served to produce a disorderly legality in which the weakness of the state was revealed and the Sovereign humiliated. Riots at the scaffold, the defiance and fortitude of the victim could mock the sovereign power. The expressive 'end' of *supplice* could thus be undercut and threatened by the means available to make it manifest. Likewise, a person who withstood procedural torture and failed to confess could neither be fully convicted nor have his property confiscated. Torture could lawfully only be used within definite limits—only so much and by prescribed methods. Anyone who could resist or perish in silence could thus retain honour and the family wealth. Procedural limits when properly applied thus prevented torture being an infallible 'means to truth'.

Punishment, because it is an artefact of social organization, thus cannot be considered purely instrumentally as a means to an end that should cease to operate when it 'fails'. Procedural torture and *supplice* failed in some considerable measure throughout the period of their application. The replacement of the *strappado* and the scaffold came about neither because they came to be perceived to be ineffective at a particular time nor because manners changed in the direction of greater 'humanitarianism'. Writers on the legal status of torture were concerned to specify 'humane' methods and limits to procedure. The notions of humanism and enlightenment have no unequivocal social location or an inherent connection with certain procedural limits.[4] Foucault (1977) is correct to look at the conditions underlying a whole regime of punishment and, in relation to these conditions, to situate the distinctive discourses that sustained it. The new punitive means introduced in the eighteenth century, the penitentiary prison, cannot be evaluated solely through the discourses of the reformers, or by means of the supposed 'ends' of punishment (correction, reform, and deterrence) enshrined in their programmes, or by the 'failure' of the resulting institutions to attain those ends. As Foucault shows, Beccaria's critique of *Ancien Régime* judicial procedure and punishments noted their 'failure' and yet did not propose imprisonment as an alternative penal method. Instead he proposed forced labour on public works.

Again, in looking at the new 'ends' set up in the means–ends relation of punishment based upon imprisonment, we cannot take those ends as the discourses of reformers like Jeremy Bentham present them. Bentham is utilizing certain social organizational means rather than 'inventing' them, and the means are certainly not confined in their application to penal policy. The objective of correcting individuals through a regime of detention becomes possible as the result of a series of changes in political and social organization. Prisons are merely one of a series of artefacts of social organization—insane asylums, hospitals, workhouses, reformatories for delinquent youth; as a means of punishment they share institutional features and regimes with forms that do not operate according to the same professed ends. That these transformations cannot be explained by the demands of an emergent capitalism is another and broader question we cannot enter into here. Suffice it to say that the regulation of labour and idleness, of madness and mental health, of sickness and social hygiene, of education and the capacities of youth arose as possibilities and became strategies because the powers and forms of the state, economic relations and national wealth, religion and the patterning of conduct changed in a complex ensemble that is not explained by a single causality or reducible to any social 'level' or the 'interests' of any social class. A change in the means of punishment is a part of this ensemble and is not explicable as the discovery of a new means–ends relation by the reformers. It is precisely such a teleological view that vitiates the explanation in D. J. Rothman's otherwise valuable *Discovery of the Asylum* (1971) and demonstrates the value of the questions Foucault asks in *Discipline and Punish* (1977).

I have stressed that the action of a means of punishment is always 'hypothetical' in its relation to specific individuals, but definite means of punishment are not thereby inconsequential in their actual effects on individuals. Means of punishment, precisely because they suppose a 'representative individual' as their object, involve definite forms of individuation. Individuals are constructed as agents before punishments and in legal procedures; they are interpellated *as* the 'representative individuals' these punishments and procedures suppose. Now whilst this may not actually secure a 'punitive effect', subjects are constructed through a certain relation to punishment and this may have effects on them.

To take an example, the effects of the inquisitorial procedure in trials for heresy. Here the subject is interpellated as not merely answerable for conduct, because outward conformity is not a sufficient defence or requirement; rather the object of inquiry is the subject's beliefs and motivations, which are not taken to be manifest givens or wholly conscious. The confession of heresy is thus conditional on a full review of the subject's beliefs and knowledge, since ignorance of doctrine can lead to heresy. A confessed heretic has a definite status, as one specifically subject to religious 'police' and limitations (on residence, confession, associations, etc.). The subject is thus interpellated as responsible not merely for conduct but for its own essence, for every thought and desire. Conduct is not merely outwardly patterned, but should be subject to comprehensive internal review. Confession has the object not merely of policing conformity, but of supervising and transforming individuals. Thus a definite form of enforcing conformity *individuates*. Indeed, heresy trials can lead to a simple man of the people being investigated, and his beliefs, thoughts, and motivations taken seriously by doctors of theology. A good example is the miller of a small village in seventeenth-century Italy whose case is examined by Carlo Ginzburg (1980). Because Ginzburg uses the trial to get at popular orally circulated beliefs, he concentrates on the figure of the miller. He therefore lays less stress on the form of examination itself, although he does recognize how remarkable it is that such attention should be paid to the beliefs of a simple uneducated man. The inquisitorial procedure used in cases of heresy could thus individuate in complex and often unintended ways.

Prison regimes were intended to individuate in specific ways by many of the reformers—to discipline and to correct but also to produce a self-governing and industrious individual of orderly habits. The intense debate about the respective merits of the Auburn and Philadelphia's 'systems' centred on their capacity to transform the prisoner into an obedient and industrious but also repentant and moral individual conscious of guilt. Prison regimes generally failed to accomplish the reforming and philanthropic goals of some of their projectors. If anything, a prolonged period of imprisonment seems to destroy the socially acquired capacities of most inmates, as Cohen and Taylor (1972) demonstrates well. The personal remodelling offered in claims for regimes based on treatment or 'behaviour modification' should be viewed with some scepticism not merely because they often repeat the very claims and methods of the penitentiary reformers but also because they tend to destroy the very notion that punishment has a limited legally specified manner and extent. Beccaria may have been wrong to suppose that we can construct a rational ratio between crimes and penalties and to identify earlier procedural limitations as mere arbitrariness, but the conversion of punishment into 'correction' is to be feared because it places previous few limits on the powers of the correctors.

If we accept that most of the penal methods are either obsolete—such as corporal and capital punishment, banishment and transportation—or substantially ineffective and used because we have no better ideas of new methods—as is the case with imprisonment and the fine—then we should be wary of 'new' methods of giving sanction to legal norms. Often such methods are presented as 'non-penal', but, just as intended penalties may not 'punish', so supposedly non-penal dispositions may in fact inflict considerable suffering and loss. The reason here is a conflict less between the 'representative' and the actual individual, than between the prospects of such organizations and practices and the shabby substance. Caution is required here—supervision, community service orders, and juvenile homes outside the prison service are probably no more ineffective than prisons and fines and can be subjected to procedural limits and inspection. The point is not to paint a rosy picture of an effective and cheap set of non-penal and non-custodial means to control or reform offenders. Painting a rosy future for supervision and 'treatment' and denouncing a new 'gulag' run by psychiatrists, social workers, etc., are parallel faults; both overestimate the effectiveness of the methods praised or damned.

To conclude: the sanctioning of legal norms does require an element of compelling force, but, as we have seen, penal methods are generally anything but effective in this capacity. Legal regulation without an element of compulsion underlying its norms is an improbable utopia. The answer to this contradiction is neither to preach the end of the principal method of punishment underlying the rest—imprisonment—because it does not work, nor to seek to 'toughen' prison regimes and lengthen sentences. We are stuck with some level of imprisonment because we have no other ultimate sanction, but we are not stuck with the present average size of prison population, with the condition of our prisons, or with the dismal efforts to educate, retrain, and resettle those offenders we end up having to send there. Knowing the limited value of our penal means we should explore the minimum extent of their use; that extent will be dictated not by the objectives of a rational penology but by what the courts, our political representatives and government officials, and the public are willing to bear. How and how much we punish is a political issue, and should not be dictated by a misplaced concern with the degree to which punishments 'work'.

Notes

1. In the case of deterrence it is not merely or even the recipient of punishment who is to be deterred; those contemplating crimes may be deterred by the fate of offenders even if, as in the case of the death penalty, these offenders have no opportunity to commit further crimes.
2. Even in these cases, there is ample ground for a judgment of failure, since punishment is not conceived as a merely purposeless ritual. 'Just deserts' theories are particularly problematic in that they fail to establish any rational relation between a crime and a particular method and extent of punishment. For example, why should execution be a more 'deserved' punishment than life imprisonment in the case of murderers. Similarly, victim satisfaction, even when it avoids simple vengeance, has no means of demonstrating that victims will be satisfied by a given punishment; they may deem it too much or too little, or

believe that no finite punishment measures the crime. Social defence supposes prolonged neutralization—typically a long prison sentence—and is therefore unlikely as a general rationale for dealing with serious offenders: only transportation and penal colonies, with minimal concern for living conditions and mortality, could offer even the mirage of a cheap solution. Social defence by means of non-penal techniques, such as surveillance and supervision or 'treatment', is another matter. On the issue of the difference between punishment and treatment see below.

3. This failure of penal servitude as a form of punishment has been evident since the days of the eighteenth-century reformers. Conservative critics pointed out that the lot of a large section of the free labouring population was harsher than any prison regime or system of labour service envisioned by the philanthropists and *philosophes* of the Enlightenment. A conservative friar, Ferdinando Facchinei, made this a central point of his criticism of *the* classic text of the reformers, Cesare Beccaria's *Dei delitti e delle pene* (1764). As Franco Venturi observes:

> Father Facchinei had already realised that hard labour would be meaningful only if it were very different from free labour, and if the condition of the convict was substantially changed in relation to the man who had to work to earn his living. Yet, one had only to look around to realise, he said, that this difference did not exist. The poverty of those who worked was such that their situation was not very different from that which Beccaria proposed should be assigned to those sentenced to hard labour. (Venturi 1971: 106)

4. Ruthven (1978), a writer firmly in the liberal humanistic tradition, is nevertheless clear that Renaissance jurisconsults were concerned to introduce procedural norms and 'humane' methods into juridical torture. For a valuable discussion of torture in early modern and Enlightenment Europe see also Peters (1985).

References

BECCARIA, C. (1764), *Dei delitti e delle pene*, trans. 1769 as *Of Crimes and Punishment*; republished in Manzoni (1964).

COHEN, S., and TAYLOR, L. (1972), *Psychological Survival* (Harmondsworth: Penguin).

FOUCAULT, M. (1977), *Discipline and Punish* (London: Allen & Unwin).

GINZBURG, C. (1980), *The Cheese and the Worms* (London: Routledge & Kegan Paul).

LANGBEIN, J. H. (1974), *Prosecuting Crime in the Renaissance* (Cambridge, Mass.: Harvard University Press).

—— (1977), *Torture and the Law of Proof* (Chicago: Chicago University Press).

MANZONI, A. (1964), *The Column of Infamy* (Oxford: Oxford University Press).

PETERS, E. (1985), *Torture* (Oxford: Basil Blackwell).

ROTHMAN, D. J. (1971), *The Discovery of the Asylum* (Boston, Mass.: Little, Brown).

RUTHVEN, M. (1978), *Torture: The Grand Conspiracy* (London: Weinfeld & Nicolson).

VENTURI, F. (1971), *Utopia and Reform in the Enlightenment* (Cambridge: Cambridge University Press).

WOOTTON, B. (1959), *Social Science and Social Pathology* (London: Allen & Unwin).

Preface: E. Rotman, 'Beyond Punishment'

A remarkable feature of penal policy discourse in the 1970s and 1980s was the speed with which 'rehabilitation' moved from being a widely shared aim of progressive thinkers to being a symbol of an outdated and reactionary approach (see Allen 1981). Many academics, policy-makers, and practitioners were persuaded that rehabilitative policies were not merely ineffectual or poorly implemented, but dangerously intrusive, authoritarian, and immoral: 'theoretically faulty, systematically discriminatory in administration, and inconsistent with some of our most basic concepts of justice' (American Friends Service Committee 1971: 12; see above, Editors' Introduction: pp. 8–10). As Rotman points out, however, the model of rehabilitation attacked by such critics was a medical model which viewed offenders as 'sick' and in need of compulsory 'cures'. This approach was in practice rare (most rehabilitative programmes involved only modest educational provision and some basic skills training), but the drastic and dehumanizing brainwashing depicted by *A Clockwork Orange* (Burgess 1962) and *One Flew over the Cuckoo's Nest* (Kesey 1962) was the image which stuck in people's minds. The idea of an authoritarian state, in white-coated therapeutic disguise, resonated widely in a cultural milieu which was libertarian in ethos, distrustful of the political process, and increasingly concerned about the threats to individual liberty and rights posed by big government.

In the decades since this sudden reversal of belief, a more nuanced understanding of the possibilities, and pitfalls, of rehabilitation has emerged. Penologists who continue to advocate rehabilitation as a proper goal of penal practice argue that rehabilitative measures can be delivered in ways which avoid the problems identified by critics. Given proper safeguards to ensure that offenders fully consent to treatment, statutory rules to prevent sentences being increased for rehabilitative purposes, and scrutiny of their implementation to avoid abuses, they have a legitimate role in the state's response to crime (see especially Morris 1974; Walker 1980). However, even the most enthusiastic supporters of this approach now claim much less for it than was once claimed. Rehabilitative measures are appropriate, and likely to be effective, only in carefully selected cases in which criminal conduct is clearly related to specific conditions such as addiction or mental disturbance. The only general role they allow to rehabilitation is the more modest role of mitigating the deleterious effect that imprisonment often has upon inmates' social skills and mental well-being (see Cullen and Gilbert 1982; Hudson 1987; Palmer 1992).

Rotman's book, from which this extract is taken, seeks to revive a richer conception of rehabilitation, and thus to reopen a normative debate which was, he believes, prematurely closed. He distinguishes different historical models of rehabilitation, and shows that some of these are more vulnerable to criticism than others. Drawing on a Continental—rather than the Anglo-American—legal tradition, he argues for rehabilitation as a constitutional right: a duty owed by the state to the prisoner. From this perspective, rehabilitation ceases to be a violation of the individual's rights. Instead, it is a social right which offenders can claim (or choose not to claim) for themselves. It is a form of help which is offered to them, not a form of coercive treatment imposed on them. It can thus be argued that rehabilitation still respects the offender as an autonomous moral agent. Moreover, since rehabilitation requires attention to 'the offender's entire life, including his or her future', rather than just to the limited facts of the offence being punished, Rotman claims that it 'incorporates a concept of justice that goes beyond the symmetrical reaction of retribution' (see also CARLEN on the need to 'do justice (between criminal, victim, and state)'; also Bottoms and McWilliams 1979, on the proper aims of probation).

Such an account must face some serious questions. How effective would Rotman's rehabilitative proposals be, given that they are still to be provided within a primarily punitive context? Should we not pay more attention to the social conditions which give rise to crime, rather than to individual rehabilitation? Is it realistic and appropriate to provide offenders with more help than is provided to disadvantaged members of the free population who have not offended (see Rusche and Kirchheimer 1968 and Mannheim 1939 on 'less-eligibility' and its tendency to inhibit reform efforts)? It is also clear that Rotman does not offer a rehabilitative justification of punishment: although some penal theorists justify punishment itself as a morally reformative process (see H. MORRIS) Rotman rejects any such 'morally oriented' conception of rehabilitation. His 'humanist' ideal of rehabilitation 'has rid itself of any punitive ingredient'; rehabilitation should be offered to offenders while they are being subjected to punishments whose own justification must lie elsewhere. Some would argue that Rotman should then be more radical than he is: that he should argue for the abolition of punishment in favour of rehabilitation rather than the provision of voluntary rehabilitation within a punitive context. Others, concerned to protect individual autonomy against state coercion, will argue that Rotman does not avoid all the objections raised against the post-war 'rehabilitative ideal'. Thus whilst the state may have a duty to offer various kinds of help to any citizen who needs it (whether or not they have broken the law), the 'offer' of rehabilitative help to someone who is being punished is all too likely in fact to pressure them into accepting that help whether they want (or need) it or not.

Rotman none the less poses a challenge to penal theory: can a subtler account of rehabilitation—which is sensitive to concerns about individual freedom and to the destructive effects of punishment as typically practised in our existing penal systems—form part of an adequate theory of punishment?

References

ALLEN, F. A. (1981), *The Decline of the Rehabilitative Ideal* (New Haven, Conn.).

American Friends Service Committee (1971), *Struggle for Justice* (New York).

BOTTOMS, A. E., and McWILLIAMS, W. (1979), 'A Non-treatment Paradigm for Probation Practice', *British Journal of Social Work*, 9: 159–202.

BURGESS, A. (1962), *A Clockwork Orange* (London).

CULLEN, F. T., and GILBERT, K. E. (1982), *Reaffirming Rehabilitation* (Cincinnati).

HUDSON, B. (1987), *Justice through Punishment? A Critique of the 'Justice' Model of Corrections* (London).

KESEY, K. (1962), *One Flew over the Cuckoo's Nest* (New York).

MANNHEIM, H. (1939), *The Dilemma of Penal Reform* (London).

MORRIS, N. (1974), *The Future of Imprisonment* (Chicago).

PALMER, T. (1992), *The Re-emergence of Correctional Intervention* (London).

RUSCHE, G., and KIRCHHEIMER, O. (1968), *Punishment and Social Structure* (New York; 1st edn. 1939).

WALKER, N. (1980), *Punishment, Danger and Stigma* (Oxford).

Beyond Punishment

E. ROTMAN

Significance of Rehabilitation

The rehabilitation of criminal offenders offers the criminal justice system a unique avenue of improvement. Despite the failures and abuses of the past, a revitalized concept of rehabilitation represents a creative opening in the repetitive mechanisms of a merely punitive system. Rehabilitation has enormous potential for humanizing and civilizing social reaction against crime.

Modern rehabilitative policies challenge the fantasy that the dark side of society can be forgotten and that deviants can be simply packed off to prisons. They propose instead to offer inmates a sound and trustworthy opportunity to remake their lives. Advocating the use of imprisonment only as a sanction of last resort, rehabilitation-oriented policies seek more effective channels of social re-entry.

Whereas the traditional punitive reaction enforces conformity to law on the basis of fear or pure calculation, rehabilitation creates in the offender the capacity for social participation and responsibility.[1] Because it aims to offer opportunities that will make crime-free life a practicable option, rehabilitation is linked indissolubly with the reorganization of the community.[2]

Rehabilitation is not incompatible with fair punishment. But rehabilitative policies rest on an assumption that it is self-defeating to try to prevent crime by using the very means one is trying to eradicate. Instead of violence and coercion, rehabilitation proceeds through purposeful constructive action. In fact, the rehabilitative idea emerged as an innovative force opposing a purely retributive justice system. But while seeking to counteract its noxious effects, rehabilitative policies recognize that criminal punishment is unlikely to be abolished in the foreseeable future. By counteracting its excesses or compensating for them, rehabilitation helps make punishment more fair. Rehabilitation is in turn enhanced by fairness in sentencing[3] and at every other stage of the criminal justice process. How fairly the offender is treated at early procedural stages has a strong bearing on the ultimate success or failure of the correctional phase.

The rehabilitative aim demands a consideration of the offender's entire life, including his or her future. It thus incorporates a concept of justice that goes beyond the symmetrical reaction of retribution and inquires into the subjective reality of the offender. Moreover, the realization of the rehabilitative aim enriches the idea of justice with the element of compassion.[4]

Rehabilitation not only enriches the notion of justice, but improves the law. The quality of law can be measured by its ability to comprehend the largest possible number of facts, and to cover in its generalizations as many situations as possible. By incorporating rehabilitation, a perfected law takes subjectivity into consideration, which would otherwise remain largely excluded from the criminal process. In a purely retributive and deterrent criminolegal system, the individual is only an abstract means to fulfill overriding social goals. Subjective aspects are considered only when relevant to establish the existence of the offence or the degree of responsibility. In contrast, the rehabilitative aim demands that the scope of the legal system be enlarged so that the future life of the offender in the community is considered in sentencing and during the correctional phases. Once the predicament of the individual human being is acknowledged as relevant, rehabilitation becomes an unavoidable humanitarian concern in the legal regulation of imprisonment. 'A prison that houses long-term offenders who have little hope of early release and no sense of usefulness to sustain their future visions cannot be anything but a jungle.'[5]

In recent times, the incorporation of the rehabilitative aim has been a major impulse for progressive reform of many European sanctioning systems. Legal developments impelled by the rehabilitative concern culminate in the recognition of rehabilitation as a right—one that in some countries has received constitutional sanction. It has become increasingly clear that a modern rehabilitative concept not only serves the social interest by preventing recidivism, but also the personal interest of the offender, who benefits from the opportunities of a crime-free life.

The rehabilitative idea introduces broader social issues into the criminal justice system, creating an area of convergence with the social welfare, public health, and educational systems. True rehabilitative action opens the apparatus of criminal justice to other fields concerned with the plight of individual human beings and their needs for solidarity and assistance. Modern rehabilitation has been seen as an extension of far-reaching social planning and reform in the area of criminal justice.[6]

Moreover, the performance of the rehabilitative task has mobilized specialists from the most diverse fields of human endeavour. Anthropology, medicine, religion, psychology, history, sports, sociology, and law have all contributed to this effort to reintegrate stranded human beings into the community as valued members.

Defining Rehabilitation

Rehabilitation needs to be redefined in a way that avoids conceptual errors made in the past (errors that are examined in detail in E. Rotman, *Beyond Punishment: A New View of the Rehabilitation of Offenders* (Westport, Conn., 1990), which explores the historical, sociological, and legal meaning of rehabilitation). For now, it is enough to emphasize that an evolved rehabilitative concept includes the perspective of the offender as well as the state. In its most advanced formulations, rehabilitation has attained the status of a right. In this way, rehabilitation clearly cannot be used as a pretext to extend punishment or coercion beyond their legal limits.

Rehabilitation, according to modern standards, can be defined tentatively and broadly as a right to an opportunity to return to (or remain in) society with an improved chance of being a useful citizen and staying out of prison; the term may also be used to denote the actions of the state or private institutions in extending this opportunity. The definition thus embraces both the offender's rights and the government's policies. Rehabilitation in prisons comprises educational opportunities; vocational training; justly remunerated work; medical, psychological, and psychiatric treatment in an adequate environment; maintenance of family and community links; a safe, fair, and healthy prison environment; *post release* support; elimination of hindrances to reinstatement in the community; and the various services directed to meeting the imprisoned offender's physical, intellectual, social, and spiritual needs, as compatible with incarceration. As this list suggests, a broad concept of rehabilitation is not limited to specific programmes but includes an adequate prison environment. Alternatively rehabilitation may take place in non-institutional settings, allowing the offender to remain in society. In fact, rehabilitation is most fully realized in the community.

Historically, the older terms such as *reform, regeneration,* and *correction* as well as more modern expressions such as *re-entry, social reintegration, re-education,* and *resocialization* have all been used to refer to the rehabilitative idea. There have been some differential nuances. For example, *reform* has been used to designate moral transformations as a consequence of punishment and *reintegration* is usually applied to the postrelease stage, but there are of relatively little importance. Following a widespread consensus in the Anglo-American penal literature on the subject, this study will adopt the term *rehabilitation* and regard other expressions as synonymous.

The literal criminolegal meaning of the word can be found in the dictionary under the sociological sense of the word *rehabilitate*. The *Webster's* definition is 'to restore (a dependent, defective, or criminal) to a state of physical, mental, or moral health'. The *Oxford English Dictionary* also includes among the meanings of *rehabilitation* the 'restoration to a higher moral state'. One should be careful, however, not to confine the concept to the sense of restoration to a pre-existing condition of adequacy. Such use would not cover the achievement of totally new social or psychological developments or the acquisition of new skills. The word *rehabilitation* should therefore be used in the technical field of penology and criminal law with a meaning broader than its dictionary definitions.

Viewed from another perspective, the dictionary definition of *rehabilitation* throws light on its conceptual structure. The term is defined as both 'the act of rehabilitation' and 'the state of being rehabilitated', thus drawing a useful distinction between the rehabilitative action and the state it produces, actual or ideal. Recognizing the dual components of the conceptual field, instrumental and teleological, facilitates the analysis and transformation of available rehabilitative models. But one should keep in mind that the division between action and goal, the means and the end, is only an artificial analytic device. In fact, the two elements remain inextricably interlinked in a dynamic and unitary process of mutual interaction.

A good way to comprehend the variety of immediate aims or outcomes pursued in rehabilitative programmes is to consult the programme evaluation literature. For example, Lipton, Martinson, and Wilks listed a number of dependent variables used to measure the effectiveness of rehabilitative outcomes: recidivism, institutional adjustment, vocational adjustment, educational achievement, drug and alcohol readdiction, personality and attitude change, and community adjustment.[7] At the instrumental level, an ever-expanding list of rehabilitative methods includes various forms of psychotherapies, guided group interaction, wilderness training, alternative schools and foster care for juveniles, family therapy, day treatment programmes, pretrial release and diversion programmes, work-released and prerelease programmes, restitution programmes, and various community assistance programmes.

Besides the positive concept of rehabilitation, there is also a negative one: the avoidance of harm and deterioration. This goal is attained mainly through noninstitutional sanctions. Even sanctions that are not specifically rehabilitative, such as fines or professional bannings, accomplish an indirect rehabilitative function in so far as they replace incarceration.

Historical Models

The history of rehabilitation can be represented by four successive models: penitentiary, therapeutic, social learning, and rights oriented. The adoption of each new model did not necessarily exclude its predecessors, which simply became less prevalent. Past models were generally retrained in a modified way, coexisting or blending with the new ones. All these models belong to the same family; that is, they are composed of similar elements and respond to similar needs of social systems. They differ in the means used to achieve social goals and in the roles and powers of the members of the rehabilitative relationship. The earlier models granted unrestricted power to the penal authorities, as in the disciplinarian penitentiary regime, somewhat mitigated by the consideration of the health of the inmate in the therapeutic model. The participation of the inmate becomes a central element of the rehabilitative system in the social-learning model and gains legal status in the rights model.

The basic elements of the penitentiary model are work, discipline, and moral education. Different concepts of psychological transformation led to two variations of the model, one approximating the monastic ideal of penance, the other associated with the individualist nineteenth-century ideal of progress through industry and personal effort. Both variations relied heavily on imprisonment to mould the character of the offender. The walls of the cellular prison not only isolated the offender from the contaminating influence of society, but supported the reformative action of religious discipline and indoctrination. Later, pentitentiary confinement was the baseline of a gradual liberalization that provided a unique system of incentives and deterrents. These carrot-and-stick reformative schemes were meant to promote habits of self-discipline and industriousness. This new disciplinary approach culminated in the adoption of the indeterminate sentence.

The same indeterminate sentencing structure was later adopted in the emergent therapeutic model. The new model assumed that offenders were sick and attempted to 'cure' them of their criminality. Most of the modern debate about rehabilitation revolves around the medical model.

Criticism of its flaws precipitated the intellectual crisis of the rehabilitative concept.

Thanks to the medical analogy, the term *treatment* (formerly applied to the administrative handling of prisoners,[8] began to be used in a medical sense. In principle, the therapeutic model can mitigate the harshness of the disciplinarian penitentiary model with the element of care. But its potential for coercion tends to overshadow its positive aspects. In fact, it has lent itself to violations of individual rights under the cloak of therapeutic intervention, what Kittrie characterized as the abuses of the 'therapeutic state'.[9] At a conceptual level, the model failed to describe a specific pathology that could help to distinguish the average type of offender from law-abiding citizens. In addition, the therapeutic model created a social stigma in the inmate, the internalization of which was bound to create a self-fulfilling prophecy. Eventually an evolved therapeutic model, aware of the social and psychological aspects of disease, paved the way to the social-learning model of rehabilitation.

Sociopsychological theory helped to correct the theoretical flaws of a unilateral therapeutic model that characterized crime as individual pathology. The resulting social-learning model views crime as the product of learned behaviour and rehabilitation as a compensation for early socialization flaws resulting, for example, from family breakup or neglect. The rehabilitative purpose is attained by transforming the traditional prison environment into a problem-solving community. The new model assumes that the capacity for law abidance can be learned through a process of human interaction, which includes participation, sharing information and feelings, and preparation for the postconfinement world. Modern European social-therapeutic experiments attempt to create social-learning environments in prisons, but community-based programmes are essential to full realization of this model's goals. It finds its most refined expression in a pedagogy of self-determination,[10] which works to emancipate the offender from compulsive criminal behaviour without adding further conditioning.

Growing respect for the dignity of offenders and for their rights led to a consideration of rehabilitation from the offenders' perspective. No longer seen exclusively as a state policy, rehabilitation became a right of the offenders to certain minimum services from the correctional authorities. The purpose of such a right is to offer each offender an opportunity to reintegrate into society as a useful human being. It includes both positive aspects, such as the provision of education and vocational training, and negative ones, related to the freedom from substandard conditions of incarceration, that is, from physical or mental deterioration incompatible with social readaptation.

The Moral Content of the Rehabilitative Process

Should rehabilitation be defined to include efforts to produce a moral change in offenders, or should it rather be confined to the acquisition of the capacity to abstain from future crimes? In other words, does the rehabilitative process aim toward inculcation of moral values or mere external conformity?

Over time, the gradual adoption of terms such as *resocialization* or *rehabilitation*, instead of *reform*, marked a shift in emphasis from the moral transformation of offenders toward their social readaptation. This new conception of the rehabilitative aim is not universally accepted. In fact, the advocates of an ethically based rehabilitation predict the failure of any efforts disconnected from a definite order of moral values.[11]

The morally oriented position disregards the fact that individual rights in modern pluralistic democracies may be violated by forced compliance with a given value system. This is an especially sensitive issue in countries where several cultural systems coexist within the same social system, as in the case of large immigrant populations. The moral approach may also lead the rehabilitating agent to a self-defeating attitude of self-righteousness and moral superiority, which will impede a genuine rehabilitative task.

The transformation of state officials into moral agents carries in itself another risk: the overextension of criminal law to moral issues irrelevant to its specific function. This function consists exclusively in protecting vital individual and social interests, embodied in the most basic prohibitions and commands of a particular legal system. Thus, the attempt to moralize the offender beyond those fundamental values necessarily transforms crime control into a paternalistic undertaking. When the coercive methods of criminal law fail to force compliance to that minimum of morality that forms the core of the criminolegal systems, rehabilitation has to seek such compliance through a learning process, rather than by becoming a subtler and more intrusive form of coercion.

Similar difficulties arise when the rehabilitative agent also holds the power of the medical doctor. The pretence of acting on a disease to obtain compliance to social patterns can be as dangerous for individual freedom as is religious or ideological indoctrination. In both cases psychological authority is used for the subtle imposition of a certain value system, contradicting the basic freedoms of modern pluralistic societies.

But while the imposition of morality or of a given idea of health should be avoided, rehabilitation may well include the offer of necessary medical assistance or of religious support and practices.

A related problem is that many offenders are members of marginal subcultural groups, affirming some values opposed to those of the larger society. The attempt to transform these people morally, without a keen understanding of the social and cultural factors of their deviance, betrays an ineffective ethnocentric approach. The implied challenge is to find a rehabilitative model capable of coping with situations in which the offender does not share the value system of the agent. Such a model should take into account the fact that deviance may result, not from disease, but from the internalization of subcultural norms. On the other hand, deviance can also be the result of an unquestioning acceptance of social values shared by the law-abiding citizen, such as the possession of certain goods or the use of aggression to reach goals. As Merton pointed out in his seminal work on the subject, the lure of socially accepted values may lead some people to abandon the institutionalized ways to attain them.[12] Past rehabilitative models tried to induce conformity to the value patterns of a given cultural system, using methods that ranged from friendly forms of persuasion to the most intrusive brainwashing procedures. Such value-loaded rehabilitative concepts have been most prevalent in times of high social consensus and cohesion.[13]

If there are grave risks in efforts to inculcate moral values, the limited goal of law abidance is also an imperfect expression of the rehabilitative aim. Mere outer conformity to the law, dictated by cunning calculation or resulting from sheer deterrence, is fragile and transient. The content of the rehabilitative enterprise cannot be so radically restricted without rendering it ineffective.

The answer to the dilemma lies in a rehabilitative action that enhances human freedom instead of narrowing it through the imposition of limiting patterns. Such an alternative model of rehabilitation excludes from its goals any imposition of moral systems based on particular religious or political ideologies. A freedom-oriented model includes an educational action directed toward self-determination and responsibility. Autonomous and responsible social conduct presupposes a certain degree of freedom from psychological and environmental determinism. Thus, an education for responsibility does not infringe the basis of a pluralistic society because it is structured in the direction of the inner freedom of the individual. Such an attitude of respect toward individual freedom generates its own methodology, which at the psychological level means the furthering of self-knowledge and deliverance from mechanically accepted patterns. Although its outcome is no longer the morality based on compulsion and normative imperatives, this procedure is by no means unrelated to morality. It generates a new morality based on the understanding and dissolution of those psychological processes of conflict and isolation that are the substance of immorality. Moral awareness in this deep sense includes responsibility and compassion.

Rehabilitative programmes are always dependent on their particular social and cultural context. Significant changes in historical models of rehabilitation reflect not only new policy-making formulas, but changes of attitudes and social practices. Today, at a time of desacralization and dissolution of social normative systems, it is futile to dream of returning to an idyllic past of uniformity. Instead, a new rehabilitative model should aim toward awakening the personal experience of social responsibility.

Anthropocentric and Authoritarian Models

To resolve the dilemma posed by the moral content of rehabilitative action, it is useful to distinguish between two general prospective models of rehabilitation: one, authoritarian and oppressive in nature, the other liberty centred and humanist.[14] The authoritarian model of rehabilitation is really only a subtler version of the old repressive model, seeking compliance by means of intimidation and coercion. Rehabilitation in this sense is essentially a technical device to mould the offender and ensure conformity to a predesigned pattern of thought and behaviour. Stultifying discipline, drugs, and even psychosurgery have been applied as part of this methodology of compulsory adjustment, which deals with the human being fundamentally as a set of reflexes. Although the distinction has typically not been made explicit, recent criticism of rehabilitation has been directed to the authoritarian model, unjustly discrediting other genuine forms of rehabilitation.

The anthropocentric or humanistic model of rehabilitation, on the other hand, grants primacy to the actual human being rather than metaphysical fixations or ideologies, which long served to justify the oppressive intervention of the state. Client centred and basically voluntary, such rehabilitation is conceived more as a right of the citizen than as a privilege of the state. A humanistic public policy regarding crime implies the idea of human perfectibility, which at the level of rehabilitation includes not only the offenders themselves, but also the society that bred them and the institutions and persons involved in their treatment.

The humanistic model of rehabilitation puts no faith whatsoever in individual change obtained through subtly imposed patterns or paradigms. Rather, it assumes that no valid transformation of the offender can be brought about merely by the action of an outside agency. Significant change will come only from the individual's own insight, which alone can dissolve the antisocial influences that conditioned his or her mind. Dialogue is essential, not to issue authoritative statements but to encourage the process of self-discovery. The social control agent needs to understand the psychological determinants leading to antisocial acts, so as to provide the key that will unlock the offender's own conscience.

The humanistic model of rehabilitation excludes all manipulative schemes to alter the offender's personality or behaviour and demands fully informed consent and willing intelligent participation. Therapy should be used only when absolutely necessary and should scrupulously respect the individual's private sphere. Therapeutic intervention should not become a further conditioning, but an intensification of inner freedom and an encouragement of self-discovery. Instead of stamping the mind of the offender with a predetermined constellation of behavioural patterns, it should become a guide toward the creative possibilities of thought and new channels of action.

The psychotherapeutic perspective of the humanistic rehabilitative models goes hand in hand with the offer of practical assistance. It rejects the naïve hope that idealistic preaching will return offenders to constructive life in a hostile society, which would accept them only on painful and abusive terms. Quite the contrary, it provides the offender with a renewed opportunity to live a crime-free life and become a useful citizen. Such a positive rehabilitative action helps create in criminal offenders a sense of social responsibility by arousing an awareness of their relationship with the rest of society.

A humanistic model of rehabilitation also includes a legal component. Not only are offenders protected against the abusive interference of the state in their rights to liberty and privacy, but a due process style is imposed on the correctional activity, which is geared toward intensifying individual freedom and self-determination. Thus the humanistic model leads to the idea of rehabilitation as a right of the offender: the state has a duty to offer him or her a rehabilitative opportunity. But while the state's rehabilitative initiatives must respect individual rights, they may nevertheless represent a significant element of governmental policies to combat crime.

Rehabilitation and Specific Deterrence Distinguished

Rehabilitation must be carefully distinguished from *specific deterrence*, the technical term for the intimidating effect of punishment on convicted individuals. At one time the two concepts may have been blurred together; in historical notions of reformative punishment, its supposed 'salutary' effects were hardly distinguishable from its intimidative value.[15] But a modern notion of rehabilitation, dissociated from the goals of punishment, goes far beyond what a behaviourist would call negative reinforcement. It encompasses a broad spectrum of constructive interventions, positive human services and opportunities that tend to reduce offenders' involvement in further criminal activity. Thus it is helpful to free the new definition of rehabilitation from such foreign bodies as specific deterrence.[16]

In its historical forms, rehabilitation encompasses various types of behavioural change through rewards and incentives for constructive action. Although admitting the legitimacy of such methods, especially significant for the treatment of certain mental disorders and insufficiencies, a liberty-centred notion of rehabilitation goes beyond positive reinforcement through immediate or even distant rewards. A true pedagogy of freedom cannot be reduced to environmentally induced change or to subtle forms of persuasion. Genuine change consists in freedom from conditioning, not in exchanging one conditioning for another, thus creating new psychological automatisms.[17] Psychotherapy in its highest sense clarifies antisocial psychological determinisms, thus facilitating a task that must be ultimately undertaken by each individual. In this way, rehabilitation becomes the product of a personal decision and not a subtle imposition.

In institutional environments it is, of course, easier to reduce change to the modification of behavioural patterns, but the limited, short-term results of behaviour modification cannot substitute for change through the intelligent apprenticeship of responsibility. Although both methods may coexist in practice, it is important to distinguish between a process of subtle imposition, influence, and conditioning and meaningful change achieved through insight into antisocial psychological determinisms. A humanistic concept of rehabilitation includes forms of psychotherapy that transcend manipulation or coercive persuasion. It also offers many opportunities for self-realization without appealing to reward or punishment. In addition to education, vocational training, and external intervention to improve work opportunities, liberty-centred rehabilitation also includes the transformation of the institutional environment and its replacement, as far as possible, by community-based alternatives. This approach culminates in the notion of rehabilitation as a right, which would preclude intrusive forms of influence and the curtailment of individual autonomy.

Rehabilitation and the Purpose of Imprisonment

Traditionally, rehabilitation has been considered to be one of the purposes of imprisonment, on the mistaken assumption that incarceration itself could be rehabilitative. This fallacy arose from a misapplication of the notion of monastic penance to the first penitentiaries. Isolation, relieved only by labour and prayer, proved to have disastrous consequences for the inmates of early nineteenth-century penitentiaries. The identification of imprisonment and rehabilitation survived this failure, however. Moreover, rehabilitation was unfairly judged to share in responsibility for the notorious shortcomings of imprisonment, becoming thus an easy prey of criticism. It was obvious that the rhetoric of rehabilitation masked a grim reality of human deterioration, which increased the ranks of criminals instead of reforming them. This distortion contributed to the crisis of rehabilitative policies in the 1970s.

In fact, rehabilitation has today a totally different nature from imprisonment.[18] A humanist notion of rehabilitation has rid itself of any punitive ingredient. Its relationship with imprisonment is only to counteract the latter's harmful effects or to find ways to avoid it altogether. It is true that in some exceptional cases the prison may act as a 'respite'[19] from the inmate's involvement in criminal social webs. Moreover, rehabilitative efforts can transform the punishment of imprisonment into an occasion to discover new existential perspectives. But imprisonment has to be justified on retributive or incapacitative grounds, never assuming a rehabilitative purpose. Interrupting a criminal career has little benefit without the creation of a purposeful rehabilitative environment, which includes the offer of meaningful opportunities. Today, rehabilitation seeks not only to transform the desocializing prison environment, but also to replace institutional confinement with non-custodial alternatives as far as possible.

Halleck and Witte denied that it is possible to create a benign prison environment without trying to rehabilitate offenders. To endure the restrictions of prison life without bitterness or aggressiveness, they explained, the offender must have hope and a sense of significance.[20]

Correctional workers share this psychological need. In this context, Irwin emphasized that dismantling the rehabilitative idea will hurt the morale of correctional officers by depriving them of a justifying philosophy that gives their work purpose and dignity.[21] In modern American megaprisons, meaningful rehabilitative action to counteract the negative effects of imprisonment should be accompanied by action at the social and cultural levels to eradicate institutional violence, neutralize the action of organized gangs, avoid the formation of prison subcultures, and overcome racial conflict.[22] Rehabilitation also requires a sentencing policy that relieves the present inhuman overcrowding of prisons.

Although rehabilitation is not the purpose of imprisonment, it is an overriding goal of a correctional system that seeks to minimize the harms of incarceration. In order to neutralize the desocializing potential of prisons, a civilized society is forced into rehabilitative undertakings. These become an essential ingredient of its correctional system taken as a whole. A correctional system 'without socialization offerings nor interest in treatment means, in fact, de-humanization and regression'.[23] The recognition that rehabilitation is needed to satisfy the social interest of enlightened crime prevention leads to a further step; its acknowledgement as a legal right of the offender.

Rehabilitation as a Right and the Principle 'Nullum Crimen, Nulla Poena, Sine Lege'

To oppose a right to rehabilitation is to ignore the due process limitation to criminal sanctions embodied in the principle *nullum crimen, nulla poena, sine lege*, inherited in substance from the Magna Carta and the post-Enlightenment codification and applied today with few exceptions in all major legal systems of the world. This principle implies not only that conduct cannot be considered criminal unless defined as such by the law before it occurs, but also that no punishment beyond what was prescribed by the pre-existent law can be imposed. Although not expressly stated in the US Constitution, this principle is embodied in the prohibition of *ex post facto* laws and bills of attainder and in the Fifth and Fourteenth Amendments.[24] 'Just as there must be a declaration of the law's intention to make an act a crime, so its punishment must be promulgated through the same process.'[25] The legislative duty to provide fair warning of punishable conduct extends, as an element of due process, to the nature and severity of the prescribed punishment. Due process of law is also violated when imprisonment includes punitive ingredients not specified by statute. This interpretation coincides with the principle established by a district court in Florida that 'the courts have the duty to protect prisoners from unlawful and onerous treatment of a nature that, of itself, adds punitive measures to those legally meted out by the court'.[26]

According to the *nullum crimen, nulla poena, sine lege* principle, the only valid purpose of imprisonment is to punish according to the law, however tautological this statement may appear. The notion of legal punishment considerably limits the possibility of adding punitive elements, whatever their motivation, to incarceration itself. The deterrent function of criminal law must flow from the normative threat of punishment and may not be left to the discretion of administrative authority. When the law wanted to make imprisonment a particularly excruciating experience, it clearly expressed that intention through the now largely abolished forms of hard labour or penal servitude. In this regard the Select Committee of the House of Lords defined in 1863 the plight of the convicted as 'hard labour, hard fare, and hard bed'. Rejecting this idea of increasing punishment by adding extra sufferings to imprisonment, later thinkers proclaimed that 'offenders are sent to prison as punishment, not for punishment'.[27] This view was mirrored in the international movement for the unification of prison sentences, which aimed to abolish the defamatory and afflictive forms of imprisonment and to reduce them to the sole loss of liberty. The question was first introduced during the International Penitentiary Congress of London and further debated in the next congress, which met in Stockholm in 1878.[28] In *Barnes* v. *Government of Virgin Islands*, the court reflected the viewpoint of enlightened modern penology when it stated that persons 'are not sent to penal institutions in order to receive additional punishment; the fact of incarceration itself is the punishment'.[29]

The principle *nulla poena, sine lege* has been invoked against an abusive notion of rehabilitation, which led to excessively discretionary sentencing practices.[30] Today, this same principle can be used as a legal pillar to support a constitutional right to rehabilitation. If imprisonment itself is the punishment, the unchecked harmful effects of incarceration on the mental and social health of the inmate represent illegal additional punishment. Institutionalization in an alienating and depersonalizing environment, without opportunities to combat degeneration or foster positive human development, is a source of various harmful effects that play no part in the design of legal sanctions. The law threatens citizens with imprisonment as the consequence of criminal conduct. That is where the deterrent function of the legal norm should stop. The law expects the citizen to foresee the loss of liberty prescribed by statute, but not the additional horrors of incarceration not intended by law. The only way to prevent or compensate for such unjustified deprivations is to carry out a positive programme of rehabilitative action.

There is thus no basis for proposing deterrent policies as a novel substitute for rehabilitation, for deterrence has always been the essence of criminal law. A right to rehabilitation does not contradict the deterrent effect of criminal sanctions as long as they do not exceed the limits marked by the due process of law. But it is a basic function of rehabilitation to prevent and counteract such abuses.

Superfluous and Impracticable Rehabilitation

Two kinds of offender may seem at first to be outside the scope of meaningful rehabilitative efforts: the socially well-adjusted and the incorrigible offender.

The first category consists mainly of certain white-collar, economic, environmental, or political criminals; civil disobedients; traffic violators; and perpetrators of regulatory offences in general, who hardly fit into a therapeutic or social-learning model of rehabilitation. As Sutherland observes, for example, the crimes of large corporations cannot credibly be attributed to the emotional instability or complexes of their chief executives.[31] Nevertheless, if rehabilitation is conceived as a counteractive force against unwanted side effects of imprisonment, it may also be necessary for originally well-socialized inmates who in the long run would desocialize without some compensatory intervention. The right to rehabilitation understood as a right not to deteriorate[32] goes beyond a utilitarian rehabilitative policy geared to preventing recidivism, and can be demanded even for so-called socially well-adapted offenders.[33]

Some white-collar criminals suffer from personality troubles, which could neutralize all sense of social responsibility, and would therefore benefit from certain forms of psychological treatment. Other types of reckless conduct arise from sheer lack of technical and professional knowledge. In some specialized areas of the economy governed by extremely complex technical rules, the provision of information on business law, economy, accountancy, cybernetics, or ecology could accomplish a preventive and rehabilitative function. A full awareness of the magnitude of damages caused by illegal behaviour in the economic field could conceivably inhibit the commission of further offences. This would be part of a new approach to moral education, based on the individual awareness of social responsibility and aiming toward self-determination.[34] In the United States, the rehabilitative function has been transferred by analogy to judicial handling of large corporations. Through probation, and also occasionally by resorting to injunctions, judicial authority endeavours to restructure the internal processes of corporations to prevent recidivism.[35] Other legal innovations accomplishing similar functions include the introduction of a public interest director and community service as a corporate sanction.[36]

Incorrigible offenders may also seem beyond the reach of rehabilitative interventions. A number of stubborn recidivists defy all efforts of reincorporation into law-abiding social life. However, this category should be treated with extreme caution because of the relativity of the concept. Perceived incorrigibility may be the result of flaws in the correctional system rather than in the offender's personality. An offender who seems incorrigible within one particular rehabilitative context may be amenable to other treatment approaches. Cases of constant rehabilitative failure are found even in the best treatment-centred institutions and in the most carefully designed community-based programmes. But most frequently, stubborn recidivism results from the unchecked negative effects of institutionalization, which include the absorption of criminal values and techniques. Incorrigibility should not lead to incapacitative confinement under the assumption that rehabilitation has failed. Incapacitation, when respecting constitutional safeguards, should be justified in its own right (that is, on the objective demonstration of the offender's dangerousness) and should be carried out within strict legal parameters. Moreover, recidivism is an insufficient criterion to measure dangerousness and does not necessarily mean incorrigibility or the failure of a particular rehabilitative policy.[37] Although a liberty-centred model of rehabilitation can coexist with exceptional incapacitative measures, the absence of tangible rehabilitative results should not be used to justify them. Indeed, when rehabilitation is recognized as a right, independent from its effectiveness,[38] apparent incorrigibility can be no obstacle to the offering of renewed rehabilitative chances. Even when the law prescribes very prolonged confinement, the maintenance of dignity and of the potentialities inherent in being human demand counteractive action and various forms of assistance. The rehabilitative response to cases of apparent incorrigibility associated with some type of mental disorders has given rise to the most conspicuous experiments of this century in 'treating the untreatable'.[39]

Sentencing and Rehabilitation

The traditional belief that rehabilitation was one of the aims of criminal punishment upheld indeterminate sentencing schemes in which rehabilitative considerations played a preponderant role. In fact, the length of imprisonment often depended primarily on the sentencing authorities' judgments on prospective rehabilitation. However, a liberty-centred concept should have no bearing on sentencing decisions. No one should endure a longer sentence in 'order to be rehabilitated',[40] nor should well-adjusted offenders receive shorter or non-incarcerative sentences just because they do not appear to need rehabilitation. In particular, giving milder sentences to white-collar criminals because of their apparent social adjustment would undermine the legitimacy of the sentencing system. Furthermore, if milder sentences are imposed in some cases on the basis of rehabilitative considerations, their denial in other cases could indirectly transform the lack of rehabilitative prospects into an increased punishment.[41]

To separate sentencing decisions from rehabilitative goals does not exclude discretionary sentencing altogether. Retributive justice is better served by individualized punishment than by fixed sentences that disregard the objective and subjective circumstances of each case. Under a rights model of rehabilitation, however, the likelihood of positive rehabilitative results cannot be used as a criterion in meting out punishment. While this model does not preclude benevolence or mercy from sentencing decisions based on other considerations, it does prohibit the use of dubious rehabilitative arguments. Furthermore, the notion of rehabilitation as right is consistent with the right of the offender to the least-restrictive sentence available, according to conditions predetermined by statute.[42] The options are not determined by rehabilitative prognoses but by explicit legal conditions, with relatively little discretion left to the sentencing authorities.

Although rehabilitative predictions should not figure in the sentencing process, longer sentences may be assigned on the basis of offenders' proven dangerousness. One of the 'dangers of dangerousness',[43] however, is the temptation to use rehabilitative chances or performances as a measure of dangerousness. Such an approach amounts to reintroducing an authoritarian concept of rehabilitation through the back door and using it for repressive purposes instead of enhancing the offender's future chances. Rehabilitation predictions should not play any role in the delicate task of balancing the rights of the individual with the need for societal protection. Recidivism has multiple causes, among which the most serious include institutionalization itself, and the ex-offender's economic and social handicaps created by the legal system.[44] Incapacitative sentences should never be a punishment for failed rehabilitation or a consequence of a poor rehabilitative prognosis. Such sentencing (e.g. for offenders with mental disorders) should be justified in its own right, on the basis of a demonstrated need for social protection and when strict legal conditions are met. Moreover, according to the rights model of rehabilitation, the sentencing authority has an obligation, derived from the basic right to freedom, of choosing the least-restrictive sanction applicable.

Rehabilitative considerations play a central role not only in the design and legislative enactment of sanctions, but also in the creation of the correctional network to which their execution is assigned. Rehabilitation requires sanctions that will favour the later reintegration of offenders into society and help increase their capacity for law abidance. In this regard, the most important policy choice in sentencing reform has to do with the use of non-custodial alternatives to imprisonment and other devices to limit the growth of prison populations. In making this legislative choice a delicate balance must be struck between vital values protected by the criminal statutes and respect for the basic rights of criminal offenders. These rights are currently jeopardized by prison sentences, given the inhuman overcrowding of correctional institutions. Overcrowding not only defeats the basic purpose of fairness, but can make criminal punishment illegal and even unconstitutional when it exceeds the penalty prescribed by the pre-existing law.

A fair sentence, essentially based on the offender's degree of culpability, contradicts neither the offender's right to rehabilitation nor governmental rehabilitative policy. Quite the contrary, in so far as a fair sentence favours the process of reconciliation between the law-breaker and the community, it may have a rehabilitative value in itself. And an unfair sentence is bound to generate antisocial reactions. Unfairness is essentially a disproportion between offence and punitive reaction. Such a disproportion is inevitable when an offender is sentenced to an overcrowded institution. The same corrosive moral effects and prison unrest that result from sentencing disparity are also produced by the current crowding of prisons.[45]

The belief that current punitive practices are not deterrent or incapacitative enough to protect the values violated by a given type of offence cannot be criticized in itself. Outstanding studies have shown that the magnitude of deterrent and incapacitative effects cannot be reliably assessed.[46] Consequently there is little sound basis for either criticizing or defending deterrent or incapacitation-oriented policy. But the deterioration and dehumanization of imprisonment in overcrowded conditions is a glaring fact immediately apparent to any observer. However coherent and balanced a sentencing system may be, it will still be unfair if the end result is unfair punishment, such as imprisonment in overcrowded institutions. In this regard, the right to rehabilitation requires sentencing and correctional policies compatible with rehabilitative prison conditions.

For this purpose, norms for directing offenders to alternative programmes should be co-ordinated with schemes to regulate prison populations directly. The Minnesota sentencing guide-lines illustrate how the interaction between the sentencing and correctional systems can be taken into account. The guide-lines complied with a legislative mandate to keep in mind the availability of correctional resources. Using a population projection model, the commission adopted a set of guide-lines intended to maintain the prison population at about 95 per cent of capacity. One motivation for this unique innovation was the sentencing commission's feeling that the state of Minnesota should not operate on an implicit policy that the prisons will be filled beyond capacity.

Notes

1. Marc Ancel, *La Défence sociale nouvelle* (Paris: Cujas, 1981), 253. For Ancel the 'pedagogy of responsibility' is a central aspect of a modern humanistic crime policy.
2. On the complementarity of rehabilitation and community reorganization, see Alden D. Miller and Lloyd E. Ohlin, *Delinquency and Community: Creating Opportunities and Controls* (Beverly Hills, Calif.: Sage, 1985), 147–84.
3. On the rehabilitative significance of fair sentencing, see Arthur Kaufmann, 'Dogmatische und kriminalpolitische Aspekte des Schuldgedankens im Strafrecht', *Juristenzeitung*, 18 (1967), 553.
4. On the relationship between love and justice, see Harold J. Berman, *The Interaction of Law and Religion* (Nashville: Abingdon Press, 1974), 99 ff. and Karl Peters, *Grundprobleme der Kriminalpädogogik* (Berlin: De Gruyter, 1960), 141 ff.
5. Seymour L. Halleck and Ann D. Witte, 'Is Rehabilitation Dead?', *Crime and Delinquency*, 23 (Oct. 1977), 379.
6. Wolfang Naucke, *Tendenzen in der Strafrechtsentwicklung* (Karlsruhe: C. F. Müller, 1975), 36. See also Peter Mrozynski, *Resozialisierung und soziales Betreuungsverhältnis* (Heidelberg: C. F. Müller, 1984).
7. Douglas Lipton, Robert Martinson, and Judith Wilks, *The Effectiveness of*

Correctional Treatment: *A Survey of Treatment Evaluation Studies* (New York: Praeger, 1975), 12.

8. Paul E. Leman, 'The Medical Model of Treatment', *Crime and Delinquency* (Apr. 1972), 204.

9. Nicholas N. Kittrie, *The Right to Be Different*: *Deviance and Enforced Therapy* (New York: Penguin, 1973), 1.

10. See Ancel, *La Défense sociale nouvelle*, 253; Albin Eser, 'Resozialisierung in der Krise?', in Jürgen Baumann and Klaus Tiedemann (eds.), *Festschrift für Karl Peters* (Tübingen: J. C. B. Mohr, 1974), 505; and Edgardo Rotman, 'L'Évolution de la pensée juridique sur le but de l sanction penale', in *Aspects nouveaux de la pensée juridique (hommage à Marc Ancel)* (Paris: Pedone, 1975), 171.

11. Karl Peters, 'Die etischen Voraussetzungen des Resozialisierungs—und Erziehungsvollzuges', in Hans Lütger (ed.), *Festschrift für Ernst Heinitz* (Berlin: De Gruyter, 1972).

12. Robert K. Merton, *Social Theory and Social Structure* (London: Free Press, 1964).

13. Francis A. Allen, *The Decline of the Rehabilitative Ideal*: *Penal Policy and Social Purpose* (New Haven, Conn.: Yale University Press, 1981), 11–22.

14. See statement by Edgardo Rotman, 'Latest Trends in Crime Policy and Their Effect on Sentencing', in *New Trends in Criminal Policy* (Proceedings of the Fifth International Colloquium), ed. International Penal and Penitentiary Foundation (Bonn: International Penal and Penitentiary Foundation, 1984), 75–8. A humanistic concept is one that recognizes in human beings their status as persons, 'irreducible to more elementary levels', and their unique worth as being 'potentially capable of autonomous judgment and action', Marian Kinget, *On Being Human*: *A Systematic View* (New York: Harcourt Brace Jovanovich, 1975), p. v.

15. Karl v. Grolman, *Grundsätze der Criminalrechts-Wissenschaft* (Giessen: Heyer, 1825), 4–5.

16. The National Research Council panel's definition explicitly rules out the effects of specific deterrence as well as those of old age or maturation. See Lee Sechrest, Susan O. White, and Elizabeth D. Brown (eds.), *The Rehabilitation of Criminal Offenders*: *Problems and Prospects* (Washington, DC: National Academy of Sciences, 1979), 21–2.

17. Edgardo Rotman, 'Las técnicas de individualización judicial frente a un moderno concepto de resocialización', *Revista de derecho penal y criminología* (1972), 114.

18. Norval Morris, *The Future of Imprisonment* (Chicago: University of Chicago Press, 1974) and John Irwin, *Prisons in Turmoil* (Boston: Little, Brown, 1980), 237–8.

19. Irwin, *Prisons in Turmoil*, 240.

20. Halleck and Witte, 'Is Rehabilitation Dead?', 372, 378.

21. John Irwin, 'The Changing Structure of the Men's Prison', in David Greenberg (ed.), *Corrections and Punishment* (Beverly Hills, Calif.: Sage, 1977), 21, 32.

22. On the possibilities and strategies of neutralizing prison violence, community-based delinquency prevention programmes, provision of new opportunity structures, and institutional and community change in general, see Miller and Ohlin, *Delinquency and Community*. On the need to focus on new loci of intervention (e.g. the family, the school, the workplace, the community), see Susan Martin, Lee Sechrest, and Robin Redner (eds.), *New Directions in the Rehabilitation of Criminal Offenders* (Washington, DC: National Academy of Sciences, 1981), 135–73 and Elliott Currie, *Confronting Crime* (New York: Pantheon, 1985), 224–78. The need to direct socializing efforts not only to individuals but also to their environment was recognized in 'The Revision of the Minimum Program of the International Society of Social Defence', *Bulletin of the International Society of Social Defence*, 26 (English–French edn. 1984). On coping with gangs at the institutional level, see John Conrad, 'Who Is in Charge? The Control of Gang Violence in California Prisons', in Robert Montilla and Nora Marlow (eds.), *Correctional Facility Planning* (Lexington, Mass.: D. C. Heath, 1979), 135–47.

23. Günther Kaiser, 'Resozialisierung und Zeitgeist', in Rüdiger Herren, Diethelm Kienapfel, and Heinz Müller Dietz (eds.), *Festschrift für Thomas Würtenberger* (Berlin: Duncker & Humblot, 1977), 371.

24. Cheriff Bassiouni, 'The Sources and Limits of Criminal Law in the United States', *Revue internationale de droit pénal*, 3–4 (1975), 301, 305.

25. Ibid. 351.

26. *Miller* v. *Carson*, 401 F. Supp. 835, 864 (MD Fla. 1975), affirmed in part and modified in part, 563 F. 2d 741 (5th Cir. 1977), See also *Barnes* v. *Virgin Islands*, 415 F. Supp. 1218 (D. VI 1976).

27. Alexander Paterson quoted by Marc Ancel, 'L'Abolition de la peine de mort et le problème de la peine de remplacement', in M. Lopez-Rey and C. Germain (eds.), *Studies in Penology Dedicated to the Memory of Sir Lionel Fox* (The Hague: Martinus Nijhoff, 1964), 9.

28. Commission Pénitentiaire Internationale (ed.), *Le Congrès pénitentiare de Stockholm* (Stockholm: Bureau de la Commission Pénitentiaire Internationale, 1879), 139–70.

29. 415 F. Supp, 1218, 1224 (D. VI 1976).

30. Marvin E. Frankel, *Criminal Sentences: Law without Order* (New York: Hill & Wang, 1973), 3.

31. Edwin H. Sutherland, *White Collar Crime* (New York: Holt, Rinehart & Winston, 1967), 257.

32. See E. Rotman, *Beyond Punishment: A New View of the Rehabilitation of Offenders* (Westport, Conn., 1990), 79, 82.

33. For a vivid testimony on the need of rehabilitative support for certain types of white-collar offenders, see Brian Breed, *White Collar Bird* (London: John Clare, 1979).

34. Rotman, *Beyond Punishment*, 7, 8.

35. Comment, 'Structural Crime and Institutional Rehabilitation: A New Approach', *Yale Law Review*, 89 (1979), 353. See also Edgardo Rotman, 'La Question de la fonction préventive du droit pénal dans la création et l'application des normes pénales économiques', in *The Sanctions in the Field of Economic Criminal Law* (Proceedings of the Kristiansand Meeting, Sept. 1983), ed. International Penal and Penitentiary Foundation (Bonn: International Penal and Penitentiary Foundation, 1984).

36. See Klaus Tiedemann, 'Le Système des sanctions en matière de délinquance pénal économique dans les divers ordres juridiques', in *The Sanctions in the Field of Economic Criminal Law*, ed. International Penal and Penitentiary Foundation (Bonn: International Penal and Penitentiary Foundation, 1984), 66.

37. Ancel, *La Défense sociale nouvelle*, 325.

38. See Rotman, *Beyond Punishment*, 120–2.

39. See ibid. 65–8, 174–6.

40. This point has been clearly addressed in Morris, *The Future of Imprisonment*.

41. On the relativity of leniency in sentencing decisions, see James Vorenberg, 'Narrowing the Discretion of Criminal Justice Officials', *Duke Law Journal*, 4 (1976), 651.

42. See Rotman, *Beyond Punishment*, 155–6.

43. Franz Exner, *Die Theorie der Sicherungsmittel* (Berlin: J. Guttentag, 1914), 59.

44. On modern legislative trends favouring the expungement of records after a certain time, see International Penal and Penitentiary Foundation (ed.), *Criminal Records and Rehabilitation* (Proceedings of the Meeting of Neuchâtel, 1979) (Neuchâtel: Editions Ides et Calendes, 1982), 36, 61, 71. See also Nigel Walker, *Punishment, Danger and Stigma* (Oxford: Blackwell, 1980), 147.

45. See testimony of Edgardo Rotman in US Congress, House Committee on the Judiciary, *Sentencing Guidelines: Hearings before the Subcommittee on Criminal Justice*, 100th Cong., 1st Sess. (1987), 175.

46. See National Academy of Science panel's report in Alfred Blumstein, Jacqueline Cohen, and Daniel Nagin (eds.), *Deterrence and Incapacitation: Estimating the Deterrent Effects of Criminal Sanctions on Crime Rates* (Washington, DC: National Academy of Sciences, 1978), 3–90.

Preface: P. Carlen, 'Crime, Inequality, and Sentencing'

Criminal conduct is no lower class monopoly, but is distributed throughout the social spectrum. Indeed, whilst 'street crimes' and burglary attract the most attention, the less visible crimes of the powerful may be argued to produce significantly greater social harm, in terms both of monetary loss and of physical injury and death (see Sutherland 1949; Braithwaite and Pettit 1990; Box 1987; Pearce 1976; Cook 1989). But the same is not true of the distribution of punishment, which falls, overwhelmingly and systematically, on the poor and the disadvantaged. Discriminatory decision-making throughout the whole criminal justice system ensures that the socially advantaged are routinely filtered out: they are given the benefit of the doubt, or are defined as good risks, or simply have access to the best legal advice (see Carlen 1983*a*; Reiman 1984; Hood 1992). Serious, deep-end punishments such as imprisonment are predominantly reserved for the unemployed, the poor, the homeless, the mentally ill, the addicted, and those who lack social support and personal assets. Increasingly, this class bias has taken on a racial complexion, as disadvantaged minority groups come to be massively over-represented in the prison population (see Hood 1992; Cook and Hudson 1993) and on death row (Amnesty International 1987: ch. 5; Bowers 1984).

Sociologists offer various explanations of why the penal system has evolved in this way, relating its shape and workings not to concerns with crime prevention, but to the goal of controlling those groups whose socially disadvantaged position makes them volatile, disaffected, and thus threatening (see Rusche and Kirchheimer 1968; Melossi and Pavarini 1981; Garland 1985; Spierenburg 1991; Katz 1989; Gordon 1992). Such explanations confront normative theorizing with penal actualities (see HIRST). In particular, they challenge 'just deserts' theorists to recognize that our penal systems do not now administer 'just deserts', and to face the problem of how we can hope to do penal justice in a context of widespread social injustice. A common charge against the 'justice model' of punishment is that in treating offenders as free, equal citizens who have chosen to commit crimes—as individuals abstracted from their social circumstances—it ignores the links between social position, crime, and punishment. In administering 'just deserts', the criminal justice system actually exacerbates the problems of social injustice and inequality (see TONRY; Hudson 1987: ch. 4; von Hirsch 1993: ch. 10 and epilogue).

Carlen is also concerned with justice—but with a broader notion of justice than that which informs the 'justice model'. We must aim to 'do justice (between criminal, victim and state) without increasing inequality' (see also ROTMAN: 2). She distinguishes four models of sentencing, and argues for that of 'state-obligated rehabilitation'. Although the sentencing aims of this approach include denunciation, crime reduction, and reconciliation, they must also give a central place to rehabilitation, as something which the state owes to the offender. To this extent, her account resembles Rotman's. A crucial difference between their accounts, however, is that while Rotman insists that rehabilitative measures should be *offered* to offenders rather than *imposed* on them, Carlen is quite willing to see them imposed on the offender if it is feasible to do so.

Two aspects of her argument should be noted. First, she emphasizes that we should avoid the narrow focus which characterizes not only the 'justice model', but many other normative accounts of sentencing—a focus which attends only to the offender and the crime. We must view law-breaking as 'part and parcel of other social problems', and attend to the social circumstances which promote criminal conduct. Criminal justice agencies should view their activities in relation to those of broader social institutions and conditions such as the labour market, urban planning, welfare provision, racial and sexual equality, and should initiate debate and action designed to highlight and deal with the social roots of criminality as well as with individual guilt (see Carlen 1983*b*). We should also address the more fundamental social institutions which determine the distribution of wealth, life chances, and status, and which thus help determine the distribution of criminal choices and penal outcomes. Penal theorizing cannot take place in a normative or sociological vacuum. It must be sensitive to the social conditions which structure law, criminality, and penality; and, as normative theory, it must be part of a larger enterprise of theorizing about the political and social institutions within which punishment can be justified (see MURPHY; Honderich 1984; Lacey 1988).

Second, Carlen insists that *feasibility* is crucial to sentencing. If courts impose sentences with which offenders cannot, given their circumstances, realistically be expected to comply (imposing heavy fines on indigent offenders, or community service orders which an offender who suffers severe social disadvantages cannot be expected to satisfy) those sentences will be not only ineffective but unjust, especially when imprisonment is the normal back-up sanction for those who fail to comply with the requirements of a non-custodial sentence. So far, advocates of the justice model could agree with her. They will, however, object strenuously to her suggestions that 'the offender could be obliged to engage in any "feasible" programme of rehabilitation or regulation' and that no such programme should be rejected 'merely on the grounds that it is an essential violation of civil liberties', or that it lies higher up the sentencing 'tariff' which seeks to match severity of punishment to seriousness of crime. For, they will insist, the state should not take this kind of coercive interest in the offender's rehabilitation. Considerations of feasibility and of rehabilitation should indeed help guide sentencers' choices between penalties of equal severity: but their primary concern must be to impose a suitably proportionate punishment (see Wasik and von Hirsch 1988). We face again a conflict between two conceptions of punishment and of government. The first is a liberal conception which requires the state to respond to offenders as rational autonomous agents, and allows it to intrude no more into their lives than is warranted by the need to impose 'just deserts'. The second is a communitarian conception which requires the state to respond to offenders as socially situated individuals who may need, and may be obliged to accept, the state's help.

References

Amnesty International (1987), *United States of America: The Death Penalty* (London).

Bowers, W. (1984), *Legal Homicide: Death as a Punishment in America 1864–1982* (Boston).

Box, S. (1987), *Recession, Crime and Punishment* (London).

Braithwaite, J., and Pettit, P. (1990), *Not Just Deserts* (Oxford).

Carlen, P. (1983*a*), *Women's Imprisonment: A Study in Social Control* (London).

—— (1983*b*), 'On Rights and Powers: Some Notes on Penal Politics', in D. Garland and P. Young (eds.), *The Power to Punish* (London), 203–16.

Cook, D. (1989), *Rich Law, Poor Law* (Milton Keynes).

—— and Hudson, B. (1993), *Racism and Criminology* (London).

Garland, D. (1985), *Punishment and Welfare* (Aldershot).

Gordon, D. (1992), *The Justice Juggernaut: Fighting Street Crime, Controlling Citizens* (New Brunswick, NJ).

Honderich, T. (1984), *Punishment: The Supposed Justifications* (rev. edn., Harmondsworth).

Hood, R. (1992), *Race and Sentencing: A Study in the Crown Court* (Oxford).

Hudson, B. (1987), *Justice through Punishment? A Critique of the 'Justice' Model of Corrections* (London).

Katz, M. (1989), *The Undeserving Poor* (New York).

Lacey, N. (1988), *State Punishment* (London).

Melossi, D., and Pavarini, M. (1981), *The Prison and the Factory* (London).

Pearce, F. (1976), *Crimes of the Powerful* (London).

Reiman, J. (1984), *The Rich Get Richer and the Poor Get Prison* (2nd edn., New York).

Rusche, G., and Kirchheimer, O. (1968), *Punishment and Social Structure* (New York; 1st edn. 1939).

Spierenburg, P. (1991), *The Prison Experience: Disciplinary Institutions and their Inmates in Early Modern Europe* (New Brunswick, NJ).

Sutherland, E. H. (1949), *White-Collar Crime* (New York).

von Hirsch, A. (1993), *Censure and Sanctions* (Oxford).

Wasik, M., and von Hirsch, A. (1988), 'Non-custodial Penalties and the Principles of Desert', *Criminal Law Review*, 555–72.

Crime, Inequality, and Sentencing

PAT CARLEN

Mass unemployment, together with the increased inequality produced by the interaction of government policy on wages, taxes,
benefit and wealth has meant that:

> the proportion of original income received by the poorest fifth of
> households in 1985 had fallen to little more than a third of its
> 1979 level—the result largely of unemployment;
> the original income share of the poorest 40 per cent had fallen by
> more than a third: reflecting the combined effect of unemploy-
> ment and low pay;
> in contrast the top fifth of households had seen their income
> share rise by an average 10 per cent.

(Byrne 1987)

Introduction

The striking increase in inequality of income and wealth which has been
a major feature of the last decade (Walker and Walker 1987) has been
accompanied by a steady increase in the prison population from 41,800 in
1978 to over 50,000 in 1988 (Home Office 1988). This is not surprising.
Whatever else prisons may be for, they have always housed large numbers of the poor, the unemployed, the unemployable, the homeless, the
physically ill, and the mentally disturbed. From time to time, also, these
staples of the prison population have been augmented by large contin-
gents of other 'problem' populations such as ethnic minority groups,
political protesters, and, most noticeably in recent years, unemployed
youth. And, as commentary on the blatant inequities of the criminal justice system, one constant jurisprudential theme has persistently centred
upon the impossibility of imposing a system of formal justice (predicated
upon an assumption of equality before the law) upon a system of substantive inequality. Nor has this concern about the relationship between
criminal justice and social justice been merely academic. In the courts
sentencers have daily wrestled with the problems of sentence feasibility

(how to punish someone who has not the wherewithal to pay a financial penalty, or who is already living in excessively punishing social conditions); and equality of sentence impact (how to impose similar degrees of penal pain or deprivation upon offenders of differing sensibilities or material means). Recently these sentencing dilemmas have become even more acute as magistrates and judges have been exhorted by government—variously—to get tough with offenders; to send fewer people to prison; to be realistic in their choice of penalties. In order therefore to elucidate some of the sentencing dilemmas and paradoxes that arise in a society where inequality is increasing, this chapter will

1. discuss the relationships between inequality, crime and punishment;
2. outline four different models of sentencing;
3. assess those models according to their capacity to develop effective measures of penal intervention without increasing inequality and its effects still further.

The fundamental implication will be that, until there is a greater recognition of the relationships between crime, criminal justice, and social justice, it is unlikely that sentences will be fashioned which will bring about reductions in law-breaking. At the most general level the argument will be that the state's right to punish is based on a contractual obligation to attempt to rectify the particular 'social problems which both occasion, and are occasioned by, lawbreaking' (Carlen 1983a: 213) and that forms of punishment which ignore that obligation, while they might fulfil other functions, will *not* reduce crime. More specifically it will be argued that there is an urgent need to re-examine the contemporary penality that

1. continues to insist that responsibility for law-breaking lies totally with individuals who have an unfettered choice as to whether or not they break the law;
2. assumes that it is only in relation to the young and the poor that sentencing dilemmas arise;
3. privileges the 'tariff' as a major guide to sentencing;
4. sees prison as the necessary and inevitable back-up to non-custodial penalties;
5. assumes that the only viable alternatives to imprisonment are those transcarceral ones that bring the pains of imprisonment into the already-straitened circumstances of the poor outside prison;
6. allows sentencers greater independence than their collective wisdom most probably warrants.

Inequality and Crime

Having reviewed sixteen major studies of the relationships between income inequality and crime, Steven Box concluded in 1987 that 'income inequality (rather than poverty alone) is strongly related to criminal activity' (Box 1987: 96) and that during the recent recession there was an increase both in conventional and white-collar crime (Box 1987: 98–102). What's more, an earlier analysis of unemployment and *imprisonment* conducted with Hale had already shown a virtual consensus that 'unemployment is related to imprisonment independently of the crime rate' (Box and Hale 1985). In Box's and Hale's own study, *even after they had excluded fine defaulters*, a significant relationship between unemployment and imprisonment was still apparent, a relationship, moreover, that could not be totally explained by changes in crime rates. But why has the recession of the 1970s and 1980s been accompanied by an increase in crime rates and a quite disproportionate increase in imprisonment?

It is often argued that if unemployment causes crime we could have expected the crime rate of the 1930s to have been similar to that of the 1980s. Instead, and as Lea and Young (1984: 90) point out, although 'the amount of unemployment in 1933 and 1981 was roughly equal (around 11.5 per cent), the amount of serious crime per 100,000 population in 1981 was over fifteen times as great as that of 1933'.

The ideological and political conditions of the 1980s are very different to those of the 1930s. Whereas the majority of unemployed in the 1930s were people who *had* experienced work and hoped to be employed again, unemployment today is concentrated amongst the young who have never known the rewards of work and who have little reason to believe that those rewards will be forthcoming in the future. Furthermore, today's unemployed have had their expectations of what they *should* receive by way of material rewards raised way beyond those of their grandparents. These higher expectations were initially raised by the short-lived 1960s economic boom and universal education, and have most recently been fuelled by daily mass media references to a world of plastic money and city financiers' six-figure salaries. Yet between 1976 and 1985 when the share of original household income of the top 20 per cent was rising from 44.4 to 49.2 per cent, the share of the bottom 40 per cent fell from 10.2 to 6.3 per cent (National Children's Home 1988: 8). During that same period unemployment trebled (ibid. 9), and by 1986 120,000 households were homeless, with 72,000 of the latter having one or more dependent children (ibid. 10).

At the same time as the poor were getting poorer (and prison), and more marginalized people who in any case were not getting their 'just deserts' were choosing to break the law, more and more of the business community, spurred on by the competitive individualism (greed) of a free market economy, also came to believe that the 'market' was somehow letting them down, and that they were therefore entitled to engage in financial crimes. (See Levi 1987: 5 on the 5 per cent annual increase in recorded fraud since 1980.) In many ways theirs was a rational choice. For though it might seem that the wealthy have much to lose by lawbreaking, the slim chances of their being caught, prosecuted, and convicted, combined with the often dispersed sources of their income and wealth, means that they can usually make the accurate calculation that in their own cases, at least, crime *does* pay. A similar calculation cannot so rationally be made by the majority of wage-earners and unemployed. However, under certain circumstances—for instance, rising unemployment and government policies that, far from bolstering the 'family' and other types of households, actually attack and weaken them to such an extent that they become the sites of increased violence—under those circumstances, increasing numbers of politically and economically marginalized people feel they have less to lose and more to gain by committing crime (cf. Kornhauser 1978). Once they do commit offences, the effects of certain sentences—especially imprisonment—result in their options being narrowed still further. Thereafter, whichever way they turn, they seem to come up against an official blockade of all legal routes out of poverty.

Examples of this narrowing options syndrome (Rosenbaum 1983) were apparent in a recent small study of thirty-nine recidivist women criminals (Carlen 1988). Several had enjoyed and successfully completed Youth Training Schemes—before being slung back into unemployment at the end of the year. No fewer than six had been involved with volunteer organizations engaged in various community projects—until cuts in local authority funding had closed them down. Many had gained some educational qualifications while in prison—and had found upon release that these were absolutely useless to them as far as employment prospects were concerned. And so on—until the combination of poverty and a narrowing of *options* for escape from it had made them believe that the only way in which they *could* take control of their lives was to commit crime. Conversely, those who had given up crime had done so not primarily through fear of another custodial sentence, but because of a change for the better in their circumstances. Their own resolve to turn their backs on crime had been a necessary but insufficient condition for their changed life-styles. It had been the 'good' probation hostel, the flat, the job, the good friend, or a newly found financial security that had enabled them to turn resolution into reality. This is neither new nor surprising. As Barbara Hudson has said:

Although there is rarely consensus in the criminological field it is more or less accepted as 'folk wisdom' that rather than being deterred from recidivism by any-thing that might be visited upon them by the agents of social control, people give up crime when they acquire bonds to the social order. . . . It could well be that present levels of unemployment are removing the opportunities for many people to acquire a stake in society, and so unemployment is encouraging them to con-tinue occasional, impulsive juvenile delinquency into more frequent, regular career criminality. (Hudson 1987: 100)

Unfortunately, sentencers have not responded to increased crime rates by providing opportunities for people to increase their 'stake in society' but have, instead, sent disproportionately more people to prison.

Inequality and Punishment

In 1976 a United Nations review of research into economic crises and crime (United Nations 1976) echoed the classic study of Rusche and Kirchheimer (1939) when it argued that in times of economic crisis societies become less tolerant and punish offenders more harshly. Two reasons were suggested. First, that at such times there is a greater perceived need to regulate and restructure the work-force. Second, that during recession police, sentencing personnel, and others in the criminal justice system really do believe that unemployed people are more likely to commit crime. (Such unfavourable stereotyping of the unemployed may well relate to the fact that as inequality increases, the anger which might more appropriately be directed at the government via the ballot box is instead visited directly upon junior police officers, social workers, and DHSS officials.)

To investigate the extent to which the posited diminution of official tolerance actually affects criminal justice personnel, Box (1987) reviewed a range of studies about police and sentencers' decision-making. His con-clusion was that, as the recession bites, each group responds by being tougher on unemployed people—the police because they see them as being more likely to commit crime; sentencers both by meting out harsher sentences *and* by imposing fines that are not realistic in terms of the offender's ability to pay. In fact, a 1984 study by the National

Association of Probation Officers (NAPO 1983, quoted in Box 1987) revealed that in Nottinghamshire unemployed people constituted about 75 per cent of fine-defaulters. A more recent study by the National Association for the Care and Resettlement of Offenders (NACRO) of unemployment and magistrates' courts found that 'although unemployed offenders were less often fined . . . some moved down the tariff to conditional discharge while others moved up . . . so that at the top end the unemployed went more often into custody.' And even if they were not sentenced directly to imprisonment, 'the unemployed were at greater risk of fine default' (Crow and Simon 1987: 48). Other people adjudged unable to pay a fine have ended up in prison through failure to complete a non-custodial order which should have been imposed only as an alternative to custody but which in fact had been imposed in place of a monetary penalty. (See NACRO 1988 for a succinct overview of research on unemployment and fine default.)

Courts and government have been uneasy about the sentencing dilemmas and patterns that have developed in the 1980s. Magistrates have feared that by moving the destitute 'down tariff' they unwittingly imply that poverty licenses crime (Carlen 1988). Judges have stubbornly refused to use the full range of non-custodial alternatives in the (unsubstantiated) belief that the public is demanding stiffer sentences all the time. The government itself has been alarmed by the expense of an ever-expanding prison-building programme which by mid-1988 had cost almost £1 billion (Home Office 1988). In 1988, therefore, proposals for more onerous 'punishments in the community' were put forward as a solution to the government's need to maintain a punitive law-and-order rhetoric while cutting a costly prison population (Home Office 1988).

Four sentencing models will now be discussed. The purpose will be to elucidate the elements of penalty from which the new proposals have been developed, and to assess their potential for reducing crime without increasing inequality.

Four Models of Sentencing

1. The general rehabilitation model
   (fitting the punishment to the offender)
2. The justice model
   (making the punishment fit the crime)
3. The community corrections model
   (bringing the pains of imprisonment into the community

4. The state-obligated rehabilitation model
   (obligation to society—denunciation
   obligation to victim—restitution
   obligation to offender—rehabilitation)

The general rehabilitation model

The general rehabilitation model of sentencing has traditionally been concerned both with punishment of the offender and with crime control. Unlike the classical theory of justice put forward by Beccaria (1963), the general rehabilitative model has always been less committed to making the punishment fit the crime and more concerned with fitting the punishment to the offender—in other words, with an individualized sentencing aimed at removing (or ameliorating) the conditions presumed to have been part-cause of the criminal behaviour.

Rehabilitationist penology was developed at the beginning of the twentieth century in England and was innovative in incorporating into sentencing a range of extra-legal criteria—medical, social, psychological, and psychoanalytical. It reached its zenith with the 1969 *Children and Young Persons' Act* (CYPA) and it was the body of criticism subsequently directed at the working of the CYPA which prepared the way for the decline of the general rehabilitation model in the 1970s and the rise of the justice model thereafter.

After 1969, rehabilitationism (called 'general' in this chapter because it embraces an eclectic mix of psychological, psychoanalytical, and positivistic theories of crime) was strongly attacked by critics from both the left and the right. Leftist critics pilloried individualized sentencing on the grounds that it discriminated against working-class youths, black people, and young girls perceived as gender-deviant. Right-wing pundits believed that the 1969 CYPA together with the introduction of more alternatives to custody (e.g. suspended sentences, deferred sentences, and community services orders) had resulted in too many younger offenders being let off too lightly. Lawyers were concerned that the lack of consistency in (individualized) sentencing was bringing the courts into disrepute; and civil libertarians of all shades of political opinion questioned the right of the state to impose 'treatment' rather than punishment on supposedly responsible citizens. In fact, and as Barbara Hudson (1987) points out, only the criticism of the civil libertarians was directed at an integral feature of rehabilitationist penology. All other criticisms could have been met without abandoning rehabilitationism or even, as Hudson suggests, 'by more and better elements of rehabilitation being incorporated into criminal justice systems' (ibid. 31). Be that as it may, the attack on reha-bilitationism united such powerful critiques from diverse political per-spectives that the growing calls for a 'return to justice' in penology met with very little resistance. While conservative thinkers hoped that a 'just deserts' model would ensure that criminals would indeed be punished and not 'let off' with a rehabilitative sentence, more liberal proponents argued that the 'net-widening' effects (Cohen 1985) of the preventive treatment of people 'at risk' could best be eliminated by a 'just deserts' model which would punish offenders for what they had done rather than for who they were. Even more importantly, it was contended on all sides that 'just deserts' sentencing would reduce crime. Conservatives claimed that the deterrent effects of *certain punishment* would be greater than those of the individualized (and therefore less certain) sentences of reha-bilitation. Liberals, on the other hand, argued that an emphasis on the principles of parsimony in punishment and proportionality of punish-ment to the crime would reduce the numbers of socially disadvantaged people drawn into the criminal justice system by the misguided policies of rehabilitationism; and that fewer people, therefore, would reoffend as a result of criminal contamination or moral debilitation.

In the rush to renounce rehabilitationism, few supporters of the justice model appeared to suspect that the 1970s attack on welfare in criminal justice might be the thin edge of the wedge as far as welfare provision in general was concerned. In future, it was agreed, the state's role in the punishment of offenders was to be concerned primarily with 'doing justice' (von Hirsch 1976) and only secondarily with 'doing good'.

The justice model[1]

The major principles of the justice model of sentencing are desert, equiv-alence, determinacy, and consistency. In 1986 the Home Office's hand-book for the courts on the treatment of offenders (Home Office 1986) clearly stated that these principles were to be preferred over those of an individualized, rehabilitationist justice. Sentencers were advised that

a sentence should not normally be justified on merely deterrent or therapeutic grounds—either that the offender will be 'cured' or that others need to be dis-couraged from similar crimes. It may be that properly reflecting the relative grav-ity of the offence, and fairness between different offenders, are more important aims in the individual case. (Home Office 1986: 7)

By 1986, however, it had already become apparent that after a decade of sentencing dominated by the justice model, crime and imprisonment rates had increased while the sentences of the courts continued to reflect the inequalities of society at large—that is they still discriminated either against or in favour of certain categories of offenders regardless of the nature of their offences. For instance, while certain women who commit trivial offences still go to prison because they are seen as being bad wives, mothers, or daughters (Carlen 1983b) others found guilty of very serious crimes still receive non-custodial sentences on the grounds that their offences result from abnormal mental or emotional states which can none the less be regarded as *normal for women* (Allen 1987). Black people also are still being treated differently by the courts—and usually more punitively. For whereas stereotypes of women result in some being made examples of and others being treated leniently, persistently unfavourable discrimination against black people has shown up in innumerable studies. In 1984, for instance, a study by Nottinghamshire Social Services compared the sentencing of black and white defendants in a juvenile court and found that there was 'a greater propensity for those in the black group to receive a custodial outcome' (16.9 per cent as against 9 per cent for the white group: reported in NACRO 1986). Two years later the Home Office (1986) reported that 'the proportion of male black prisoners is about double those in the comparable age groups in the general population' (NACRO 1986); and, furthermore, that even though black prisoners had fewer previous convictions than white prisoners, they were serving on average longer sentences and some of this difference was statistically significant (ibid.). Finally, and turning now to income inequality, the sentences of white-collar criminals who commit large tax frauds remain disproportionately lenient when compared with the sentences of poor and unemployed offenders (see Cook 1988, 1989a, 1989b).

Barbara Hudson, in a passionate and elegant denunciation of the justice model, has explained precisely *why* 'just deserts' sentencing *is* consistently unjust:

What deserts-based sentencing means . . . is building on class-based definitions of serious crime, ignoring class-differential vulnerability to the acquisition of a 'bad' record and imposing an arbitrary, blind 'fairness' at an advanced stage of the criminal justice process. Ignoring the 'non legal' factors in sentencing means, ignoring the fact that in all its stages, criminal justice is a complex process of negotiation. . . . By modesty demurring that social injustices can be dealt with by the criminal justice system, justice model reformers are building those very injustices into the heart of the system, by privileging the factors they most strongly influence—the nature of the charge faced by a defendant, and the length of the previous criminal record—as the only factors relevant in sentencing. (Hudson 1987: 114)

Unless there is an entirely new approach to punishment it is unlikely that implementation of the Home Office's new 'punishment in the community' proposals will either diminish present injustices or decrease crime and imprisonment rates.

The community corrections model

The government's Green Paper *Punishment, Custody and the Community* (Home Office 1988) was published in July 1988. Its main proposals were that

1. more offenders convicted of less serious crimes should be 'punished in the community' rather than sent to prison;
2. offenders should be made to pay as much as they can to provide financial compensation to their victims;
3. to increase public confidence in court orders which leave offenders in the community, the regulations governing community service and probation orders should be strengthened, while day centre projects should offer 'strict and structured regimes' aimed at reducing the offending of young adult offenders;
4. 'a new sentence might be developed to include
    - compensation to the victim;
    - community service;
    - residence at a hostel or other approved place;
    - prescribed activities at a day centre or elsewhere;
    - curfew or house arrest;
    - tracking an offender's whereabouts;
    - other conditions, such as staying away from particular places' (Home Office 1988: 13).

The penal principles underlying the proposals were clearly stated. Retribution and general deterrence, still the dominant planks of what in effect remained a 'just deserts' policy, were in future to be buttressed by an individualized sentence designed to incapacitate offenders according to their circumstances. There was a new emphasis on reparation both to community and victim.

When an offence is so serious that a financial penalty alone is inadequate, the government considers that the penalty should, where possible, involve these three principles:

- restrictions on the offender's freedom of action—as a punishment
- action to reduce the risk of further offending; and

– reparation to the community and, where possible, compensation to the victim. (Home Office 1988: 2)

Unfortunately, present inequalities of wealth and income will make it impossible to fashion each offender's penalty in accordance with the foregoing principles. Rather, it is likely that as far as non-custodial sentencing is concerned offenders will fall into three main groups. The largest will be comprised of those poorer people who, unable to pay a financial penalty or make compensation to the victim will receive a tough punishment involving close surveillance in the community. In this group will be those whose social circumstances make them least able to cope with any further punishment in the community (punishment, that is, beyond that already inflicted by unemployment and poor to non-existent housing) and who are therefore the least likely to be deterred from crime by stiffer penalties. Another group will contain first-time or other 'not-at-risk of recidivism' offenders who will most probably not reoffend whatever non-custodial penalty is imposed. And a third will consist of better-off 'professional' or 'white-collar' criminals who, having paid a not-too-onerous fine (and maybe compensation), will either be excused 'punishment in the community' altogether, or discover that, within the comfort of their well-off homes and supportive environments, 'punishment in the community' is no punishment at all.[2] Furthermore, if present punitive sentencing practices continue, the tightening-up of the non-custodial alternatives to prison will merely result in sentencers imposing tougher alternatives regardless of the appropriateness or feasibility of the sentence and in offenders then breaching the conditions of unrealistic orders, and ending up in prison anyhow. Non-imprisoned, 'professional' or 'white-collar' criminals, on the other hand, having weighed the light costs of their crime against its very profitable rewards, might well conclude that crime *does* pay and have little incentive to change their ways in the future. In short, although there was much to welcome in the government's proposals to reduce the prison population and fashion more socially productive penalties for crime, their implementation would be unlikely to produce the desired reductions in crime and imprisonment rates unless accompanied by other, more radical reforms.

State-obligated rehabilitation

The term 'state-obligated' rehabilitation (though not the model developed here) is taken from F. T. Cullen and K. E. Gilbert (1982) who, in their book *Reaffirming Rehabilitation*, were among the first to warn that a renaissance of the justice model of sentencing might not be the best way to reduce crime and prison populations. Arguing that where rehabilitationism had previously failed it had done so because of the state's lack of commitment to it, they suggested that

Liberal interest groups should embark on efforts to transform enforced therapy into a programme of state-obligated rehabilitation that takes seriously the betterment of inmates but legitimates neither coercion in the name of treatment nor neglect in the name of justice. (Cullen and Gilbert 1982: 246)

In their programme of liberal reforms Cullen and Gilbert proposed that prison administrators should be obliged to offer treatment to every inmate and that 'all prisoners should be invited to enter a parole contract' whereby they 'agree to complete certain rehabilitation programmes and in exchange are given the exact date on which they will be paroled' (ibid.).

The notion of state-obligated rehabilitation could also be profitably extended to non-custodial penalties, though in the model developed below it would be assumed that, in order to be rehabilitated, offenders would need to be convinced not only that their own behaviour had been reprehensible but also that the state's treatment of them had been *just*— in terms of impact in relation to their *offence* and in terms of sentence feasibility in relation to their *social circumstances*.

A fundamental assumption of state-obligated rehabilitation would posit that as both offender and state might be more or less responsible for the breakdown of social relations which had resulted in crime, both had an obligation (more or less) to take action to reduce the likelihood of similar rupture in future. Such a conception of reciprocal obligation might also displace the punishment/treatment dichotomy:

Imagine for a moment that the court was really concerned only with considering ways in which the living conditions of the accused could be so changed that either he was improved or society was protected from him—and the whole meaning of the term punishment evaporates at once. (Pashukanis 1978: 177)

Furthermore, in a model of state-obligated rehabilitation, displacement of questions about the state's right to punish would not be replaced by ones about the state's right to treat. Instead, the state's duty to intervene would be based upon an obligation to do justice (between criminal, victim, and state) without increasing inequality. For as Nicola Lacey has recently argued:

if individuals have a fundamental interest in the maintenance and development of a peaceful just society to which they belong and through which many of their interests are realised and indeed constructed, the alleged moral boundaries which dictate that individuals never be used merely as a means to social ends begin to dissolve. (Lacey 1988: 172)

Lacey herself recognizes that at present we are nowhere near achieving the ideally just society which she specifies as being preconditional to a just criminal law but concludes that

given the limited extent to which present society is committed to the equal pursuit of the welfare and autonomy of all its citizens, the best option may nonetheless be to support at least some of its practices of punishment, in the absence of any realistic prospect of getting anything better in the near future. (Lacey 1988: 196)

Yet it may be that in order to get something better at any time in the future there is a need constantly to call into question the practices of the present.

State-obligated Rehabilitation: Sentencing Principles

The major principles of state-obligated rehabilitation should be

1. that imprisonment is an extreme form of punishment, to be used only in exceptional cases and *never* as back-up to a non-custodial court order;
2. that denunciation, crime-reduction, rehabilitation, and reconciliation (between community, offender, and victim) should be the major aims of sentencing (see Blom-Cooper 1988);
3. that punishment should be a primary aim of sentencing only if offender and court are agreed that a rehabilitative element would be redundant in a particular case;
4. that so long as the state fulfilled its obligation to rehabilitate in a particular case the offender could be obliged to engage in any 'feasible' programme of rehabilitation or regulation (including, for instance, urine testing of drug-takers or electronic monitoring of other offenders). For *no* rehabilitative or regulatory programme would be rejected out of hand on the grounds of its being an essential violation of civil liberties or on the grounds of its being essentially lacking in feasibility. Rather, it would only be rejected on the grounds of its non-feasibility in a specific case;
5. that attempts to achieve greater equality of sentence impact should only be qualified by the court's recognition that in a specific case an offender's circumstances rendered the appropriate degree of punishment non-feasible.

Towards State-obligated Rehabilitation: Suggested Sentencing Reforms

Sentencing to promote good rather than to impede evil

Implicit in the government's Green Paper *Punishment, Custody and the Community* (Home Office 1988) was the notion that greater use of non-custodial alternatives to prison is justified only if such alternatives bring many of the pains of imprisonment into the community. This is a retrogressive view. The aim of judicial intervention into offenders' lives should be to help them create living conditions in which they will be more likely to choose to be law-abiding in the future. Close surveillance, punitive work schemes, curfews, and so on are not necessarily the types of interventions that will increase all offenders' capacity to change their behaviour. Indeed a radical approach to rehabilitative sentencing might not concentrate on the individual offender at all. Rather, it might see law-breaking as part and parcel of other social problems. For example,

excessive numbers of alcohol-related crimes in one area might result not only in increased treatment facilities for those with a drink problem, but also in intensive programmes designed to educate the public about the dangers of alcohol and, in addition, the levies on those benefiting from its manufacture and sale might be increased. Or, in a different example, excessive youth crime might result in public debate about, and investigation and remedy of, the work and leisure opportunities for the youth in that area as well as a review of police practices in relation to youthful offenders. (Carlen 1983*a*: 214)

When individual sentences *are* being considered, however, the notion that rehabilitation is only for poorer offenders should be abandoned. Every offender should have the chance to say if he or she thinks that there should be an element of rehabilitation in the sentence and in certain cases of recidivism an offender might even be coerced into accepting a rehabilitative order. (For instance, a recidivist business criminal might be required to attend compulsory training sessions on company and/or tax law as a condition of a disqualification being lifted after a period of time. Similar re-educative orders might be made in relation to driving offences, certain sexual offences, and other offences based on undesirable behaviour patterns of habits.) No order should be imposed, however, until the court has been assured by the probation service that, in the light of the offender's circumstances, such an order is *feasible*.

Sentence feasibility, social circumstances, and the tariff

Although the traditional jurisprudential concern about the difficulties of assessing the impact of the same sentence on offenders in different circumstances continues to be discussed by leading writers on sentencing (e.g. Walker 1980; Ashworth 1983) the academic focus upon sentence *impact* has not been matched by a similar focus upon sentence *feasibility*. And there is a difference between the two. Whereas the principle of equality of impact raises questions about the possible inequality of pain or deprivation suffered by different offenders awarded the same punishment, the notion of sentence feasibility raises questions about the likelihood of extremely disadvantaged offenders being able successfully to complete *any* very demanding non-custodial order. Yet though this latter concern has been largely ignored by academic lawyers, it has traditionally been a major concern of the probation service who have been especially enjoined to advise the court as to the feasibility of individual offenders being put on probation or given a community service order. In recent years, however, the punitive 'just deserts' model has so dominated the courts that probation officers fear that if they advise against any available non-custodial order on the grounds of its non-feasibility, their clients will be given a custodial sentence instead. (The numbers of mentally ill and homeless prisoners suggests that their fears are not groundless.) The fundamentally punitive tenor of *Punishment, Custody and the Community* (Home Office 1988) is likely to increase those fears. This is ironic, because if some of the proposals in the Green Paper are adopted it will be more important than ever before that courts take seriously the issue of sentence feasibility.

When the Green Paper was published in 1988 it was hailed by certain of the mass media as evidence of a new, 'get tough' approach to offenders. This characterization was rooted in the government's stated determination 'to increase the public's confidence in keeping offenders in the community' (Home Office 1988: 2) and the implication that probation services should in future attempt to impress sentencers by making all orders subject to strict and punitive enforcement. (No evidence was presented to support the claim that public and sentencers actually *do* currently lack confidence in the non-custodial alternatives to imprisonment; nor was there discussion as to whether any such lack of confidence might not be more properly attributed to the ignorance and prejudice of the sentencers than to failures on the part of probation.) But it was the eagerness to woo sentencers to non-custodials by presenting them with a mix of orders designed to hurt rather than help that finally over-ruled the Green Paper's reiterated contention that an over-punitive approach won't work—either in terms of reduction of the prison population or in terms of crime control. For although on pages 11 and 12 the Green Paper's authors seemed to be of the opinion that, because of their unenforceability and adverse side-effects, tracking, electronic monitoring, curfews, and intermittent custody would be undesirable adjuncts to existing non-custodial penalties, three of these newly mooted forms of surveillance (the exception being electronic monitoring) were mentioned without demurrer on page 13 as possible components of a new non-custodial sentence, and finally reappeared again in the Appendix as part of specimen 'pick'n' mix' programmes which might well be offered to the courts. In October 1988 the Home Secretary announced that the electronic monitoring of persons on remand before trial would be implemented for an experimental period. If the proposals put forward in the Green Paper were indeed to result in a new order then it should also become mandatory that no persons considered for a non-custodial penalty end up in custody purely because their social circumstances might render such an order impractical. Conversely people who might desperately need the help which the probation service can give should not be denied assistance because the relevant order would also push them 'up tariff'.

The problem of sentence feasibility and social circumstances comes about primarily in two ways. First, because so many people are currently enduring domestic situations fractured by the pains of unemployment, low wages, and poor housing. Second, because many areas of the country lack the communal facilities which provide for a decent standard of public life. Thus, while certain offenders might be perfectly willing to attempt compliance with specified non-custodial orders, their probation officers might rightly calculate that, given the tensions and frustrations already existing in their homes, the clients would be unlikely to complete any order involving constant home calls, curfews, or house arrest. Similarly, in other cases officers might know that while a lack of childminding facilities would prevent some parents from doing community service, a dearth of public transport would equally prevent some other clients from getting to and from suitable schemes. Additionally it might also be unrealistic to expect emotionally and mentally damaged recidivist clients to complete a punitive, as opposed to a supportive, order. It would be desirable, therefore, that sentencers be obliged to accept a probation officer's assessment of the non-feasibility of a rigid non-custodial sentence in certain cases, and that, in the cases of offenders bearing multiple social disadvantage, they should attempt to do least harm by making orders that are totally supportive and non-punitive.

A slightly different problem in relation to sentence feasibility arises when a probation officer, though believing that a first or minor offender's social circumstances are such that he or she could benefit from some type of probation assistance, is reluctant to recommend an order that will push the client 'up tariff'. In fact, the whole notion of the 'tariff' in relation to an offender's record—i.e. 'the recommended sentence being the next one higher than the last one served' (Hudson 1987: 50)—would be abandoned in a reformed system that did not see offenders' records as pushing them inexorably towards imprisonment. (Indeed, it is likely that a radically reformed sentencing programme would abandon the term 'non-custodial alternatives' altogether in favour of some term connoting a more positive form of social regulation—cf. Shaw 1987: 14.) Certainly in a state-obligated model of rehabilitation it should be the expectation that all offenders would be offered any rehabilitative help that they might need, and that acceptance of it would not disadvantage them if they were to appear in court again in the future. Under the present system it is evident that tariff sentencing involving the '"when all else has failed" use of imprisonment can . . . be inappropriately punitive to the petty persistent offender, the very offender that most reformers and policy makers think should be kept out of prison' (Hudson 1987: 50).

Equality of sentence impact[3]

The principle of equality of impact in sentencing suggests that whilst it is just to impose the same sentence on two equally culpable offenders for two equally grave offences, it is unjust to do so if the two offenders have such differing 'sensibilities' that the sentence would have a significantly different effect on each of them. (Ashworth 1983: 283)

Even on a state-obligated model of corrections, many offenders, as well as being deemed suitable for some kind of rehabilitative element in their sentences, would also be judged as culpable and deserving of punishment. In some cases, moreover, the court would decide that though questions of rehabilitation did not arise, punishment would be necessary both to symbolize the state's abhorrence of the crime and to deter this offender and his/her potential imitators in the future. In such cases it is likely that the fine would remain the most favoured sentencing option and it is in relation to monetary penalties that questions of sentence impact are at their most difficult.

The 1986 edition of *The Sentence of the Court* (Home Office 1986) advised sentencers that though they should reduce a fine for an offender of very small means they should not increase it 'because an offender is very affluent'.

Parliament has provided specifically that a magistrates' court must, in fixing the amount of a fine, 'take into consideration among other things the means of the person on whom the fine is imposed. . . .' Specifying the correct approach, the court has said that 'in principle, the amount of the fine should be determined in relation to the gravity of the offence, and then—and only then—should the offender's means be considered, to decide whether he has the capacity to pay such an amount.' It is therefore clearly not correct sentencing practice to increase the level of a fine beyond what would otherwise be appropriate if that sum is more than the offender can be fairly required to pay within a reasonable time. (Home Office 1986: 25)

It is this approach which has led many people to argue that the relatively small fines imposed on the very rich are derisory rather than denunciatory and deterring. At the same time, it is not an approach (being advisory rather than mandatory) that has prevented sentencers from imposing unrealistically high fines on poorer offenders. Yet, as has already been argued, in order for rehabilitation to have any degree of success in terms of reducing law-breaking, it is necessary that offenders should see their sentences as being *just*—just, that is, according to the principle that sentences for the same offences should have equal impact on different offenders.

   A partial solution to the problem of differential sentence impact on offenders of differing means is to be found in the day fine system of some European countries (see Shaw (1989) for a more detailed discussion of day fines). This could well be used in England to calculate fines in the cases of all but the very poor and the very rich. Andrew Ashworth (1983) gives a succinct description of the procedures involved.

For this system the courts must obtain information about the offender's annual income, together with information about his liabilities and any capital he may possess. In general the day fine is assessed at one thousandth of his annual income. Once this calculation has been completed the court can order him to pay so many day fines, the number being calculated according to the seriousness of the case. Thus the two factors, the seriousness of the case and the offender's means, are determined quite independently of each other, and both the number of day fines and the amount of each are announced in court. (Ashworth 1983: 288)

But, even if this system were to be introduced into the English courts, there would still be problems in relation to those too poor to pay a fine and those too rich to suffer deprivation as a result of any fine a court would be likely to impose.

According to Peter Young (1987), Sweden has adopted a very realistic approach to petty fine default and it is quite common to remit fines in Sweden:

Swedish judges argued that the contact an offender has with the court both at the stage of prosecution and at the stage of default is sometimes seen as 'punishment' enough. This was seen to be the case especially for first offenders. Also the opinion was expressed that when the sum of money defaulted on is small then it is simply neither financially nor administratively worthwhile to pursue the offender to the bitter end of imprisonment. [Furthermore] the Swedish judges could not see why their lenient attitude necessarily led to disrespect for the court or the criminal law. Indeed it was forcibly contended that to pursue to the bitter end of imprisonment those who had defaulted on small fines was more liable to create disrespect because it is absurd. (Young 1987: 287)

Quite so. But what about poverty-stricken offenders who commit more serious offences and rich ones whose wealth often appears to license their crime?

In reality, it is likely that offenders too poor to pay a fine are also those suffering from other social disadvantage and, under a system of state-obligated rehabilitation, the court would have a duty to make an order that was at least in part rehabilitative. If in addition the court were to consider it desirable to include an element of retribution in the sentence, a community service order might be imposed with a condition of deferral until such time as the offender was receiving sufficient support to make the order feasible. At the other end of the scale, a progressive (rather than arithmetical) approach to day fines would help ensure that the final sum exacted would hurt the offender despite his or her great wealth (Ashworth 1983: 291). In the cases of professional and corporate criminals, moreover, deprivation of the profits of crime together with disqualification orders in relation to certain forms of business involvement could be combined with realistically heavy fines to punish and deter. Already-existing 'disabling' measures might also be taken more frequently and more forcefully against not so wealthy white-collar and corporate criminals, and other 'respectable' recidivists such as drunk drivers. (See Levi 1989 for discussion of disqualification orders for fraudsters.) As Ashworth says, 'it will be virtually impossible to achieve equality of impact, but . . . it is fairer to move some distance towards the principle of equal impact than to ignore it altogether' (ibid.).

A more democratic approach to sentencing

It has by now become commonplace for penologists to acknowledge that little can be done to establish a coherent sentencing policy aimed at reducing the prison population until judges and magistrates lose their power to subvert it by sending more and more people to gaol. Equally, it is also widely contended that no constitutional issue concerning the independence of the judiciary would arise merely as a result of their discretion being structured in a more efficient and democratic way. On the contrary, having to negotiate patterns of sentencing with other professionals might help judges shed some of the politico-moral prejudices of their class, prejudices from which their judgments have seldom been free (see Griffith 1977). As for lay magistrates, the intricacies of sentencing are such that lay persons should not be expected to bear the responsibility without firm guide-lines as to practice. To ensure that central policy is supported by the appropriate local facilities, regional and central review committees should be set up to monitor both the sentencing practices of local courts and the local facilities for community corrections. For, if punishment is to be in the community it seems only just that communities should have some say in the types of programmes they are prepared to support.

A Sentencing Council of the type advocated by Andrew Ashworth would go far towards helping sentencers make more informed judgments. The task of such a body, composed of a variety of criminal justice personnel, would be

to produce . . . sets of declared sentencing ceilings for different grades and types of offence, which have their basis in certain relativities between offences, together with declared principles for use in calculating the precise sentence beneath that ceiling, principles to deal with persistent offenders, multiple offenders, breaches of peace, suspended sentences and so forth. (Ashworth 1983: 449)

A state-obligated rehabilitation model might go even further. It might specifically require

1. that prosecutors have the power to waive prosecution and ask for a rehabilitative order when an offender (having admitted guilt) is clearly in need of assistance and when no public good would be served by prosecution (see Carlen 1983a);
2. that probation officers have the duty to object to the supervision of certain orders on grounds of their non-feasibility and that sentencers be required to justify in open court any over-ruling of a probation objection;

3. that *all* sentences be justified in open court and that where a sentencer wishes to make a particular rehabilitative order but cannot because of lack of facilities, a record to that effect be made and sent to a regional sentencing review committee.

Summary and Conclusions

The major arguments of this chapter have been that

1. The criminal justice system should be used not only to punish criminals but also to redress some social injustices, or, failing that, to ensure that at least its sentencing policies do not increase social inequality.
2. Because fear of punishment is but one factor amongst many more positive ones which result in offenders becoming law-abiding, a purely punitive approach to sentencing (especially one involving imprisonment as the ultimate sanction) will do little to decrease crime and will certainly increase the prison population.

The specific reforms suggested in the latter part of the chapter have not been intended as a blueprint for a radically changed sentencing policy. They have merely been put forward to highlight four of the major impediments to a more rational approach. These impediments are

1. the continuing dominance of the justice model, even in the government's proposals for community-based punishments;
2. the reluctance in practice for the courts to elevate sentence feasibility to a major sentencing principle;
3. the similar reluctance, in practice, to ensure that the rich pay for their crimes; and the concomitant failure of courts to use to the full the already existing disabling measures that would limit the opportunities of rich business and other 'respectable' criminals to reoffend in future;
4. the failure of governments to limit sentencing discretion and make criminal justice more democratic.

Implementation of a state-obligated rehabilitation model of sentencing would not be cheap. On the contrary, in the short term its full implementation would most likely cost as much as the present housing and maintenance of a prison population of over 50,000. But with a much reduced prison population, the initial costs of community schemes could be met. Once the initial capital outlay had been made, community projects would be much cheaper to run than the labour-intensive gaols. But there is no *very* cheap way of paying for the problems caused by the positive relationship between crime and inequality. The choice is between continuing to squander millions of pounds on prisons, or developing a rational system of criminal justice which could use the savings ensuing from a heavily reduced prison population to regenerate the communities where, too often, victim and offender continue to live in fear, poverty, and isolation long after the sentence of the court has been pronounced.

Notes

1. A thoroughgoing critique of the justice model is to be found in Hudson (1987).
2. See for instance NACRO (1988:1) on the way in which electronic monitoring has been used abroad:

> The limited evidence available indicates that electronic monitoring is used most often for male offenders who have their own home, a telephone and a job; who have committed non violent offences; and are able to pay the fees charged for the hire of the monitoring equipment and supervision by a probation officer or other supervisor.

3. A full discussion of all aspects of equality of sentence impact is to be found in Ashworth (1983).

References

ALLEN, H. (1987), *Justice Unbalanced: Gender, Psychiatry and Judicial Decisions* (Milton Keynes, Open University Press).

ASHWORTH, A. (1983), *Sentencing and Penal Policy* (London, Weidenfeld & Nicolson).

BECCARIA, C. (1963), *On Crimes and Punishment* (Indianapolis, Ind., Bobbs-Merrill; 1st published 1764).

BLOM-COOPER, L. (1988), *The Penalty of Imprisonment* (London, Prison Reform Trust).

BOX, S. (1987), *Recession, Crime and Punishment* (London, Tavistock).

—— and HALE, C. (1985), 'Unemployment, Imprisonment and Prison Overcrowding', *Contemporary Crises*, 9: 208–28.

BYRNE, D. (1987), 'Rich and Poor: The Growing Divide', in A. Walker and C. Walker (eds.), *The Growing Divide: A Social Audit 1979–1987* (London, Child Poverty Action Group).

CARLEN, P. (1983a), 'On Rights and Powers: Some Notes on Penal Politics', in D. Garland and P. Young (eds.), *The Power to Punish* (London, Heinemann).

—— (1983b), *Women's Imprisonment: A Study in Social Control* (London, Routledge & Kegan Paul).

—— (1988), *Women, Crime and Poverty* (Milton Keynes, Open University Press).

COHEN, S. (1985), *Visions of Social Control* (Cambridge, Polity Press).

COOK, D. (1988), 'Rich Law, Poor Law: Differential Responses to Tax and Supplementary Benefit Fraud', unpublished Ph.D. thesis, University of Keele.

—— (1989a), 'Fiddling Tax and Benefits: Inculpating the Poor, Exculpating the Rich', in P. Carlen and D. Cook (eds.), *Paying for Crime* (Milton Keynes), 109–27.

—— (1989b), *Rich Law, Poor Law: Differential Responses to Tax and Supplementary Benefit Fraud* (Milton Keynes, Open University Press).

CROW, I., and SIMON, F. (1987), *Unemployment and Magistrates' Courts* (London, NACRO).

GRIFFITH, J. (1977), *The Politics of the Judiciary* (London, Fontana).

Home Office (1986), *The Sentence of the Court* (London, HMSO).

—— (1988), *Punishment, Custody and the Community*, Cm. 424 (London, HMSO).

HUDSON, B. (1987), *Justice through Punishment* (London, Macmillan).

KORNHAUSER, A. (1978), *Social Sources of Deliquency* (Chicago, Ill., University of Chicago Press).

LACEY, N. (1988), *State Punishment: Political Principles and Community Values* (London, Routledge).

LEA, J., and YOUNG, J. (1984), *What is to be Done about Law and Order* (Harmondsworth, Penguin).

LEVI, M. (1987), *Regulating Fraud: White-Collar Crime and the Criminal Process* (London, Tavistock).

—— (1989), 'Fraudulent Justice? Sentencing the Business Criminal', in P. Carlen and D. Cook (eds.), *Paying for Crime* (Milton Keynes), 86–108.

NACRO (1986), *Black People and the Criminal Justice System* (London, NACRO).

—— (1988), *NACRO Briefing: Fine Default* (London, NACRO, Sept.).

NAPO (1983), *Fine Default and Debtors Prisons* (London, National Association of Probation Officers).

National Children's Home (1988), *Children in Danger* (London, National Children's Home).

PASHUKANIS, E. B. (1978), *Law and Marxism: A General Theory* (London, Ink Links).

ROSENBAUM, M. (1983), *Women on Heroin* (New Brunswick, NJ, Rutgers University Press).

RUSCHE, G., and KIRCHHEIMER, O. (1939), *Punishment and Social Structure* (New York, Russell & Russell).

SHAW, S. (1987), *Conviction Politics: A Plan for Penal Policy* (London, Fabian Society).

—— (1989), 'Monetary Penalties and Imprisonment: The Realistic Alternatives', in P. Carlen and D. Cook (eds.), *Paying for Crime* (Milton Keynes), 29–45.

United Nations (1976), *Economic Crises and Crime* (New York, United Nations Social Defence Research Institute).

VON HIRSCH, A. (1976), *Doing Justice* (New York, Hill & Wang).

WALKER, A., and WALKER, C. (1987), *The Growing Divide: A Social Audit 1979–1987* (London, Child Poverty Action Group).

WALKER, N. (1980), *Punishment, Danger and Stigma* (Oxford, Blackwell).

YOUNG, P. (1987), 'Punishment, Money and the Legal Order: An Analysis of the Emergence of Monetary Sanctions with Special Reference to Scotland', unpublished Ph.D. thesis, University of Edinburgh.

Preface: H. Bianchi, 'Abolition: Assensus and Sanctuary'

Most of the authors represented in this collection regard punishment as an essential feature of any modern state. They differ on how it is to be justified, on what its aims should be, on how far we should try to limit its scope and severity: but they agree, more or less reluctantly, that punishment is a necessary weapon in the state's armoury. However, more radical voices can also be heard, arguing that punishment cannot be justified at all; that we should aim not simply to reform or limit our penal practices and institutions, but to abolish them (Mathiesen 1974, 1986, 1990; Christie 1977, 1981; Abel 1982; Hulsman 1981, 1982, 1986, 1991; Cohen 1985, 1991; Bianchi and van Swaaningen 1986; de Haan 1990; Duff 1994).

Though 'abolitionists' do not speak (any more than do the members of any other 'school') with one voice, some common themes characterize abolitionist thought, and are visible in Bianchi's essay. One is a critique of the concept of 'crime' (Hulsman 1986; Christie 1977): instead of seeing 'crime' as an individual's culpable disobedience to some supposedly shared moral norm, we should conceptualize it as a matter of 'conflict' between members of the community. Another theme is that we should 'civilize' our responses to crime: our model should be the civil law's resolution of disputes, rather than the criminal law's punishment of crime. A third is 'informal justice' (Abel 1982; Matthews 1988): rather than having our conflicts 'stolen' by the professionalized institutions of the formal law (Christie 1977), we should resolve them within the communities in which they occur, by informal procedures involving the parties to the conflict and their community. And finally there is the theme of reconciliation: we should look not for 'retributive' justice, but for 'reparative' or 'restorative' justice which will reconcile the 'offender' to the community.

Bianchi sketches both an abolitionist critique of our current penal institutions and an alternative model for dealing with 'crime'. It is an ideal model; and, as with any such ideal, it leaves us with the problem of how we might move from here to there. But even on the assumption that such a goal might one day be reached, as the final stage of a long process of legal, political, and social change, does it command the moral force that abolitionists ascribe to it?

Some of the ideals which inform abolitionist thought also figure in certain theories of punishment. For instance, those who portray punishment as a communicative process of moral reform insist that it should reconcile offenders with their victims and their communities; and they may also portray punishment as a mode of reparation, which can repair those relationships which crime damages (see H. MORRIS; Duff 1992). One reason why they make *punishment* central to their accounts is the belief that crime must be condemned: punishment aims to communicate to criminals a justified criticism of their crimes. One reason why Bianchi and other abolitionists object to punishment is that they object to any such 'imposition' of our moral views on others, and to what they see as the pretence that the criminal law embodies the genuinely shared values of the community. A critic might reply in turn that a community which was not willing to condemn some kinds of conduct would be a community not worth living in. Durkheim (1984), for example, argued that wherever people believe passionately in the values of their community, they will be moved to punish those who violate them. The abolition of punishment would thus be at the expense of the collapse of the collective conscience. But perhaps Durkheim failed to imagine a world in which shared values could be upheld by more positive rituals, and in which violators might be sanctioned in non-penal ways (see Garland 1990: ch. 3). It is precisely around this issue that abolitionist discourse revolves.

Although Bianchi favours a 'civil' process of dispute resolution, rather than a criminal process of conviction and punishment, he also recognizes that we will still need analogues of some aspects of the criminal process. There will still be a role, though a changed one, for officials like judges, prosecutors, and police. There will still be a role for compulsory detention: those who present an immediate danger to others must be quarantined; those who refuse to negotiate their disputes must be detained until they are willing to negotiate; those whose seriously injurious conduct has aroused strong passions must be offered (required to accept?) 'sanctuary' pending reparative negotiations. But even if these kinds of detention are, as Bianchi insists, more humane and civilized than our existing prisons, a critic might object that they are liable to intrude more seriously on individual liberty than would a just system of punishment—which at least limits the severity of punishment to what is proportionate to the seriousness of their crime. Furthermore, while the professional specialists of the centralized apparatus of the criminal justice system might be seen as 'stealing conflicts' from local communities, it should also be remembered that one function of the legal state is to protect individuals from what might well be the far more oppressive and unrestrained responses of their local communities (see Christie 1981: 109–13; Walker 1969: 3, who describes the first aim of a sentencing system as being 'to protect offenders and suspected offenders against unofficial retaliation'). Once more, the persuasiveness of the abolitionist ideal depends upon a vision of public conduct and attitudes which differ from those which exist today.

Abolitionist arguments challenge the conventional assumption that punishment is a necessary feature of any modern society. They force us to look more critically at the operations of our existing penal institutions, and at the assumptions upon which they depend. And, perhaps above all, they offer a forceful critique of contemporary penality. But whether we should accept their positive ideal of a non-punitive and informal system of civil justice depends on a variety of deep normative and practical questions. Should we abandon the very concept of crime, as wrongdoing to which the community should respond with condemnation? Even if the punishments imposed by our existing penal institutions are too often neither just nor beneficial, would punishment have no part to play in a morally better system? Can we realistically hope to develop genuinely informal modes of justice—procedures which would be genuinely participatory, but which would not themselves become oppressive (see Abel 1982; contrast Cain 1985; de Haan 1990)? These are the fundamental issues raised by the abolitionist approach.

References

ABEL, R. (1982) (ed.), *The Politics of Informal Justice* (New York).

BIANCHI, H., and VAN SWAANINGEN, R. (1986) (eds.), *Abolitionism: Towards a Non-repressive Approach to Crime* (Amsterdam).

CAIN, M. (1985), 'Beyond Informal Justice', *Contemporary Crises*, 9: 335–73.

CHRISTIE, N. (1977), 'Conflicts as Property', *British Journal of Criminology*, 17: 1–15.

—— (1981), *Limits to Pain* (London).

COHEN, S. (1985), *Visions of Social Control* (Cambridge).

—— (1991), 'Alternatives to Punishment: The Abolitionist Case', *Israel Law Review*, 25: 729–39.

DE HAAN, W. (1990), *The politics of Redress: Crime, Punishment and Penal Abolition* (London).

DUFF, R. A. (1992), 'Alternatives to Punishment—or Alternative Punishments?' in W. Cragg (ed.), *Retributivism and its Critics* (Stuttgart), 43–68.

—— (1994), 'Penal Communications: Recent Work in the Philosophy of Punishment', forthcoming in *Crime and Justice: An Annual Review of Research*.

DURKHEIM, E. (1984), *The Division of Labour* (1893), trans. W. D. Halls (London).

GARLAND, D. (1990), *Punishment and Modern Society: A Study in Social Theory* (Oxford).

HULSMAN, L. (1981), 'Penal Reform in the Netherlands I', *Howard Journal*, 20: 150–9.

—— (1982), 'Penal Reform in the Netherlands II', *Howard Journal*, 21: 35–47.

—— (1986), 'Critical Criminology and the Concept of Crime', *Contemporary Crises*, 10: 63–80.

—— (1991), 'The Abolitionist Case: Alternative Crime Policies', *Israel Law Review*, 25: 681–709.

MATHIESEN, T. (1974), *The Politics of Abolition* (London).

—— (1986), 'The Politics of Abolition', *Contemporary Crises*, 10: 81–94.

—— (1990), *Prison on Trial* (London).

MATTHEWS, R. (1988) (ed.), *Informal Justice* (London).

WALKER, N. (1969), *Sentencing in a Rational Society* (Harmondsworth).

Abolition: Assensus and Sanctuary

HERMAN BIANCHI

Part I. Major Objections to the Prevailing System

In order to design effective strategies of abolition and to project workable alternatives of law, we need to agree on what we are opposing.

What we in our western societies understand by a criminal law system is a state-run organization, possessed of the monopoly to define criminal behaviour, directed towards the prosecution of that behaviour which it has defined—irrespective of the wishes or needs of a possible victim or plaintiff—and which has at its disposal, pre-trial and post-trial, the power to keep its prosecutees and convicts in confinement.

Representatives and managers of the criminal law system cherish the pretension that their organization could protect society from such a dangerous threat as criminality. In fact, however, the organization, since it was established in its present form about the end of the 18th century, has, in every respect and on all counts, failed to accomplish what it promises. Quite the reverse. For a long time the criminal law organization has been escalating dangerously. Any enhancement of the punishing power of the organization has so far led to more rather than less criminality. A nation that builds more prisons and imposes more repressive punishment usually provokes criminality.

In order to do the job it has undertaken and to find continuous public support for that, the criminal law organization must always keep alive a negative stereotype of 'the criminal'. It must maintain its stigmatizing power. At best the managers of the system are unable, or unwilling, to prevent the media from feeding the negative stereotype of 'the enemy of society'.

This negative stereotype is a direct result of the system's ideology. Since the 'war against crime' is continually being waged by its managers and their supportive politicians, an 'enemy-image' is constantly being produced. When nations and their rulers prepare for warfare, they begin by invoking a negative image of the enemy: the little yellow man, the American capitalist imperialist, the Soviet communist imperialist, etc. By doing so, their people will forget that they are dealing with human beings, and almost anything goes. In a former publication I compared the way the State creates moral panic waves in order to legitimize its expansion with the myth of the Lord of the flies (*de Vliegengod*, 1967. Dutch translation of W. Golding's *Lord of the Flies*, Faber 1954.).

The origin of the negative stereotype of the offender is ominous. It stems directly from the medieval Inquisition. In the old law system of Europe there was not even a shadow of public prosecution for wrongful acts committed between free citizens. Such acts were considered to be injuries and causes of conflict, for which damage to body and property had to be repaired, and the extent of the reparation was to be fixed by negotiation. The Inquisition, however, introduced the prosecutor (ecclesiastical at first, then later on, when the state had gradually come to accept this system, a public prosecutor). The Inquisition created the image of the heretic, a subhuman enemy of the church (later, of the state) for whom there was no salvation or penitence, and against whom the most infernal punishment was permitted because he was going to hell anyway. Sooner or later the evolving European states accepted the heretic definition of social dissidence from the church (including England), called him a criminal, and gradually grew to ignore the old legal system of the country, by which most crime-conflicts were solved through negotiation. Our present criminal law system—Anglo-Saxon as well as Continental—is still based on the old Inquisition, but in a secular form.

The results of this negative image have been disastrous, and twofold. Because the old negotiation procedures of conflict-regulation fell into disuse, the prosecutee and convict cannot contribute in any regular way, and by their own free will, to the improvement of the situation. Even the most docile convict, who is prepared in the most masochistic way, and without complaint, to endure the punishment that is imposed upon him, cannot contribute to his own social salvation. From then on the stigma he received makes it impossible for him to recover the status he had before he was degraded. The victim does not profit at all from our criminal law either, for the system largely ignores him or her. Even the certainty that the criminal is being punished is not much help in gaining reparation for the harm done.

The other destructive result of this negative image is the reality that most adaptation, probation, and therapy programmes have failed. Why should society take back into its midst a person who was depicted as the *enemy* of society? And most forensic psychiatry failed because it was imposed upon an unwilling 'patient' who, with good reason, did not believe that therapy would help him to be reintegrated into society, since the stigma of 'being sick' makes the original criminal stigma even worse, and is, even more difficult to wipe out. The 'criminal' stigma is always a social life sentence, for any convict.

Adaptation and therapy programmes have even strengthened the destructive power of the criminal law system. That is why abolitionists do not favour the so-called 'medical model' either.

The rules of our present criminal law system are very much at variance with our general legal system. The latter is built upon the idea that the set of rules it comprises is meant for the settlement of disputes, regulation of conflicts, and the construction of society—in short, the realization of peace and justice. The criminal law system, however, is rather *destructive* to society. Its rules differ so much from the legal system that it is even ignored by authors of general introductions to the philosophy or theory of law. They do not know what to do with criminal law and where to place it. Criminal law has its own basic philosophy, entirely outside the legal system. Criminal law is like war, and this phenomenon is not treated in our legal philosophy either. That is the reason why all attempts to 'humanize' the criminal law system have failed so far: you cannot 'humanize' a war either, can you? Abolitionists do not favour the humanization of the criminal law system as a goal in itself, but as a way of recalling the legal system to deal with wrongful acts, the rule of law, and the cancelling of a derailment of the general legal system.

In fact, the present criminal law system denies human rights. During the American and French revolutions, human rights were being defined (not because there were no human rights before, but because they were in greater jeopardy then than ever before). Our present criminal law system was then definitely introduced, and these rights were declared to be inalienable, except for those being prosecuted. They received very little from this horn of plenty of human righteousness, except the right not to be cruelly punished 'unnecessarily'. Mere indictment is sufficient to deprive anyone who is prosecuted of his human dignity. He no longer has freedom of the press, no privacy for his mail, no freedom to group together or meet, no freedom for sexual and human contact. He is even deprived of the pursuit of happiness (in his case, to try to repair the harm he has done), and thereby be accepted as an honest citizen.

Our present system of criminal law prosecutes mainly those who are already the underprivileged and deprived categories of our population: racial minorities, young people, the socially weak and defenceless—and until recently (though the moral panic on AIDS can update it again) sexual deviants. For several centuries the managers of the system had been clearly showing a constant preference to prosecute the weaker, so the question may be asked if the rulers of our societies have ever been interested in real crime-control. One gets the impression that they prosecuted the weak in order to legitimize their own conduct. Rulers will never prosecute their own class associates. Or at least, it is very exceptional.

In the present structures of criminal procedures the 'criminal', or perpetrator of crime, is treated as an *object* of prosecution. Being an object is a total denial of his human dignity. Human beings should never be made into objects, since it is a basic human right to be a subject and bearer of rights. At our trials the culprit has to defend himself, not so much against his victim, as against the whole of society, which in the Netherlands is represented by an all powerful public prosecutor. Such a charge is too much for any human being. The defendant is, moreover, deprived of his natural surroundings and he is not allowed to bring in for his defence his friends and relatives. They may be witnesses, but not an intimate support group. Very few people have learned to defend themselves in such important matters without the immediate help of their kin. Only people with higher education have learned to speak up for themselves, and as a result they are less likely to be the object of prosecution because they generally have the means, and the socio-linguistic and verbal skill, of defence.

The term *trial* in the English language is living evidence of the obscure and sad origin of criminal law. *Trial* means that people had to be *tried* on the purity of their souls (if they ever could), and the term goes back to the days of the Inquisition and ordeal.

Part II. The Aims of an Abolitionist Perspective

Our first aim is that criminal law should be brought back into our general legal system, back under the rule of law. The criminal law system barely deserves the beautiful name of justice, since it is a derailment of our legal system. We must learn all over again to apply the rules of a normal legal system, which for centuries, in the best of our western traditions, were used for the settlement of disputes and the regulation of conflicts between—if possible—*equal* parties. The main problems of our strategy have to be defined in legal terms. It has been the deficiency of penal reform so far that the legal system of civil and administrative law has been neglected, whereas attention has been paid exclusively to the problems of social disorganization, prison reform, psychological stress, and psychiatric therapy. As long as the present system is kept intact, all reform will be co-opted by it, and reform will eventually strengthen it, as is so vividly described by Thomas Mathiesen in his theory of positive and negative reforms (*The Politics of Abolition*, Martin Robertson, London, 1974).

Crime in abolitionist thought has to be defined in terms of *tort*. Indeed, we do not have to devise an entirely new system of rules. We already have one, waiting to be applied and adapted. Lawyers and jurists are the allies of abolitionists, since they are capable, and hopefully willing, to develop new concepts of tort which would be suitable for the regulation of crime conflicts, and rules for the settlement of disputes arising from what we used to call 'crime'. The skills of psychologists, psychiatrists, and social workers must be adapted and rewritten for conflict-regulation, whereby personality problems would become secondary—if even that. The new system would no longer be called criminal law but *reparative law*.

If a new system of rules were being tried out, we would have an excellent opportunity to 'clean up' the stereotype of the 'delinquent'. He would no longer be the—suitable enemy of society (if the managers of the criminal law system and their political friends do not place him in that role); he would no longer be a 'sick' person (if he is no longer made sick by degradation and incarceration, or labelled as sick by a psychiatry that went astray); no longer deviant (if not labelled as such by control-agencies). (See Nils Christie, 'Suitable Enemies', in H. Bianchi and R. van Swaaningen (eds.), *Abolitionism: Towards a Non-Repressive Approach to Crime*, Free University Press, Amsterdam 1986, 42–54.) In the abolitionist perspective a 'criminal', or a 'delinquent', is a person who has committed a liability-creating act, as a result of which he is in a difficult, and not always enviable, but certainly not hopeless, position in which he has to participate in a discussion on the harm he has done, and how it can be *repaired*. He is thus no longer an evil-minded man or woman, but simply a debtor, a liable person whose human duty is to take responsibility for his or her acts, and to assume the duty of repair.

To the abolitionist movement the main concepts of the system of reparative law no longer stem from guilt and culpability. We want to replace them largely by concepts like debt, liability, and responsibility. We do not deny, of course, that ethical concepts like guilt and culpability exist and are of great importance, but we doubt if they can be defined or be used in criminal law proceedings, or even be applied in legal proceedings anyway. They can most certainly *not* be used in the 'trial' proceedings as we have them now. A trial, and any other criminal procedure, is based on a false premiss of *consensus*. When, during a trial, a verdict or sentence is pronounced and a person convicted, such proceedings are based on the pretence that there is consensus on the interpretation of norms and values. This is done quite undemocratically, however, because the convict's peer and social groups have no real influence on the definition process. Those countries that have jury trials are not very much better off. What is purported to be consensus is just power exerted by one group over another. It smacks of class justice. Some radical criminologists are therefore in favour of a *dissensus* model instead of the traditional consensus model. The disadvantage of the dissensus model is, however, that it can really only be used in political trials, or those criminal proceedings which have a political character. The dissensus model is in fact a civil war *in statu nascendi*, and will turn into a consensus model whenever one of the parties has beaten the other. For abolitionist procedures an *assensus* model is preferable. Using such a model we admit that the last word on good and evil, on guilt and culpability, can never be pronounced without violence. It is better therefore to discuss these problems of ethics and morality without imposing our own views on the other person. In other publications I have tried to outline such a model (*Justice as Sanctuary: Toward a New System of Crime Control*, Indiana University Press, Bloomington, Indiana, USA, 1994). In our culture the assensus model is very common (e.g. western parliament), and in other cultures it is common in cases of harmful acts and injury. We should consider such a model for the resolution of criminalized conflicts as well. But it comprises a new set of rules, and we must first practice its use in order to master the process eventually. Once these rules are mastered, we will discover that guilt and culpability are so interwoven in our social and cultural system that we can never blame just one person, as we still do in our criminal law system. Dostoyevsky argued that each of us is guilty towards all. And we have to share responsibility. That is why a liable person has a human right to help to shoulder his responsibility. This should be a legal right as well!

The ideas of punishment and punitive response to liability acts must wither away entirely. The very thought that one grown up human being should ever have a right, or duty, to punish another grown up human being is a gross moral indecency, and the phenomenon cannot stand up to any ethical test. The punitive response should be replaced by a call for responsibility and for repair, and punishment should be replaced by reconciliation. Punishment is destructive to society because it is violent: reconciliation serves society, and is a lesson in humanity.

The institution of prison and imprisonment has to be abolished as a retributive form of punishment. No trace should be left of this dark side of human history. In our constitutions, amendments, articles, or paragraphs should be inserted to read: 'imprisonment, in whatever form, is not tolerated in this country and nation'. We can use terms that were applied when servitude and slavery were constitutionally abolished.

We must discuss answers to a number of problems, which may not be so difficult in themselves, but for which people will continue to demand an answer, and rightly so. The *first* question is: what are we going to do with the persons who create an *immediate danger* to our bodies and our lives? It is true that there are very dangerous people who are never prosecuted. Although presidents who are playing wargames in the Pacific, in Central America, and in Libya, or who are helping to terrorize European airports, are a much greater danger to people's safety than any 'ordinary criminal' whatsoever, we do not lock *them* up. We let them do their dangerous deeds in the political, military, and economic spheres. But that is not an answer to the question. I agree that we have the right, and the duty, to protect ourselves and others against danger. But at the same time I wonder if the number of dangerous people would be so great if the criminal law system no longer degraded its prosecutees, mutilating them by incarceration and mental injury; if the state no longer provoked criminality by its bad example of punitive violence; and if the media no longer whipped up public opinion against 'criminals'. Perhaps, if we improve our legal system, the number of dangerous people will be so small that, even in a large country like the United States, two or three small places of quarantine will be sufficient, and certainly not the huge store of hundreds of thousands of human beings which that country has today. The person taken into quarantine, however, would legally enjoy all medical and social help, and his treatment would be controlled by strict rules in order to avoid the abuse which could readily creep in. Any such person in quarantine would have the legal right of a trustee, a non-professional person from outside, of his own choice. Any extension of his stay would have to be controlled, not by an institutional board, but by the court. No extension could be imposed without plentiful legal aid for lawyers. A government deputee would have to report to parliament or the state council, annually, on any of the people in quarantine.

The *second* question that arises is: what are we going to do when a person refuses, and *continues to refuse, to negotiate* about the injury he has caused, or in which he has participated? In that case he should be invited to negotiate, not seven times, but seventy times seven. If his refusal is due to the unreasonable demands of the other party (whether the defendant refuses or the plaintiff), the case can be brought before court. If only the defendant is to be blamed for negotiations not taking place, he may be kept in custody for debts, but again under the strictest rules, lest his case be abused. The defendant must be released as soon as he or she is willing to reopen negotiations. The defendant in custody has every right to be accompanied by, or to receive, whomsoever he wishes. Such custody must be under the permanent control of a public representative. But again, in the abolitionist movement, we feel sure that if the state no longer set a bad example of violence by the repression of criminality (which is unsuccessful anyway), and if we were all able to develop a set of rules which would allow people to do justice to others and to themselves, hopefully the number of conscientious refusers would remain very small indeed.

The present system of criminal law has a very authoritarian character and is entirely devoid of democracy. Far too much power is in the hands of the prosecutor and the judge. There simply cannot be a 'fair trial', quite apart from the fact that the word trial as such must be abolished, if too much power is in the hands of one party. The abolitionist perspective wishes to bring the conflict back to the community wherever possible. This implies that we want negotiations on conflict to take place out of court as much as possible. The *third* question that arises is: are there any tasks left for *judges*? The help of a judge would only be invoked if the disputing parties were unable to come to a settlement by themselves. From the sociology of law we have learned that this is the practice already in civil and administrative cases; so why not in criminal cases? The role of the judge, therefore, would be far more that of a *mediator*, insisting that parties comply with his mediation. The judge would no longer be a person who, godlike or fatherlike, pronounces verdicts on morality, when one person, or party, is found guilty.

The role of the *prosecutor* poses the *fourth* question. It has to be redefined. He would no longer be a prosecutor, except in those cases where he would be allowed to make a public complaint, because there is no identifiable victim. In such cases a process of negotiation would be impossible otherwise. His new task, however, would be of an equalizing nature. As a public representative he would see to it that neither defendant nor plaintiff abuses the situation. If any of the parties is weaker he would stand by. The new name for his role would be that of *praetor*, a word in Roman law for the man who enabled legal action, and observed that it ran smoothly.

Fifthly, what about the *police*? In the old days, in western society, when we still had at our disposal an infra-judiciary, negotiative system of conflict solution, we could dispense with the police. As a matter of fact, there were hardly any police before 1800. But there were still old rules and customs for tracking down thieves and culprits; there were sanctuaries and asylums for outlaws; the church often offered aid in conflict regulations; and the communities were much smaller and knew people face-to-face. Our present criminal law system has only gradually crept into our society, and has become more and more anonymous.

Nowadays, social conflicts are on a larger scale and more intricate. We could not do without the police to trace those who have committed wrongful acts, and should be invited to settle the disputes. The population is too large—although more face-to-face relationships in district neighbourhood life are growing up again—and most conflicts are between more than two people. Therefore a simple convocation of the disputing parties is not always possible—but still, in a great many cases, it *is*. As long as the police do not set a bad example of violence and counter-violence (the police must be *less* violent than criminals, not *more*), so long as they are not racially biased, nor partial in class or generation conflict, nor allow themselves to be politically abused, but accept gratefully all kinds of parliamentary control and take citizen's wishes seriously in their activities and power, and do not allow the organization to be more military than at present: *then* the police would be very welcome to help the citizens to build up a better system of injury control, and to help the citizens—who will have to play an active role themselves as well—to settle their disputes.

Part III. Some Guide-Lines for Alternatives

The abolitionist movement firmly believes that at the present time we have to have confidence that people have come of age sufficiently in order to settle their disputes by themselves, and that they are not in need of any bureaucratic organization to take their conflict out of their hands.

People were able to settle their disputes themselves in the past in our own culture, and they are still able to do so in other cultures.

Therefore we should avoid falling into the trap of bureaucracy by abolishing the existing one and handing it over to another professional bureaucracy of any kind. Professional solutions have to be very restricted in number. Servo-mechanisms have to be built into any new system we devise, such as community control and non-professional activity, in order to prevent any new professionalism from arising.

Any abolitionist movement has to be very careful not to co-opt the power of an old system which is very strong and efficient. We have seen this happen in attempts to bring 'diversion'-solutions into the old system, or, rather, half-way into it. This type of conflict solution whereby, in some cases, with the agreement of the public prosecutor, no court action will be taken so long as the parties come together to settle their disputes, e.g. by reparation, has in fact strengthened the system, because it provided the public prosecutor with the opportunity to extend his power into those areas which he had previously left unnoticed. It by no means diminished his power. He just made neighbourhood centres work for him, in order to take minor cases off his hands.

An abolitionist should not offer the authority in power an elaborate blueprint of the alternatives, because that also relieves citizens of the possibility of building up a system according to their own real needs and feelings of justice. And a blueprint is also the safest way to create a new bureaucracy of professionals (see Mathiesen's *The Politics of Abolition*, Martin Robertson, London 1974).

What follows is, therefore, not a blueprint, nor an elaborate and entirely considered system, but a few proposals whereby some answers to some questions are considered, and some new (or rather old) institutions are offered for consideration. In order to give clarity to the intricacy of the problems, we will separate the conflicts into four types.

1. *Minor cases of injury*, such as petty theft, minor robbery, insult, quarrel, and row. These are the typical cases where *neighbourhood centres* offer the best solution. The citizens who claim to be victims, and want to be plaintiffs, may settle the dispute with the defendant. Often the offenders are not detected (just like in the existing system), or are too young. If the offenders do not get punished, but simply have to repair damage and restore or return what was stolen, if they no longer have to be deterred by punishment, there is good reason to expect that this petty criminality will gradually diminish. It should be remembered how provocative the power of punishment is, certainly for young people, more so than a

deterrent. Moreover, restoration of damage is a lesson in good citizenship. The word 'crime' should gradually disappear from our language. We should not forget that the stigmatizing power of language may be very harmful for good citizenship, that also implies an immediate, preventive interference at the very moment a crime is being committed.

2. *Slightly more serious cases of injury*, such as burglary and housebreaking, not too serious violence, petty fraud, swindling, arson without causing death, scuffles, scrapes, and that sort of thing. Here the neighbourhood is of great importance as well. We should not forget that most harmful acts do not stand by themselves, but are committed between people who usually know each other quite well, or between groups and in neighbourhoods. There should be boards of citizens who bring the parties together. The San Francisco *Community Board* Programme is a good example of this. We should no longer consider any party as an individual who has to defend himself or herself all alone. He should be allowed to take his intimate groups with him, because conflicts might be discussed more easily and negotiated upon in a familiar setting. In the negotiation discussions (palavers) in the neighbourhood centres, the other side of the conflict has to be party to the considerations. The other elements of the conflict will not lead to a diminution of the actors' guilt (as is now the case), since, in those discussions, it is not guilt that is under consideration but the best way of finding a solution to the conflict.

Sometimes the conflict may have difficult judicial aspects, so often lawyers and jurists will have to take part in the discussions. Here *civil law alternatives* play an important role. If the conflicting parties of defendant and plaintiff require it (although it may very often be very difficult to distinguish the one from the other), a social worker may help. But usually groups are quite capable of handling their own affairs, and feel no need to be labelled as helpless.

3. The third category are the *serious cases*, where murder or manslaughter is involved, very serious violence, rape, arson with a fatal result, and killing with political aims. These injuries are very serious, and people get very emotional about them. On the one hand an abolitionist will argue that people's emotions are whipped up by the media too often, and that politicians abuse the feelings aroused by such injuries for their own end. None the less, abolitionists agree that emotions are justified and have to be respected. They are human, and they will never disappear, and they do not need to. But emotions should not prevent attempts to bring conflict towards some kind of regulation. For long-term impris-

onment does not bring the victim back to life either (to say nothing of the death penalty), and the humiliated or mutilated victim does not get his or her health back as result of this sort of punishment. And the so-called 'satisfaction', which the victim or his next of kind might receive from the certainty that the 'criminal' is suffering is far more destructive to the soul of the victim than any attempt by the actor to do some possible good, to show the slightest sign of repentance, or to try to improve the situation of his victim. The argument that severe punishment would deter criminals has been so often shown by scientific research to be entirely unjustified, in all cases of any seriousness, that it needs no further consideration in any abolitionist article, were it not that politicians still abuse that argument so often for improper purposes.

Penitence and reconciliation are, and always have been, the royal way to improve a difficult situation. It is the sole and proper way for actor and victim (and their kin) to overcome the regrettable event.

But emotions are still there, and if they do not have an outlet, or if they are not controlled and appeased, they may lead to an outburst, to lynching or to destructive and violent self-help by the people involved. Lynching takes place more often in racial repression than in cases of 'ordinary crime', and happens more often in Hollywood movies than in reality. In the old days in Europe we had a system of blood vengeance. Historical research has found evidence, however, that active blood vengeance did not occur frequently. People were far too scared of the escalatory effects of the system. There were no public prosecutors, so people had the opportunity to do justice to themselves, but they needed some kind of sting for unwilling parties: that was the threat of blood vengeance, which was usually sufficient to bring parties to the palaver hall. We should not forget that, even in cases of very serious and heinous acts, there is often much more at stake than just that act. And this has to be considered also in palavers and negotiations. Such circumstances and aspects have a better chance of being discussed there than during trials.

But emotions remain, and very often, immediately after a serious violent act, public reactions can be so violent that the actor needs some protection in order to survive for the later negotiations—not only him but his intimate group too if he has one. In the old days *sanctuary* served as a place of refuge where the perpetrator of a serious offence could go and live for a while in safety until negotiations could begin. Sanctuaries were in use in England and France until the 17th century. In the Netherlands and many other European countries they were available in a secular form until the end of the 18th century, when they were abolished to make room for our modern criminal law system. The sanctuaries were often churches, and the church often helped the parties to become reconciled. In England, and many other countries, the kings often granted to abbey churches the privilege of sanctuary, so convinced were they of its wholesome effect. We should reintroduce sanctuaries in our societies: places of refuge, having the right of immunity, outside state control, where actors of violent acts have the right of asylum whilst awaiting negotiations, either within the place of sanctuary or in a *civil court*. That would be much better than a trial. Perhaps once again there is a role for the churches here? In America revival of the *Sanctuary Movement* was initiated by the churches, which wanted to offer sanctuary to refugees from Central America. But at universities also interest in the reintroduction of sanctuaries is growing (i.e. Stastny and Tyrnauer, Universities of Vermont and Montreal). In Geneva, Switzerland, the World Alliance of Reformed Churches too has set out plans for conference on sanctuary. But why only the churches? We need secular places of refuge as well! I tried to outline some basic conditions for the establishment of sanctuaries for communal offenders in my book *Justice as Sanctuary* (1994).

4. Those cases where *no individual victim* can be found i.e. transgressions of order. These comprise such divergent acts as traffic offences, drunk-driving, offences against licensing acts, trading in contraband, economic offences, environmental offences—and, in my view also, the preparation of a war. If these offences are just the abuse of a received licence (like drunk-driving), *administrative measures* will suffice. Imprisonment is ridiculous. If a person continuously, and in spite of receiving a warning, abuses his licence he is bound to lose it. It is not such a problem. Such administrative measures seem to have more deterrent effect than imprisonment. If actors, with or without violence, claim a political excuse for their activity, they would be better to argue their case before a *political body*—like parliament—other than before a judicial body, like the court.

Although the abolitionists are in favour of handling disputes out of court wherever possible, we would still need a judiciary. For if it ever happens that negotiations get out of hand, and one of the parties is in danger of being victimized, he should have the right of appeal to a court. That too is justice.

Part IV. Action and Research

The existing criminal law system is powerful. It is being backed by very powerful political and economic interests, and it is constantly being whipped up by the media, who, again, have commercial interests. For the time being we have to put up with the idea that a system which took several centuries to become what it is now will not disappear overnight, and that it will take several decades for it to be abolished and replaced by a more just, justified, and efficient system of reparation and reconciliation.

The new system has to be borne by the people, and they have to relearn what has been lost through the activity of the criminal law bureaucracy: how to cope with problems in their own community; they have to be reskilled, as Raymond Shonholtz puts it.

For the coming decades we have to live with the reality that two different systems will operate side by side—a *two-system system*. It may look odd, but for the abolitionist movement this oddness may turn out to be a benefit. Let us learn from what happened in Italy in the mid-1970s. There a group of psychiatrists, inspired by the ideas of one of them, Franco Basaglia, argued that the immense storehouse of psychiatric institutions made the patient sick instead of making him well. It is freedom that cures, they said, and our patients have to be brought back into their communities, because such communities have immense resources for healing their own deviants. All right, said the Italian government, which had been irritated for a long time by this sort of progressive thinking. And a bill was passed through parliament closing many large institutions and suspending their subsidies. The result was disastrous. The patients were simply sent back to the communities, but the latter had long since forgotten how to cope with these problems. They had to relearn what they had not been used to for more than a hundred years. The Italian government laughed up its sleeve when psychiatrists began again to beg for subsidies and the reopening of the institutions. This ill-intended generosity on the part of the government meant a serious set-back for progressive psychiatry in the country. Such a thing must not happen to the abolitionist movement of criminal law!

It is alright for criminal law to continue in those communities which are not yet well prepared to cope with their conflicts, and for the criminal law system to be available for those perpetrators of harmful acts who prefer to go on being called 'criminal' in the criminal law system, rather than being free citizens who declare themselves liable and responsible for their acts, and who want to make amends for the harm they have done. It seems to some people that the dull passivity of imprisonment is to be preferred to taking on responsibility.

A risk that may occur is that the authorities may offer subsidies for building up 'self-help' programmes in communities. There is a mortal danger in subsidies. They are quite often the most effective instrument for a bureaucracy to control the activities of its citizens (although this statement is not true of all subsidies). But subsidies lead in many cases irrevocably to professionalization, and professionals usually tend to create a new bureaucracy. Thus the system would have co-opted the abolition proposals, and neutralized them.

There is another risk; forewarned is forearmed. This is the so-called 'cave-in-model'. Penal reformers have often fallen into that trap in the last eighty years or so, as I have described in my article 'Pitfalls and Strategies of Abolition' (H. Bianchi and R. van Swaaningen (eds.), *Abolitionism: Towards a non-Repressive Approach to Crime*, Free University Press, Amsterdam, 1986, 147–56). Authorities will often argue: 'Yes, abolitionists, we think you are right. We do indeed have an inefficient and unnecessarily cruel system of crime control, and we should see to it that the smallest possible number of people are affected by it. In particular, let us prevent young people from falling victim to it: let us, for a start, save the children.' Then everyone will be happy, for we all seem to agree that children should be saved rather than adults. Several times in the last century it was like that with penal reform. The effects of this are, however, dysfunctional for abolition. For, what the authorities really have in mind is to save their prosecutors' power for what they call 'the war against hard core criminality', and it is they who define what that is. After a while, it turns out that they are prosecuting just as many people as before, because their prosecutory man-power has remained the same—or may even have increased. In the end, it turns out that just as many young people are being prosecuted as before, or even more, and they are not saved anyway. Most sweet promises by a criminal law bureaucracy to adopt an abolitionist policy, are the treacherous song of the Pied Piper.

The abolitionist movement should remain aware that, as long as the criminal law bureaucracy has the monopoly of crime definition and certainly if it remains the only authority to define hard core criminality, its power will just grow if we allow it a cave-in model. The abolitionist movement should devise its strategy for saving both violent offenders and non-violent young delinquents. Sanctuaries for serious actors are needed as much, if not more, than centres for young people, if we really want an abolitionist movement to be effective in the end.

Some people will wonder whether or not an abolitionist can still do any good within the system *without* strengthening it. Yes and no. I should like to give one illustrative example. A few years ago in the Netherlands some people were active in obtaining permission for inmates to have television sets in their cells. The prisons' administration were in favour of that, because it kept the inmates quiet, and away from any rebellious thinking. In this way it strengthened the system. But better information from the outside world will also keep them aware of their rights as citizens, make them critical of their situation, and fit to contest it. There is no doubt that the most powerful and effective action the abolitionist movement can achieve in its struggle against the prison institution is the total abolition of any restriction of human rights imposed on inmates, both on remand and after conviction. Imagine the prison authorities being obliged to grant inmates the right of free association, and not only inside their own institution or prison, but all prisoners in any one state or nation: a sort of national council of prison inmates! That would be very threatening to the system, and a lot of exertion would be needed to obtain that constitutional right. I think we must just start with—perhaps less way-out—initiatives in order to achieve the abolition of punitive laws and measures.

Many statements in this article are still in need of continued research. The abolitionist movement should try to get allies among criminological researchers, and among progressive social movements too. Criminology has predominantly been a *repressive* science. What we need in this field is a science directed towards *emancipation*, anticipating the coming changes in society.

References

BIANCHI, H. (1986), 'Pitfalls and Strategies of Abolition', in H. Bianchi and R. van Swaaningen (eds.), *Abolitionism: Towards a Non-Repressive Approach to Crime* (Free University Press, Amsterdam, 1986). 147–56.

—— (1994), *Justice as Sanctuary: Towards a New System of Crime* (Indiana University Press, Bloomington, Indiana, 1994).

CHRISTIE, N. (1986), 'Suitable Enemies', in H. Bianchi and R. van Swaaningen (eds.), *Abolitionism: Towards a Non-Repressive Approach to Crime* (Free University Press, Amsterdam, 1986), 42–54.

MATHIESEN, T. (1974), *The Politics of Abolition*, Martin Robertson, London, 1974.